AN ABRIDGED
MALAY-ENGLISH DICTIONARY

(ROMANISED).

BY

R. J. WILKINSON,
F.M.S. Civil Service.

KUALA LUMPUR:
PRINTED AT THE F.M.S. GOVERNMENT PRESS.
1908.

PREFACE.

In preparing this abridged edition of a larger work my aim has been to supply a full Malay Vocabulary in a book of conveniently small size.

I have followed the phonetic system of romanised spelling prescribed by the Federated Malay States Government, but have added a good many variants to assist persons accustomed to other orthographical rules.

R. J. WILKINSON.

NOTE ON THE SPELLING OF ROMANISED MALAY.

The recommendations of the Committee appointed by the Federated Malay States Government in 1904 to lay down rules for romanising Malay may be summarised as follows:

(i) The Roman letters used should be given their English values as regards consonants and their Italian values as regards vowels;

(ii) The peculiar Malay indeterminate vowel should be represented by *ĕ*;

(iii) The peculiar Arabic letters ذ, ض and ط should all be represented by *dz*;

(iv) Words like سهاج, بهارو, بهاي, etc., should be always written with the *h* between two letters a—e.g., *sahaja*, *baharu*, *bahaya*, etc.;

(v) In selecting the vowel for use in final consonants we should follow the following convention:

(a) *ong* (not *ung*), *oh* (not *uh*), *ok* (not *uk*), *um* (not *om*), *un* (not *on*), *ul* (not *ol*), *up* (not *op*), *us* (not *os*), *ur* (not *or*), *ut* (not *ot*), *u* (not *o*);

(b) *eh* (not *ih*), *ek* (not *ik*), *ing* (not *eng*), *im* (not *em*), *in* (not *en*), *il* (not *el*), *ip* (not *ep*), *is* (not *es*), *ir* (not *er*), *it* (not *et*), *i* (not *e*).

But if the penultimate vowel is *e* or *o*, the final should contain *e* or *o* in preference to *i* or *u*—e.g., *pohon* (not *pohun*), *kotor* (not *kotur*), *gesel* (not *gesil*).

AN ABRIDGED
MALAY-ENGLISH DICTIONARY
(ROMANISED).

aadzim, Ar. august, sublime; *sultánu'l-aadzim*, the august sultan— i.e. the Sultan of Turkey in contradistinction to local Malay rulers.

aalam, Ar. all-knowing; omniscient; *wa'llahu aalam*, God knoweth best.

aalan, Ar. the subscribers (to a newspaper).

abad, Ar. eternity; the endless future, in contradistinction to the endless past (*azal*).

abadi, Ar. eternal.

abadiat, Ar. eternity.

abah-abah, tackle, gear, harness.

abaimana, the lower orifices of the body.

abang, elder brother; a cousin older than oneself.

abau, a large tortoise.

abdi, Ar. a slave.

abělur, Pers. crystal.

abjad, Ar. the alphabet according to the numerical values of the letters as used in divination.

aboe, Ch. sir; a respectful form of address to Chinese headmen.

abok, see *habok*.

abrak, Ar. mica.

abu, I. Ar. father of—e.g. in proper names such as *Abu-bakar*. II. ashes, cinders; *ular abu*, a name for the hamadryad.

abuan, a share, a portion.

abur, *měngabur*, to lavish.

achan, to get into a person's way; to obstruct (unintentionally or in teasing).

achar, I. Hind. pickles; preserves in vinegar. II. (Kedah) a sink; a rubbish-hole.

achara, Skr. a rule of conduct; a religious observance.

achat, (Kedah) a small leech.

Acheh, Acheen.

achi, I. *achi-achi*, the lever by which the boom of a Malay boat is turned round and round so as to fold up the sail; also *charhi*. II. done! agreed! *sudah achi*, it is settled; *ta'-achi*, it is off.

achu, to menace; to attempt or appear to attempt without fully carrying out—e.g. to raise one's arm to strike without actually striking; to essay; to assay, to test, to try.

achuan, a mould or matrix.

achum, mischief-making, tale-bearing; *měngachum*, to libel, to slander.

ada, to be; to be present; to exist; to be at home (to a visitor); to exist in connection with, to appertain to, to have; *ada orang*, there are people present; *ada laut, ada-lah pěrompak*, where there are seas, there are pirates; *sahaya ada duit*, (colloquial) I have money, I am rich; *adakan* and *měngadakan*, to create, to call into existence, to appoint; *kěadaan*, state, existence, condition of life, position; *tiada*, is not; there is not; *ta'-dapat-tiada*, there cannot but be; there must be; must.

adab, Ar. respect; courtesy; manners (especially propriety in behaviour to one's elders or superiors); *děngan a.*, courteously, respectfully; *biadab*, lack of manners; disrespectful.

Adam, Ar. a proper name, Adam; *nabi A.*, Adam, the common ancestor of all men; *anak A.*, or *bani A.*, humanity, mankind.

adang, I. obstruct; intercept; barring a passage; opposing a barrier to; *měngadang*, to interpose between; to keep something off; *m. musoh*, to keep the foe at a distance; to keep off enemies. II. *adang-adang*, at times, sometimes; = *kadang-kadang*.

adas, *adas manis*, aniseed; *a. pědas*, fennel.

adat, Ar. custom; customary law; customary behaviour; proper behaviour; courtesy; law; *a. Měnangkabau*, the (customary) law of Menangkabau; *sěpěrti adat-nya*, as was his custom; *běradat*, in accordance with custom; proper, courteous.

adek, younger brother or sister; cousin younger than oneself; a term of endearment to one slightly younger than oneself; *a. běradek*, near relatives; *měngaku a. běradek*, to accept as a brother or sister—i.e. to terminate a closer relation in a friendly manner, or to set a limit to possible relations; *a. sa-pupu*, a (younger) first cousin.

adi, Skr. excellent, noble, eminent; an expression usually met with in titles—e.g. *adipati*, *adiraja*.

adib, Ar. respectful—the adjective of *adab*, q.v.

adika, see *andeka*.

adikara, Skr. majestic.

adil, Ar. just, fair, honest—used of superiors being just to their subordinates or of a judge being impartial.

adinda, younger brother or sister; a more courteous variant of *adek*, q.v.

ading, younger brother or sister; a variant (in Malayo-Javanese literature) of *adek*.

adipati, Skr. an ancient exalted title used in Java.

adiraja, Skr. very royal; royal by descent; a component part of many Malay titles of distinction; also *diraja*.

adiwarna, Skr. glowing with colour, resplendent.

adoh, alas! oh! an exclamation of pain, sorrow, or regret.

adohi, alas! oh! = *adoh*.

adok, stirring up; thoroughly kneading or mixing; *champur adok*, a mixture; miscellaneous.

adu, I. contest, competition; to sue (in court); to refer for decision; *běradu*, to make (crickets) fight; *měngadu*, to contend, to compete; *měngadukan hal*, to represent one's case; *aduan*, a lawsuit; the plaintiff in a case. II. *běradu*, to sleep (of a prince); *pěraduan*, a couch, a bed, a bedroom.

adun, I. finery in dress; *adunkan pěngantin*, to deck out a bridegroom. II. *adunan*, dough; *měngadun*, to knead.

adzab, Ar. sorrow, pain, trouble; also *azab*.

adzmat, Ar. awful, terrible, awe-inspiring; also *asmat*.

afiat, Ar. health; good health; *sehat dan a.*, id.

afrit, Ar. an evil spirit.

agah, to crow, of a baby.

agak, conjecture, guessing; *agak-agak*, approximately, about, as far as one can guess; more or less; *agak-nya* —id.; *agak gěrangan*, if by any chance.

agal, (Kedah) an unidentified species of tortoise.

agam, masculine, manly, big, stout, tall.

agama, Skr. religion; *a. Islam*, the Muhammadan religion; also *igama* and *ugama*.

agan, *mati běragan*, to die without visible cause; to seem alive in death =*mati běrakan*, from *akan*.

agar, I. Hind. in order that, so that =*supaya*. II. *agar-agar*, a kind of seaweed used for making jelly.

agas, a sandfly.

ageh, a share agreed upon; the share to be allotted to anyone.

agok, a neck-ornament worn by women and children.

agong, large, great, main (in certain expressions only); *tiang a.*, the main-mast; *layar a.*, the mainsail, *a. alam*, a prince of the earth.

agus, Jav. fair, handsome.

ah, ah! oh! an exclamation of pain or anguish.

ahad, Ar. *hari ahad*, Sunday; the first day of the week; *Allahu ahad*, God is one.

ahli, I. Ar. versed in, expert in; II. Ar. a variant of *ahlu*, q.v.

ahlu, Ar. family; people; men who do or are versed in anything; *ahlu'n-nujum*, astrologers; *ahlu'l-kuran*, experts on the Koran.

ahmak, Ar. dense, stupid, unintelligent.

aho, ho! there! an interjection of summons or to call attention.

ahwal, Ar. things, matters, events, occurrences; *sěgala hal ahwal pěrkara itu*, all the facts of the case.

ai, yes, yes! an interjection of eager approval.

aib, Ar. a shame, a disgrace; *měm-běri a.*, to put to shame; to disgrace.

ain, Ar. *ain-ul-banat*, the name of a cloth sometimes mentioned in romances.

aiyar, Ar. a swindler, a cheat.

ajaib Ar. wonderful, miraculous, strange; *běnda yang ajaib*, a curio; an extraordinary article.

ajak, invitation, suasion to do anything; *měngajak*, to invite.

ajal, Ar. allotted time; destiny; alloted span of life; *tiada sampai ajal-nya*, his time (to die) has not yet come.

ajar, I. teaching, instruction; *ajar-kan*, to teach; *bělajar*, to learn; *pě-lajaran*, learning; the thing taught or learnt; *pěngajaran*, the act of teaching; the process of teaching; the lectures of anyone; *pěngajar*, a teacher. II. Skr. *ajar-ajar*, devotees; ascetics; disciples of an ascetic teacher.

aji, I. Jav. royal; *rama a.*, or *bapa a.*, sovereign father, sire; *kakang a.*, royal brother; *sang-aji*, king, ruler, sacred majesty. II. *měngaji*, to read (the Koran); to study (religion); to study generally.

ajnas, Ar. miscellanies; sorts; *tuh-fatu'l-ajnas*, "a gift of various articles," a common expression in epistolary language to describe the letter itself.

ajok, mimicry, imitation; ridicule by mimicry; *měngajok*, to take off.

ajun, widest from the mark; last in the competition.

akal, Ar. intelligence, understanding, mind; *běrakal*, intelligent; *a. baligh*, maturity, years of discretion; *pan-jang a.*, resourceful.

akan, to, approach to; motion towards; intention to; *budak yang akan měngaji*, a boy about to study; *akan-daku*, to me; *akan-dia*, to him; *akan-akan*, like, resembling, very similar to; *sa-akan-akan*, almost exactly like; *běrakan* = *běragan*—v. *agan*.

akar, root, fibre; a climbing or creeping plant; *tiada rotan akar pun běr-guna*, if you cannot get a rattan any fibre will be useful (half a loaf is better than no bread), prov.; *bĕrak ır*, to take root.

akas, lively, nimble, graceful.

akat, Ar. to settle; to conclude; to put through; *a. nikah*, to settle the details of a marriage; *a. barang*, to deal in goods, to trade.

akbar, Ar. most great, almighty; *Allahu akbar*, God is almighty.

akek, Ar. agate, cornelian; coral.

akhbar, Ar. news; a newspaper.

akhir, Ar. last; the end; *akhir-nya*, in the end; *akhir-zaman*, for ever; to the end of time.

akhirat, Ar. eternity, the life to come.

aki, *to' aki*, (Perak) grandfather.

aksara, Skr. letter, alphabetical symbol.

aku, I. I, me, myself; *akandaku*, to me; *aku sĕmua*, we; *aku sakalian*, id. II. *mĕngaku*, to admit, to accept (a fact).

al, Ar. the.

alabangka, Port. a crowbar.

alah, to be worsted; to lose (a contest); *ala bısa oleh biasa*, theory is worsted by practice, prov.; *alahkan* and *mĕngalahkan*, to vanquish, to bring into subjection.

alahan, a dried up river-bed.

alaihi, Ar. upon him; to him.

alaikum, Ar. upon you; to you.

alam, Ar. the world.

alamat, Ar. sign, token.

alan-alan, a jester; a buffoon; a clown.

alang, I. cross, across; *a. balai*, the cross-beams over an audience-hall. II. slight (in importance), of little account; *a. kĕpalang*, id.; *bukan alang-alang* of no little importance, important, weighty; *a. alangan*, half-hearted, slight; *alang-kah*, is it of no importance that...—a semi-sarcastic interrogative enhancing the force of a statement.

alap, sedate, slow, quiet.

alar, the child of a slave (of the class known as *ulur*).

alas, I. foundation, basis, framework, stand; *a. kaki*, a footstool; *a. baju*, the lining of a coat; *a. pĕ'ana*, a numnah; *a. rumah*, the foundations of a house. II. Jav. *alasan*, the jungle.

alat, Ar. equipment, appurtenances; *a. kĕrajaan*, regalia; *a. pĕrang* and *a. sĕnjata*, military equipment; *alati* and *mĕngalatkan*, to fit out.

aleh, change of position, moving, shifting; also *kaleh*.

alek, *olak-alek*, backwards and forwards.

algoja, Port. an executioner.

ali-ali, a sling; *rajut a.-a.*, the socket of a sling.

alif, the name of the first letter of the alphabet.

alim, Ar. wise, learned; *orang a.*, a savant.

alin, medicinal rubbing; the use of an embrocation.

aling, *ulang aling*, motion to and fro, backwards and forwards.

alir, flowing; floating down stream; *mĕngalir*, to flow; *mĕngalirkan*, to set floating; *tali alir*, a floating line used for catching crocodiles.

alis, Jav. the eyebrow.

alit, touching up the edge of anything with colour; colouring the edge of the eyelid.

alkari, Port. sealing-wax.

alku, a go-between, a pimp.

Allah, Ar. God.

allahumma, Ar. my God; O God!

almari, Port. a wardrobe, an almeirah.

almas, Ar. a diamond.

alongan, Jav. a pool, a mere.

alpa, Skr. carelessness, negligence; to treat with carelessness; also *lĕpa*.

alti, clever, smart.

alu, I. a pestle, a pounder. II. *mĕngalu-ngalukan*, to welcome; to receive a guest with assiduous attention. III. *ikan alu-alu*, a large fish (unidentified).

alun, I. ground-swell; long rolling waves; *bĕralun* and *mĕngalun*, to roll-up, of the sea; to be tempestuous. II. Jav. *alun-alun*, the esplanade in front of a Javanese palace.

alur, the channel of a river; the hollowed-out bed of a stream.

alwat, Ar. aloes-wood.

ama, I. a gnat, an atom. II. Ar. *ama baad*, well then after that... an opening to a Malay paragraph.

amah, a Chinese nurse.

amal, Ar. good works; meritorious deeds in the eyes of God.

aman, Ar. peace, safety; mercy, forgiveness.

amanat, Ar. security; fidelity.

amang, I. tourmaline, wolfram. II. *mĕngamang*, to threaten, to menace.

amar, Ar. order, command, edict; the commands of the Deity.

amat, exceeding, very; *'ĕramat*, surpassingly; *amati, amat-amati* and *mĕmpĕramat-amati*, to look very closely at; to devote careful attention to.

ambai, a fixed riverine purse-net.

ambal, I. *ambalan*, a procession; *bĕrambal-ambalan*, in procession, trooping after. II. a rug.

amban, bamboos lashed to a boat's side to increase its stability.

ambang, the lintel of a door; *mĕngambang*, to just seem to rest on the horizon, of the sun or moon; to remain motionless in the air, of a bird; *chinta ambang-ambangan*, "wishing" when the moon just appears over the horizon—a most propitious time according to Malay belief.

ambar, I. Ar. ambergris. II. insipid, tasteless, vapid.

ambil, taking over; taking and retaining (and not merely picking up); *a. pĕdoman*, to set the course by the compass; *a. angin*, to take an airing, to go for a walk; *mĕngambil*, to take; *mĕngambil akan mĕnantu*, to take as a son-in-law; to give one's daughter in marriage to; *mĕngambil di-hati*, to take to heart; to bear a grudge over.

ambin, a scarf to support a burden borne on the back.

ambohi, hullo, oh! an exclamation of astonishment.

ambong, I. a sort of native knapsack. II. *mĕngambong*, to surge up, of waves. III. *ambong-ambong*, a seashore shrub (*scæv. la koenigi*).

ambul, rebounding by the force of elasticity; *mĕngambul*, to rebound (*e.g.* as a ball).

ambur, = *hambur*.

ambus, *mĕngambus*, to run away.

amin, Ar. amen; be it so! *mĕngaminkan*, to keep repeating the word amen.

amir, Ar. an emir; a chief; *amiru'l-muminin*, Commander of the Faithful.

amok, a furious attack; an "amuck"; *mĕngamok*, to run amuck; to attack furiously.

ampai, hanging and waving loosely; *ampaian kain*, a clothes-line; *ampai-ampai*, a small stinging jelly-fish— c.f. *lampai*.

ampat, see *ĕmpat*.

ampong, drifting, to drift—cf. *apong, lampong*, etc.

ampu, holding up by pressure from below; *mĕngampu*, to hold up, to support (as corsets hold up the breasts).

ampuan, *tĕngku ampuan*, a raja's principal wife.

ampul, *mĕngampul*, to swell out; to be blown out.

ampun, pardon, forgiveness; *mĕminta a.*, to ask forgiveness; *ampuni, ampunkan* and *mĕngampunkan*, to forgive.

amput, (vulgar) sexual congress.

amra, Hind. the hog-plum.

amris, Ar. *urat amris*, the muscles and veins at the side of the throat; the throat.

anai-anai, the white ant; the termite.

anak, child, offspring, issue; the young of an animal; the native (of a place); the relationship of an accessory to a principal object or of a component part to a whole; *a. anakan*, a puppet, a doll, an image; *a. angkat*, a child by adoption; *a. anjing*, a puppy; *a. ayam*, a chicken; *a. ayer*, a rivulet; *a. bini*, family, wife and family; *a. buah*, the people under the charge of a native headman or chief; *a. buangan*, a foundling; *a. chuchu*, descendants; *a. dagang*, a foreigner; *a. dara*, a maiden; *a. dayong*, an oarsman; *a. gahara*, a legitimate child; *a. gampang*, an illegitimate child of doubtful paternity; *a. gĕnta*, the clapper of a bell; *a. gobek*, a betel-nut pounder; *a. gula*, syrup; *a. gundek*, a son by a secondary wife; *a. haram*, an illegitimate child; *a. jari*, a finger; *a. kĕmbar*, a twin; *a. kunchi*, a key; *a. laki-laki*, a boy, a son; *a. lidah*, the uvula; *a. murid*, a pupil; *a. nĕgĕri*, a native of the country; *a. orang*, other people's children (especially their daughters); *a. panah*, an arrow; *a. pĕrahu*, a boatman; *a. pĕrĕmpuan*, a girl, a daughter; *a. piatu*, an orphan; *a. raja*, a prince; *a. rambut*, the fringe of hair over the forehead; *a. roda*, the spoke of a wheel; *a. sulong*, the eldest-born; *a. sumbang*, a child of incest; *a. sungai*, a small tributary stream; *a. tangga*, a step, a rung of a ladder; *a. tĕlinga*, the external gristly portion of the ear; *a. tĕruna*, a bachelor, an unmarried youth; *a. tiri*, a step-child; *a. tunggal*, an only child; *bĕranak*, to be possessed of a child, to bear a child; *mĕmpĕranakkan*, to beget; *pĕnganak*, a sort of drum; *pĕranakan*, born in the country, natives.

anakanda, son—a respectful and endearing form of *anak*.

anakda, son—a variant of *anakanda*.

anam, see *ĕnam*.

ananda, son—a variant of *anakanda*.

anang, my son; a variant of *anak* occurring in Malayo-Javanese literature.

anbia, Ar. prophets; the plural of *nabi*.

anchai, to let go.

anchak, a rough wide-intersticed creel or basket of bamboo in which offerings are placed for evil spirits; *buang a.*, to make such offerings.

anchar, Jav. the upas-tree (*antiaris toxicaria*).

anchok, the pairing of animals.

anchong, a glazed earthenware pot.

anchu, I. a large raft. II. cross-beams under a *nibong* flooring.

anda, Skr. the musk-glands in a civet; *a. kĕsturi*, the name of a Malay sweetmeat.

andai, I. the hook to which the sheet of a Malay sail is attached. II. *andainya*, possibly. III. see *handai*.

andak, *mĕngandakkan layar*, to reef a sail.

andal, *undok andal*, in swift succession (of work).

andam, Pers. the dressing of the hair above the forehead; the fringe of a bride.

andang, I. a torch of dry leaves. II. *andang-andang*, the yard on a ship or boat.

andar, Ar. *mati andar*, to die unavenged.

andas, a block with a flat surface; an anvil.

andeka, I. Jav. you—a pronoun of the second person used in addressing people of rank. II. descent; the dignity of a hereditary non-sovereign chief; also (in Perak) *adika*.

andoh, support by means of a sling; *andohan sĕkochi*, the slings under a boat at the davits; *tali andoh*, the lashings of a gun-carriage.

andoman, Skr. a (Kedah) variant of *hanoman*, q.v.; see also *doman*.

andong, the dracoena of gardens (*cordyline terminalis*).
andun, Jav. *mĕngandun pĕrang*, to make war = *mĕngadu pĕrang*.
andur, a buffalo-sleigh.
aneka, Skr. kinds, species; *sĕrba a.*, of different kinds, various; also *neka*.
angan, thoughts, ideas, the mind, usually *angan-angan*; *siti juga di-angan-angan*, my lady is ever in my thoughts.
angek, (Kedah) *ungak-angek*, bobbing up and down.
angga, tine of a deer; *mĕrangga tandok*, with branching horns.
anggai, a sign (in very high-flown language), = *isharat*.
anggal, buoyant, lightly laden; light (of sickness).
anggap, a challenging invitation at a game; *bĕranggap-anggapan*, in turns, turn and turn about.
anggar, reckoning, calculation; *anggaran pĕlayaran*, navigation (as a science); *mĕmbuat anggaran*, to take bearings; *anggaran burong*, the perching place of a bird.
anggara, see *angkara*.
anggau, clutching at anything; putting out the hand to seize.
anggĕrek, an orchid.
anggĕrka, *baju anggĕrka*, a long overcoat or surtout.
anggit, fastening together; *rotan pĕnganggit atap*, a rattan for fastening ataps; *rotan anggit*, the rattan binding outside a drum.
anggok, to nod the head; also *ĕnggok*.
anggota, Skr. limbs; the members of the body.
anggul, to lift at the bows, to pitch (of a boat).
anggun, fastidious, affected in manner or dress.
anggur, I, transplanting. II, Pers. the vine, grapes, (by simile) grape-shot, shot; *ayer a.*, wine; *buah a.*, grapes; *tarok a.*, a vine-shoot.

III, better, rather, it were better that.
angin, a wind, a breeze, a current of air; *a. barat*, a west wind; *a. darat*, a land breeze; *a. gila*, an uncertain wind; *a. puting bĕliong*, a whirlwind; *a. sakal*, a head-wind; *a. sĕlĕmbubu*, an eddying wind; *a. timba ruang*, a wind on the beam; *ambil a.*, to go for an airing; *chakap a.*, vapouring, empty talk; *di-atas a.*, west, countries from which ships used to come in the south-west monsoon; *di-bawah a.*, Malaya, Burma, etc., countries to which people come from the west during the south-west monsoon; *kĕpala a.*, flighty; *kĕreta a.*, a switch-back railway, (sometimes) a bicycle; *makan a.*, to set well in a breeze (of a sail), to take an airing; *mata a.*, the direction from which the wind is blowing; *mĕnjaring a.*, to waste time; *pĕrchaya a.*, vain hopes or expectations; *pĕnyakit a.*, a generic name for internal diseases which it is hard for a native doctor to diagnose; *pokok a.*, a storm-cloud; *anginkan*, to dry in a current of air.
angka, Skr. a numerical figure, a cypher; *a. dua*, the figure two, the reduplication-mark.
angkap, a variant of *anggap*, q.v.
angkara, Skr. violence, gross brutality or disrespect, violence to a girl or woman; *hina a.*, a low brute; *sĕtua a.*, a fabulous monster of great strength.
angkasa, Skr. the regions of the air, the heavens; *dewa a.*, a celestial deity; *unggas a.*, a bird of the air.
angkat, raising, lifting, bringing up; *anak a.*, an adopted child; *angkat-angkat*, gait, bearing; *angkatkan*, to raise, to lift; *angkatan*, an expeditionary force; *angkatan raja diraja*, the hearse at a sovereign's funeral; *bĕrangkat*, to go (of a prince).
angkau, see *ĕngkau*.
angkit, raising (small light objects),

picking up; *bĕlat angkit-angkit*, chicks.

angkoh, proud, haughty.

angkok, the figure-head of a native boat.

angkup, tweezers, forceps.

angkut, raising piecemeal, picking up one at a time; *mĕngangkut*, to keep picking up and removing; *angkut-angkut*, the mason-bee.

anglo, Ch. a brazier.

anglong, a pavilion, a summer-house.

angsa, Skr. a goose.

angsana, the ansenna-tree; also *sĕna*.

angsoka, Skr. the name of a tree (*pavetta indica*?)

angsur, progress in short stages; in instalments.

angus, see *hangus*.

angut, day-dreaming—e.g. under the influence of opium.

ani, *mĕngani*, to arrange the pattern on a weaver's loom.

aniaya, Skr. oppression, injustice, wrong.

aning-aning, a large wasp.

anja, halliard.

anjak, to shift one's position slightly; edging away.

anjal, *mĕnganjal*, to spring back into its original position (of a flexible body).

anjang, *kĕtam anjang-anjang*, a variety of crab.

anjiman, Eng. *kapal anjiman*, an East Indiaman (ship).

anjing, a dog; dog, as a term of abuse; *anjing-anjing*, the muscle of the calf; *a. ayer*, an otter; *a. hutan*, a wild dog; *anak a.*, a puppy; *gigi a.*, the canine teeth; *gĕmbala a.*, a dog-boy.

anjir, Pers. the fig.

anjong, a projecting upper-floor room; a sort of covered verandah over a porch or drive.

anjur, *mĕnganjur*, to project, to stretch out.

anum, Jav. fair, handsome; *ratu a.*, the handsome prince; Sira Panji.

anur, a (Kedah) variant of *andur*, q.v.

anta, I. Skr. existence, entity, nature; *bĕranta indĕra*, divine; *bĕranta loka*, earthly, mundane; *anta kĕsoma*, flowery; the name given to a Malay dish (made of *kĕledek*). II. Skr. *naga anta-boga*, the great serpent.

antah, the husk; the outer skin of grain.

antak, to tap the ground with the cushion of the foot, the heel remaining stationary.

antan, a pestle.

antap, heavy for its size; of great specific gravity.

antar, = *hantar*.

antar-antar, a ramrod; a pounder.

antara, Skr. space between; time between; *di-antara*, during the interval between; in the space between; among; *ingat antara bĕlum kĕna*, think before you are involved in anything (look before you leap), prov.

anteh, *mĕnganteh*, to spin (thread).

antĕlas, Ar. satin.

antero, Port. the whole; *a. Kĕlang*, the whole of Klang—i.e. the district and not the mere town.

anti, *untak anti*, convulsive movement; also *ĕntak-anti*.

antil, *untal-antil*, swaying loosely.

anting, hanging down and swaying; pendulous; *untang-anting*—id. of many objects swaying at a time; *anting-anting*, an ear-pendant; *burong anting-anting*, racquet-tailed drongo (*dissemurus platurus*).

antok, I. *mĕngantok*, to be drowsy or sleepy. II. colliding; *bĕrantok*, to collide; *gigi bĕrantok*, chattering teeth; *tĕrantok*, in collision; *sudah tĕrantok baharu tĕngadah*, to look up after the collision (to shut the stable-door after the steed has been stolen), prov.

antul, *mĕngantul*, to bound back, to fall back.

antun, *bĕrantun*, to be particular about one's dress.
antup, Jav. the sting of an insect.
anu, such-and-such; *si-anu*, so-and-so; *di-kampong anu*, at such-and-such a place.
anugĕrah, Skr. favour; grace; the gift of a superior to an inferior; *anugĕrahi*, to bestow, to confer a favour on.
anun, a (Kedah) variant of *anu*.
anyam, plaiting; basket and mat-work; *mĕnganyam*, to plait.
anyang, to sweep up rubbish into heaps.
anyek, *onyak-anyek*, vacillating, undecided; shaking (as a loose tooth).
anyut, see *hanyut*.
apa, what; *dia orang apa*, what is he? *apa-buat*, what are you doing? *apa-apa*, whatever; *apa-bila*, when, whenever; *apa fasal*, why? *apa guna*, what is the use? *apa-kala*, when, whenever; *apa-lagi*, what then? *apa-lah*, please—i.e. as much as you please; *khabari apa-lah*, tell me something (whatever you like); *apa-macham*, how; what kind of; in what way; *apa sĕbab*, why; *apa-tah*, what...? *barang-apa*, whatever; *bĕbĕrapa*, in some quantity; some, several; *bĕrapa*, in what quantity; how many, how much? *bĕtapa*, how, why? *kĕnapa* and *mĕngapa*, why? *siapa*, who? *tiada mĕngapa*, or (colloquially) *tidak apa*, no matter, never mind.
apabila, when; whenever.
apak, Jav. foul, fetid (of odour).
apakala, when, whenever.
apam, Tam. a thin cake.
apas, striking, effective (of costume).
apek, I. spruce, smart, neat. II. *chakap upak-apek*, tale-bearing; mischievous or inconsistent talk.
api, fire; a light; a light-house; *api-api*, a generic name for a number of trees of the mangrove class; *asap a.*, smoke; *bara a.*, live embers; *batu a.*,

flint; *bunga a.*, sparks, fireworks; *di-makan a.*, burnt; *gobek a.*, a fire syringe; *gunong a.*, a volcano; *kapal a.*, a steamship; *kayu a.*, firewood: *kĕreta a.*, a railway; a steam tramway; *laut a.*, the fiery sea (hell); *pĕriok a.*, a bomb, a shell; *sĕmut a.*, a long black stinging ant; *bĕrapi*, flaming.
apilan, a gun-shield.
apit, wedging between two surfaces (not connected by a hinge); *apitan*, a printing-press; *mĕngapit*, to press between two surfaces; *tĕrapit*, wedged in between.
apiun, Ar. opium.
apong, drifting, floating; floatsam, driftwood; *laksana apong di-tĕngah laut*, like driftwood on the waves (helpless), prov.
apum, a cake resembling (but not identical with) the *apam*.
apus, = *hapus*.
ara, a generic name for trees of the fig type; *mĕnanti ara ta'-bĕrgĕtah*, to wait for the fig to lose its sap (an endless wait), prov.
Arab, Ar. Arabian, Arabic; *nĕgĕri A.*, Arabia; *bah-sa A.*, Arabic.
arah, direction; *a. ka-laut*, towards the sea; *sa-kĕliling a.*, on all sides, in all directions; *ta'-tĕntu a.*, in confusion.
arai, *arai jĕmarai*, hanging loosely.
arak, I. *bĕrarak*, to march in procession; *pĕrarakan*, a processional car; II. Ar. arrack; rice-spirit; spirits generally.
arakian, furthermore.
aral, Ar. an obstacle; a difficulty; a hindrance.
aram, I. suspicion. II. *aram tĕmaram*, dimmed in lustre; clouded over (as the moon).
arang, charcoal; *kayu a.*, ebony; *a. batu*, coal; *a. di-muka*, defilement; shame, disgrace.
ararut, Eng. arrowroot.
aras, I. rising to a level with;

měngaras a., to rise to the cloud-line. II. a term in chess.
arash, Ar. the throne of God.
archa, Skr. an image; a bas-relief.
ari, I. Jav. younger brother or sister; = *adek*; *ari-ningsun*, id.; = *adinda*. II. *ari-ari*, the pubes. III. Ar. halter. IV. = *hari*.
aria, (nautical) lower away!
arif, Ar. learned, erudite.
arifin, Ar. wise men; the wise—plural of *arif*.
aring, I. foul-smelling. II. the small piece of worked steel at the top of the blade of a *kěris* (it corresponds in some respects to the guard on a foil).
arip, Jav. sleepy.
aris, I. a bolt-rope. II. Ar. a husbandman.
arit, Jav. a slightly curved knife used for tapping trees.
Arjuna, Skr. the hero Arjuna.
arkian, see *arakian*.
arnab, Ar. a rabbit.
arong, wading through water; fording; *měngarong*, to wade through water; to ford; to traverse; *bělayar měngarong*, to put out to sea; *měngarong darah*, to wade through blood (a metaphor for great slaughter); *arongan*, a crossing, a channel (a metaphor for the deep central part of the sea).
arpus, catgut.
arti, see *hěrti*.
aruan, a fresh-water fish (*ophiocephalus* sp.)
aruda, Port. rue (*ruta graveolens*).
arwa, a saw-edged knife.
arwah, Ar. the vital elements in a man; the soul; the spirits of the dead; *makan a.*, a feast in honour of the dead; *těrbang a.*, loss of consciousness.
asa, Sk. hope; *putus a.*, hopelessness; *hilang a.*, id.
asad, Ar. a lion.
asah, grinding down, whetting; filing (the teeth); *batu a.*, a whetstone; *asahkan*, to whet, to grind down.
asai, a fruit-weevil.
asak, pressing in or pressing down; ramming into a small space.
asal, Ar. origin; *a. usul*, history; origins; lineage; *asal-nya*, originally; *asalkan* (or simply *asal*), if, provided that, if only.
asam, acid, sour; acid fruits; *laksana asam děngan garam*, like acids and salt (which go well together), prov.; *limau a.*, the lime.
asap, smoke, vapour; *asapkan*, to fumigate; to perfume with incense; *pěrasapan*, a censer.
asek, giddy behaviour.
ashik, Ar. enamoured; in love; lover.
asin, salt, saline.
asing, distinct, separate, apart; *orang a.*, another person, a different person; *asingkan*, to set apart; to discriminate.
askar, Ar. soldiery.
asmara, Skr. love; sexual love.
asoh, *měngasoh*, to nurse; *pěngasoh*, a nurse.
asok, (Kedah) masked dancer.
Asrafil, Ar. the archangel Israfel.
astaka, a dais.
astakona, Skr. an octagonal pattern.
astana, = *istana*.
asu, *gigi asu*, the canine teeth.
asut, stirring up enmity, egging on to a quarrel; *měngasut*, to egg on, to stir up.
atap, roofing; thatch of palm-leaf; *a. ayan*, a corrugated iron roof; *a. batu*, *a. gěnting*, or *a. sisek těnggiling*, a tiled roof; *a. gajah měnyusu*, a covered way.
atar, *minyak atar*, otto of roses.
atas, position above; with reference to; about; *di-atas*, above; *ka-atas*, upward, to a place above.
atau, Skr. or.
atong, *těratong-atong*, riding at anchor.
atur, setting in order; arranging;

aturan, regulations; *aturkan*, to set in order.
atus, (Kedah) to filter; to rinse.
aulia, Ar. a saint; the saints.
aum, (onomatopœic); *mĕngaum*, to growl (as a tiger), to murmur (as a crowd).
aur, a generic name given to many large bamboos.
aus, to be worn away by friction.
auta, false, lying.
awak, body, person, self; contents; you, thou (in Johor and Pahang); *a. pĕrahu*, the crew of a ship.
awal, Ar. beginning; first; *a. musim*, the beginning of the season.
awan, cloud; cloud-like pattern; *a. mĕngandong hujan*, a rain cloud; *a. timbul*, pattern in relief; *a. tĕnggĕlam*, an incised pattern.
awang, I. young fellow, young man, youth. II. *awang-awang* or *awang-awangan*, the lower heavens; the space between earth and sky.
awar, = *hawar*.
awas, keen sight; second sight.
awat, I. why, what, wherefore. II. the ridge between plough-furrows; *mĕmĕchah a.*, to cross-plough.
ayah, I. father, sire; *a. bonda*, parents. II. Hind. an Indian nurse.
ayahanda, sire (in court language).
ayak, sifting; *mĕngayak*, to pass through a sieve; *ayakan*, a sieve.
ayam, a generic name for fowls; *a. bĕlanda*, a turkey; *a. dĕnak* or *a. hutan*, a jungle fowl; *a. itek*, poultry; *a. jantan*, a cock; *a. kasi* or *a. kĕmbiri*, a capon; *a. mutiara*, a guinea-fowl; *a. pĕgar*, the fire-back pheasant (*lophura rufa*); *ayam-ayam*, a watercock; *anak a.*, a chicken.
ayan, Eng. corrugated iron.
ayapan, victuals.
ayat, Ar. verse of the Koran.
ayer, water, liquid, juice, sap; *a. bah*, a flood; *a. batu*, ice; *a. gula*, syrup; *a. kĕras*, spirits; *a. madu*, honey; *a. mata*, tears; *a. mawar*, rose-water; *a. minum*, drinking-water; *a. muka*, expression of face; *a. pasang*, the rising tide; *a. pĕloh*, perspiration; *a. surut*, the falling tide; *a. tawar*, fresh water; *a. teh*, tea; *a. tĕrjun*, a waterfall; *buang a.*, to ease oneself; *mata a.*, a spring; *tanah a.*, territories.
ayo, an interjection of greeting.
ayoh, alas! an exclamation of sorrow.
ayok, (coarse) sexual congress.
ayu, Jav. fair, handsome.
ayun, to rock, to sway; *bĕrayun* or *mĕngayun*, id.; *ayunan*, a hammock; a cradle.
ayut, (coarse) sexual congress.
aza, Ar. honoured; in honour (of God).
azab, Ar. sorrow, pain, trouble; also *adzab*.
azal, Ar. the beginning of time; the endless past.
azimat, Ar. a talisman.
aziz, Ar. dear, darling.
azmat, Ar. awe-inspiring; also *adzmat*.

B

ba, the name of the second letter of the alphabet.
baada, Ar. after; *baada-hu*, after that.
bab, Ar. a chapter; a main division of a book.
baba, a Straits-born Chinese; a foreigner born in Malaya.
babad, Jav. a chronicle, a history.
babak, set, series; *sa-babak*, of one series; similar, identical.
babang, agape; gaping wide.

babar, astretch; expansion; *těrbabar*, spread out; astretch.

babas, driven out of its course (of a ship).

babi, a pig; pig as a term of abuse; *b. buta*, recklessness; *b. hutan*, a wild pig; *b. kawan*, the half-grown wild pig; *b. nangui*, the young wild pig (striped); *b. tunggal*, the full-grown boar; *bulu b.*, a sea-urchin; *burong b.*, the adjutant (bird); *gila b.*, epilepsy.

babil, wrangling, altercation; *běr-babil*, to dispute.

babit, interference; dragging third parties into a dispute.

babok, dull, dense, stupid.

babu, a Javanese nurse.

babur, broad-bodied.

bacha, reading; the utterance of formulæ, prayers or incantations; *mèmbacha*, to read; *tanda bachaan*, vowel-points; diacritical marks.

bachang, see *machang* or *ěmbachang*.

bachar, loquacious.

bachin, stinking, fetid.

bachir, *bochor-bachir*, very leaky, constantly running.

bachul, timid, spiritless; *ayam b.*, a cock that will not fight.

badak, a generic name for the rhinoceros and tapir; *b. api*, a fabulous rhinoceros; *b. hěmpit = b. kěrbau*; *b. kěrbau*, the Sumatran rhinoceros; *b. raya*, the Javan rhinoceros (r. *sondaicus*); *b. tampong*, the tapir; = *těnok*.

badam, Pers. the almond; *b. china*, ground-nuts.

badan, Ar. the body (in contradistinction to the soul); cf. *tuboh*.

badang, a large bamboo tray or sieve.

badar, Ar. the moon; the name of a plain near Mecca.

badek, a small knife.

badi, the evil influences affecting a place; also *bahadi*.

badok, I. clumsy; bulky. II. the name of a fish.

badong, Jav. a gorget worn by a child.

badui, Ar. a Bedouin; a wandering scoundrel.

badut, Jav. a jester.

bafta, Pers. woven fabrics.

bagai, kind, species, variety; like— the Penang equivalent for *sěpěrti*; *bagai-bagai*, sorts, kinds; also *pělě-bagai*; *běrbagai-bagai*, of different sorts; *sa-bagai*, like, resembling.

bagaimana, how? in what way?

bagal, awkward, clumsy; too tall, too big.

bagan, a platform for drying fish; a scaffolding; (Penang) a landing-place.

bagas, continuous (of a gale).

bagau, a plant (*xyris indica*).

baghal, Ar. a mule.

bagi, (Penang) to, for, towards; to give.

bagimana, = *bagaimana*.

baginda, Sk. king, prince, ruler; your majesty.

bagini, in this way; thus.

bagitu, in that way; so.

bagong, clumsy, awkward (of the build of a boat).

bagu, *bagu-bagu*, a slice or natural sub-division of a fruit.

bagur, big for one's age; overgrown.

bagus, fine, handsome.

bah, *ayer bah*, flood water; inundation.

bahadi, the evil influences (supernatural) haunting a place; also *badi*.

bahaduri, Pers. knightly, gallant.

bahagi, to divide; to allot; *bahagian*, a division, a share.

bahagia, Skr. blessing; *běrbahagia*, fortunate, blessed.

baham, holding in the mouth; chewing; mouthing; mastication; also a coarse equivalent for eating.

bahan, I. a chunk or large lump (especially of wood). II. drubbing, soundly thrashing.

bahana, noise; the confused murmur of many sounds.

bahang, the glow of fire; glowing, hot.
bahar, Ar. the sea; *bintu'l-bahar*, a mermaid.
bahara, a weight; cf. *bara*.
bahari, Pers. excellent, noble, worthy.
baharu, new; newly; just; just then; not till then; then; *tahun b.*, the new year; *baharu ia datang*, he has just come; also *baru*.
bahas, I. knocking up against. II. Ar. debate, discussion.
bahasa, Skr. language; fitting language; politeness; manners; *b. Mĕlayu*, the Malay language; *tiada tahu b.*, to lack manners; *kurang b.*, id.; *jalan b.*, idiom; *juru b.*, an interpreter: also *basa*.
bahaya, Skr. danger, peril; *marabahaya*, id.; also *baya*.
bahkan, of a truth; yes; verily; moreover; a strong affirmative.
bahtĕra, Skr. a vessel; an ark; an argosy—a poetic equivalent for a ship.
bahu, I. the shoulder; *tĕrchabut-lah sĕndi bahu-nya*, his shoulder was put out of joint. II. (Dutch) a measure of superficies (a *bouw*).
bahwa, Skr. the story is, the facts are, namely, to wit—a word used to open a paragraph or the words of a statement; *bahwa-sanya* or *b. sasunggoh-nya*, id.
baïd, Ar. far, distant; *karib dan b.*, near and far; relatives and strangers.
baiduri, Skr. an opal; a generic name for a number of precious stones —such as opals, cat's-eyes, etc.
baik, good, excellent; useful; well; *tuan ada b.*, are you well; how are you; how do you do; *baik-baik*, carefully; *jaga b. b.*, take care; *baik...baik...*, both...and...—e.g. *baik jantan baik bĕtina*, both men and women; *baik-lah*, all right; very well; *sa-baik-baik*, however well; as well as possible; *baiki* or *mĕmbaiki*, to repair, to mend.

bairup, Eng. a beacon; a buoy; a trigonometrical station.
bait, Ar. house; *baitu'l-mal*, the treasury; *baitu'llah*, God's house; *baitu'l-mukadas*, Jerusalem.
baja, I. steel; the process of tempering; improving by manure; *kalau asal baja yang baik*, if of good steel to start with; *tanah yang tiada bĕrbaja*, unmanured land. II. a preparation of burnt coconut shell used for staining the teeth.
bajak, I. (Malacca, Singapore) a plough; = (Penang) *tĕnggala*; *mata b.*, the ploughshare. II. Jav. a pirate.
bajan, Skr. a basin; better *bĕjana*.
bajang, an evil spirit; a familiar spirit.
bajau, a sea gipsy.
baji, a wedge; *b. bĕlah*, a wedge for forcing open a fissure; *b. rapat*, a wedge for filling an interstice so as to keep an object in position or steady.
bajik, Jav. *kĕbajikan*, virtue, merit, good deeds.
bajing, Jav. a squirrel.
baju, an outer garment, a coat, a jacket, a tunic; *b. dalam*, a singlet; *b. hujan*, a mackintosh, a rain coat; *b. panas*, an overcoat; *tangan b.*, the sleeve of a coat.
baka, I. heredity; inherited character. II. Ar. eternal, lasting; *dari nĕgĕri yang fana ka-nĕgĕri yang baka*, from a perishable to an imperishable country (from earth to heaven).
bakai, (Kedah) *mandi bakai*, to wash in fresh water after bathing in the sea.
bakal, I. hereditary social position; *b. laksamana*, of a laksamana's family. II. Jav. materials for construction.
bakap, a fish (unidentified).
bakar, burning; to burn; *mĕmbakar*, to burn, to roast; *tĕrbakar*, burnt.
bakarat, Ar. virginity.
bakat, tide-rips; masses of driftwood and seaweed marking the point

of contact of two currents or the highest point of the beach reached by the tide; traces of an eruptive disease.

bakau, mangrove-swamp; a generic name for mangroves; *ular b.*, a species of viper (*lachesis purpureo-maculatus*).

bakdul, a bearing-rein.

bakek, a pepper; *piper chaba*.

bakhil, Ar. covetous, avaricious.

bakhtiar, Pers. fortunate.

baki, Ar. balance left over; surplus; remainder.

bakir, turned sour (of milk).

bakok, stupid, inattentive, dense.

bakong, a large white-flowered lily-like plant (*crinum asiaticum*).

bakti, Skr. meritorious service; devotion; *bĕrbuat b.*, to show devotion to God; to earn merit in God's sight; *bĕrbakti*, devout; *kĕbaktian*, devotion.

bakul, a basket, a hamper; *mĕnjunjong b.*, to carry a basket on the head.

bakup, closed by inflammation (of the eyes); "bunged up."

bala, I. Ar. misfortune, injury; *tolak b.*, a propitiatory offering or sacrifice. II. Sk. army, soldiery; *b. tĕntĕra*, an army.

balah, disputing, quarrelling, wordy war.

balai, I. a hall of audience; the court of a *pĕnghulu*; (Penang) a police-station. II. *halai-balai*, upsetting, confusing; confused, disorderly.

balairong, a large hall of a type mentioned in romances; a hall of general assembly; *b. agong*, id.

balak, (Dutch) a baulk, a large piece of timber.

balam, I. the Malay ground-dove (*geopelia striata*), usually known as *tĕkukur*. II. dimly visible, hazy (as distant hills); *balam-balam*, id. III. *mĕmbalam-balam*, to paddle with short quick strokes.

balang, I. a bottle with a long narrow neck. II. a missile; to hurl a missile. III. Jav. mournfulness = *walang*. IV. to paddle quickly = *balam*.

balar, I. albino whiteness; pinkness; *kĕrbau b.*, a pink buffalo. II. *chakar balar*, scratched all over; covered with abrasions.

balas, sending back; return; requital; revenge; *balasi*, to requite; *mĕmbalas*, to send back—e.g. *m. tabek*, to return a salutation; *m. surat*, to reply to a letter.

balasan, Ar. balm, balsam.

balau, *pokok balau*, a large tree (*swintonia* sp.)

Balchi, Baluchi, *nĕgĕri B.*, Baluchistan.

baldi, Hind. a horse-bucket.

balek, position behind; in rear of; the reverse; *di-balek*, behind; *b. adab*, disrespect; *bolak-b.*, backwards and forwards; *bĕrbalek*, to return; *tĕrbalek*, upside down, reversed.

balgham, Ar. mucus, phlegm.

bali, I. Ch. the cabin of a junk. II. Balinese; *Pulau B.*, Bali.

baligh, Ar. adult, mature; *akal b.*, years of discretion; puberty.

baling, revolution; *bolang-b.*, chain-shot.

baloh, the wooden frame of a drum; *balohan*, the skeleton of a howdah.

balok, I, Port. a small sailing craft. II. *mĕmbalok*, to "string" for choice of positions.

balong, I. the comb of a cock; *b. kulit*, patches of bark sticking out loosely from the trunk. II. *balong bidai*, an evil spirit of the water.

balu, widowed.

balun, to beat with a rattan.

balur, hard skin, such as that which forms under the yoke in a bullock; untanned hide; jerked meat.

balut, I. enwrapping, enwinding, *b. rokok*, to roll up a cigarette; *di-balut-nya surat*, he wrapped the letter in the envelope (of yellow silk). II. inflamed, red (of the eyes).

bam, cross-tree; cross-piece; the bar of a bullock-cart.
bambang, flat and broad (as a mirror).
bambu, bamboo; better *buloh* and *aur*.
bambun, the Malayan mongoose.
bami, Ch. a dish of vermicelli, prawns and pork.
banang, large (in certain compound expressions only).
banar, *sinar banar*, resplendent.
banat, I, *mĕmbanat*, to thrash. II. wild, forest-covered = *bĕlĕntara*. III. Ar. *ainu'l-banat*, a precious cloth.
banchi, I. toll, census, enumeration per capita. II. Tam. adze. III. Jav. hermaphrodite.
banchoh, mixing up; kneading up (flour, etc.).
banchut, I. projecting; *tĕrbanchut mata*, with the eye thrust out intently (of a lizard on a wall). II. Batav. to futilize = *bantut*.
bandang, *ikan bandang*, a fish (*chrysophrys hasta?*)
bandar, I. Pers. a sea-port; *shahbandar*, harbour-master; a Malay officer controlling the coast and shipping. II. *bandaran*, a water-course; *bandar ayer*, id.
bandarsah, a private mosque or chapel.
bandĕla, a bale.
bandera, see *bĕndera*.
banding, comparison; *tiada sa-banding*, incomparable; *bandingkan*, to compare.
bandok, nervous, self-conscious.
bandong, I. a connected pair—e.g. *balai bandong*, two halls connected by a passage; *tĕlur dua sa-bandong*, two yolks in one egg.
bandu, Skr. friend, associate, companion.
bandul, Eur. the pendulum of a clock.
bandut, to bind, to fasten; to bind up.
bang, I. Pers. the call to prayer.

II. Jav. red; *Batek b.*, a pattern of sarong in which red predominates.
bangai, *tĕrbangai*, left unfinished; incomplete (of a work).
bangar, I. putrid (of long stagnant water). II. *ingar bangar*, great uproar.
bangat, speed; extreme speed; extremely soon; *bangat-bangat* or *b. amat*, very quick; in a very great degree indeed.
bangau, the Malay egret (*bubulcus coromandus* and *herodias intermedia*).
bangbang, Jav. red; *kĕtara bangbang wetan*, the eastern glow appeared.
bangĕlas, opened out; unpartitioned.
bangĕlo, Eng. bungalow.
bangkai, a dead body; a carcase—cf. *mayat* (which is respectful).
bangkang, I. wide apart (of the points of horns, etc.); *tandok b.*, horns, the points of which are wide apart; *kala b.*, the black forest scorpion. II. Jav. contradictoriness. III. unfinished, left incomplete.
bangkar, tough, hard; set stiff (in death).
bangkas, yellow flecked with black (as the colour of a fighting-cock).
bangking, a large round lacquered box.
bangkir, *bongkar-bangkir*, turning everything upside down (as in a disorderly search).
bangkit, rising up; *b. bĕrdiri*, to rise and stand erect; to stand up; *bĕrbangkit*, to rise; *bĕrbangkit-lah kĕtakutan*, a panic arose.
bangkong, *parang bangkong*, a short broad-bladed Bugis chopping knife.
bangku, Port. a bench, a stool, a seat without arms or back.
bangkut, stunted in growth; stumpy.
bangsa, Skr. race, family, good birth; *bahasa mĕnunjokkan bangsa*, a man's manners show his descent, prov.; *b. China*, the Chinese; *bĕrbangsa*, of birth; nobly born.

bangsai, decayed, rotten, falling to pieces (of wood).
bangsal, a shed; *b. kuda*, a stable or stall.
bangsat, vagrant, mean, despicable; *orang b.*, a vagabond.
bangsawan, Skr. of good birth, noble; the word is also used of a native opera company.
bangsi, a native flute or flageolet.
bangun, to rise, to get up; shape, bearing; *jatoh b.*, falling and rising; stumbling along; *těrlalu takut bangun-nya*, bearing himself like a man in great fear; *bangun-bangun*, shape, form; *bangun-bangunan*, a turret or crow's nest in a stockade; a scaffolding; *bangunkɩn*, to make a person get up; *měmbangur*, to rise; to recover damages for the loss of a murdered relative.
bani, Ar. *bani Adam*, the children of Adam; mankind.
banian, see *běnian*.
baning, the tortoise (*testudo emys*).
banir, a buttress-like projection at the base of the trunk of certain trees.
banjar, row, rank, file; *běɩbanjar*, arranged in rows; *taman banjaran sɑri*, the Old-Javanese garden of the hesperides.
banji, Ch. glazed earthenware lattice-work.
bantah, quarrelling, altercation; *běrbantah*, to dispute; *bantahan*, quarrelsome, given to contradicting; *pěrbantahan*, an altercation.
bantai, cutting up a slaughtered animal; quartering; *pěmbantai*, a butcher.
bantal, a pillow, a cushion; *bantal-bantal*, a short horizontal patch of rainbow light.
bantang, *bunting bantang*, advanced pregnancy.
banteng, the Bali ox (*bos sondaicus*) when domesticated.
banting, dashing down, beating together; threshing padi against the sides of a wooden tub; *měmbanting*, to dash against; *sapěrti ombak měmbanting diri-nya*, like waves dashing into each other, prov.
bantu, aid, assistance; *měmbantu*, to succour, to aid, to help.
bantun, uprooting; pulling up the foundations.
bantut, frustration; rendering abortive; nipping in the bud.
banyak, much; many; a quantity; *b. orang*, a number of persons; *orang b.*, the populace; *sa-banyak*, the same number as, as many as, as much as; *kěbanyakan*, most; the majority; the common people; common.
banyu, Jav. fermented coconut water used in dyeing silk.
bapa, father; *mak b.*, or *ibu b.*, parents.
bapang, my father—a Javanese (first person singular possessive) form of *bapa*.
bara, I. embers; *b. api*, live coals. II. *tolak bara*, ballast (see *bahara*). III. *sara-bara*, higgledy-piggledy. IV. Hind. big, great, main (in certain nautical expressions).
barah, abscess, tumour.
barai, an edible salt-water shell-fish.
baran, low swampy undergrowth; *babi b.*, wild pig infesting such undergrowth.
barang, things in general; luggage; one's belongings; anything; any; would that in some way; *b. apa*, whatever; *b. barang*, (1) things, belongings, luggage; (2) ordinary, common; *b. bila*, whenever; *b. kali*, perhaps; *b. siapa*, whoever; *sa-barang*, whatever.
baras, Ar. leprosy.
barat, I. west; *b. těpat*, due west; *orang b.*, Kelantanese (as described in Pahang). II. *sěsat barat*, very much astray; confused. III. *ikan barat-barat* (*triacanthus brevirostris*).
barau, *ikan barau-barau*, (*triacanthus blochii*); *burong barau-barau*,

the yellow crowned bulbul (*trachycomus ochrocephalus*).
barek, mottled, veined, variegated.
Bari, I. Ar. God the Creator. II. *baribari*, fruit-flies.
baring, lying down at full length; *bĕrbaring*, to lie down; *baringkan*, to place in a recumbent position.
baris, a line, a row, a file (of soldiers); *b. sipahi*, a line of troops.
baroh, low land; the land lying below one.
barong, I. a booth, a stall. II. a road between hills; a pass or col.
baru, I. new; = *baharu*. II. a seashore tree (*hibiscus tiliaceus*); *ikan daun b*. (*drepane punctata*).
barus, *kapur b*., camphor.
barut, a long bandage; a bodice worn by children; to bandage or swathe in cloth.
barzakh, *alam b*., Hades.
basah, wet, moist; *b. kuyup*, wringing wet; *kain basahan*, clothes used for bathing in; old clothes; *basahkan*, to wet.
basal, jaundice.
basau, hard (when it should be soft), e.g. of a boiled potato.
bashah, Turk. a pasha.
basi, musty, stale, mouldy.
basoh, washing; *sapĕrti ayer basoh tangan*, like water for washing one's hands (a cheap and little-prized article), prov.; *basohkan*, to wash.
basong, I. a pointed excrescence near the root of a tree. II. an envelope of bark for raw sago. III. half seasoned (of wood).
bata, I. *batu bata*, a brick; *atap b*., a tiled roof. II. *bata-bata*, in doubt; *kĕbata-bataan*, perplexity.
Batak, an aboriginal tribesman; a Battak; *mĕmbatak*, to lead a nomadic life.
batal, Ar. futile, useless; *mĕmbatalkan*, to bring to nought.
batang, a tree-trunk; a shaft; a handle; a rod; *b. ayer*, a watercourse; *b. hidong*, the bridge of the nose; *b. joran*, a fishing-rod; *b. kayu*, a tree; *b. leher*, the neck; *b. pĕngayoh*, the handle of a paddle.
batara, see *bĕtara*.
batas, the ridges round wet padifields.
batek, the process of painting sarongs; *kain b*., a painted (Javanese) sarong.
bati, *sa-bati*, inseparably connected; bound together.
batil, a metallic cup or small bowl.
batin, I. a tribal chief (of aborigines, *orang laut*, etc.). II. Ar. esoteric: inner; hidden.
batir, *batir-batir*, a gold band fastening a *kĕris* scabbard to its belt.
batoh, a gambler.
batok, a cough; *b. kĕring*, phthisis; *b. lĕlah* or *b. sisek*, whooping-cough.
batu, stone, rock; mile-stone, mile; native anchor; *b. api*, flint; *b. arang*, coal; *b. asah*, whetstone; *b. bata*, brick; *b. bĕlanda*, crystal; (diamond) paste; *b. bĕrani*, magnet; *b. bĕsi*, granitic rock; *b. chanai*, grindstone; *b. daching*, the weight on a balance; *b. duga*, a plummet; *b. gĕliga*, a bezoar; *b. kail*, the weight on a fishing-line; *b. karang*, galena ore; *b. kĕpala*, crown of the head; *b. las*, emery; *b. lintar*, fossil stone implements; *b. roboh*, débris; *b. sauh*, a native anchor; *b. sĕmpadan*, boundary-stone; *b. uji*, touchstone; *ayer b*., ice; *chap b*., lithography; *gula b*., loaf-sugar.
bau, smell, odour; *bau-bauan*, perfume; *bĕrbau*, to be scented; to smell of.
bauk, a beard under the chin; *chambang b*., a full beard; *janggut b*., id.
baung, I. curved (as a plantain or chairback—i.e. concave on one side, convex on the other). II. *ikan baung*, (*bagrus* sp.)
baur, *champur baur*, much mixed up; also *champur gaul*.

bawa, conveying; *mĕmbawa*, to bring, to carry, to convey; *b. diri*, to take oneself off, to be off; *b. iman*, to accept the Muhammadan faith; *b. jalan*, to lead the way; *b. lari*, to carry off, to run away with; *b. mati*, to retain till death; to carry to one's grave; *b. pĕrgi*, to take away; *pĕrgi b.*, to fetch.

bawah, below, under; *ka-bawah*, downward; *di-bawah*, below; *dari-bawah*, from under.

bawal, *ikan bawal*, the pomfret; (*stromateus* sp.)

bawang, a generic name for onions, leeks, etc.; *b. Bĕnggala* or *b. Bombai*, imported onions; *b. China*, garlic; *b. merah*, the local onion.

bawasir, Ar. piles, hæmorrhoids; also *wasir*.

bawat, drooping; *mata b.*, drooping eyelids, sleepiness.

baya, I. *sa-baya*, of the same age. II. Skr. danger; = *bahaya*.

bayak, bulkiness, extreme corpulence.

bayam, spinach.

bayan, I. *burong bayan*, the parroquet (*palæornis longicauda*). II. Ar. clear, obvious; *tĕrbayan-lah nyata*, id. III. Jav. a waiting-maid at a court.

bayang, shadow, image, vague outline; *tĕrbayang*, imaged vaguely, shadowed forth.

bayar, payment, paying; *mĕmbayar*, to pay.

bayoh, plurality of wives.

bayong, *pisau b.*, a small knife.

bayu, I. Skr. the wind, the breeze; Vayu, the Æolus of the old Javanese mythology; *di-puput bayu*, waving in the breeze. II. a slave; a submissive pronoun of the first person.

bayur, a name given to several trees.

bea, customs dues; *pĕbean*, a customs-station.

bĕbal, stupid, dull, dense; *orang yang bĕbal*, a fool.

bĕban, a burden, a load.

beban, wicked, perverse, disobedient.

bĕbang, a stoppage (in the anus or uterus).

bebas, free behaviour; familiarity; making oneself at home.

bĕbat, girdling, wrapping round.

bebek, Jav. duck; = (Malay) *itek*.

bechak, I. muddy, slushy. II. Ch. a jinrikisha.

bechang, *bechang-bechok*, the sound of quarrelling.

bechek, Jav. slushy; = *bechak*.

bechok, *bechang-bechok*, the sound of quarrelling.

beda, Skr. distinction, difference; *sĕkarang ini beda tĕrlalu*, things are very different now; *mĕmbedakan*, to distinguish between, to differentiate; *pĕrbedaan*, distinction, difference; also *beza*.

bedak, division into equal parts.

bĕdak, a cosmetic face-powder; *bĕr-bĕdak*, powdered with cosmetic.

bĕdal, a swishing blow with a light rattan.

bĕdan, reddish itchy spots.

bedar, an ancient one-masted type of ship.

bĕdara, Skr. a name given to several trees; *b. China*, the jujube; *buah b.*, (1) the fruit of this tree; (2) a name of a Malay sweetmeat.

bĕdĕbah, Pers. ill-starred, accursed.

bedek, *mĕmbedek*, to look fixedly through one eye; to aim.

bĕdia, a spangle.

bĕdil, *obat bĕdil*, gunpowder.

bĕdok, a big drum used for calling people to mosque; = (Kedah) *gĕndang raya*.

bĕdong, a swaddling-cloth for a newly born child.

bĕdukang, *ikan bĕdukang*, a freshwater fish (unidentified).

bega, pointing at, aiming at; *mĕmbega*, to aim at.

begak, foppish, dandified.

begal, highway robbery.

begap, robust; square-set.
bĕgar, Ar. stiff, hard; hard and proud.
bĕgawan, Skr. blessed—a title given to minor deities and to heroes who have given up kingship for asceticism.
bĕgok, a goitre.
bĕhina, Pers. excellent, important; *tiada b.*, not to attach importance to; *mĕmbĕhinakan*, to pay attention to; to care about; also *bena*.
bĕjana, Skr. a basin; also *bajan*.
bejar, Pers. out of humour.
beka, *bĕrbeka*, to gossip, to discuss; to talk over a matter.
bĕkal, supplies for a journey; stores, provisions; *pĕrbĕkalan*, id.
bĕkam, a slight bruise or discoloration of the skin.
bekang, a kind of cake.
bĕkas, impression, trace, mark; the wrapper, garment or receptacle in which a thing is contained; *b. mĕnangis*, traces of weeping; *b. baubauan*, a scent-bottle; *b. pinang*, a sireh box; *b. tuboh*, a garment.
bĕkat, tightly filled up; *pĕnoh b.*, id.
bĕkil, *ikan bĕkil*, an edible marine fish (unidentified).
bĕku, coagulated, congealed, frozen; *ayer b.*, ice; *b. didalam hati*, one's heart standing still; one's blood running cold.
bĕkukong, *ikan bĕkukong*, a marine fish (*chrysophrys calamara*).
bĕla, sustenance; nourishing; bringing up; *mĕmbĕla*, to bring up (a child); to support (a relative); to keep (a familiar spirit).
bela, atonement by blood; blood-offering; suttee.
bĕlachan, a preparation of prawns and small fish (it is used as a relish for curry).
bĕlachu, unbleached calico cloth.
bĕladau, a broad curved dagger.
bĕlah, splitting in two; cleaving; halving; side; *sa-bĕlah*, a side; *sa-bĕlah sana*, on that side, in that direction; *sa-bĕlah tangan*, one hand; *sa-bĕlah mĕnyabĕlah*, on both sides; *sa-bĕlah kanan*, the right-hand side; *sa-bĕlah kiri*, the left-hand side.
bĕlahak, making noises in the throat after eating.
bĕlai, dalliance; *bĕlu-bĕlai*, to converse, to chatter.
bĕlajar, see *ajar*.
bĕlak, mottled (as the grain of certain timbers).
belak, openging out folds or creases; holding a fold open.
bĕlaka, altogether, quite.
bĕlakang, back, behind; *di-bĕlakang*, in rear; subsequent; *mĕmbĕlakang*, to have one's back turned to.
bĕlalah, given up to gluttony.
bĕlalai, trunk, proboscis.
bĕlalak, to have a fixed look about the eyes.
bĕlalang, a generic name for grasshoppers, stick-insects, leaf-insects, etc.; *mata b.*, prominent eyes.
bĕlam, *chĕlum bĕlam*, over familiarity; tramping in and out of a house as though it was one's own.
bĕlambang, a truss; a lath.
bĕlanak, *ikan bĕlanak*, a marine fish (*mugil* sp.)
Bĕlanda, Dutch; *orang b.*, a Dutchman; *nĕgĕri b.*, Holland; *ayam b.*, a turkey; *ayer b.*, mineral water; *kuching b.*, a rabbit.
bĕlandong, too loose (of garments).
bĕlang, striped; *b. chĕchak* or *b. bĕrintek*, spotted.
bĕlanga, an earthenware cooking-pot.
bĕlangkas, the king-crab.
bĕlanja, expense; cost of sustenance; salary; *bĕlanjakan*, to expend.
bĕlantan, a club or cudgel.
bĕlantara, (Kawi) *hutan bĕlantara* or *rimba b.*, the wilds of the forest.
bĕlantek, see *lantek*.
bĕlar, mischievous.
bĕlaram, a variant of *balgham*, q.v.

bĕlas, I. a word utilised in forming the numerals from eleven to nineteen: it suggests that having counted all the fingers, the counter goes back (*balas*) counting them again; *sa-bĕlas*, eleven; *dua b.*, twelve. II. pity, mercy, sympathy; *b. kasehan*, id.

bĕlasah, caning, thrashing with a rattan.

bĕlat, a large screen of bamboo or bertam used in fish-traps; fish-traps in which such screens are used.

bĕlati, Skr. European (of goods); imported from afar; *tali b.*, hempen rope; *tĕmbakau b.*, tinned tobacco.

bĕlatok, a generic name for woodpeckers; also *pĕlatok*.

bĕlau, I. (Dutch) blue. II. *bĕlau-bĕlau*, blinking, shimmering; trying to the eyes.

bĕlĕbas, a lath laid horizontally along *atap*; a ruler; a cross-piece in a loom.

bĕlĕbat, single-stick play; slashing.

bĕlĕbau, belabouring, swishing.

bĕlĕda, a sweet gruel.

bĕlĕdoh, see *bĕludoh*.

bĕledok, *chengkok bĕledok* (Penang) zigzag.

bĕlĕdu, I. Port. velvet. II. *burong bĕlĕdu*, a bird (unidentified).

belek, looking closely into anything, examining carefully (as a watchmaker examines the works of a watch).

bĕlek, turning the upper eyelid up or the lower eyelid down.

bĕleko, Ch. a sort of glutinous syrup.

bĕlĕmak, Jav. an owl.

belen, a wooden roller used in making pastry.

bĕleng, Jav. potsherd.

bĕlĕngas, sticky (of the body).

bĕlĕnggu, shackles, fetters.

bĕlengket, linked together.

bĕlengset, exposed (of the inside of the eyelid) as the result of injury or disease.

bĕlera, a weaver's "sword"; *ular b.*, a sea-snake; also *ular bĕlerang*.

bĕlerang, sulphur; *asap b.*, sulphur fumes (used medicinally); *ular b.*, a sea-snake.

bĕleter, (Kedah) to chatter; = (Malacca) *mĕrepet*.

bĕli, purchase, buying; *mĕmbĕli*, to purchase.

bĕlia, Skr. *muda bĕlia*, young and fresh; in the bloom of youth.

bĕliak, exposing the whites of the eyes.

bĕlian, I. *hantu bĕlian*, the tigerspirit in incantations. II. the billian tree.

bĕliau, "what's-his-name," "so-and-so" (when speaking of someone whose name one knows but does not wish to utter).

bĕlibis, the whistling-teal (*dendrocygna javanica*).

bĕlida, *ikan bĕlida*, a marine fish (*notopterus kapirat*).

bĕligu, Jav. the wax gourd (*benincasa cerifera*).

bĕlikat, the shoulder-blade.

bĕliku, a sharp bend in a river's course.

bĕlimbing, ridged longitudinally; a descriptive name given to the leathery turtle (*dermochelys coriacea*), and also (*buah bĕlimbing*) to a well-known fruit (*averrhoa bilimbi*).

bĕlin, a small edible eel (unidentified).

bĕliong, a native hatchet; *puting b.*, a waterspout.

bĕlisah, fidgeting.

bĕlit, twining round, coiling round; *mĕmbĕlit*, to coil round.

bĕlitong, *siput bĕlitong*, a shell (unidentified).

bĕlodok, projecting, prominent (of the eyes).

beloh, stupid.

bĕlohan, = *balohan*; v. *baloh*.

belok, luffing, going on the opposite tack; going about; turning.

bĕlok, Eng. a (pulley) block.

bĕlolok, fallen in quantities (of fruit).
bĕlong, *bĕlah bĕlong*, an insect which makes a loud noise at night and is believed to bring bad luck; also *bĕlah bĕlum*.
bĕlongkang, a river-boat in use at Palembang.
bĕlongkeng, a small edible snail.
bĕlongsong, a cloth fabric.
bĕlontok, a fish (*gobius viridipunctatus*).
bĕlu, Jav. *bĕlu bĕlai*, to chatter, to converse.
bĕluam, a mendicant's wallet.
bĕlubur, a rice-bin.
bĕludal, a dry, crisp native cake.
bĕludoh, *tĕrbĕludoh*, filling the landscape; looming large.
bĕlukang, an edible marine fish.
bĕlukap, a mangrove (*rhizophora mucronata*).
bĕlukar, secondary jungle.
bĕlulang, a dry pelt; a patch of hardened skin.
bĕlum, not yet; not; *b. pĕrnah*, never yet; *sa-bĕlum*, before (conjunction).
bĕlumpai, not yet; = *bĕlum sampai*.
bĕlungkur, *ikan bĕlungkur*, a fish (unidentified).
bĕlunjur, to stretch oneself; to extend the lower limbs.
bĕluntas, a sea-shore shrub with lilac flowers (*pluchea indica* or *conyza indica*).
bĕlus, free to go in and out; unobstructed; loose in a socket.
bĕlusok, *ikan bĕlusok* a fish (unidentified).
bĕlut, to desert; to go over to the enemy.
bĕlut, *ikan bĕlut*, an eel.
bem, to puff out the cheeks.
bĕmbam, to roast in hot ashes.
bĕmban, a tree (*clinogyne grandis*).
bembeng, lifting a globular object on the flat of the hand.
bĕna, a tidal bore.
bena, Pers. caring about; taking to heart—a special use of *bĕhina*, q.v.

bĕnah, an insect-pest; a blight.
bĕnak, I. dull, slow of apprehension. II. marrow, brains.
bĕnam, *tĕrbĕnam*, buried in sand or mud; (more rarely) immersed in water, drowned.
bĕnang, thread; a thread-like line; *b. mas*, gold thread; *b. arang*, a charcoal line drawn by carpenters to guide them in their cutting or carving.
bĕnar, true, right, accurate; *bĕnarlah sapĕrti kata tuan*, what you say is true; *bĕnarkan*, to confirm; *kĕbĕnaran*, truth, accuracy, verification.
bĕnara, a washerman, a dhoby.
benchah, a morass; a muddy place; slushy, swampy.
bĕnchana, Skr. mischief-making, trouble, slander; *mĕmbĕnchanakan*, to slander.
benchang, to scull.
bĕnchi, hatred; to hate; *b. dan marah dan dĕngki*, hate, anger, and spite; *bĕnchikan* or *mĕmbĕnchikan*, to hate; (rarely) to arouse hatred in another; *pĕmbĕnchi*, a talisman or simple to cause another person to hate a third party—e.g. to cause a girl to hate a rival suitor.
bĕnda, Skr. thing, article; *mata b.*, things of value; gems, curios.
bĕndahara, Skr. the title of a very exalted Malay state official, usually ranking next to the heir-apparent; *pĕrbĕndaharan*, treasury.
bĕndahari, Skr. a treasury officer.
bĕndala, Port. a bandolier.
bĕndalu, a misletoe shrub.
bĕndang, a stretch of rice-fields; *buat b.* (Penang) to plant *padi*.
bĕndari, Hind. a sea-cook.
bĕndawat, a stay, a lashing; cordage in a ship.
bĕndĕla, see *bandĕla*.
bĕndĕlam, a vessel made of a coconut shell cut into two unequal parts, the smaller serving as a cover to the larger.

bĕndera, Port. a flag; *tiang b.*, a flagstaff.
bĕndĕrang, I. *tĕrang bĕndĕrang*, all pervading (of brilliant light). II. *tombak bĕndĕrang*, a spear with a tuft of horse-hair attached to it; a spear of state.
bĕndĕrong, a passage in a prince's audience rooms.
bĕndi, Hind. a carriage on two wheels; a "bandy."
bendi, Hind. *sayur b.*, the okra or *beni* fruit; "ladies' fingers"; *kachang b.*, id.
bĕndir, a kind of gong used by hawkers.
bĕndong, a dam, a dyke.
bĕnduan, Hind. a transported convict.
bĕndul, the beam at the threshold of a door; the threshold.
bĕneh, seed; grain for use as seed.
bĕngah, holding one's head up; stuck up; conceited.
bĕngal, temporary dullness of hearing—e.g. when water gets into the ear.
bĕngang, singing noises in the ear.
bĕngap, artificial dullness of hearing —e.g. when cotton is put in the ear.
bĕngeh, (Kedah) to hiss (of a cat).
bĕngek, to catch one's breath; to pant.
benggal, knobby, protuberant; *b. benggul* or *b. bĕnggil*, id.
Bĕnggala, the presidency of Calcutta.
Bĕnggali, a native of the presidency of Calcutta.
bĕnggil, a small knob or protuberance; a small bump or swelling.
benggul, a large low-rising bump or protuberance.
bĕngis, cruel, heartless; *kĕbĕngisan* or *pĕmbĕngisan*, indifference to the sufferings of others.
bengkah, to strike and let go one's weapon; to hit an opponent's top with one's own.

bĕngkak, inflamed, swollen; a swelling.
bĕngkalai, unfinished, incomplete (of work).
bĕngkalis, the name of a fish (unidentified).
bengkang, *bengkang bengkok*, zigzag.
bĕngkar, opening out (as a spring).
bĕngkarak, unfinished—a coarse equivalent of *bĕngkalai*.
bĕngkarong, the skink; *mabuia*.
bĕngkawan, a lath; a numeral co-efficient for ataps.
bĕngkayang, gorged, glutted with food.
bengkeng, angry, irritable, peevish; savage (of an animal).
bĕngkil, a bump or protuberance.
bengkok, crooked, bent; *bengkang-bengkok*, zigzag.
bengkong, I. girdle. II. crooked— cf. *bengkok* and *bengkang*.
bĕngkuang, see *mĕngkuang*.
bĕngkudu, see *mĕngkudu*.
bĕngkunang, a name for the *napoh* (*tragulus napo*).
bĕngok, *tĕrbĕngok*, with bowed head and contracted shoulders (as a man in a state of dejection).
bĕngong, confused—cf. *bingong*.
bengut, twisted, awry.
bĕnian, I. a coffer. II. Hind. a trader or merchant from India. III. a banyan or singlet.
bĕning, clear, limpid—a variant of *hĕning*.
benjil, bumpy (of the forehead).
benjul, a slight bump or swelling.
bĕnta, a small ulcer on the upper lip.
bĕntala, Skr. the earth.
bĕntan, relapse; the return of sickness.
bĕntang, spreading out, extension; *mĕmbĕntang* and *mĕmbĕntangkan*, to spread out (a carpet); to pitch (a tent).
bĕntangur, a name given to a number of trees yielding good timber (*calophyllum* sp.)

běntar, sa-běntar, a moment; an instant; sa-běntar di-sini, sa-běntar di-sana, one moment here, another there; děngan sa-běntar, in a moment, at once.
běntara, Skr. a herald, a marshal of the court.
běntas, to tear up and dash down; di-běntas-nya sa-buah bukit kapada hulubalang, he tore up a hill and dashed it on the troops.
benteh, to lock shins, to trip up.
benteng, a fort, a battery; b. sasaran, a target.
bentes, a variant of benteh, q.v.
běntok, curve; a numeral co-efficient for curved objects such as rings, fish-hooks, etc.; sa-puloh běntok chinchin, ten rings.
běntur, bowing, bending, "giving"; = lěntur.
běnturong, the bear-cat (arctictis binturong).
běnua, a large expanse of country; an empire; a continent; the mainland, as against an island; b. China, China; orang b., aborigines.
běnuang, rusa běnuang, a variety of the deer cervus unicolor; also (Kedah) gěnuang.
běnyai, insipid (of badly cooked rice).
benyek, soft, through over-boiling (of rice).
benyut, twisted, awry.
beo, the name given (in Java) to the tiong, or mynah.
běra, flushed, crimsoned, inflamed (of the face); a face-ache, neuralgia.
běragan, see agan and akan.
běrahi, love, passion; běrahikan, to be in love with.
Běrahman and **Běrahmana,** Skr. a Brahmin.
běrai, chěrai-běrai, scattered, broken up, dispersed (as a defeated army).
běrak, flushed—a variant of běra, q.v.
berak, to ease oneself.
běrakah, self-important, stuck up.
běraksa, I. kuda běraksa or burong běraksa, a legendary Pegasus. II. pokok běraksa (cassia fistula).
běram, a generic name for liquors made of fermented rice-spirit.
běramin, bakul běramin, a globular basket hung from the roof to protect its contents from rats.
běranda, Port. verandah.
běrang, běrang-běrang, the otter (lutra sumatrana).
berang, I. anger, wrath; hati yang b., angry feelings, passion. II. ular berang, a venomous snake (probably one of the sea-snakes).
běrangai, pěrahu běrangai, a Malay piratical craft furnished with a boarding gangway and grappling irons.
běrangan, I. realgar; = warangan; b. puteh, white arsenical oxide. II. a generic name for oaks and chestnuts.
běrangsang, exciting, rousing to courage.
běrangta, Jav. love, passion.
běrangti, a variant of běrangta, q.v.
běrani, courage, bravery; batu b. or běsi b., magnetic iron.
běranta, see anta.
běrapa, how much; see apa.
běras, rice (without the husk, but uncooked); cf. padi and nasi.
běrat, heavy, weighty; weight; kěpala b., heavy, dull-witted; kěběratan, pregnancy; burden; měmběratkan, to hinder, to handicap, to interfere with.
běrata, an idol; měmuja b., to worship idols.
běrdus, corpulent, obese.
berek-berek, burong berek-berek, the bay-backed bee-eater (merops sumatranus).
běrěmbang, pokok běrěmbang, a seaside tree (sonneratia acida).
běrěmi, the native water-cress (herpestes monniera).
běrěnang, to swim; see rěnang.
běreng, běreng-běreng, a small Chinese gong.

běrěnga, larvæ of insects—e.g. as visible on decayed animal matter.

běrěngau, a musical instrument (only mentioned in ancient literature).

běrěnggil, serrated, crenelated (of the appearance of a mountain range against the sky-line).

beret, *cheret-beret*, continually flowing.

bergok, Ar. a veil worn by female hajis.

běrhala, an idol.

běri, giving, bestowal; to give; *měm-běri*, to give, to allow; *měmběri tahu*, to give information of; *měmběri tabek*, to greet, to salute; *pěmběrian*, gift, grant, dowry.

běrida, Skr. veteran, experienced.

běringin, the waringin tree (*ficus benjamina*).

běrita, Skr. news, information; = *warta*; *pěmběrita*, a news-giver; a newspaper.

běrkas, a tied bundle; a bale of otherwise disconnected objects.

běrkat, Ar. blessing.

běrkek, *burong běrkek* (Singapore, Malacca) the snipe; = (Penang) *burong tětirok*.

běrkok, *burong běrkok*, the large green pigeon (*butreron capelli*).

Běrma, I. Skr. Brahma. II. redness, especially when caused by suffusion of blood. III. Burma; *orang B.*, a Burmese.

běrnas, springing up quickly (of young plants); swelling, expanding rapidly.

běrniaga, to trade; *pěrniagaan*, trade, business.

běroga, *ayam běroga*, a name for the jungle-fowl (*gallus ferrugineus*).

běrohi, arrowroot.

běrok, the pig-tailed monkey (*macacus nemestrinus*); *sěrah b.* or *b. měnghantar hasil*, the mumps.

běrombong, funnel-shaped.

běronok, a name given to several edible sea-worms—e.g. *colochirus anceps, haplodactyla molpadisides*, etc.

běroti, a lath (in lattice-work).

běrsat, gone astray (of food which gets into the windpipe).

běrseh, clean, free from impurities; *běrsěhkan*, to clean.

běrsil, to emerge, to come suddenly into view.

běrsin, to sneeze; *jambu b.*, the guava fruit.

běrsut, scowling, a black look (as the result of unpleasant thoughts).

běrtam, a well-known palm (*eugeissona tristis*).

běrteh, to toast rice in the husk; *běras b.*, toasted rice.

běruang, the Malayan bear (*ursus malayanus*).

běruas, the wild mangosteen.

běrudu, a tadpole.

besan, the relationship between people whose children have intermarried.

běsar, large, great; *hari b.*, festival, holiday; *hati b.*, arrogance; *tuan b.*, the head of an office; *běsarkan* and *měmběsarkan*, to enlarge; *kěběsaran*, grandeur, greatness; pride.

beser, incontinence of urine.

běsi, iron; *b. běrani*, magnetic iron; *b. batang*, bar iron; *b. kawi*, manganese; *b. lantai*, sheet iron; *batu b.*, granite; *pandai b.* or *tukang b.*, a blacksmith; *pukul b.*, to shoe a horse; *tahi b.*, rust.

běsing, whizzing, singing through the air (of a projectile).

besok, to-morrow; also *esok*.

běstari, well-bred, accomplished.

běsut, a contraction of the brows; = *běrsut*.

běsuta, a silken fabric from Surat.

beta, Skr. slave, servant; your servant, I.

bětah, restored to health; convalescent.

bětak-bětak, a skin-disease.

bětapa, how; in what manner; what, why.

bětara, Skr. a title given in old Java

to major divinities and to reigning princes of great power.

bĕtari, a grass(*sorghum saccharatum*).

bĕtas, ripping open, splitting open (as a seam gives way under strain).

bĕtek, *buah bĕtek*, the papaya fruit (*carica papaya*).

bĕteka, Ar. a plant name (*citrullus edulis*).

bĕti, *bĕti-bĕti*, a tree (*eugenia zeylanica*).

beti, Skr. a female slave; a palace attendant—the feminine of *beta*.

bĕtina, female, feminine (of animals), and (familiarly) of human beings; *kuda b.*, a mare.

bĕting, a sand bank or mud bank.

bĕtis, the leg (between knee and ankle); *buah b.*, or *jantong b.*, the calf.

bĕtok, I. burnt (by acids). II. the name of a fish (unidentified).

bĕtong, large (in certain connections only)—e.g. *katak b.*, a large species of frog; *buloh b.*, a large bamboo; *tĕbu b.*, a large sugar-cane; and *rumput b.*, a large grass.

bĕtul, correct, true, straight; *bĕtulkan*, to correct, to set right; *mĕmbĕtulkan*, id.

bĕtutu, an edible fish (unidentified).

bewak, a Kedah variant of *biawak*, q.v.

beza, difference; = *beda*.

bi, Ar. with, in; *bi'smi'llah*, in God's name; *bi-hi*, on him, with him.

bia, tolls, duties; *bian-bian* or *pĕbian*, a customs-station.

biadab, Pers. disrespectful, discourtesy.

biak, prolific, reproductive.

biang, I. lascivious. II. *biang-biut*, zigzag.

biapĕri, Pers. a merchant, a trader.

biar, I. to permit, to allow, to let; may; no matter if; *biar-lah*, never mind, let it alone; *biar puteh tulang jangan puteh mata*, let the bones whiten but not the eyes (better death than shame), prov.; *biarkan*, to permit, to concede, to allow. II. *cha-ching biar-biar*, intestinal worms.

bias, to be driven out of its course (of a ship).

biasa, Skr. acquaintance with a person or thing; accustomed to; practised in; *ia tĕlah biasa dĕngan aku*, he is an acquaintance of mine; *biasa-lah tangan-ku mĕmĕgang kalam*, my hand became accustomed to holding a pen.

biawak, a generic name for monitor and other large lizards.

biaya, Skr. cost, expenses; outlay.

bibi, Hind. lady, mistress.

bibir, lip, edge, rim; *b. mata*, eyelids.

bibit, to carry a light object in the hand; also *bimbit*.

bichara, Skr. opinion; discussion; deliberation; a judicial proceeding; *tĕmpat b.*, a police court; *bĕrbichara*, to discuss, to debate about.

bichu, a screw-jack.

bida, a damsel about a court; a maid of honour.

bidaah, Ar. deceitful, treacherous.

bidadari, Skr. a nymph of heaven; a fairy; a houri.

bidai, chicks, blinds, hanging screens of split rattan or bamboo.

bidak, Ar. a pawn at chess.

bidal, I. a thimble. II. a proverbial saying; a dictum of an ancient sage; an aphorism.

bidan, Skr. a midwife.

bidang, I. spacious, extending; a numerical co-efficient for things that are spread out—e.g. sails, mats, etc. II. a palm-cabbage.

bidara, see *bĕdara*.

bidas, a blow given by an elastic or flexible body when tension is removed.

bidok, a fishing boat; *kutu b.*, the beetles infesting ill-kept lockers, etc., in boats.

biduan, Skr. a musician, a singer or dancer.

biduanda, Skr. a royal messenger, a herald.

bidur, a slab (of tin).
bighair, Ar. separate, distinct from.
bijak, Sk. learned, sage, prudent; *b. laksana*, id.; = *bijaksana*.
bijaksana, Skr. learned, prudent; chaste; also *bijak laksana*.
bijan, (*sesamum indicum*).
bijeh, grains of alluvial tin.
biji, a seed; a grain; a numerical co-efficient for small objects; *b. mata*, eyeball.
bikin, to make; to do.
bikir, Ar. virginity, virgin.
biku, I. a saw-edged pattern, a zig-zag pattern. II. (Pali) a mendicant Buddhist priest.
bila, when; *apa-bila*, id. (relative); *bila-mana*, whenever; *barang-bila*, as often as.
bilah, a numeral co-efficient for blade-like objects—e.g. knives, chisels, daggers, hatchets, needles, etc.
bilai, a weal.
bilal, Ar. the muezzin of a Malay mosque.
bilalang, see *bĕlalang*.
bilang, recounting, enumeration; to repeat, to say, to tell; *sa-bilang*, each, every; *bilangan*, enumeration, tale; *chukup hari bilangan*, when the tale of days was complete; *mĕm-bilang*, to count, to number; *tĕrbilang*, famous; talked about.
bilas, washing in fresh or scented water after a bath in common water.
bilau, *kachau-bilau*, in confusion; higgledy-piggledy, topsy-turvy.
bilek, room, apartment.
bilis, I. *mata bilis*, blear-eyed. II. *ikan bilis*, a fish (unidentified).
bi'llahi, Ar. by God.
biludak, *ular b.*, a venomous snake; a viper?
bilur, a scar, a weal.
bimbang, anxious, uncertain, irresolute, nervous.
bimbit, to carry lightly in the hand; also *bibit*.

bin, Ar. son of; *Puteh bin Mat*, Puteh, son of Mat.
binasa, Skr. ruin, destruction; *ikut rasa binasa*, to give way to one's passions is destruction, prov.; *binasa-kan* or *mĕmbinasakan*, to destroy, to ruin.
binatang, an animal; *b. yang liar*, wild animals; *b. yang jinak*, domestic animals.
binchana, see *bĕnchana*.
binchang, *binchang ayam*, a knot or fastening of great strength; a coiled knot.
binchul, a slight bump or swelling.
binchut, a variant of *binchul*.
bindu, a turning-lathe.
bingas, growling, menacing (of a wild beast).
bingit, uneasy; indisposed, out of sorts.
bingka, *kueh bingka*, a Malay cake.
bingkai, rim, border; rattan binding on edge, rim or border.
bingkas, springing back (of a spring); rising to attention; resuming a proper position.
bingkis, I. a complimentary gift accompanying a letter; *surat bingki-san*, id. II. *bungkus-bingkis*, all kinds of parcels and packages.
bingong, mazed, confused, disconcerted; dull, muddle-headed.
bini, wife (less courteous than *istĕri*); *anak b.*, family; *bĕrbini*, to be married; *bĕrbinikan*, to marry, to take to wife.
binjai, the name of a common fruit-tree (*mangifera coesa*).
bint, Ar. daughter; *bintu'l-bahar*, mermaid—cf. *binti*.
bintang, a star; a heavenly body; a decoration; *b. bĕrasap* or *b. bĕrekur*, a comet; *b. bĕridar*, a planet; *b. kĕ-bĕsaran*, the star of an order of knighthood; *bĕrbintang-bintang*, full of small holes (through which light penetrates: of a roof).
bintangur, see *bĕntangur*.

bintek, *bĕrbintek-bintek*, covered with small spots of prickly heat.
binti, Ar. daughter of; *Baidah binti Hasan*, Baidah, daughter of Hasan—cf. *bin* and *bint*.
bintil, a stye in the eye.
bintit, a small swelling (such as that caused by the bite of a mosquito).
biola, Port. a violin.
birah, a name given to a number of aroids (chiefly wild); *b. kĕladi* (*colocasia antiquorum*)
birahi, see *bĕrahi*.
biram, a poetic word for an elephant; *b. bĕrjuwang* a war-elephant.
biras, the relationship between two people who have married sisters; close connection by marriage.
birat, a scar on the mouth.
birau, *kachau-birau*, in extreme confusion.
bireh, a fence; a parapet; the gunwale of a ship—in literature only.
biri, I. *kambing biri-biri*, a sheep. II. *sakit biri-biri*, beri-beri.
biring, light red or yellow (of a fighting cock).
biru, I. blue. II. *haru biru*, disturbance, uproar, confusion.
bisa, I. venom; blood-poison; *ular b.*, a venomous snake. II. (Batavia) can, able to; = *boleh*.
bisai, dandified, dainty.
bisat, (Penang) *tiada bisat*, not to care; = *tiada indah*.
bisek, to whisper; to speak in whispers; *bĕrbisek*, id.
bisi, Skr. immodest, unchaste; a term of abuse.
bising, loquacious, chattering.
bismi, Ar. in the name of.
Bisnu, Skr. Vishnu.
bisu, dumb, mute.
bisul, a boil, a superficial abscess.
biuku, a species of tortoise (unidentified).
bius, Pers. *obat bius*, a stupefying drug; an anæsthetic.
biut, *biang-biut*, zigzag.

bobos, leaky (through having a very big hole in its bottom).
bochok, an awning over a child's cradle.
bochong, an earthenware vessel shaped something like an hour-glass.
bochor, leaky (not as strong as *bobos*, q.v.)
bodi, see *budi* II.
bodoh, stupid, dull, dense; *orang b.*, a fool; *kĕbodohan*, stupidity.
bodok, Eng. a gaff; a boat-hook.
boga, I. Skr. *sĕmpana pĕrgam boga*, a kind of pleasure boat. II. Skr. *antaboga*, the great serpent.
bogam, I. pieces of gold or silver leaf on a head ornament (*tajok*). II. great—a rare equivalent of *bĕsar*.
bogang, *tĕlanjang bogang*, stark naked.
bogi, Eng. *kĕreta bogi*, a buggy, a hooded vehicle.
bogok, a large black caterpillar.
bogot, horrid, ugly—in the expression, *hitam bogot*, horridly black (of Papuans).
bohok, (Penang) a puddle.
bohong, lie; lying; false; *bohong samata-mata*, altogether untrue; *pĕmbohong*, a liar.
bojot, very much entangled; hopelessly mixed up.
bok, I. Jav. mother; = *ĕmbok*. II. a kind of carpet.
bokcha, Turk. a bag, scrip or wallet.
bokong, worn the wrong way; front and back interchanged.
bokop, closed by inflamation (of the eyes); = *bakup*.
bokor, a metal bowl or basin with a flat rim.
bokot, veiling, enshrouding; covering or wrapping up.
bol, see *bul*.
bola, Port. a ball; a cricket ball, football, billiard ball, or tennis ball.
bolak, *bolak-balek*, there and back; backwards and forwards; *bolak cha-*

kap, going back on one's word, prevarication.

boleh, able to, can; power to; *sa-boleh-boleh-nya*, the best of his ability; *mana b.*, how can this be so; impossible; *apa boleh buat*, what is to be done? there is an end of it.

bolong, black; blue black; tarring, blackening.

bolos, stripped off, fallen off (of a coiled string falling off a top, of leaves falling off a tree, of hairs falling off, etc.)

bolot, roughly or hastily wrapping up a parcel—cf. *balut*.

bolu, Port. sponge-cake.

bom, Eur. the shafts of a carriage; the boom of a ship.

bomantara, Skr. the firmament; the vault of heaven.

bomba, Port. a pump; the hose of a fire-engine; a fire-engine; *juru bomba kain*, a dhoby.

Bombai, Bombay; *měmbuang ka-něgěri B.*, to (penally) transport.

bomoh, a native doctor; a practitioner of magic, a sorcerer.

bonchol, a knob-like protuberance.

bonda, mother (in respectful language); = *ibu'nda*; *ayah b.*, parents.

boneka, Port. a puppet, a doll.

bonggol, a dome-shaped protuberance; a hump; also *bongkol*.

bongkah, a piece, a block.

bongkak, pride; arrogance; self-assertion; overbearing manner.

bongkal, a measure of weight for precious articles; 1⅓ oz. approximately.

bongkam, *azimat pěmbongkam*, a drug or talisman to silence a hostile witness.

bongkang, spread out to its full length (of a dead body) in contradistinction to being huddled up.

bongkar, heaving up, turning up the soil, weighing anchor; *b. kota*, to blow up a fort; *měmbongkar*, to heave up; *m. sauh*, to weigh anchor; *m. bukit*, to dig up a hillock; *bongkar-bangkir*, turning everything topsy turvy.

bongkas, rising up (as the roots of a tree when the tree is blown down, or as the buried portion of a stake or pile when the pile is knocked down); heaved up; thrust up.

bongkeng, lying forward, face downwards and knees drawn up (of a dead body).

bongkok, hump-backed; *b. baharu bětul*, "the hump-back who has just become straight" (a beggar on horseback), prov.; *měmbongkok*, to stoop, to humble oneself.

bongkol, a hump; = *bonggol*.

bongkong, I. *bongkong kayu*, a parasitic growth on the trunk of a tree; II. a Malay cake made in a wrapper of banana leaf.

bonglai, a ginger used in medicine (*zingiber cassumunaar*).

bongok, heavily built, clumsy.

bongsu, younger-born.

bonjol, projection outward—cf. *bujal, běnjul*, etc.

bonyor, soft, sappy, juicy, tender.

bopeng, pockmarked; also *mopeng*.

bor, (Dutch) an auger.

borak, I. insipid (of tobacco); also *boyak*. II. Ar. a mysterious flying animal; the animal upon which Muhammad made his journey to heaven.

borang, Jav. a caltrop; = *ranjau*.

bordu, Port. the gunwale (sometimes the hatches).

boreh, a yellow ointment for the body.

borek, spotted (with fairly large spots); *ayam b.*, a spotted fowl.

boren, a kind of coral.

boria, Hind. a topical song.

borong, wholesale; by the gross; *měmborong* or *měmběli borong*, to buy up wholesale so as to command the market.

boros, profuse, prodigal, extravagant, reckless in money matters.

bosa, *tali bosa*, a rope attached to a ship's cable to stop it when sufficiently run out.
bosan, satiety, nausea.
boseta, Port. a basket.
bosor, greed, gluttony.
bostan, see *bustan*.
bota, Skr. a goblin, an evil spirit of man-devouring propensities.
botak, bald at the back of the head; baldness of the crown.
botan, the rose peony.
boya, I. Port. a buoy; also *bairup*. II. a (Penang and Kedah) variant of *buaya*.
boyak, weak; insipid (of tobacco); also *borak*.
Boyan, the isle of Bawean between Java and Borneo; *orang B.*, a "Boyanese."
buah, fruit; a spherical or nearly spherical object; a descriptive prefix or numeral co-efficient for objects of a more or less spherical or cubical appearance such as houses, hills, eggs, baskets, stones, countries, towns, etc.; *b. chatur*, chessmen; *b. hati*, the heart (especially as a term of endearment); *b. kĕras*, the candle-nut; (*aleurites moluccanus*); *b. mĕlaka*, a sweetmeat of soft dough; *b. pala*, nutmeg; *b. pĕlir*, the testiculi; *b. pinggang*, the kidneys; *b. timbangan*, weights; *anak b.*, dependents, people under a pĕnghulu; *buah-buahan*, fruits in general, fruits of all sorts; *bĕrbuah*, to bear fruit.
buai, rocking, swaying, swinging (as a cradle); *bĕrbuai*, to be swinging; *buaian*, a swinging cradle.
bual, bubbling up; loquacious (especially boastfully loquacious); braggart.
buana, Skr. the world, the universe; *paku b.*, nail from which the universe hangs—a Javanese royal title; *sangga b.*, prop sustaining the universe (a similar title); *sĕri tĕri-buana*, light of the three worlds (another title).

buang, throwing away, discarding; *mĕmbuang*, *buangkan*, or *mĕmbuangkan*, to expel, to get rid of; *b. ayer*, to obey a call of nature; *b. ayer darah*, dysentery; *b. diri*, suicide; *b. ingus*, to blow the nose; *b. nyawa*, to give up one's life; *b. undi*, to cast lots; *champak b.*, a javelin; *para b.*, a window or aperture (in a Malay house) through which rubbish is thrown out; *tĕrbuang*, exiled, abandoned, discarded; *anak buangan*, a discarded child, a foundling.
buas, wild, fierce (of animals); *singa yang maha-buas*, a most ferocious lion.
buat, doing, making; *bĕrbuat* or *mĕmbuat*, to make; *buat-buat*, to feign; pretence, shamming; *buatan*, make —e.g. *buatan Inggĕris*, of English make; *pĕrbuatan*, act, deed.
buaya, a crocodile; *b. tĕmbaga* or *b. katak*, the common crocodile (*crocodilus porosus*); *b. sĕrunai*, *b. jĕnju-long*, *b. nyĕnyulong* or *b. jolong-jolong*, the gavial (*tomistoma schlegeli*); *ikan korek tĕlinga b.*, the fish (*gastrotoceus biaculeatus*); *lidah b.*, the aloe (*aloë ferox*).
buboh, setting, placing, affixing; *mĕmbuboh* or *mĕmbubohkan*, to lay, to affix; *mĕmbuboh tanda tangan*, to attach one's signature; *mĕmbuboh chap*, to seal.
bubok, a weevil, a wood-maggot; *di-makan b.*, worm-eaten.
bubong, a variant of *bumbong*, q.v.
bubu, a small fish-trap of bamboo and rattan.
bubul, the repairing of nets; *mĕmbubul* to mend (a net).
bubur, rice-broth; *b. susu*, rice boiled in milk.
bubut, I. a name for coucals and crow-pheasants (*centropus eurycercus* and *centropus bengalensis*). II. the throat-halliards (in rigging); *bubutan*; id.
buchu, a corner or angle.

budak, a boy or girl; a child of several years in age.
budi, I. Skr. wisdom, prudence; understanding, mental disposition; *akal b.*, or *b. bichara*, id.; *hilang b.*, loss of discretion; throwing discretion to the winds; *b. bahasa*, tact; *bĕrbudi*, discreet, intelligent, wise. II. Skr. the peepul-tree (*ficus religiosa*); *daun b.*, the leaf of that tree (a name given to a peculiar fig-leaf-like pattern or border).
budiman, Skr. wise, prudent—cf. *budi*, I.
budu, a pickle (small fish preserved in brine with their scales and entrails).
bueh, foam, froth.
bugil, *tĕlanjang b.*, stark naked.
Bugis, the name of a people from the Celebes.
bujal, projecting outward (of a navel).
bujam, a pouch made of *mĕngkuang* leaf.
bujang, single, unmarried (used of widows, widowers, and divorced persons as well as of persons who have never been married).
bujangga, I. Skr. a monster of the winged-dragon or winged-man type. II. an unmarried man; = *bujang*.
bujok, I. coaxing; soothing—better, *pujok*. II. *ikan b.*, a fresh-water fish (*scolopsis ciliatus*).
bujur, extension of length relative to breadth; long, straight, stretching; *bujur lalu, lintang patah*, those that fall straight get through, those that fall across (the channel) get broken (and get through), (all is fish that comes to his net), prov.; *b. bulat*, elliptical; *b. tĕlur*, oval; *lintang b.*, diagonal.
buka, opening, exposing, revealing; undoing, unharnessing, untying, unfolding; *mĕmbuka*, to open, to unfold or undo; *m. jalan*, to open out a road; *m. kain*, to take off one's clothing; *m. layar*, to unfurl sails; *m. pintu*, to open a door; *m. puasa*, to end a fast; *m. rahasia* to reveal a secret; *m. topi*, to take off one's hat.
bukan, no, not; there is not; it is not; *bukan barang-barang pĕrĕmpuan*, no ordinary woman; *yang bukan-bukan*, that do not really exist; impossible, wrong.
bukat, troubled, disturbed (of water).
bukit, a hill; *anak b.*, a hillock; *kaki b.*, the foot of a hill; *orang b.*, aboriginal tribes dwelling in the mountains; *pĕnara b.*, the level ridge at the crest (of a range).
buku, a joint (in a finger, on the ankle, wrist, etc.); a knot (in wood); the lumpy or disagreeable part of anything; (by metaphor) the sting of a remark; *kĕna b.*, to come across the nasty part of anything, to run up against the wrong spot; *b. jari*, the knuckles; *bĕrbuku*, clotted, in lumps.
bul, globular; bubble-like; *jambu b.*, a fruit (*eugenia malaccensis*).
bulai, I. albino. II. a variant of *bĕlalai*.
bulan, the moon; a month; the period of gestation; *sa-hari b.*, the first day of the month; the one-day-old moon; *ĕmpat bĕlas hari b.*, the 14th day of the month; the full moon; *b. pĕrnama*, id.; *b. timbul*, the new moon; *b. tĕrang*, moonlight.
bulang, I. enwinding, enwrapping; binding on with wrappings as the spurs of a fighting-cock are fastened on; *mĕmbulang taji*, to fasten on the spurs of a fighting-cock. II. a generic name for a number of thorny shrubs (*canthium* sp., etc.); *bulangan*, id. III. *bulang-baling*, rolling over and over; a name given to chain-shot.
bular, whitish discoloration of the eye; *buta b.*, blindness accompanied by such discoloration.
bulat, roundness; smoothness of surface; freedom from angularities; *b. bujur* or *b. panjang*, elliptical; *b.*

pipeh, flat and round (as a coin); *b. torak*, cylindrical; *kayu b.*, round logs stripped of branches; *masak b.*, cooking whole; *pusat b.*, the centre of a circle; *sĕluar b.*, pyjamas; *tĕlanjang b.*, stark naked; *sa-bulat-bulat*, altogether; *dĕngan sa-bulat-bulat hati*, with my whole heart.

buli, *buli-buli*, a small flask or bottle.

bulir, I. *anak bulir*, an illegitimate child. II. ear (of padi); cluster.

buloh, bamboo; a generic name for many bamboos; *b.* **bangsi**, a reed pipe; *b. pĕrindu*, (1) a sort of Jew's harp; (2) a singing bamboo of legend; *sa-pĕrdu b.*, a clump of bamboo.

bulu, wool; feathers; the hair of the body; *b. kĕning*, the eyebrows; *b. landak*, the quills on a porcupine; *b. liang roma*, the fine hairs on the body; *b. roma*, id.; *b. tĕngkok*, the mane (of a horse); *ulat b.*, the hairy caterpillar; *hati bĕrbulu*, to get angry.

bulugh, Ar. maturity, puberty.

bulur, extreme hunger, starvation; *mati b.*, to die of hunger.

bumbong, the ridge of a roof; rooflike; *bumbongan*, a roof; *tulang bumbong*, the ridge-pole; *bĕrbumbong* or *mĕmbumbong*, to swell up.

bumbu, Jav. mixed spices; condiments; = *rĕmpah*.

bumbun, a hut in which a hunter hides when decoying game.

bumi, Skr. the earth; the soil of the earth; the ground; *jatoh ka-bumi*, to fall to the ground; *pĕtala b.*, the folds or layers of which the earth is said by Malays to be formed; *mangku-bumi*, a regent.

bun, I. (Dutch) a metal pail. II. *sa-tali bun*, a string (of pantuns).

bunchis, (Dutch) French beans.

bunchit, swollen, blow out, distended (of the stomach).

bundar, rounded, globular.

bunduk, Ar. bastard.

bunga, a flower; an ornamental pattern or design; *b. api*, sparks, fireworks; *b. ayer mawar*, the rose; *b. karang*, a coralline sponge; *b. kuku*, the base (of the finger nail); *b. pala*, mace; *b. rampai*, flower-petals mixed with scented leaves; *b. wang*, interest on money.

bungar, *bungaran*, first fruits.

bungkus, rolling up a thing (as a package or parcel); *bungkusan*, a package; *mĕmbungkus*, to make up a parcel.

bungsil, a very young coconut (used as a plaything by children).

buni, *orang bunian*, invisible elves (of the forest).

bunoh, killing, murdering; erasing; *mĕmbunoh*, to kill; to put an end to; *mati di-bunoh*, murdered; destined to a bad end; *pĕmbunoh*, a manslayer, a murderer; *pĕmbunohan*, killing; slaughter.

buntak, short, stumpy; beamy (of a boat).

buntal, a generic name for fish that distend their bodies with air when caught (*b. pisang*, tetrodon lunaris; *b. batu*, tetrodon fluviatalis).

buntang, I. starting out of the head (as the eyes of the man who is being strangled). II. a weaver's rod.

buntar, dome-shapped; roughly hemispherical; *b. bayang-bayang*, rounded with wavy edges.

buntat, a gall-stone; a petrified substance found in animal or vegetable substances; a bezoar.

buntil, a clothes-bag.

bunting, enceinte, pregnant, pregnancy; *b. sarat*, advanced pregnancy.

buntu, blocked (of a road or watercourse).

buntul, the ring on a *kĕris* sheath.

buntur, sated with food, glutted.

buntut, the posterior; the stern; the fundament.

bunut, *hujan bunut*, very heavy rain.

bunyi, sound, noise; meaning, accent;

intonation; děmikian bunyi-nya, of the following tenor; bunyi-bunyian, strains of music; běrbunyi, to sound; měmbunyikan to enunciate, to pronounce.

bupati, Skr. a title of distinction; lord of the earth.

bura, spitting out; ejecting; pillorying; ular naga b., a snake (probably naia sputatrix, the black cobra).

burai, gushing out (as entrails from a wound in the stomach).

burhan, Ar. demonstration, proof.

buri, Jav. back, behind; di-buri, in rear.

burit, posterior, stern; buritan, the stern of a ship; měmburit, to commit an unnatural offence.

burj, Ar. castle; sign of the zodiac.

burok, worn, decayed (of vegetable and manufactured articles, but not of animal matter—cf. busok); burokkan, to wear out.

burong, a bird; b. dewata, the bird of paradise; tembak b., bird-shooting.

buru, hunting, the chase; měmburu, to hunt; pěmburu, hunter; hantu pěmburu, the wild huntsman, an evil spirit; pěrburuan, sport, the game hunted; anjing pěrburuan, huntingdogs.

burun, kambing burun, a name for the serow of the Malay Peninsula (nemorrhoedus swettenhami).

burut, hernia, rupture, hydrocele.

busana, Skr. raiment, ornamental dress.

busar, a bow, an arc; the bow for cleaning cotton; sěpěrti kapas di-busar, like cotton after cleaning (pure white), prov.; sěpěrti busar Ranjuna, like the bow of Arjuna (a simile for a beautiful arm); also busur.

busi, Hind. rice-bran.

busok, decayed (of animal matter); putrid, stinking; bau b., a bad smell; hati b., a bad disposition; nama b., an extremely bad name.

busong, dropsical inflammation; b. darah, an aneurism.

bustan, Pers. a garden; a pleasaunce; a park.

busur, a bow; a variant of busar, q.v.

busut, an ant-hill.

buta, I. blind; b. larangan, myopia; b. tuli, blind and deaf; pukul b. tuli, striking recklessly. II. see bota. III. buta-buta, a tree (cerbera odollam). IV. China b., a muhallil.

butang, Eng. a button; b. dasi, a stud.

butir, a grain, particle; a numeral co-efficient for small round objects (such as gems).

butoh, the penis.

butu, a variant of butoh, q.v.

buyong, a water-jar (of portable size).

buyut, flabby of flesh; pěrut b., flabby obesity.

Ch

chabai, Skr. long pepper (piper longum).

chabak, a wound left by the removal of a bit of flesh.

chabang, bifurcation; the main branches of a tree; běrchabang, forked (as the tongue of a snake); běsi tiga ch., a trident.

chabar, faint-hearted.

chabek, tearing; torn; a rent; chobak-ch., tattered.

chabir, tearing, torn; chobar-ch., torn about all over.

chabit, a varriant of chabek, q.v.

chabok, I. Pers. a whip; II. a festering ulcer (especially in the lower leg).

chabul, outrageous behaviour; licentious violence; unseemly language; bĕrbuat ch., to commit an outrage (especially rape); mĕnchabuli, id.

chabut, plucking out; a royalty; mĕnchabut, to pull out; to drag out; to uproot; tĕrchabut, pulled out; drawn (of a sword).

chacha, a formula for reducing to submission.

chachah, I. pricking a pattern; bĕrchachah, tattooed. II. a Malay soup.

chachak, implanting; sticking in the ground; ch. lari (slang), to make a bolt of it.

chachar, an eruptive disease; small-pox; ch. ayer, measles or chicken-pox.

chachat, a flaw, a defect, a blemish.

chachau, to confuse; to throw into disorder.

chachi, a small lever used to roll up a sail.

chachil, small for its purpose.

chaching, a worm; ch. pipeh, the tape-worm.

chadang, reliance; a stand-by; a reserve fund or war-chest.

chadar, Hind. a rug, sheet, or shawl.

chaeng, picked to pieces; minced.

chagak, the swivel of a swivel-gun (lela).

chagar, relying; trusting; a Malacca form of mortgage in which the mortgagee is given the usufruct of land in lieu of interest.

chagu, a disease of the toes.

chagut, Jav. the chin.

chah, an interjection; a cry for hurrying on buffaloes.

chahar, diarrhœa, purging.

chahari, to seek—v. chari.

chahaya, Skr. lustre, brilliancy, glow; ch. mata, light of the eyes (a term of endearment); bĕrchahaya, to glow, to shine.

chakah, wide (of an angle); obtuse.

chakang, forming a very open curve.

chakap, to speak; to undertake; bĕrchakap, to speak; pĕrchakapan,

speech, utterance; ch. angin, empty boasting.

chakar, scratching; ch. balar, scratched all over; mĕnchakar, to scratch (as a fowl).

chakĕra, Skr. a discus, a quoit.

chakĕrawala, Skr. the revolving vault of heaven.

chakok, indirect (of a blow); given at a curve; golok ch., a curved chopper.

chakup, catching in the open mouth (as a dog catches a biscuit).

chakus, mĕnchakus, to carry a burden suspended from a stick that rests on the shoulder.

chalak, I. likely to take place. II. affectation; airs.

chalar, a long scratch on the skin; bĕrchalar, scratched.

chaling, cholak ch., or cholang ch., in a tangle, in disorder.

chalit, smearing, smudging.

chalong, I. a small ladle. II. pisau ch., a small knife resembling a pisau wali.

chalu, Hind. the run of a steamer.

cham, recognition by sight; chamkan, to recognise.

chamar, burong ch., a sea-gull; also chĕnchamar.

chamau, a generic name for tree-dracœnas.

chambang, whiskers; ch. bauk, a full beard.

chamchah, Hind. a spoon.

champah, insipid, tasteless.

champai, a variant of chapai, q.v.

champak, I. casting away, discarding; champakkan, to throw away—e.g. a cigar-end. II. a skin eruption; measles.

champang, sculling or paddling from the bows of a boat.

champing, chompang ch., tattered at the edge; torn.

champong, shattered at a stroke (as a tree struck by lightning).

champur, mixing, mingling; ch. baur,

utterly mixed up; in confusion; *ch. gaul,* id.; *champuran,* components of a mixture; *champurkan,* to mix up, to mingle; *bĕrchampur,* in solution with; mixed with.

chamti, see *chĕmĕti.*

chan, Ch. a Chinese conical basket.

chanai, whetting; a stone roller; smoothing or polishing or grinding by means of a roller; *kĕris baharu di-chanai,* a newly sharpened *kĕris.*

chanang, a gong with a shallow rim and no hemispherical knob in it; *chanangkan,* to proclaim by beat of gong.

chanar, a generic name for the plants known as *smilax.*

chanchang, sticking up, rising to a point (as certain forms of native head-dress).

chanda, I. *ta'-chanda* to care nothing about; = *ta'-indah.* II. the strip of wood at the stern of a boat to which a rudder is attached. III. a variant of *sĕnda,* q.v. IV. *si-chanda-kia-mana,* what slanderer. V. *chanda-pĕti,* a secretaire; a box divided into compartments; a cabinet.

chandal, I. difficult; = *sukar.* II. Hind. loose, foul-mouthed, ribald. III. jarring; = *janggal,* q.v.

chandan, a variant of *chĕndana,* q.v.

chandang, *bĕrani chandang,* not knowing when one is beaten; obstinate courage.

chandat, a kind of hook with several unbarbed points sticking out in different directions (it is used to fish up sunken cables; or, in small size, for catching cuttle-fish).

chandek, I. a recognised concubine of a prince—as distinct from an inferior wife (*gundek*) or casual mistress (*jamah-jumahan*). II. a fixed riverine purse-net.

chandi, I. a monument; a memorial pillar or building. II. restive (of a horse); forward (of a woman).

chandit, that extremity of a native anchor to which the cable is not attached.

chandong, *parang chandong,* a chopper in which the handle and blade are in one piece and not fastened together.

chandu, prepared opium.

chang, I. carrying pick-a-back. II. Ch. a square lift-net. III. (Kedah) panniers for an elephant.

changak, to look round hastily (as a frightened man).

changap, a notch or dent for fitting together two pieces of wood.

changgah, a forked punting-pole (used for propelling a boat up-stream by pushing against tree-boughs, snags, etc.)

changgai, an artificial finger-nail or nail-protector (worn really as an ornament).

changgek, *chonggang-changgek,* an up-and-down bobbing motion (such as that of a Chinese kowtowing).

changgong, I. inharmonious; incongruous; out of place; unnatural. II. a snag in a river. III. astonishment; better *chĕngang.*

changip, *chungap-changip,* panting, out of breath.

changit, *chongak-changit,* restless up-and-down movements (of the head).

changkal, deep (of water).

changkat, I. a low hillock; a piece of rising ground. II. a shallow.

changkeh, uneven, irregular; *chongkah ch.,* all ups and downs; all crooked.

changking, lifting up (by seizing a boy's elbows and raising him in the air).

changkir, I. a small glass cup of Arab make. II. *chongkar ch.,* of all sizes and shapes (as the component parts of a heap of firewood).

changkis, a (Penang and Kedah) variant of *changkeh.,* q.v.

changkok, a crook; a pole with an iron hook at the end such as is used for managing elephants.

changkong, squatting.
changkul, a large hoe used for digging.
changkup, scooping up with the palm of the hand.
changok, *měnchangok*, to sit with curving neck (as a hawk on a bough).
chantas, severance by a single blow from a heavy cutting instrument; lopping, pruning.
chantek, pretty, good-looking; neat, nicely got up; well-groomed.
chanting, a sort of bamboo bucket (used for getting water out of a ship's well).
chantum, coming back together again; folding back again.
chap, Ch. printing; "chopping"; a Chinese chop or seal for use with ink; *chapkan*, to print; *pěrkakas ch.*, apparatus for printing; a press; *tukang ch.*, a printer; *ch. batu*, lithography; *ch. timah*, printing in metallic movable type.
chapa, a plant (*blumea balsamifera*).
chapah, a rough unpainted washtub (of Burmese make), a wooden plate.
chapai, to grasp; to attain to; to reach; to grip; *měnchapai*, id.; *hěndak měnchapai bulan*, to wish to get hold of the moon (a proverbial description of mad ambition).
chapak, inattention; omitting to notice, either through preoccupation or deliberately; to slight, to overlook.
chapal, a sort of shoe consisting of a leather sole with a band over the instep and a thong passing between the big toe and its neighbour.
chapek, lame, limping, halt.
chapiau, Port. a hat; *ch. lipat*, a cocked hat.
chaping, a metallic plate (used to cover the nudities of a very young female child).
chapok, a gross form of insult.
chapul, a (Kedah) variant of *chabul*, q.v.
chara, way, custom, manner, style,

wise; *mĕmakai chara pĕrĕmpuan*, to dress as a woman; *ch. China*, in the Chinese language or in the Chinese way.
charang, the minor boughs and branches of a tree.
charbi, Hind. grease used for lubrication.
charek, tearing; a rent; *chorak-charek*, frayed, tattered; *charekkan*, to tear up; *mĕncharek-charek*, id.
chari, seeking for; looking for; *charikan*, to search for anything; *mĕnchari*, to seek; *pĕrĕmpuan mĕnchari*, (Penang) a prostitute; *pĕncharian*, a source of livelihood.
charok, a runnel; a running ditch; the puncturing of a gutta tree.
charut, obscene language; *mĕncharut*, to use obscene language.
chat, Ch. paint; *sapu ch.*, to paint; the process of painting.
chatang, Ch. a rattan-basket-cosy.
chatok, I. the blow of a pick; the peck of a bird. II. sitting bolt upright.
chatu, doling out in niggardly quantities.
chatur, Skr. chess; *main ch.*, to play chess; *buah ch.*, chessmen; *tapak ch.* chequered; *loh ch.* or *papan ch.*, a chess-board.
chaung, sunken—of the cheeks (through loss of teeth).
chaus, thin by emaciation.
chawak, I. a dimple. II. a leash.
chawan, Ch. a tea-cup.
chawang, bifurcation, branching off; a branch—cf. *chabang*.
chawat, a loin-cloth; *bĕrchawat*, to wear as a loin-cloth is worn; to wear a loin cloth; *kĕmudi ch.*, a rudder (on European lines).
chawis, ready, prepared.
chayer, thin (of liquids); watery; *lumpur ch.*, very watery mud; *bubur ch.* thin broth.
che' "Mr."—a title given to otherwise untitled Malays.

chĕbai, *chĕbek-chĕbai*, pouting.
chĕbak, excavation (in quarry work); digging out by side-long blows.
chĕbek, *chĕbek-chĕbai*, to pout.
chĕbis, *sa-chĕbis*, a tatter, a shred.
chebok, a coconut scoop; ladling up water with this scoop; cleansing from fœcal defilement; *ta'-bĕrchebok*, a term of abuse; "dirty beast."
chĕbur, plunging heavily into water; plunging into a flaming mass; *mĕnchĕburkan diri*, to plunge, to cast oneself into.
chĕchah, dipping (a pen into ink); immersion followed by immediate withdrawal; *sa-chĕchah*, a moment; also *chichah*.
chĕchak, I. *bĕlang ch.*, speckled. II. see *chichak*.
chĕchap, touching (food) with the finger and then applying the finger to the lips; tasting.
checher, dropping away in driblets; *bĕrchecheran*, id.
chĕdas, to smooth a plait by passing a rattan over it.
chĕdĕra, Skr. a flaw, a defect; *mĕndatangkan ch.*, to reflect upon someone, to injure (somebody's) reputation.
chĕding, thin and out of condition.
chĕdok, sunken (of the cheeks and eyes).
chedok, scooping up; baling up; ladling up.
chega, wary (of a bird or fish).
chĕgak, erect; = *tĕgak*.
chĕgar, a rapid; a water-race.
chĕgok, *sa-chĕgok*, a gulp; = *sa-tĕgok*.
cheh, a somewhat contemptuous exclamation of disbelief or disgust.
chĕkah, split open; splitting under pressure (as a mangosteen); cf. *chĕkeh*.
chĕkak, I. holding between the thumb and forefiger; *sa-chĕkak*, as much as can be held between the thumb and forefinger; a pinch; *bĕrchĕkak pinggang*, with waist belts tied together (used of two adversaries who tie themselves to each other in single combat so that the one or the other must perish). II. reliable (of a workman).
chĕkal, strength, resisting-power.
chĕkam, a sharp-pointed stick (used for making holes in the ground for hill-padi cultivation); *sakit ch.*, a festering sore under a toe-nail.
chĕkang, tight; tightly stretched; taut; *rangak ch.*, a shell (*pteroceras chiragra*).
chĕkap, skilful, expert; *kĕrja suatu ta'-boleh chĕkap*, he is no good for any work.
chĕkar, Hind. hard a-port or hard a-starboard (of the steering-wheel).
chĕkau, reaching out for anything.
chĕkeh, cracked by pressure; slightly split—cf. *chĕkah*.
chĕkek, *mĕnchĕkek leher*, to seize by the throat; to garotte; *mati tĕrchĕkek*, death by choking; *chĕkek kĕdadak*, violent vomiting (invoked as a curse on an enemy).
chekel, stingy, miserly.
chŏki, Ch. small Chinese playing-cards; "chicky-cards."
chŏkit, to pick away small morsels; to pick to pieces.
chĕkok, to force food down a child's throat; *ch. chĕkek*, the struggle for breath by a choking man.
chŏku, denting with the finger-nail, pressing a mark.
chĕkup, covering with the palms of the hands.
chĕkur, a medicinal plant (*kœmpferia galanga*).
chĕkut, to pick up between the tips of the thumb and three fingers.
chĕla, censuring, blaming; finding fault; *chĕla mĕnchĕla*, to abuse; *nama yang kĕchĕlaan*, a bad name.
chĕlaga, I. soot, fine cinders (adhering to a torch). II. *chĕlaga kĕmudi*, the tiller.
chĕlah, crevice, fissure, crack, cleft;

ch. batu, the space between two boulders; *ch. dinding*, a crevice in a wall; *ch. gigi*, the line between adjoining teeth; *ch. gunong*, a gully or ravine; *ch. jari*, the space between two fingers.

chělak, antimony-powder (used to darken the fringe of the eye).

chělaka, ill-starred; ill-omened; bringing bad luck; a term of abuse; *orang ch.*, a scoundrel; *yang tĕrlalu bĕsar chĕlaka ku lihat*, the greatest infamy of all that I saw.

chĕlakuti, (Patani) betel-nut scissors; = *kachip*.

chĕlam, (onom.) *chĕlum-chĕlam*, stamping; tramping.

chĕlana, trousers (loose above but tight round the calf).

chĕlap, (onom.) *chĕlup-chĕlap*, the sound of splashing.

chĕlapah, soiling, dishonouring.

chĕlapak, astride; sitting on the fork; sitting astride; also *chĕlĕpak*.

chĕlapek, a preparation of dried fish and herbs.

chĕlari, *kain chĕlari*, a thin fabric of shining silk with gold thread.

chĕlaru, (Kedah) disorderly, confused.

chĕlas, *chĕlus-chĕlas*, the sound of a man coming in and out; free, familiar.

chĕlatu, the flying ant; better *kĕlĕ-katu*.

chele, *kain chele*, a cloth fabric imported from Southern India.

chĕledang, *chĕledang-chĕledok*, a swaggering, rolling gait (affected by abandoned women).

chĕledok, see above—s.v. *chĕledang*.

chĕlĕguri, a shrub (*clerodendron disparifolium*); also *sĕlĕguri*.

chĕleh, idle, lazy, sluggish.

chĕlek, lifting the eyelid; seeing; *si-buta baharu chĕlek*, a blind man who sees for the first time (a beggar on horseback), prov.

chĕlĕmpong, Jav. a musical instrument (wire strings played like a harp); the sound of strumming.

cheleng, Jav. a pig; = *babi*; *ch. alas*, a wild pig, = *babi hutan*.

chĕlĕngap, agape; open-mouthed.

chĕlengkang, *ch.-chĕlengkok*, motion in curves or waves.

chĕlengkok, see above—s.v. *chĕlengkang*.

chĕlĕpa, (Kedah) a sireh-box.

chĕlĕpak, sitting astride; = *chĕlapak*.

chĕlĕpek, (onom.) the sound made by mud bespattering a surface.

chĕlĕpok, (onom.) the sound of a heavy mass of mud falling on anything.

chĕlichi, covetous.

chĕlis, chopping into small pieces.

chĕlomis, weak, sickly.

chĕlong, a sort of elephant trap.

chĕlum, (onom.) *ch.-chĕlam*, tramping, stamping.

chĕlup, steeping in; saturation in; dyeing; *di-chĕlup merah*, dyed red; *chĕlupkan*, to saturate, to dye.

chĕlupar, garrulous.

chĕlur, immersion in boiling liquid; scalding.

chĕlus, coming in and out familiarly; slipping on and off readily (of a ring); *ch.-chĕlas*, free, familiar.

chĕmar, I. pollution, dirt; *bĕrchĕmar kaki*, to dirty one's feet—i.e. to take vigorous measures. II. a variant of *chamar*, q.v.

chĕmara, Skr. a pendant of horsehair (under the blade of a spear); a yak-tail; a chignon; *kayu ch.*, a name sometimes given to the casuarina.

chĕmas, anxiety, nervousness; *jangan-lah ch.*, don't be nervous.

chĕmat, I. fastening together with a pin or spike; fastening ataps. II. towing; *tali pĕnchĕmat*, a tow-rope.

chĕmbul, a casket; a small box; *laksana chĕmbul dĕngan tutup-nya*, like a casket and its cover (exactly suited one to another), prov.

chĕmburu, suspicious, jealous.
chĕmĕngkian, a fruit (used medicinally as an aperient).
chemer, extremely dim-sighted; nearly blind.
chĕmĕrlang, glittering, radiant, shimmering.
chĕmĕti, Tam. a whip.
chĕmidu, nervous; self-conscious; timid and retiring.
chĕmok, I. a pod; II. (Kedah) to quarrel.
chĕmpa, *bunga chĕmpa*, a flower (unidentified); *chĕmpa raya*, id.
chĕmpaka, Skr. the champak tree (*michelia champaca*); *ch. biru*, the frangipanni (*plumiera acutifolia*).
chĕmpana, a litter; also *jĕmpana*.
chĕmpĕdak, a jack-fruit (*artocarpus polyphema*); *ch. ayer* (*artocarpus maingayi*).
chĕmpĕlek, pitch and toss.
chĕmpĕlong, (onom.) the sound of a heavy body falling plump into water.
chĕmpĕrai, a generic name given to a number of sea-shore shrubs, notably *champereia griffithii* and *cansjera rheedii*.
chĕmpĕrling, the tree-starling (*calornis chalybeius*); *mata ch.*, very red eyes; also *pĕrling*.
chĕmping, *sa-chĕmping*, a very small bit; a morsel.
chĕmpong, carrying between both arms (as a bale of firewood is carried).
chĕmuas, dirt on the face (after a meal); greasy.
chĕmuchup, love-grass; burrs.
chĕmus, sick of, sated with—stronger than *jĕmu*.
chena, old and hardened (of a fighting-cock).
chĕnangau, a malodorous flying bug very destructive to padi.
chĕnangga, Skr. a birth-mark; a congenital deformity.
chĕnangkas, a heavy cutlass.
chĕnchala, a Kedah name for the fantail fly-catcher (*rhipadura*, spp.); elsewhere *murai gila*.
chĕnchalok, a relish made of small prawns.
chĕnchang, slashing, slicing, chopping, cutting.
chĕncharu, a fish (*caranx boops*); also *jaru-jaru*.
chĕnchawan, the socket of the knee; *minyak ch.*, the oily matter in the patella.
chencheng, running as hard as one can; tearing away.
chĕnchodak, the Kedah and Penang name for the fish *belone strongylura*; elsewhere *todak*.
chĕnchurut, the musk-rat; = *tikus turi*.
chĕndala, Skr. harlot, profligate; immodest.
chĕndana, Skr. sandal-wood (*santalum album*).
chĕndawan, a generic name for poisonous fungi (mostly *agarici*); *mabok ch.*, poisoned by fungi; (by metaphor) love-sick—of a woman.
chĕndayam, pleasant to look at; fair; beautiful.
chĕndĕra, I. Skr. a race of fairies. II. deep (of sleep); = *nyĕdar*.
chĕndĕrai, a generic name given to several plants—viz. one croton (*c. argyratus*) and three *grewia*.
chĕndĕramulia, Skr. a tree bearing an edible fruit (unidentified).
chĕndĕrasari, a bird (unidentified).
chĕndĕrasuri, a tree (unidentified).
chĕnderawaseh, the bird of paradise.
chĕndĕrus, (Penang) removing rancidity from oil.
chĕnduai, seduction; enticing women by magic art.
chendul, a kind of thin broth with cakes of dough floating in it.
chĕnela, Port. a slipper.
chĕngal, the name of a tree (*balanocarpus maximus*) usually known by the Kedah form of the word, *chĕngai*.

chĕngang, astonishment; *tĕrchĕng-ang*, bewildered with surprise.
chengeng, whining continually (of young children).
chenggek, *bĕrchenggek*, to perch; = *bĕrtenggek*.
chĕngi, a nasal twang.
chĕngis, a repulsive odour about food.
chĕngkam, gripping between finger and thumb.
chĕngkang, I. wakeful, sleepless. II. barring the passage—cf. *sĕngkang*.
chĕngkarok, a sweetmeat made of boiled rice.
chĕngkau, a variant of *chĕkau*, q.v.
chĕngkeh, the clove-spice (*eugenia caryophylla*); *buah ch.*, a clove.
chengkeh, walking on the side of one's foot.
chengkek, thinner at the centre than at the extremities (of a post).
chĕngkelat, a variant of *sĕngkelat*, q.v.
chĕngkĕling, a variant of *sĕngkĕling*, q.v.
chĕngkĕra, hollow-eyed; sleepless-looking.
chĕngkĕram, earnest money, an advance.
chĕngkĕrek, a cricket; *bĕradu ch.*, to make crickets fight.
chĕngkĕreng, I. a tree (*erythrina stricta*). II. an abscess.
chĕngkĕrma, Skr. moving over an area; spreading as news; wandering.
chengki, Ch. a run of luck; good luck.
chengkok, I. twisted; *ch. bĕledok*, zigzag. II. a leaf-monkey (*semnopithecus femoralis* or *s. cristatus*).
chĕngkolong, withdrawing a small amount from a large; drawing on a deposit.
chĕngkong, hollow, sunken (of the eyes).
chĕngkuas, shaggy, unkempt.
chĕngkurai, I. a silk fabric. II. *bĕrchĕngkurai*, crumbling to fragments, breaking up into picees.

chĕngong, gazing in open-mouthed astonishment—cf. *chĕngang*.
chĕnok, *minyak chĕnok*, a vegetable oil obtained from the tree *diplocnemia sebifera*; also *minyak kawang*.
chenok, *burong chenok*, a malkoha (*ramphococcyx erythrognathus* or *rhopodytes sumatranus*).
chĕnong, a fixed steady look at anything.
chĕntayu, a variant of *jĕntayu*, q.v.
chĕntong, I. a ladle (consisting of a bamboo receptacle with a handle rising vertically up from it). II. an erectile tuft of feathers on a bird's head; an erectile crest.
chĕnuram, a declivity; a precipitous incline—cf. *churam*.
chĕpat, speedy, quick; rapidity of movement.
chepeh, soft and pendent (of buffalo-horns).
cheper, a kind of metal saucer or plate on which a bowl (*batil*) rests.
chepoh, a club-foot.
chĕpu, a flat round box of wood (used as a receptacle for toilet requisites); *chĕpu-chĕpu*, the truck of the mast; *puting chĕpu-chĕpu*, the foot of the mast.
chĕpua, a blush of shame; a guilty look.
chĕrabah, ugly (of a child).
chĕrachak, sticking up in points.
chĕrachap, Malay castanets (bamboos beaten against each other).
chĕrah, clear, unobstructed (of the view); *ch. chuacha*, clear daylight.
chĕrai, severance, separation, divorce; *bĕrchĕrai*, to separate from; to be divorced from; *chĕraikan*, to separate (one person from another); *ch.-bĕrai*, broken up, scattered (of a defeated army).
chĕrakin, a sort of Malay medicine chest.
chĕramah, talkativeness—cf. *ramah*.
chĕrana, Skr. a deep salver or bowl on which are placed the various

vessels used for holding the requisites for betel-chewing; *měnyorongkan ch.*, to pass round this bowl so as to allow guests to help themselves to areca-nut, sireh-leaf, lime, etc.

chěranchang, lying point upwards.

chěrang, a clearing in the forest; *ch. rimba*, id.

chěranggah, branching into points; *rusa běrchěranggah*, a deer of many tine.

chěrani, a rich cloth.

chěrat, a plug-hole.

chěratok, squatting in a row; perched in a row (as birds on a telegraph-wire).

chěrawat, Skr. an arrow of fire.

chěrcha, Skr. abuse, insult, reviling; *kěna ch.*, to be reviled.

chěrchak, I. slightly pockmarked—cf. *chěchak*. II. a variant of *chěrcha*.

chěrdas, I. foolish cunning. II. a buffalo-whip.

chěrdek, clever; sharp-witted; bright; intelligent; *měndatangkan ch.*, to sharpen the wits.

cherek, a kettle; a vessel for boiling water.

cheret, diarrhœa; looseness of the bowels; *ch. beret*, to run continuously.

chěrewet, fussiness; fussy and interfering behaviour.

chěrgas, reliable (of work); a thing you can depend on.

chěri, Hind. *gělang chěri*, a bangle.

cheri, a gong the sides of which slope inwards.

chěria, I. Skr. fidelity. II. cleared, brightened (of the countenance).

chěridawan, cries; shouts in unison; vocal music; chorus singing.

chěriga, I. being on one's guard; wary, watchful. II. a cutlass; a broad-bladed short sword or dagger.

chěrita, I. a story, a narrative; *ch. zaman dahulu*, a tale of old times. II. (onom.) *běrchěrita*, to twitter (of the magpie robin).

chěrlang, shining, resplendent—cf. *chěměrlang*.

chěrmai, a tree (*phyllanthus distictous*); it yields a small round acid fruit.

chěrmat, care; delicacy of touch; neatness in appearance or dress.

chěrmin, a mirror; *ch. mata*, the pupil of the eye; an eye-glass; *ch. těropong*, the lens of a telescope.

chěrna, Skr. assimilated, digested.

chěroboh, rough, rude, coarse, violent, vulgar.

chěroh, a second pounding of rice (to whiten it).

chěrok, I. a corner; an out-of-the way part of the room where things are placed that one does not need; the space under a wardrobe or between it and the wall; a hidden nook. II. a bamboo funnel used in milking.

chěrpělai, Tam. the imported Indian mongoose.

chěrpu, Tam. sandals, clogs; *bawah ch.*, position beneath the sandals (of a prince), the position of a subject—cf. *kaus* and *duli*; *měnjunjong ch.*, to acknowledge the rule of a prince.

chěrubah, a (Kedah) weapon.

chěruchup, burrs, love-grass.

chěrup, to lap up water; the sound of lapping water.

chěrut, I. tight compression; strangling; the sensation caused to the wearer by tight clothes or tight boots. II. cheroot; also *chěrutu*.

chěrutu, a cheroot.

chětai, *běrchětai-chětai*, tattered.

chetak, the wooden cases in which type is kept; the work of a compositor.

chetek, shallow; *elmu-nya ch.*, his learning was shallow.

chětěra, I. Skr. *payong ch.*, an umbrella with a hanging fringe. II. Skr. a story; = *chěrita*.

chětěri, Hind. tent, awning, canopy.

chětěria, Skr. a kshatriya; a member of the princely or warrior caste; a warrior.

chěti, Tam. a chetty; a moneylender; *di-pĕgang ch.*, in the hands of money-lenders.

chĕtus, (onom.) *chĕtus api*, to strike a light.

chewe, a term by which animals are spoken of (especially at sea) if the mention of their names is believed to be likely to attract their attention and cause injury or disaster.

chi, Ch. a measure of weight used in weighing opium; a tenth of a tael.

chiak, a sparrow; a finch.

chiar, crying continually (of a child).

chiau, I. disarranged (of dress). II. a long oar (worked standing).

chichah, steeping; dipping (e.g. food into gravy) so as to saturate; also *chĕchah*.

chichak, a lizard; also *chĕchak*.

chichek, shuddering at; feeling a strong aversion to; looking down upon with disgust.

chichit, great-grandchild.

chika, colic (during the night).

chikar, see *chĕkar*.

chikil, see *chekel*.

chili, chili; red pepper.

China, Chinese; *orang Ch.*, a Chinese; *nĕgĕri Ch.* or *bĕnua Ch.*, China; *ch. buta*, the *muhallil* or intermediate husband necessary to make the re-marriage of divorced persons legal; *main ch. buta*, blind man's buff; *lada ch.*, capsicum (*piper chaba*), also called *chabai*; *bunga ch.*, a name given to gardenias and sometimes to cultivated varieties of the *ixora*.

chinchang, see *chĕnchang*.

chinchau, Ch. a cold sweet jelly.

chinchin, a finger-ring.

chinchu, Ch. the "chinchew" or owner's agent on a ship.

chinda, great-grandson; a polite variant of *chichit*.

chingam, a sea-shore plant (*scyphiphora hydrophyllacia*).

chinta, Skr. loving desire; regret; longing; *bĕrchinta*, to be in love; *bĕrchintakan*, to pine for; *pĕrchintaan*, sorrow, regret.

chintamani, Skr. a fabulous gold-yellow snake, the finding of which is believed to betoken good fortune in love; *ular ch. gajah*, a name given to light forms of the viper *lachesis wagleri*.

chinting, Ch. a revenue officer employed by the farms in the Straits.

chipai, a monkey (*semnopithecus melalophos*).

chipan, I. a battle-axe. II. (Perak) a tapir.

chiri, the coronation formula used in certain Malay States. [It would appear to be Pali].

chirit, a variant of *cheret*, q.v.

chis, an interjection of vulgar and contemptuous disbelief or disapproval—stronger than *cheh*.

chita, I. Skr. feeling, emotion; *suka-chita*, joy; *duka-chita*, sorrow; *mĕn-chita*, to fix one's thoughts upon a talisman in order to get its magical aid; to call into existence by will-power. II. Hind. *kain chita*, chintz.

chiu, I. a state cushion; a cushion for a royal divan. II. Ch. spirituous liquor.

chium, to smell; to kiss (in the Malay way); *mĕnchium*, id.; *pĕnchium*, the sense of smell.

chiup, a bladder made by blowing out a fowl's crop.

choba, attempting, trying, testing; "please," "just"; *choba tanya kapada guru*, please ask the teacher; *chobai*, to hold a test; *chobakan*, to put to the test; *pĕnchoba*, a trial or test.

chobak, *chobak-chabek*, tattered or torn at the edge; frayed.

choban, a needle of horn or bamboo used in repairing nets.

chobar, rent down the middle, torn; *ch.-chabir*, much torn.

chobek, *sa-chobek*, a pinch.

chobis, *sa-chobis*, a splinter, a fragment from the edge.

chodak, *mĕnchodak*, to hold the head aloft (as a swimming snake).
choek, a soup-plate or bowl of Chinese make.
chogan, Pers. an ensign—better *jogan*; a portent in the heavens.
chogo, Jav. blockhead, fool.
chokar, a game resembling draughts.
choket, the abstraction of a very small quantity; picking a piece.
chokin, a bathing cloth (used by Chinese coolies).
chokmar, a mace.
chokok, the cry of a latah-subject when excited.
cholak, *ch.-chaling*, confused, entangled.
cholang, *ch.-chaling*, confused, entangled.
cholat, a dig with the elbow or hand—cf. *cholet*.
cholek, prizing out with a point; digging out with a pin; *mĕncholek*, to scrape out with a pointed instrument; *pĕncholek api*, a lucifer match.
cholet, a dig with the point of the finger—cf. *cholat*.
choli, Hind. a tight-fitting native corset or bodice worn next the skin by Indian women.
cholok, a fuse of cloth steeped in oil.
choma, see *chuma*.
chombol, the knob on a door.
chomek, a cuttle-fish.
chomel, I. dainty, pretty. II. babbling; unable to hold one's tongue.
chomot, defiled with dirt.
chompang, *ch.-champing*, torn, tattered at the edge, frayed.
chompes, injured by the loss of a corner or projection.
chompoh, Ch. a cook.
chondĕrong, inclining; leaning; *ch.-hati*, mental leanings; inclinations; also *chondong*.
chondong, leaning to one side; out of the perpendicular; *ch.-hati*, personal inclination; also *chondĕrong*.

chonet, a slight upward projection of the tip of anything; tip-tilted; also *chotet*.
chongak, turned upwards (of the face); holding his head up (of a buffalo sniffing when alarmed); pointing up (of the beak of a bird).
chonggah, projecting unevenly; sticking out in all sorts of directions; also *chongkah*.
chonggang, *ch. chongget*, bobbing up and down (as a sandpiper picking up food, or as a man climbing a difficult hill).
chongget, see *chonggang*.
chongkah, projecting unevenly; out of line (of a projection); also *chonggah*.
chongkak, a generic name for cowrie shells (*cypraeae*); *main ch.*, a game played with these shells; *papan ch.*, the board used for playing this game.
chongkang, *ch. kĕlalak*, topsy-turvy (at sixes and sevens).
chongkar, *ch.-changkir*, of all sizes and shapes (as the component parts of a heap of firewood).
chongkeng, sticking out in all directions (as the points of a caltrop).
chongok, *mĕnchongok*, to sit stiffly erect.
chonteng, smearing (anything) on a surface; *muka tĕrchonteng arang*, a face smeared over with charcoal; (by metaphor) disgraced.
chontoh, a model of an object to be copied; a sample; a specimen.
chorak, the general colouring (of a sarong); the prevailing hue in a design.
choram, a variant of *churam*, q.v.
chorang, cheating at games; *pĕnchorang*, a cheat.
chorek, the long linear markings in the grain of certain woods.
choreng, streaked with long vertical streaks (as a man on whom paint

has fallen); *ch. moreng*, covered with streaks.

chorong, I. a sireh tray or platter. II. a cylindrical funnel; the chimney of a lamp.

chorot, I. bringing up the rear; *pĕn-chorot*, the hindmost. II. Jav. the spout of anything; *ch. cherek*, the spout of a kettle.

chotek, *sa-chotek*, a very small portion; a pinch; a bite.

chotet, tip-tilted; = *chonet*.

chotok, I. the small fleshy protuberance at the base of a bird's beak. II. projecting above the surface (of a low flat rock).

chua, not pleasing, unsatisfactory.

chuacha, Skr. clear (of the atmosphere); *tĕrang ch.*, bright daylight.

chuai, to hold in little esteem; of little account.

chual, cloth in the first stage of its manufacture.

chuali, excepting, saving; *kĕchuali*, id.; *kĕchuali kĕbanyakan*, some; a number of.

chuani, a kind of cloth.

chuar, sticking up (of long objects, such as masts); cf. *chuat*.

chuat, sticking up (of short objects); cf. *chuar*.

chubit, pinching, pressing between finger and thumb; *mĕnchubit*, to pinch.

chucha, abasing or silencing one's foe (especially by magic arts).

chuchi, cleansing; *bĕrchuchi*, to clean, to cleanse; *kĕtam ch.*, a plane.

chuchoh, I. setting anything alight; putting fire to anything. II. teasing, verbal annoyance.

chuchok, piercing; driving a point into anything; threading a needle; piercing with a needle; perforating; *manek tanggal daripada chuchok-nya*, pearls fallen from their strings; *ch. kajang*, making *kajang* mats by running a piece of bamboo through pandanus leaves to hold them together; *ch. sĕnjata*, the leader of a charge; *bĕrchuchok-ch.*, in strings; *mĕnchuchok*, to pierce, to perforate.

chuchong, a variant of *chuchu*.

chuchu, grandchild; *anak ch.*, descendants.

chuchunda, grandchild—a respectful form of *chuchu*.

chuchur, I. trickling; flowing in small quantities; *chuchuran atap*, the edge of a roof; *chuchuri*, to let water fall or drip on anything; to anoint. II. a generic name given to cakes of hard-backed pastry. III. a bird (*podargus javanensis?*)

chuchut, Jav. the shark.

chuit, a playful tap or blow with the finger; a movement of the finger hinting "go away"; the wagging of a bird's tail.

chuka, Skr. vinegar.

chukai, toll; tax; impost; *timbang ch.*, the payment of dues; *mĕlarikan ch.*, to avoid the payment of an impost.

chuki, a game resembling draughts.

chuku, Tam. dried gambier-root.

chukup, completion, sufficiency; quite, fully; full; *ch. sa-ratus hari*, a full hundred days; *sudah ch.*, it is enough.

chukur, shaving; *tukang ch.* (Straits) a barber; *mĕnchukur*, to shave; *pisau pĕnchukur* or *pisau pĕnyukur*, a razor.

chula, Skr. the horn of a dragon; magical or supernatural horn.

chulan, *bunga ch.*, a flower (*aglaia odorata?*)

chulas, inert, sluggish, slow, idle—a stronger expression than *malas*.

chulim, a pipeful of tobacco or opium.

chuma, vain; useless; idle; gratuitous; *chuma-chuma*, uselessly; *pĕr-chuma*, id.

chumbu, coaxing, love-making, verbal endearments; *chumbuan*, loving

words; bĕrchumbu-chumbuan, flirtation, the exchange of endearing expressions.
chun, Ch. an inch (approximately).
chunam, long delicate pincers for extracting wax from the ear, for working in the precious metals, etc.
chunda, grandchild—a respectful equivalent of chuchu.
chundang, kĕchundang or pĕchundang, conquest; the position of the defeated, relative to the victor.
chungap, ch.-changip, panting, short of breath.
chungkil, the use of a pointed instrument for extracting foreign bodies—(e.g. as a tooth-pick is used); gouging; pĕnchungkil gigi, a toothpick.
chupak, a measure of capacity; a quarter of a gantang, or, approximately, the capacity of a half-coconut-shell; sĕpĕrti chupak hanyut, like a floating chupak-measure—a half-coconut-shell (which rocks greatly when it floats)—a simile for loose swagger; chupak is used also of the bowl of a mortar or opium-pipe.
chupar, garrulous—cf. chĕlupar.

chuping, the lobe (of the ear or nostril); ch. tĕlinga, the lobe of the ear.
chupu, a variant of chĕpu, q.v.
chupul, not long enough (for the purpose in view); inadequate owing to shortness.
chura, jesting; joking; not taking seriously.
churah, emptying out; churahkan, to empty out, to pour out.
churai, loose, severally, one at a time.
churam, sloping; a declivity; a precipitous incline—cf. chĕnuram.
churat, gushing out violently (of liquid).
churi, I. theft; stealing; stealthy removal; stealth; churi-churi, stealthily, surreptitiously; mĕnchuri, to steal; pĕnchuri, a thief; kĕchurian, theft. II. to flow (as water or blood).
chus, an interjection coarsely enjoining silence.
chut, a Kedah variant of chus, q.v.
chutam, an amalgam of gold, silver and iron.
chutap, a waist-buckle of shiny black material.
chuti, Hind. leave of absence; furlough; bĕrchuti, to be on leave.

D

daba, hawa-daba, odour, smell; suspicion.
dabir, Ar. a writer, a scribe.
dabong, mĕndabong, to file the teeth.
dabus, a broad round shaft of wood with a short spike set like a spear-head at its extremity; main d., to stab oneself with this awl.
daching, a steel-yard of Chinese type; anak d., batu d. or buah d., the weight on a steel-yard.
dada, breast; chest; seat of feeling; mĕnĕpok d., to beat the breast; bĕrpĕrang bĕrdada, to fight in the open.

dadah, I. a native medicine-box. II. = dadak, q.v.
dadak, chĕkek kĕdadak, violent vomiting; violent sickness (often invoked upon the head of a scoundrel).
dadap, a metallic shield of a type only mentioned in romance.
dadar, I. a thin pancake or omelet of Malay make. II. mĕndadar, to distribute charity.
dadeh, curds; ayer d., whey.
dadok, mĕndadok, to beg; to solicit alms.
dadong, I. (Kedah) crooning a child

to sleep. II. (Riau Johor) exposing for fermentation.

dadu, I. Port. a die, dice; *main d.*, to play with dice. II. roseate; *mega d.*, the roseate clouds. III. *bĕrdadu*, to gossip. IV. *sĕri d.*, a variant of *soldadu*, q.v.

daeng, I. dried fish; *minta darah pada daeng*, to ask dry fish for blood —(to get blood out of a stone), prov. II. a Bugis title of distinction.

daerah, Ar. district, outlying dependency.

dafnah, Ar. the laurel.

daftar, Ar. a tabular list; a roll; a register of attendance.

daga, *mĕnduga*, to do uphill work; to make an effort.

dagang, a stranger; a foreigner; *pĕrahu d.*, a vessel from elsewhere; a trading ship; *dagangan*, commercial products; *d. sĕntĕri*, the stranger as an object of pity—a depreciatory description of himself often used by a writer; *d. piatu, d. yang miskin* and *d. yang hina*, id; *d. yang rawan* and *d. yang rayu*, id. (in love poetry).

daging, flesh, meat; *d. ular sawa*, the flesh of the python; *d. darah* or *darah dan daging*, flesh and blood (close relationship or intimate friendship, such as "blood-brotherhood").

dagok, *hantu d.*, clouds on the horizon of weird and changing form (believed by the Malays to be ghosts of murdered men).

dagu, the human chin; the "chin" or corner of certain Malay knives and choppers, this "chin" being one of the corners near the handle.

dah, done—a colloquial abbreviation of *sudah*, q.v.

dahaga, thirst; thirsty; *lapar d.*, hunger and thirst; *mĕnghapus d.*, to assuage one's thirst.

dahagi, extreme covetousness.

dahak, phlegm; mucus (from the mouth).

daham, (onom.) "hum" (in the expression "hum and haw"); *bĕrdaham*, to hum and haw; to hesitate before speaking.

dahan, I. a minor bough or branch of a tree; *harimau d.*, a large tiger-cat or small leopard (*leopardus macrocedus*). II. *pĕndahan*, an obsolete weapon mentioned in romance.

dahana, *mĕndahana*, to beg, to importune for gifts; see also *dana*.

dahi, the brows; the region of the eyebrows; *sa-hari bulan dahi-nya*, his brow was as the new moon.

dahshat, Ar. panic, alarm; *mĕmbĕri d.*, to rouse panic, to terrify.

dahulu, before; *zaman d.*, past ages; *adat d. kala*, customary law; *dahuluĭ* to anticipate, to be too quick for; *bĕrdahulu-dahuluan*, pressing on, one trying to get in front of the other— cf. *hulu*.

Dajal, Ar. Antichrist; the false Messiah.

dak, no, not—an abbreviation of *tidak*.

daka, *tiang d.*, the wooden supports upon which rests the plank hiding away the body in a Malay grave.

dakap, embracing, drawing to the breast; *bĕrdakap*, to embrace; *mĕndakap*, id.; *bĕrdakap-dakapan*, exchanging embraces.

dakar, perversity, obstinacy in doing wrong; offensive arrogance.

dakhil, Ar. trusty.

daki, I. filth, dirt; *mĕmbuang d.*, to clean, to wash. II. ascent, climbing up; *mĕndaki*, to ascend.

daksina, Skr. the south.

daku, me—a form taken by the word *aku* (I, me) after the words *akan* and *dĕngan* and verbs ending in *kan*.

dalal, Ar. agent, broker, go-between.

dalalah, Ar. a female go-between.

dalam, I. interior, inside; in, while, during; *ka-dalam*, inward; *di-dalam*, inside; position in; *di-dalam hati*, mentally to oneself. II. depth, deep; *tĕrlalu dalam ayer-nya*, its waters were very deep; *měndalamkan*, to deepen. III. Jav. princely dwelling, court; *bahasa d.*, the language of the court.

dalang, the story-reciter (who also works the figures) at a Malay shadow-show; the author (in stories written for use with shadow-shows).

daleh, subterfuge, quibble, equivocation.

dalek, *dolak-d.*, shilly-shallying.

dalil, Ar. the elucidation of the Koran by commentaries; the whole of the standard commentators.

dalima, see *dělima*.

dalong, a large platter for feeding a numerous party.

dalu, a mistletoe.

dam, I. (Dutch) *main dam*, draughts. II. Ar. a religious penalty. III. a whiff or puff at a pipe.

damai, settlement; bringing about a good understanding; *damaikan*, to effect a settlement; *běrdamai*, to be at peace; *pěrdamaian*, a settlement of differences; a treaty of peace.

damak, the dart of a blow-pipe; *tabong d.*, the quiver for such darts.

damal, slow to move; difficult to sail or row (of a boat).

daman, the sheet of a large sail.

damar, resin; "dammar"; a torch of resinous wood.

damba, desire for; wish to possess.

damdam, spite, grudge; *měnaroh d.*, to bear a grudge.

dampar, cast ashore; being aground; *těrdampar*, stranded.

dampil, contiguity, proximity; *běrdampil-d.*, in close proximity—cf. *damping*.

damping, juxtaposition; contiguity; contact; *běrdamping*, to be hard by; to come next.

dan, I. and, furthermore. II. ability or time to manage anything; *ta'-dan*, it cannot be done. III. (Naning) your servant; I.

dana, Skr. gift, charity; *měrapu d.*, to go a-begging—cf. *dahana*.

danau, a mere, a pool, a tarn, a lake.

dandan, the projecting platforms or galleries on a native ship; *d. haluan*, the prow platform.

dandang, a large copper boiler.

dandi, I. small Tamil cymbals (a musical instrument often mentioned in literature). II. spotted, mottled; *rusa d.*, a deer with spotted markings.

dang, a title given in old romances to ladies about a court—cf. *dayang*.

dangau, a temporary lean-to erected when camping out for watching padi-fields.

dangdang, a (Kedah) variant of *dandang*, q.v.

dangkal, dry; lacking in juiciness.

dangkap, a variant of *dakap*, q.v.

dangkar, I. *dongkor-d.*, bundling out bag and baggage. II. a variant of *dakar*, q.v.

dangking, *dongkang-d.*, (Kedah) extremely emaciated; cadaverous.

dangok, *měndangok*, to have the head thrust forward.

dani, a (Kedah) variant of *dandi*, q.v.

danta, Skr. ivory; *asmara d.*, beautiful white teeth.

danu, *ular d.*, (Kedah) a rainbow.

danur, putrid emanations from a dead body; a putrefying corpse.

dap, I. a sort of tabor. II. a sword with a long blade and a bamboo hilt covered with skate-skin.

dapa, a slave-messenger sent as a gift with a proposal of marriage.

dapat, obtaining, getting, acquiring; managing; *hutang mas dapat dibayar*, a debt in money may be paid; *lěmak dapat ka-orang*, the fat goes to others; *dapati* and *měndapat*, to obtain, to get; *kědapatan*, the acquisition of anything; *pěndapatan*, the thing acquired; the proceeds; *měndapatkan*, to come across, to meet; *ta'-dapat-tiada*, it must be; must; *unjokkan surat ini, ta'-dapat-tiada* *di-tolong-nya*, show him this letter and he must help you.

dapur, I. a Malay kitchen; an oven; a brick-kiln; *rumah d.*, a cook-house; *juru d.*, a cook; *d. tanah*, a mud-oven. II. *dapur-dapur susu*, the outer-portion of the breast; *d.-d. kubur*, the grave mound (in contradistinction to the head-stone).

dar, Ar. abode.

dara, Skr. unmarried; maiden; maidenhood; *bini dan dara*, matrons and maids; *anak d.*, a virgin; *bĕr-dara*, virgin.

darah, blood: *buang d.*, blood-letting; *buang ayer d.*, dysentery; *d. puteh*, "white blood"—i.e. royal blood; *daging d.*, (one's own) flesh and blood, near relatives; *bĕrdarat*, bleeding, suffused with blood.

darai, (Kedah) sexual impotence in the male.

darat, land; dry land (as opposed to water); the interior (as opposed to the coast); *naik ka-dwrat*, to land (from a vessel); *daratan*, dry land; *mĕndarat*, to go inland.

dari, from; out of; of (in the sense of "made of"); in the matter of; than; *d. sini*, hence; *d. situ*, thence; *daripada*, from, out of, regarding; than.

darjah, see *darjat*.

darjat, Ar. rank; grade; emblem of distinction.

darwi, crumbling to pieces.

darya, Pers. sea, ocean, river; *wakil d.*, the lord of the waters.

das, the sound of a shot, *raja ini datang, bĕrapa das tembak*, when this prince arrives how many "guns" are we to give him.

dasa, Skr. ten; *sa-dasa*, a batch of ten.

dasar, ground-work; materials of construction; prevailing element in a design; the essence of anything.

dasi, *butang d.*, a collar-stud.

dastur, *layar d.*, a studding-sail.

datang, coming, approach; *daripada Allah datang-nya*, it comes to us from God; *datangkan* or *mĕndatangkan*, to bring on; to cause; *m. sĕmbah*, to bring a respectful greeting; *m. fikiran*, to invite reflection; *kĕdatangan*, the coming; *k. maut*, the coming of death; *mĕndatangi*, to attack; to meet a hostile assault.

datar, smooth, level; = *rata* and *natar*.

datia, Skr. a Titan; a giant.

datok, grandfather; a senior; a title of distinction; a joss or idol; the tutelary spirit of a *kĕramat* or wonder-working spot; *d. nenek*, ancestors.

datong, a variant of *datok*, q.v.

daulat, Ar. majesty; the sanctity which invests the office of a king; the mysterious kingly power which does not die with a sovereign, but abides so as to punish any degenerate successor (according to Malay belief); *daulat tuan-ku*, your majesty!—an exclamation of homage; *di-timpa d.*, struck down by the power of offended majesty.

daun, a leaf; a blade of grass; the submerged screen in an outshore fish-trap *(jĕrmal)*; *d. buntut*, the short outer pocket of this screen; *d. pĕnjarang*, the long inner pocket over which the fish first pass; *d. chĕki*, "chicky" cards; *d. teh*, tea, tea-leaves; *d. kayu*, the leaf of a tree; *mĕndaun kayu*, as the leaves of the forest in number.

daup, beamy and heavy (of a boat); heavy and sullen (of a face).

dawa, Ar. a lawsuit; *kĕna d.*, to be sued.

dawai, wire; *d. gĕlang*, very thick wire.

dawat, Ar. ink; *tĕmpat d.*, or *bĕkas d.*, an inkstand.

daya, I. resource, stratagem; *d. upaya*, resources, means; *apa-kan d.*, what can one do? *mĕndayakan*, to

deceive by a stratagem. II. *barat d.*, the south-west.
Dayak, Dyak.
dayang, a damsel, a young girl; *awang dan d.*, young men and maidens; *dayang-dayang*, attendants in a court.
dayong, an oar; the breast fin of a fish; *anak d.*, an oarsman; *batang d.*, the shaft of an oar; *daun d.*, the blade of an oar.
dayu, a low moaning sound; *měn-dayu-d.*, to rumble in the distance.
dayus, Ar. a despicable coward.
děbak, (onom.) a smacking sound.
děbap, (onom.) a slapping sound.
děbar, the beating or throbbing of the heart; *běrděbar-děbar-lah rasa hati-nya*, he felt his heart throb violently.
děbas, (onom.) the hiss of rushing air.
děbek, (onom.) the bleating of goats; also *ěmbek*.
děbok, a variant of *děbak*.
děbong, (onom.) a thumping sound.
děbop, a variant of *děbap*.
děbu, dust; haze—cf. *lěbu*.
děbum, (onom.) a thumping sound.
děbur, (onom.) the sound of a landslip or heavy crumbling fall.
děbus, a variant of *děbas*.
děching, (onom.) a chinking sound.
děchit, (onom.) a twittering or squeaky sound.
dědah, open, exposed (especially of indecent exposure).
dědai, *běrdědai-d.*, in long, straggling, disorderly lines—cf. *děrai*.
dědak, I. bran; padi husk; II. *měn-dědak*, to crowd, to press on.
dědam, *běrdědam*, to be crowded together.
dědap, a generic name given to a number of trees (*erythrina*, spp.) that bear very bright scarlet flowers and that are used to provide supports for the pepper plant; *ikan pari d.*, a ray (*eurogymnus asperrimus*).

dědar, a touch of illness.
dědau, *měndědau*, to shout, to cry out.
děgam, (onom.) a slamming sound.
děgap, *běrděgap-d.*, to heave quickly (of the breast).
děgar, I. *chakap běrděgar-d.*, boastful talk. II. *bunyi běrděgar-d.*, reverberation.
děgil, stiff-necked, obstinate, perverse.
děgum, (onom.) a booming sound.
děgup, (onom.) a duller variant of *děgap*.
děhaga, see *dahaga*.
děhagi, see *dahagi*.
děham, see *daham*.
děhana, see *dahana*.
děhulu, see *dahulu*.
dek, a variant of *adek*, q.v.
děkah, (onom.) the sound of loud laughter; *těrtawa běrděkah* or *těrtawa běrděkah-děkah*, to laugh heartily.
děkak, a variant of *děkah*.
děkam, to crouch for a spring (of a beast of prey).
děkan, the bamboo-rat (*rhizomys sumatrensis*).
dekar, *pěndekar*, a master of fence; a champion warrior.
děkat, near, hard by; *d. ka-darat*, near the shore; *děkati* and *měnděkati*, to approach; *měnděkatkan*, to bring close.
děkunchi, a variant of *těmu kunchi*.
děkus, the blowing of a porpoise.
děkut, (onom.) calling pigeons; *buloh d.*, the bamboo instrument used to call pigeons for snaring.
děIah, an edible salt-water-fish (unidentified).
děIaki, a (Kedah) variant of *laki-laki*.
děIapan, eight; the number eight; *d. bělas*, eighteen; *d. puloh*, eighty.
dělima, Skr. the pomegranate; *batu d.*, the ruby; *d. měrěkah*, a split pomegranate (showing its red contents), a simile for ruby lips.
dělinggam, a variant of *sědělinggam*.

děmah, dry-poulticing; hot dry applications to a diseased part.
děmam, fever; d. kura, benign tertiary fever; d. kěpialu, violent malarial fever accompanied by delirium; d. kěpialu kětulangan, rheumatic fever; d. běrlat or d. běrsělang, mild intermittent fever; d. sěsěma, influenza; d. rabu kěmbang, fever in lung disease.
děmap, gluttonous.
děmi, by, with, on, at (when); sa-orang děmi sa-orang, one by one; děmi běrbunyi gěnta, when the bell rang; d. Allah, by God.
děmikian, thus, so, in this way.
děmit, young; child (an expression often used by medicine-men to describe the patient).
děmpak, broad, beamy (of a boat).
děmpang, I. hollow-sounding, resonant; chakap běrděmpang-d., boastful talk. II. going across to; visiting; stopping at.
děmpir, cracked-sounding (of a gong).
dempok, proximity, approach.
děmpul, tow for caulking boats.
děmukut, (Kedah) broken pieces of rice husk; chaff; = lěmukut and mělukut.
denah, an evil spirit causing diseases in the feet.
děnai, a wild-beast track.
děnak, decoy; ayam d., a jungle-fowl (gallus ferrugineus).
děnching, (onom.) the chink of coin.
děnda, Skr. a fine; kěna d., to incur a fine, to be fined; děndakan, to fine.
děndam, I. longing; rindu d., loving, longing. II. a grudge; = damdam.
děndan, order, arrangement; plaiting, design, style; běrděndan, to plait; awan d., plait-ornament.
děndang, I. a name sometimes given to the crow (corvus macrorhynchus); d. ayer, a bird (phalacrocorax carbo); burong pěděndang (heliopais personata). II. timun d., a bitter inedible gourd. III. Spanish fly.

dendang, the droning chorus to a Malay quatrain.
dendeng, jerked meat.
děngak, a variant of dongak or dangok.
děngan, I. with; along with; in conjunction with; in accordance with; on, by (in imprecations); d. nama nabi Allah, by the name of the prophet; d. surohan raja, in accordance with the prince's order; masing-masing děngan kěhěndak-nya, everyone as he pleased. II. your servant; I.—cf. dan.
děngar, listening to; hearing; choba d., please listen; di-děngar-nya, in his hearing; děngari, měněngar, měnděngar, děngarkan and měněngarkan, to listen to, to hear; pěněngaran, the sense of hearing.
děngkang, loud laughter; = děkah.
dengkel, shrivelled up internally (of fruit).
děngki, aversion, spite, envious hatred; měnaroh d., to nurse a grudge; běrasa d., to feel spiteful.
děngkong, the baying of dogs.
děngkur, snoring, běrděngkur or měnděngkur, to snore.
děngok, těrděngok, squat, shortened (of the neck).
děngong, (onom.) humming; the sound of a Jew's harp or of a humble-bee; the twang of a bow-string; droning or buzzing in the ear; the hum of a kite or top; běrděngong, to give out a humming sound.
děngu, I. běrděngu or měnděngu, to draw in one's breath before muscular effort. II. dull, stupid; also dungu.
děngus, měnděngus, to snort; to sniff.
děngut, the cry of a quail.
deni, this; = dia ini.
děntam, (onom.) a slamming sound.
děntum, (onom.) a deep booming sound.
denu, that; = dia itu.

děnyut, the throbbing of a boil.
děpa, a Malay fathom; the span from finger-tip to finger-tip of the outstretched arms—cf. děpang.
děpan, front; = hadapan; di-děpan, in front.
děpang, to stretch out the arms; a cruciform position.
děpun, the lining of a garment.
děra, chastisement; punishment.
děrai, běrděrai-d., in long straggling line; trailing away—cf. dědai.
děrak, (onom.) a cracking sound.
děram, (onom.) a rumbling sound; měnděram, to rumble (as thunder).
děrang, (onom). a clanging sound (such as that of a bell).
děrap, (onom). a crackling or rapping sound; the sound of small arms firing.
děras, I. speed; rapidity of motion; těrlalu děras lari-nya, he ran very fast. II. Ar. měnděras, to study the Koran.
děrau, (onom.) the sound of a heavy shower approaching.
děrawa, Skr. gula děrawa, syrup (often pronounced di-rawak).
deret, a row, a long line; běrderet-d., in long lines (as people fleeing along the road from a stricken city).
děrhaka, Skr. traitorous; treason, betrayal; ada-kah patut kita děrhaka akan-dia, is it right that we should betray their confidence; měnděrhaka or běrbuat d., to turn traitor; to betray.
děrham, Ar. a small silver coin or gold coin from Turkey or Persia.
děring, I. (onom.) a ringing sound. II. the trumpeting of an elephant.
děrita, Skr. tiada měnděrita, insupportable; unbearable; unable to contain oneself any longer.
děrji, Hind. a tailor.
děrma, Skr. alms; gifts to the poor; charity; favour; gift to a subordinate; měmběri d., to distribute charity; jikalau ada děrma kurnia tuan-ku, by the favour and kindness of my lord.
děrmawan, Skr. open-handed, charitable.
děrni, the threshold or sill of a door; pintu d., a light screen-door.
děrong, (onom.) a sonorous clang (such as that of a deep-toned bell).
děru, (onom.) the roar of a storm, or of a crowd, or of an inundation; měnděru, to roar.
děrum, I. (onom.) the sound of a tree falling heavily. II. a word of command to make an elephant kneel; děrumkan, to make an elephant kneel.
děrut, (onom.) a dull scraping sound.
děrwis, Pers. a dervish.
desa, Skr. region, country; sa-desa něgěri, every country and town; everywhere; měndesa něgěri, id.; běrtandang d., to go wandering from place to place.
děsar, (onom.) běrděsar, to hiss (as water falling on hot iron).
děsau, (onom.) the swish of rain falling on bamboos.
děsing, (onom.) the whizzing sound made by a projectile.
děsir, a variant of děsar.
děstar, Pers. an unstarched headcloth; a turban.
děsur, a variant of děsar.
dětas, (onom.) the rustle of paper.
dětek, (onom.) the cracking of a twig.
děting, (onom.) the twang of a stretched string when struck.
dewa, Skr. a "deva"; a minor divinity; a fairy; a demi-god.
dewana, Pers. courtly, royal.
dewangga, Skr. a rich cloth often mentioned in romance.
dewasa, Skr. time, period, date.
dewata Skr. godhead, divinity, d. mulia raya, the greatest of gods; burong d., unggas d., manok d. or paksi d., the bird of paradise.
dewi, Skr. a minor goddess; a fairy.

di, I. at, in; *di-sini*, here; *di-sana*, there; *di-dalam*, inside; *di-luar*, outside. [By an idiomatic use of this word, it forms a passive—e.g. *kapal di-tunda jongkong*, a ship in tow of a dinghy—i.e. a ship towed by a dinghy; *di-děngar-nya*, in his hearing; heard by him.] II. Skr. noble—an abbreviation of *adi* in certain titles—e.g. *dipati* for *adi-pati*, *diraja* for *adi-raja*, etc.

dia, he, him, she, it; = *ia*, when following an *n*; *akan-dia*, to him; = *akan-ia*. [This form of *ia* is often also used emphatically.]

diam, I. silence; being silent; *diamlah ia*, he was silent; *diam-diam*, silently; *diamkan* or *měndiamkan*, to silence. II. residence, abode, dwelling; *diam-lah ia di-Mělaka*, he lived at Malacca; *diami*, to inhabit; *kědiaman*, abode; *tempat kědiaman*, place of abode, home.

dian, a candle; *kaki d.*, a candle-stick; *sinar d.*, the light of a candle; *lilin d.*, the wax of a candle; *burony kaki d.*, a large sandpiper (*totanus calidris*).

diang, toasting; heating before a fire; *běrdiang*, to heat at a fire (used remedially after a confinement).

diat, Ar. blood-money; expiatory payment; a fine for violating some religious injunction.

dibaj, Pers. a rich brocade.

dideh, effervescing, boiling up; *měndideh*, or *měnideh*, to boil up; to be boiling hot; *ayer měndideh*, boiling water.

didek, nurturing, fostering, bringing up (used of men bringing up animals).

didis, *měndidis*, to hash.

dikau, a form of the second personal pronoun—you, thou, thee.

dikir, Ar. *běrdikir*, to chant verses; *pědikir*, a singing (and dancing) girl.

dikit, *sa-dikit*, a little; *sa-dikit banyak*, a fair amount; *běrdikit-d.*, sparingly.

din, Ar. faith; the faith of Islam.

dina, Skr. poor, mean, humble, of little account; *hina d.*, id.

dinar, Ar. a coin (usually of gold); *d. mas*, id. [The coin is mentioned in literature only.]

dinding, screening; a light partition; a party-wall; *dindingan*, serving as a screen or partition; *dindingkan*, to screen off; *pěndinding*, screening; protective; *doa p.*, prayers or formulæ protective against evil spirits.

dingin, cold, chilly—cf. *sějok* (which is only relative coolness); *dinginkan*, to chill.

dini, *dinihari* daybreak, dawn.

dipati, see *di*.

diraja, see *di*.

dirgahayu, Skr. long life, majesty and dominion (an expression of homage addressed to a ruler).

diri, I. self; *diri-ku*, I myself; *diri-nya*, himself, herself, itself, themselves; *di-dalam d.*, to oneself, mentally; *měmbawa d.*, to run away; *měmbuang d.*, to commit suicide; *minta d.*, or *mohon d.*, to beg leave to depart; *diri*, is sometimes used as a pronoun of the second person. Cf. also *sěndiri*. II. *dirikan*, to erect, to put up; *měndirikan*, id.; *běrdiri*, to stand erect: to get up; *těrdiri* set up; standing erect; upright.

dirus, irrigation; the flowing of water; *měndirus ayer*, to water.

diwal, Pers. a wall; the thick outer wall of a palace or fortress.

diwan, Pers. a court of justice; a bench; a board.

diwani, Pers. authorised by government; minted; a minted coin.

doa, Ar. prayer; incantation, magical formula; *d. pěngaseh*, a charm to arouse love; *d. pěndinding*, a formula protective against evil spirits; *minta d.*, to pray.

dobi, Hind. a dhoby; a laundryman.

dodol, *kueh d.*, a cake made of rice-flour, molasses and fruit.

dodot, *mĕndodot*, to take whiffs at a pipe.
doga, see *duga*.
dogang, support by a rope—e.g. as a rope is tied to a tree when the tree is felled to prevent it falling on the woodsmen, or as Malays hang out to windward in a racing boat by holding on to ropes (*tali dogang*) attached to the mast.
dogel, tail-less (of a fowl).
dogeng, a (Kedah) variant of *dogel*.
dogol, a (Kedah) variant of *dongkol*.
dok, a colloquial shortening of *dudok*.
dokoh, a gold crescentic breast-ornament worn at marriages and great ceremonies.
dola, Skr. a "dhooly"; a litter or stretcher.
dolak, *d.-dalek*, shilly-shallying.
dolat, a variant of *daulat*.
domah, *pĕndomah*, a gift (sent by a raja).
doman, I. *pĕdoman*, a compass; II. Skr. *hantu d.*, a dog-faced spirit; a (Kedah) survival of the Hanuman legend.
domba, Pers. a sheep.
domol, (Kedah) snout; = *monchong*.
dondang, a lullaby; a swinging cradle.
dondon, pattern or colour in clothing; *sa-dondon*, of similar pattern (of a sarong and baju).
dongak, *mĕndongak*, to sit with head raised and pushed forward.
dongeng, I. Jav. a tale for chanting. II. *mĕndongeng*, to importune (of children).
dongkang, *dongkang-dongkang*, skin and bone.
dongkol, hornless or with downward-curving horns (of a bullock); combless (of a cock).
dongkor, *d.-dangkar*, bundling out bag and baggage.
dongok, disproportionately broad; uncouth; badly proportioned.
donia, Port. a lady.

dorong, stumbling forward; *tĕrdorong*, fallen forward; tripped up; fallen.
dosa, Skr. a sin; an offence against religion or morality, but not necessarily an offence against statute law; *bĕrdosa*, sinful.
dua, I. two; *d. bĕlas*, twelve; *d. puloh*, twenty; *d.-dua*, two by two; *kĕdua*, both; *yang kĕdua*, the second; *mĕnduakan*, to have two of—e.g. *mĕnduakan laki*, to commit bigamy; *mĕnduakan Allah*, to worship more gods than one; *bĕrdua*, in a party of two; *bĕrdua dĕngan*, in company with (someone else); *pĕndua*, a fellow or match. II. a variant of *doa*, q.v.
duai, *ipar duai*, a brother-in-law or sister-in-law.
dubur, Ar. the buttocks.
dudok, sitting, to sit; to keep doing something; to continue; to reside; situation, position; *dudokkan*, to seat; *kĕdudokan*, position; *tĕmpat kĕdudokan*, residence; *tĕrdudok*, seated.
dudu, following immediately behind.
dudun, pressing on (of a crowd).
dudur, a plant (unidentified.)
duga, probing, fathoming, sounding; *laut yang dalam dapat di-duga, hati manusia siapa tahu*, a deep sea may be sounded, but who can fathom a man's thoughts? *batu pĕnduga*, the lead on a sounding-line.
dugal, nausea; the feeling of a bad sailor as the sea begins to be rough.
duit, (Dutch) a cent, a doit; (Singapore) a quarter-cent; (Penang) a cent; *d. cent*, small currency; *bĕrduit*, to have money.
duka, Skr. grief, sorrow, mental anguish; *hati yang d.*, a sorrowful heart; *suka dan d.*, happiness and grief; *mĕnanggong d.*, to suffer sorrow; *d.-chita*, feelings of sorrow; *kĕdukaan*, id.
dukan, Ar. a shop.
dukat, (Dutch) a ducat.
dukong, carrying on the hips (as a

Malay woman carries her child); *měndukong*, to carry in this way; *dukongan* or *kain dukongan*, a support for the child.

duku, a well-known fruit (*lansium domesticum*); *kěra d.*, the slow loris (*nycticebus tardigradus*).

dukun, a native doctor.

dulang, a large low-rimmed platter or tray; *pěndulang mas*, a large platter used in washing for gold.

duli, Skr. dust; the dust under a sovereign's feet; (by metaphor) the position which a subject occupies and to which he can address himself; *ka-bawah d.*, the form of address of a subject to a sovereign; *d. yang-dipěrtuan*, a royal title.

dum, a tree; the date-palm?

dungu, dull-witted, dense, stupid; also *děngu*.

dunia, Ar. the world; *pěridaran d.*, the chances and changes of mortal life.

dupa, Skr. incense; *měmbakar d.* or *pasangkan d.*, to burn incense.

dura, anxiety; mental restlessness; *běrhati d.*, disquieted.

Durga, Skr. the goddess Durga; *dewi Durga Sakti* or *dewi Durga Kěsoma*, id.

durhaka, a variant of *děrhaka*, q.v.

duri, a thorn; *ada-kah duri di-pěrta-jam*, does one sharpen thorns.

durian, the well-known fruit, the "durian."

durja, Skr. countenance, visage—a poetic equivalent for face (*muka*);

d. běrsěri, a bright countenance; *d. muram*, a clouded visage; *jamjam d.*, expression; a poetic equivalent for *ayer muka*.

durjana, evil, wicked, treacherous; *měntěri d.*, a traitorous councillor.

dusi, *měndusi*, to be perpetually crying (of young children).

dusta, Skr. false, lying; *běrbuat d.*, to deceive, to tell a lie to; *běrdusta*, id.; *měndusta*, false—e.g. *chěmara měndusta*, false hair.

dusun, a village, a hamlet; a grove; *kěpala d.*, a village headman.

duta, a messenger, an envoy.

duyong, I. the dugong (*halicore dugong*); *ekur d.*, the tail of the dugong; forked, treacherous; *minyak tangis d.*, the tears of the dugong —a potent love-philtre. II. *měnduyong*, to totter, when about to fall; to hover, when about to perch.

duyun, *běrduyun-duyun*, crowding forward, pressing forward.

dzabah, see *zabah*.

dzaif, Ar. weak, feeble.

dzakar, Ar. the male organ of generation; also *zakar*.

dzarab, Ar. to multiply arithmetically.

dzarah, see *zarah*.

dzarurat, see *zarurat*.

dzat, see *zat*.

dzikir, Ar. chanting God's praise; also *dikir*.

dzu, Ar. possessing, endowed with; also *zu*.

E

eban, flinging out of the way.

ebek, a sun-sail; also *embek*.

ebeng, *měngebeng*, to sway the body (as a dancing girl).

edah, speaking across a distance.

edan, Jav. mad; = *gila*; *e. kěsmaran*, madly in love; = *gila běrahi*.

edar, see *idar*.

egah, walking with a waddling or affected gait.

eh, an interjection of wonderment; what?

eja, Ar. spelling, to spell; *měngeja*, to spell; to read slowly spelling out the words; *ejaan*, spelling.

ejek, *měngejek*, to tease.

ejit, mockery; a variant of *ejek*.
ekhlas, = *ikhlas*.
ekur, tail; extremity; a numeral coefficient for animals; *e. mata*, the corner of the eye; *e. pulau*, the point (of a riverine island) that is furthest downstream; *pokok e.* (Penang) gutta; *bĕrekur-e.*, in Indian file, one holding on to the other (as children in certain games); *bintang bĕrekur*, a comet.
ela, I. Eur. an ell; a yard. II. a variant of *hela*.
elah, Ar. stratagem, contrivance, device; *habis daya tipu elah*, at the end of his wiles, tricks and resources; *olah e.*, extreme duplicity; full of dodges.
elak, evasion; getting out of the way; dodging a blow; *bĕrelak*, to get out of the way; *elakkan*, to evade, to dodge (a blow).
ĕlat, see *lat*.
elat, better *elah*, q.v.
ĕlis, better *lis*, q.v.
elmu, Ar. knowledge, scholarship, science; magic art; also *ilmu*.
ĕlok, better *lok*, q.v.
elok, beauty, excellence, charm; handsome, fine; *orang yang elok rupa-nya*, a man of handsome appearance; *maha-elok*, very beautiful or fine; *kĕelokan*, beauty; excellence.
ĕlong, see *long*.
ĕlut, see *lut*.
ĕmak, see *mak*.
ĕmarah, see *marah*.
ĕmas, see *mas*.
ĕmat, see *mat*.
ĕmbachang, the horse-mango (*mangifera foetida*), also *machang* and *bachang*.
ĕmbak, case, instance, time; *sa-ĕmbak*, once; *dua ĕmbak*, on two occasions.
ĕmbal, not quite dry; still damp; still moist.
ĕmbalau, lac; solder; sealing-wax.
ĕmban, an arrangement of ropes enabling a porter to secure a burden borne on the back.
ĕmbarau, an artificial embankment.
ĕmbas, likeness, close resemblance; *ĕ. tupai*, like a squirrel.
ĕmbat, a long swishing stroke; *kĕna ĕmbat*, to be caned.
embek, a sun-snail; also *ebek*.
ĕmbek, *mĕngĕmbek*, to bleat (as a sheep or goat).
embeng, a variant of *ebeng*, q.v.
ĕmboh, *ta'-ĕmboh*, unwillingness; no; I won't; *ĕ.-ĕmbohan*, although; admitting that; yet.
ĕmbok, I. Jav. mother; a respectful designation for old ladies. II. *mĕng-ĕmbok*, to throb; also *mĕngĕmbut*.
ĕmbun, dew; *ĕ. asap*, haze; *ĕ. bĕtina*, dew in small drops; *ĕ. jantan*, dew in large drops; *kĕring ĕ.*, when the dew dries up—i.e. about 7.30 a.m.; *bĕrĕmbun*, to be falling (of dew); *mĕngĕmbun*, to fall in thin drops (of spray).
ĕmbus, to blow (of wind); *ĕmbusan*, bellows.
ĕmbut, a variant of *ĕmbok* II.
ĕmpama, see *umpama*.
ĕmpang, barring; damming; stopping the course or flow of anything; a weir, a dam.
ĕmpap, (onom). the sound of a flat object falling on a soft surface; *sa-pĕlĕmpap*, the width of the hand when the palm is laid flat on the table.
ĕmpat, four; *ĕ. bĕlas*, fourteen; *ĕ. puloh*, forty; *kĕĕmpat*, all four; *yang kĕĕmpat*, the fourth; *bĕrĕmpat*, with three others (making four in all).
ĕmpĕdal, = *pĕdal*.
ĕmpĕlas, = *mĕmpĕlas*.
emper, Jav. a pent-house, a shed.
ĕmping, rice plucked, crushed and cooked before it has attained maturity; *pĕngĕmping* or *lĕsong pĕngĕmping*, a pounder for young rice; *masak pĕrĕmping*, just ripe enough to be cooked as *ĕmping* (as growing rice).

ĕmpoh, overflowing; *rĕbus ta'-ĕmpoh*, boiling without overflowing (playing with fire yet escaping unsinged), prov.
ĕmpok, a soft spot in fruit.
ĕmpu, *pĕrĕmpuan*, a woman.
ĕmpul, *mĕngĕmpul*, to beat about against adverse winds (of a ship).
ĕmpulur, a plant (unidentified).
ĕmpunya, possession; *yang ĕ.*, whose; *mĕmpunyaï*, to possess, to own.
emul, officious questioning, importuning; *mĕngemul*, to importune; to intrude.
enak, delicious, delightful, most enjoyable.
ĕnam, six; *ĕ. bĕlas*, sixteen; *ĕ. puloh*, sixty; *kĕĕnam*, all six; *yang kĕĕnam*, the sixth.
ĕnau, = *nau*.
ĕnchal, *ĕnchal-ĕnchal*, jumping a naughty child up and down by pulling his ears.
ĕnchang, I. an equivalent of *ĕnchal*. II. *ĕ.-ĕnchok*, crooked, awry, zigzag.
ĕnche', Mr.; an honorific prefix; often written *inche*.
encher, watery.
ĕnchok, see *ĕnchang*.
endah, see *indah*.
ĕndak, see *hĕndak*.
ĕndal, I. *mĕngĕndal*, to walk with the head and shoulders held back and the breast and stomach thrust forward. II. stuffing in; = *asak*.
ĕndap, crouching; keeping oneself concealed while watching; *mĕngĕndap*, to spy; to lurk on the watch; *tĕrĕndap*, crouching, watching.
ĕndas, Jav. the head.
endel, *buang e.*, a sweep of the right arm in dancing.
ĕndong, to console children; to soothe a child.
ĕndul, a swing support, a hammock, a cradle, a sling for an injured arm.
engar, = *ingar*.
ĕnggak, a basket for holding *ĕmping*.

ĕnggal, *ĕnggok-ĕ.*, swaying, bobbing up and down.
ĕnggan, unwillingness; objection to; *ĕ. bĕrchĕrai*, unwilling to separate.
ĕnggang, a generic name for large hornbills (especially *dichoceros bicornis* and *buceros rhinoceroides*).
ĕnggat, as far as; *ĕ. ini*, thus far.
ĕnggil, *ĕ.-bĕrĕnggil*, serrated (of a mountain ridge).
ĕnggok, to nod the head; also *anggok*.
ĕngkap, *ĕ.-ĕngkip*, rising and falling; up and down.
ĕngkau, you (familiarly); *bĕrĕngkau*, to use the expression *ĕngkau* (instead of a more formal one) when addressing a man—cf. *kau*.
ĕngkip, *ĕngkap-ĕ.*, up and down—v. *ĕngkap*.
ĕngku, a princely title of the second grade (the highest being *tĕngku*).
engsel, (Dutch) a hinge.
engsut, gentle propulsion; edging off someone.
ĕngut, = *ngut*, q.v.
ĕnjak, *mĕngĕnjak*, to tread down; *pĕngĕnjak*, the sole of the foot.
ĕnjal, to be forced down on one's seat; to be pushed back (as a restless child).
ĕnjĕlai, = *jĕlai*, q.v.
ĕnjut, *mĕngĕnjut*, to tug (as a fish tugs at a line).
ĕntah, an expression of doubt and interrogation; perhaps; I do not know; I cannot tell; *jawab-ku, ĕntahlah tuan*, I replied, I do not know, sir; *ĕ. bĕrtĕmu, ĕntahkan tidak*, perhaps we shall meet, perhaps not.
ĕntak, ramming down, pounding down; *ĕ.-anti*, convulsive up-and-down movements.
ĕntang, I. *ta'-ĕntang*, carelessness, recklessness, indifference to circumstances; = *ta'-indah*. II. = *tang*, q.v. III. to set down; = *lĕtak*.
entek, *mĕngentek*, to winnow rice by shaking it and giving an occasional side-jerk every now and again.

ěnyah, = *nyah*, q.v.
epeh, chattering; continually talking; *orang e.*, a chatterbox.
epek, outer posts used to keep the screens in position against the skeleton framework of a large fish-trap (*bělat*).
epok, a small bag or receptacle used for carrying about the requisites for betel-chewing.
erak, edging away slightly.
ěram, = *ram*, q.v.
erang, I. Jav. black; blue-black; extremely dark red. II. *e.-erut*, twisted, awry.
ěrang, = *rang*, q.v.
erap, = *irap*, q.v.
ěrap, = *rap*, q.v.
ěrat, *rat*, q.v.
erau, visiting (for the purpose of condoling and assisting) a recently bereaved person.
erek, = *irek*, q.v.
eret, pulling back, drawing back; *mengeretkan*, to draw back (anything).
erong, I. a small cup of Chinese porcelain. II. *erong-erong*, the scupper holes in a ship. III. slanting, askew; *pahat e.*, a chisel (the edge of which is cut at an angle).
Eropah, Europe.
ěrti, meaning, signification; *ě. kitab*, the meaning of a book; *ě. pěrkataan*, the meaning of a word; *ěrti-nya*, that is to say; its meaning is; *ěrtikan*, to interpret, to explain; *běrěrti*, to bear a meaning; *měngěrti*, to understand.
erut, twisted, bent, awry; *e. hujong hidong-nya ka-kiri*, the point of his nose pointed slightly to the left; *erang-e.*, zigzag; much out of the straight line.
ěsa, a variant of *sa*, one (in certain expressions—e.g. *yang ě.*, the one, the only). [As a numeral and article, the form *sa* is used.]
esak, = *isak*, q.v.
ěsang, *měngěsang*, to blow the nose.
esek, a disease causing the skin to become dry and scaly.
esok, to-morrow; *e. lusa*, to-morrow or the day after; *kě-esokan hari*, the morrow; also *besok*.
ěstu, = *sětu*, q.v.
esut, gentle propulsion; edging off—a variant of *engsut*.
etong, see *hitong*.

F

faedah, Ar. profit, advantage, gain.
fajar, Ar. dawn.
fakir, Ar. a poor man; a mendicant (especially a religious mendicant); also *pakir*.
falak, Ar. astrology.
fana, Ar. mortal; corruptible; perishable; to die; *dari něgěri yang fana ka-něgěri yang baka*, from a perishable to an imperishable world—from earth to heaven; also (colloquially) *pana*.
faraid, Ar. observances (especially obligatory religious observances).
faraj, Ar. *pudendum muliebre*.
Farsi, Ar. Persian; *bahasa F.*, the Persian language.
fasal, Ar. paragraph, article, section, minor sub-division; concerning; *apa f.*, why; *f. itu*, for that reason; therefore.
fatihah, Ar. the confession of faith; the first *sura* of the Koran.
feel, Ar. deed, work, behaviour, conduct; character, as shown in manner; *feel-nya sěpěrti pěnchuri*, he behaves like a thief.
fi, Ar. in, at, upon, regarding; *fi'l-alam*, on earth; in the world.
fikir, Ar. to think; also *pikir*.

firasat, Ar. a horoscope; a book on astrology; astrological work; also *pirasat*.

firdaus, Pers. paradise; fairyland.

firman, Ar. order, command; the word of God; *bĕfirman*, to speak (of God); *sĕpĕrti firman Allah*, in accordance with God's word; also *pĕrman*.

fitnah, Ar. calumny, slander; *kĕna f.* to be slandered; also *pĕtĕnah*.

fuad, Ar. heart; the seat of the feelings, = *hati*.

fulan, so-and-so; *si-fulan*, id., usually pronounced *si-polan*.

G

gabas, coarse; roughly done (of work).

gabok, bulky; short and thick (of a a monitor-lizard).

gabus, easily cut (of wood); cutting (of a knife), sharp, sharpening. II. *ikan gabus*, a fresh-water fish (*ophicephalus*, sp.)

gada, Skr. a club; an obsolete weapon mentioned in old romances of Indian origin.

gadai, pawning; giving in pledge; *pajak g.*, a pawn-shop; *bĕrgadai*, to pawn.

gading, ivory; the tusk of an elephant; *gading-gading*, the ribs of a boat; *aur g.* or *buloh g.*, the large bamboo (*bambusa vulgaris*); *punai g.*, the pink-headed pigeon (*ptilopus jambu*).

gadis, an unmarried girl, a maiden— a Sumatran equivalent of *anak dara*.

gadoh, tumult; noisy disturbance; loud dispute; *bĕrbuat g.*, to create a disturbance; *pĕrgadohan*, an altercation; a noisy dispute; *bĕrgadoh*, to take part in a row.

gadong, a climbing plant the tubers of which yield a narcotic poison (*dioscorea dæmonum*).

gaeng, a shallow fin-keel of wood.

gagah, pluck, determination, forcefulness; *g. pĕrkasa*, valiant and strong; *gagahi*. to force by menaces, to threaten; *mĕnggagahi*, id.

gagak, the Malayan jungle crow (*corvus macrorhynchus*).

gagang, the stalk or stem of a flower or leaf.

gagap, an impediment in one's speech; stammering, stuttering; *orang g.*, a stammerer.

gagau, groping about for anything; searching with the hand; (of an elephant) picking up with the trunk.

gah, dignity, fame, importance, distinction, greatness; a sense of greatness, pride.

gahara, legitimate; of royal birth on both sides; *anak g.*, a legitimate child; *raja yang g.*, a prince of fully royal descent.

gahari, = *ugahari*, q.v.

gaharu, *kayu gaharu*, agila wood (a fragrant and valuable wood used for burning as incense).

gahir, (Kedah) lust, longing, covetousness.

gajah, the Indian elephant (*elephas maximus*); a descriptive epithet meaning "large"; *g. bĕrjuang*, a fighting elephant; *g. lalang*, a tame elephant; *g. mĕnyusu*, a covered way between a Malay house and its kitchen or outhouses; *g. mĕta*, a rogue elephant; *g. mina* (literally) a "fish-elephant"; (in Javanese design) a monster with the head of an elephant and the body of a fish; a name given to the whale when it is met with—one specimen locally obtained is the hump-backed whale (*megaptera boops*); *badak g.*, the large rhinoceros (*rh. sondaicus*); *main g.*, to play chess.

gaji, I. Eur. wages, pay; *orang g.*, a paid employee; *makan g.*, (Straits Settlements) to be in the pay of. II. *gagi-gagi*, a saw—usually *gĕrgaji*.

gajus, *buah g.*, the cashew (*anacardium occidentale*).

gala, I. *tiada bĕrgala*, unlimited, unbounded. II. *gala-gala*, a mixture (pitch and resin) used for caulking boats—more commonly *gĕgala*.

galah, a pole (for poling a boat); a mooring-pole; a long pole (one of a pair) for thrusting down the submerged screen in a *jĕrmal*; a stick for knocking down fruit from trees; *g. pasir*, the short poles used for punting a boat over shallows; *g. lobok*, long poles for use in deep places; *g. bujang*, ordinary punting-poles of medium length; *g. changgah*, punting-poles provided with a forked end for resting against snags, tree-trunks, etc.

galak, menacing, threatening, bluffing; uxorious, lascivious.

galang, a bar or roller laid athwart the path; *g. pĕrahu*, the rollers on which a boat rests when hauled ashore; *g. tĕmalang*, such rollers when resting on others, to which they are at right angles; *tupai g. pĕrahu*, a squirrel (*sciurus rafflesii*); *galangan*, a slipway; *galangkan*, (1) to lay a boat on rollers; (2) to interpose a bar to a descending blow; *mĕnggalang*, to be in the way, to obstruct—cf. *alang*, *palang* and *malang*.

galas, carrying on the back by means of a sling or support.

galek, *golak g.*, the wrong way about.

gali, digging; *mĕnggali*, to dig; *galian*, a surface-mine; *pĕnggali*, a spade.

galir, I. flowing or running rapidly but unevenly; *pĕrkataan yang g.*, fluent but foolish talk—cf. *alir*. II. *kain g.*, the curtain used in a puppet-show.

galoh, Jav. a princess; *g. di-Daha*, the Princess of Daha, Chandra Kirana (Panji Samerang), the betrothed of Sira Panji.

galur, rebounding, going back; *ombak g.*, receding waves; *susur g.*, tracing back.

gamak, I. a preliminary act; a threatening gesture; *mĕnggamak*, to start doing something by way of a threat. II. guessing at; approximately estimating; *gamak-gamak*, approximately; more or less.

gamam, restlessness (as the result of excitement); *gopoh g.*, eager haste.

gamat, an edible sea-worm; *g. pisang*, a sea-worm (*stichopus variegatus*).

gambang, a Javanese musical instrument.

gambar, representation, picture, statue, model; *g. di-larek*, a polished image; *g. tulisan*, a sketch; *tĕrgambar*, imaged, pictured, represented.

gambir, gambier (*uncaria gambir*).

gamboh, a professional dancing-girl from Java or Madura; *bĕrgamboh* or *bĕrmain g.*, to dance (of such girls).

gamĕlan, a Javanese orchestra.

gamgam, (Kedah) *naik g.*, to get angry, to flare up.

gamis, Ar. a shirt.

gamit, turning in the fingers or lips; swaying backwards; beckoning; *mĕnggamit*, to beckon with the fingers.

gamoh, a large vessel for storing water.

gampang, light; of little account; *anak g.*, a child of doubtful paternity.

gan, (Kedah) putting off a creditor.

gana, I. Ar. mighty (of God). II. Skr. *sangyang g.*, Ganesha, the Hindu deity. II. *guna-gana*, confused; mentally befogged.

ganas, fierce (of animals); man-destroying; *harimau g.*, a man-eating tiger.

ganchang, nimble, agile.

ganchu, a crook; a long stick with a hook at the end for pulling down fruit or branches laden with fruit.

ganda, I. fold (in expressions such as "two-fold," "three-fold"); *sa-kali g.*, once; *g. běrganda*, time after time; over and over again; *gandakan*, to repeat, to double. II. Skr. perfume, fragrance—a component part in the name of many plants.

gandam, coloured by betel-chewing (of the teeth).

gandan, *gěbar g.*, a rich, embroidered coverlet for a couch.

gandar, the lever of a rice-pounder (*lěsong hindek*); *g. chinchin*, the claws (in a ring) which hold the gem in position.

gandariah, a plant (unidentified).

gandarokam, a plant (unidentified).

gandarusa, a medicinal plant (*justicia gandarusa*).

gandasuli, a plant (*hedychium coronarium*).

gandek, a frontal ornament worn by a bride.

gandewa, Skr. a bow (used by heroes of romance).

gandi, Skr. a bow; = *gandewa*; *main g.*, archery.

gandin, a mallet.

gandis, = *kandis*, q.v.

gandong, light logs attached as outriggers to a native boat to give it greater steadiness.

gandu, *buah gandu*, a hard black fruit (unidentified) used as a ball or marble in some children's games.

gandum, Pers. corn, wheat; *těpong g.*, flour.

gang, a brazier's chisel; *g. bulat*, id., with a rounded edge; *g. ranchong*, id., with a sharp-cut point.

Gangga, Skr. the deified Ganges; a fabulous monster; *bětara G.*, the deified Ganges.

ganggang, roasting before the fire—cf. *panggang*.

ganggu, importunity; worrying; constant questioning; insistence.

ganggut, grazing; cropping the grass.

gangsa, Skr. bell-metal, bronze.

gangsi, (Kedah) *měnggan-si*, to perfume cloth with incense-smoke; = *měngukup*.

ganja, I. bhang or Indian hemp (*cannabis sativa*). II. the peculiar guard-like piece at the top of a *kěris* blade; *kěris g. iras*, a *kěris* with the guard and blade in one piece.

ganjak, edging forward slightly; shifting one's seat forward.

ganjal, a (Kedah) variant of *ganjil* —cf. also *gasal*.

ganjapuri, a (Kedah) variant of *kachapuri*.

ganjar, a long pike used as an emblem of rank.

ganjat, abnormal, extraordinary.

ganjil, uneven, odd (of a number).

gantang, I. a measure of capacity. II. *guling g.*, rolling over and over.

ganti, substitution; changing the one thing for another; stead, instead; *g. rugi*, compensation for injury; *gantian* or *pěrgantian*, a substitute; *gantikan* or *měnggantikan*, to substitute, to replace; *běrganti*, in place of; *běrganti-g.*, in turns, successively replacing.

gantong, suspension, dependence, hanging; *gantongkan*, to hang anything up; *běrgantong*, in dependence on; hanging; *běrgantong rambut sa-hělai*, hanging by a single thread; *těmpat buleh běrgantong*, home; a place to which one can attach oneself.

ganyah, *gonyoh-ganyah*, to rub down; to scrub vigorously.

ganyut, only superficially cooked; raw or hard inside.

gapah, *gopoh-gapah*, very great haste; hurry-scurry.
gapil, *měnggapil*, to carry off quietly or unconsciously.
gara, = *gahara*.
garak, *guling-garak*, rolling about uneasily.
garam, salt; *ibu g.*, brine, coarse-grained salt; *měmbuboh g.*, to flavour with salt.
garang, fierce, savage, passionate, quick-tempered; *měnggarang*, to fly into a passion.
garau, hoarse, raucous, harsh (of the voice).
garfu, Port. a table-fork.
gari, I. handcuffs. II. Port. *malau g.*, (Kedah) sealing-wax.
garing, I. a kind of satchel or basket. II. crisp and dry (of food).
garis, scratching; *běrgaris*, scratched.
garok, scraping, grating, scratching; *měnggarok*, to scratch; also *garu*.
garu, scratching—a variant of *garok*.
garut, = *garok*, q.v.
gas, Eng. *minyak g.*, kerosene oil; *kěreta g.*, a motor-car; = *kěreta "engine."*
gasak, striking a blow; *g. lari*, (slang) to abscond; to "clear out."
gasal, (Kedah) odd, uneven of numbers; = *ganjil*.
gasang, incontinence; lustful excitement; impetuous passion of any sort.
gasing, a spinning-top.
gat, a variant of *měaat*, q.v.
gatal, itchiness; lust; *sakit g.*, the itch (as a disease); *miang g.*, extremely itchy or lascivious.
gaul, *champur g.*, very much mixed up or confused; = *champur baur*.
gaung, sound dulled or confused by echo; reverberation.
gawa, see *pěnggawa*.
gawai, a tool or instrument; *pěgawai*, an agent; a district officer.
gawar, a token or mark placed across a road to signify that passage is prohibited; *gawar-gawar* or *gěgawar*, quarantine; *tembak g.*, to fire in the air so as to warn robbers off the premises.

gaya, Skr. conduct, manner, tone; *rupa g.*, appearance and ways; *g. usul*, manner and bearing; *běryaya*, affectedly; *tiada běrgaya lagi*, to lose all consciousness.
gayam, *buah g.*, the Otaheite chestnut.
gayang, light-headed; unstable; a sense of weakness.
gayat, nervous fear; giddiness when looking down a great precipitous height.
gayong, I. a vessel made of half a coconut shell with a handle attached. II. *běrgayong*, to fence or box; also *main gayong*.
gayut, hanging from a rope or bough (as a monkey).
gaz, Pers. a measure of length mentioned in old romances; it represented about 33 inches.
gěbar, a coverlet or counterpane; *g. gandan*, a rich embroidered coverlet.
gebeng, I. a long native boat with a rudder of the European type. II. Eng. cabin.
gěbu, delicate in texture; *g. chantek*, daintily pretty; *pasir g.*, fine light sand.
gědabir, loose folds of skin (the dewlap of an ox, the gills of a cock); also *gělambir*.
gědang, great, large; = *běsar* (in Sumatran Malay).
gěděbong, I. a sort of bamboo box or receptacle. II. a square piece of cloth with a pouch on it.
gěděmbai, a (Kedah) variant of *kělěmbai*, q.v.
gěděmi, a (Kedah) variant of *gěmi*, q.v.
gědok, a (Kedah) variant of *bědok*, q.v.
gědombak, a single-membrane drum.

gĕdong, an office, store or magazine; a "godown."

gĕdubang, an Achehnese broadsword.

gĕdubil, (Kedah) *muka g.,* brazen-faced.

gĕgai, loosely put together; lacking in stiffness or strength.

gĕgak, noise, uproar (especially the din of battle); *g. gĕmpita,* extreme uproar; an insupportable din.

gĕgala, = *gala-gala.*

gĕgaman, Jav. weapons; armed soldiery.

gegap, a variant of *gĕgak,* q.v.

gĕgar, quivering; shaking; a thrill.

gĕgas, a movable hatch or planking in a Malay boat.

gĕgasing, a variant of *gasing,* q.v.

gĕgat, a small insect which bores holes in clothes, books, etc.

gĕgawar, see *gawar.*

geger, noisy panic; the clamour of fear or anxiety.

gĕlabir, = *gĕlambir.*

gĕlabur, to fall "plump" into water.

gĕladak, the deck of a ship.

gĕladir, a large movable piece of planking in a ship's side—removed to facilitate loading.

gĕlagah, a wild sugar-cane (*saccharum glaga*).

gĕlak, laughter; *tĕrtawa gĕlak-gĕlak,* peals of laughter.

gĕlakak, a prolonged chuckling laugh.

gĕlam, I. a tree (*melaleuca leucodendron*). II. the name of a tribe of the orang laut. III. *burong gĕlam,* a name given to the bird *ardetta cinnamomea.*

gĕlama, a generic name given to a number of fish including *gerres oyena* and (*g. panjang*) *otolithus argenteus.*

gĕlambir, loose folds of flesh (the dewlap of an ox, the gills of a cock); also *gĕdabir.*

gĕlang, a bracelet or anklet; *g. chĕri,* a bangle; *g. kaki,* an anklet; *g. kana,* a (Javanese) armlet; *g. kunchi,* a key-ring; *dawai g.,* wire wrapped round a cylindrical surface—e.g. round the neck of a bottle of wine; *pĕrgĕlangan,* the circumference of the wrist; the wrist; *pĕnggĕlang,* id.; *pĕrgĕlangan kaki,* the ankle.

gĕlanggang, an enclosure for cocks to fight in; a circular space; *g. ayam,* the fighting-ring for a cock; *g. susu,* the dark circle round the teat.

gĕlap, darkness, obscurity; surreptitious, secret; *g. katup,* pitchy darkness; *g. gulita,* id.; *chandu g.,* smuggled chandu; *mata-mata g.,* a detective.

gĕlar, the bestowal of a title or designation; *gĕlaran,* a title; *gĕlari,* to bestow a title; *bĕrgĕlar,* entitled; possessing a title.

gĕlasar, *mĕnggĕlasar,* to slip or slide forward, as a man who loses his footing in a slippery place.

gĕlatek, = *jĕlatek,* q.v.

gĕlatok, *mĕnggĕlatok,* to chatter (of the teeth).

gĕlebar, to flap continuously—cf. *kibar.*

gĕlĕbau, a monkey (unidentified).

gĕlĕcha, a light quilt-mattrass.

gĕlĕdang, *mĕnggĕlĕdang,* to stretch out the arms at right angles to the body.

gĕlĕding, *mĕnggĕlĕding,* to become warped (of wood).

gĕlĕdoh, a variant of *bĕludoh,* q.v.

gĕlĕgak, I. boiling up, bubbling over (of hot water). II. a heavy wooden sounding-block.

gĕlĕgar, a girder; a rafter; a beam on which a floor or ceiling rests.

gĕlĕgata, a kind of nettle-rash.

gĕlĕgut, = *gĕlugut.*

gelek, bending a limb; arching the neck; closing the hand; bowing the head; *mĕnggelekkan leher,* to arch the neck (of a long-necked bird).

gĕlĕkak, *mĕnggĕlĕkak,* to crumble away (as the plaster on a wall).

gĕlĕma, phlegm; mucus in the throat.
gĕlĕman, *gĕli-g.*, the nervous sensation excited by a rasping noise.
gĕlĕmat, decking over the bows and stern of a boat.
gĕlĕmbong, a bubble; anything blown out with wind; *gĕlĕmbongan*, a blown-out bladder made of a chicken's crop; *mĕnggĕlĕmbong*, to be puffed out (of the cheeks).
gĕlĕmpang, outstretched (as a man lying on the ground with his arms extended at full length).
gĕlĕmpok, *gĕlĕmpok gĕmok*, extremely fat.
gĕlĕmpong, a spongy kind of lint used for staunching the flow of blood.
gĕlenggang, a medicinal plant (*cassia alata*).
gĕlĕntang, *guling g.*, rolling over and over; = *guling gantang*.
gĕlĕntar, *mĕnggĕlĕntar*, to quiver, to tremble. Cf. *kĕtar*, *gĕmĕtar*, etc.; also *gĕlĕtar*.
gĕlĕnyar, tingling; *mĕnggĕlĕnyar*, to tingle.
gĕlepek, to lie slackly upon anything (as a sail lying slackly against a mast).
gĕlĕpong, *mĕnggĕlĕpong*, to fall heavily into water.
gĕlĕtar, *mĕnggĕlĕtar*, to quiver, to tremble. Cf. *kĕtar*, *gĕmĕtar*, etc.; also *gĕlĕntar*.
gĕletek, *mĕnggĕletek*, to tickle.
gĕlĕtek, *mĕnggĕlĕtek*, to wriggle, to squirm.
gĕlĕting, = *lĕting*.
gĕli, ticklishness; the desire to laugh; *g. hati*, lightheartedness; *g. gĕman* or *g. gĕlĕman*, the nervous sensation created by a rasping or scraping noise; *pĕnggĕli hati*, things that rouse mirth or enjoyment; humorous tales.
gĕliang, *mĕnggĕliang*, to sway about; to writhe, to wriggle.
gĕliat, twisting, straining; *mĕnggĕliat*, to turn and twist as a man stretching himself.

gĕlibat, = *kĕlibat*.
gĕliga, see *guliga*.
gĕligin, a cross-rod in a weaver's loom.
gĕligis, *mĕnggĕligis*, to shudder.
gĕligit, to keep biting—cf. *gigit*.
gĕlinchir, slipping away to the side; a side-slip; *tĕrgĕlinchir*, slipped— e.g. *tĕrgĕlinchir kaki-nya lalu jatoh*, his foot slipped and he fell.
gĕlinchoh, stumbling; to stumble.
gĕlindong, a reel; a shuttle; a roller.
gĕling, a slight sidelong shake of the head (meaning "no," just as a nod means "yes").
gĕlinggam, = *sĕdĕlinggam*, q.v.
gĕlingsir, side-slip; = *gĕlinchir*, q.v.
gĕlintar, = *halintar*, q.v.
gĕliong, I. Eur. a galleon. II. a variant of *gĕliang*.
gĕlip, = *kĕlip*, q.v.
gĕlisah, *mĕnggĕlisah*, to fidget, to move restlessly.
gĕlisai, *mĕnggĕlisai*, to disturb, to confuse, to create ill-feeling.
gĕlisek, a (Kedah) variant of *sĕlisek*.
gĕlita, = *gulita*, q.v.
gĕliut, *gĕliang-g.*, swaying and twisting—cf. *gĕliang*.
gĕlobok, (onom.) *mĕnggĕlobok*, to bubble up (of boiling water).
gĕlodar, I. *mĕnggĕlodar*, to struggle for freedom; to try to get loose. II. turbid (of water).
gĕlogok, enquiry with menaces; trying to get information by "bluff."
gĕloh, = *kĕloh*, q.v.
gĕlohok, extensive perforation; gaping with holes.
gĕlojoh, gluttony.
gĕlok, a mug or drinking bowl made of coconut shell.
gĕlomang, wallowing with a wet body in a powdery substance; *bĕrgĕlomang*, to roll one's wet body in dust, flour, etc.
gĕlombang, long rolling waves, billows; *g. bunga lĕpang*, waves

with white crests; *g. kĕpala kĕra*, choppy waves; *g. mangkok*, an eddy; a whirlpool; *hĕmpasan g.*, breakers; the surf-line.

gĕlomor, *mĕnggĕlomor*, to dirty.

gĕloneng, a small gong forming a part of the Javanese *gamĕlan*.

gĕlong, I. a cutting or channel; the navigable channel for entering a river. II. a double or multiple loop of rattan. III. (Kedah) an elephant-track; = *dĕnai*.

gĕlongsong, = *kĕlongsong*, q.v.

gĕlongsor, *mĕnggĕlongsor*, to slip down forward. Cf. *gĕlingsir* (which is a side-slip); also *gĕlunchur*.

gĕlopak, = *kĕlopak*, q.v.

gĕlorah, Ar. stormy, troubled; trouble or care generally; also *gĕlurat*.

gĕlosok, vigorous washing or scrubbing; an intensive form of *gosok*.

gĕlosor, = *gĕlongsor*, q.v.

gĕlotak, *mĕnggĕlotak*, to remove a hard rind or husk from a fruit.

gĕluga, a red dye; *kayu g.*, the tree (unidentified) from which this red dye is obtained.

gĕlugur, *asam g.*, a tree with orange acid fruits used in flavouring curries (*garcinia atroviridis*). [The word is also used to describe fluted patterns in art.]

gĕlugut, *mĕnggĕlugut*, to shiver; to quiver; to chatter (of the teeth).

gĕlulur, *mĕnggĕlulur*, to slip down (of a sarong).

gĕlumat, = *gĕlĕmat*, q.v.

gĕlumur, = *gĕlomor*, q.v.

gĕlunchur, *mĕnggĕlunchur*, to slip down forward; also *mĕnggĕlongsor*.

gĕlup, *mĕnggĕlup*, to fall out (of the teeth).

gĕlupar, = *kĕlupar*, q.v.

gĕlupas, = *kĕlupas*, q.v.

gĕlupur, = *kĕlupur*, q.v.

gĕlurat, Ar. care, anxiety, trouble; also *gĕlorah*.

gĕlut, *bĕrgĕlut*, to strive, to contest, to compete—especially in boat-racing (*bĕrgĕlut lanchang*).

gĕma, echo, reverberation.

gĕmak, = *gĕmap*, q.v.

gĕmal, a clump, a cluster; *bĕrgĕmal-g.*, in clusters (of small stalks).

gĕmala, a talisman; a luminous bezoar; also *kĕmala*.

gĕmalai, *lĕmah g.*, extreme lassitude; also *kĕmalai*.

gĕman, nervous quivering; *gĕli g.* the nervous feeling created by a rasping noise.

gĕmang, ungraceful bulk; disproportionately thick.

gĕmap, *tĕrgĕmap*, taken aback; thunderstruck.

gĕmar, pleasure, satisfaction; *gĕmari*, to like; to take pleasure in; *kĕgĕmaran*, delight.

gĕmas, anger, envy, annoyance.

gĕmaung, the murmur of a crowd.

gĕmbak, a tuft of grass; a lock of hair; also *gombak*.

gĕmbal, = *kĕmbal*.

gĕmbala, Skr. a man employed to look after animals; *g. anjing*, a dog-boy; *g. ayam*, a poultry-tender; *g. gajah*, a mahout; *g. kambing*, a shepherd or goat-herd; *g. kuda*, a groom.

gĕmbar, = *kĕmbar*, q.v.

gĕmbira, passion, fire, excitement; *naik g.*, to become inspirited; *suara g.*, a rousing voice.

gĕmbol, a hemispherical excrescence; a bump.

gĕmbong, = *kĕmbong*.

gĕmbur, loose (of unrolled earth); unfinished (of a road).

gĕmbut, I. surface motion (the agitating cause being below the surface); the movement of sand when an animal is digging underneath; the movement of bed clothes over a sleeper; the throbbing of the fontanel. II. a canopy borne by an elephant. III. a golden betel-nut box.

gĕmĕlai, = *gĕmalai*.

gĕmĕlan, = gamĕlan.
gĕmĕlatok, gĕlak g., prolonged chuckling laughter.
gĕmĕlĕgut, = gĕmĕlugut.
gĕmĕlĕtak, (onom.) continuous crackling—cf. gĕmĕrĕtak.
gĕmĕlĕtap, (onom.) continuous tapping—cf. gĕmĕrĕtap.
gĕmĕlĕtok, a variant of gĕmĕlĕtak.
gĕmĕlugut, continuous shivering and trembling.
gĕmĕntam, (onom.) a crashing sound.
gĕmĕntar, trembling all over; also gĕmĕtar—cf. gĕntar, kĕtar, etc.
gĕmĕrĕchak, (onom.) the plash of oars or paddles.
gĕmĕrĕchek, (onom.) a slight splashing sound.
gĕmĕrĕnchang, (onom.) continual clanking or clanging.
gĕmĕrĕncheng, (onom.) continual ringing or tinkling.
gĕmĕrĕsek, (onom.) continual rustling or crackling.
gĕmĕrĕtak, (onom.) continuous crackling—cf gĕmĕlĕtak.
gĕmĕrĕtap, (onom.) continous tapping—cf. gĕmĕlĕtap.
gĕmĕrlap, glittering, shimmering, sparkling; gĕmĕrlapan, id.
gĕmĕrotok, (onom.) a continuous clatter.
gĕmĕtar, trembling all over; also gĕmĕntar—cf. kĕtar, gĕntar, etc.
gĕmi, ikan gĕmi, the sucking-fish.
gĕmilang, shining, dazzling, glittering; gilang g., resplendent, radiant.
gĕmok, fat, plump; rich (of soil); gĕlămpok g., extremely fat.
gĕmpa, an earthquake; a cataclysm.
gĕmpal, average (in size or build).
gĕmpar, noise, clamour; disturbing rumours or sounds.
gĕmpita, Skr. uproar, noise; gĕgak g., extreme uproar.
gĕmuroh, the roll of thunder; the roar of many waters; the murmur of an angry crowd; thunderous.

genang, I. genang-g., a native sweetmeat. II. to flow (of tears); = linang.
gĕnap, complete, full, even; dua puloh g., a full score; sa-gĕnap, every; sa-tĕlah g., on the completion of.
genchok, giving a twisting motion to the pounder when pounding rice.
gĕndala, hindrance; obstruction; difficulty; aral g., id.
gĕndang, a native drum; g. batak, a name given to certain instruments of the monochord and primitive zither type; g. kĕling, a drum (both sides of which are beaten by the drummer); g. mĕlela, a drum (one side of which is beaten with the hand and the other with a drumstick); g. raya, a large drum used to summon people to mosque.
gĕndap, juru g., the leading drummer in a Malay band.
gĕndĕrang, a war-drum, state-drum or processional drum—cf. gĕndang.
gĕndir, a Javanese musical instrument mentioned in literature.
gĕndis, Jav. sugar.
gĕndit, a belt, a girdle; also kĕndit.
gendong, a variant of kendong, q.v.
gĕndut, heavy and pendulous (of the stomach).
gĕneh, the teeth in a cow-elephant corresponding to the tusks in the male.
gĕnggam, grasp; seizure in the closed hand; sa-g., a handful; gĕnggamkan, to seize in the closed hand; to seize in its talons (of a bird).
genggang, a fabric of cloth.
genggeng, carrying an object by seizing a small portion of it between the teeth; siput g., a shell (nautilus pompilius).
genggong, a sort of Jew's harp made of bamboo.
genjang, awry; crooked; aslant not parallel; out of line; g.-gĕnjut, zigzag.
gĕnjur, = kĕnjur.

gĕnjut, I. aslant, awry—v. *genjang.*
gĕnta, Skr. a bell; *mĕnggoyang g.* or *mĕnggĕrakkan g.,* to ring a bell.
gĕntala, a magic wheeled car (in contradistinction to a flying chariot); *naga g.,* a fabled dragon of monstrous size.
gĕntar, quivering, shaking, trembling —cf. *kĕtar* and *gĕmĕntar.*
gĕntas, plucking (a flower); breaking a stalk.
gĕntat, shrunken or withered on one side (of fruit).
gentel, a small pellet; rolling up a pellet between the thumb and finger-tips.
gĕnting, I. extremely slender; *g. bukit,* a very low ridge joining two lofty hills; *pinggang g.,* wasp-waisted. II. *atap gĕnting,* a tiled roof.
gĕntong, a large earthenware tub or jar.
genyut, not meeting; not in line.
gĕpoh, *gĕpoh-gĕpoh* (Kedah) a padlock.
gĕpok, a small round tobacco-box of silver.
gĕra, reminding; drawing attention to.
gĕrabang, *gĕrabang pari,* strips of salted skate preserved for food,
gĕrachang, = *kĕrachang.*
gĕragas, to comb down the hair over the forehead into a sort of fringe.
gĕragau, a small shrimp.
gĕrah, = *kĕrah.*
gĕraham, a molar tooth; *g. bongsu,* a wisdom tooth; also *gĕrham.*
gĕrai, a sleeping-dais or platform.
gĕrak, motion, movement; *g. hati,* impulse; *bĕrgĕrak,* to move, to stir; *mĕnggĕrakkan,* to give motion to.
gĕram, I. warmth (of anger, courage or passion); *mĕmbĕri g.,* to excite; *naik g.,* to become excited; *mĕnggĕram,* id. II. (Dutch) the framework of a house.
gerang, extreme eagerness, zest, keenness.

gĕrang, I. an oily cosmetic obtained by burning coconut-husks and other vegetable substances. II. see *gĕrangan.*
gĕrangan, perchance, perhaps—an expression suggesting doubt or interrogation; *bulan pĕrnama gĕrangan jatoh daripada langit yang kĕtujoh,* can it be that the full moon has fallen from the seventh heaven.
gĕrangau, = *gĕrĕngau.*
gĕrapai, *mĕnggĕrapai,* to fumble with the hands; to feel about.
gĕrapak, bluffing, startling, attempting to frighten.
gĕrau, a palace cook; a chef.
gĕrayang, *mĕnggĕrayang,* to go about picking up odds and ends.
gĕrbak, to spread (of an odour).
gĕrbang, spread out; extended; *pintu g.,* the main gate; *mĕnggĕrbang,* to open or spread out; to be dishevelled (of hair).
gĕrbong, = *kĕrubong.*
gĕrda, = *gĕroda.*
gĕrĕbak, a noisy clapper used to frighten squirrels and birds from fruit-trees.
gĕrĕdak, (onom.) a heavy bumping or rattling sound.
gĕrĕdam, (onom.) a heavy repeated slamming sound.
gĕrĕdok, (onom.) a duller variant of the sound represented by *gĕrĕdak,* q.v.
gĕrĕdum, (onom.) a deeper variant of the sound represented by *gĕrĕdam,* q.v.
gĕrĕgak, I. *g.-gĕrĕgau,* opening and closing the hands; darting about in search of food. II. a bamboo clapper, = *gĕrĕbak.*
gĕrĕgau, *gĕrĕgak-g.,* opening and closing the hands; see *gĕrĕgak.*
gĕrĕhak, (onom.) coughing up phlegm.
gĕrĕham, = *gĕrham.*
gĕreja, Port. a church.
gerek, I. boring; *mĕnggerek,* to bore. II. eagerness, keenness; = *gerang.*

gĕrĕmut, *mĕnggĕrĕmut*, to throb (of a boil).
gĕrĕnchang, (onom.) a continually repeated clanging noise.
gĕrendeng, snappish, irritable.
gĕrenek, tremulous and low (of a voice).
gĕrĕngau, clawing; scratching; scraping.
gĕrengseng, I. a brass vessel used in cooking. II. Jav. *kain gĕrengseng wayang*, a pattern of sarong much referred to in literature.
gĕrĕntam, (onom.) *mĕnggĕrĕntam*, to stamp the feet; also *gĕrĕtam*.
gĕrĕnyau, over-talkativeness.
gĕresah, (Kedah) longing, pining.
gĕrĕtak, (onom.) rapping; tapping; clacking; *kĕna g.*, to get "whacked"; *mĕnggĕrĕtakkan kuda*, to urge on a horse by rapping the heels against its sides.
gĕrĕtam, (onom.) *mĕnggĕrĕtam*, to stamp the foot in anger; also *gĕrĕntam*.
gĕrĕtok, (onom.) a sound such as that of a carpet being beaten.
gĕrgaji, a saw; *yu g.*, the large saw fish; *habok g.*, saw dust; also *gaji-gaji*.
gĕrgasi, Skr. a tusked man-eating demon; a name given to the aborigines of Kedah.
gĕrham, a molar tooth; *g. bongsu*, a wisdom tooth; also *gĕraham*.
gĕrhana, Skr. eclipse; *kĕna g.*, to suffer eclipse—a metaphor for a great man under calamity.
gĕri, a nervous movement; an involuntary or unconscious gesture.
gĕriang, *g.-gĕresah*, intense longing.
gĕrichau, *mĕnggĕrichau*, to chatter (of a shrilly twittering bird).
gĕrigi, tooth-edged; regularly serrated—cf. *gigi* and *gĕrigis*.
gĕrigis, jagged; irregularly serrated —cf. *gigi* and *gĕrigi*.
gĕrim, (Dutch) *kain gĕrim*, a coarse flannel cloth.

gĕrinda, *batu gĕrinda*, a whetstone; a stone used for filing teeth.
gĕrindam, I. a (Kedah) variant of *gĕrinda*. II. = *gurindam*.
gĕring, illness; sick (of a prince); *g. hulu*, a prince's head-ache.
gĕrinjam, an ear-cleaner.
gĕrit, I. (onom.) a scraping sound; the gnawing of a mouse—cf. *kĕrit*. II. *akar gĕrit-gĕrit*, a generic name for a number of rubber-vines belonging to the order *apocynaceæ*.
gĕrlap, = *kĕrlap*.
gĕrling, = *kĕrling*.
gĕrmang, *mĕnggĕrmang*, to bristle up (of short hair).
gĕrmit, (Penang) an auger; a drill.
gĕrobok, I. Jav. a crockery chest. II. *mĕnggĕrobok*, to bubble up (of boiling water).
gĕroda, Skr. *burong gĕroda*, the eagle or "garuda" of Vishnu.
gĕrodak, (onom.) a sound such as that of stones thumping against the sides of a box.
gĕrodi, Tam. an auger; also *gurdi*.
gĕrogoh, a barrel-like trap for prawns.
gĕroh, constitutional bad luck; persistent misfortune.
gĕrok, a wrapper used to prevent a heavy fruit (such as a *nangka* or *chĕmpĕdak*) falling to the ground through its own weight.
gĕronchong, = *kĕronchong*.
gĕrondong, = *gondong*.
gĕrong, (onom.) *mĕnggĕrong*, to growl (of a wild beast).
gĕronggang, hollow; lacking in kernel or core.
gĕronggong, I. the name of a tree (*cratoxylon arborescens*). II. a stinging medusa or jelly-fish much feared by Malays.
gĕronyot, a twinge of pain.
gĕropoh, (onom.) *mĕnggĕropoh*, to splash about.
gĕrsek, gravel, coarse sand; also *kĕrsek*.

gĕrtak, a bridge.
gĕru, *mĕnggĕru*, to trumpet (of an elephant).
gĕrugul, *hantu gĕrugul*, an evil spirit of the forest.
gĕruit, *mĕnggĕruit*, to wriggle out (as a worm leaving its hole).
gĕrun, panic, alarm; *kambing g.*, the Malay serow (*nemorhœdus swettenhami*).
gĕruning, a large lizard (unidentified).
gĕrup, a portion of a Malay loom in which the comb (*sisir*) is fixed.
gĕrus, rubbing off asperities; sandpapering; polishing.
gĕrut, *ikan gĕrut-gĕrut*, a fish (*pristipoma hasta*).
gĕrutu, = *kĕrutu*.
gĕrutup, (onom.) the noise of artillery fire.
gesek, rubbing or scraping a sharp edge against anything (used especially of playing the violin); *mĕnggesek biola*, to play the violin—cf. *gesel* and *geser*.
gesel, rubbing two sticks or other light bodies together—e.g. in ignition by friction—cf. *geser* and *gesek*.
geser, scraping past each other (as two ships striking each other at an extremely acute angle)—cf. *gesek* and *gesel*.
gĕta, Skr. a sleeping-platform; a divan; a broad sofa or couch; *g. kĕrajaan*, a royal divan; *g. pĕraduan*, a state bed.
gĕtah, latex or gum produced by trees; gutta; caoutchouc; bird-lime; gum; *pokok g.*, a caoutchouc-yielding tree; *burong di-gĕtah*, a limed bird; *g. ipoh*, the poisonous sap of the *ipoh* (*antiaris toxicaria*) used as dart-poison; *g. jĕlutong, dyera costulata*; *g. pĕrcha, dichopsis gutta*; also *g. taban merah*; *g. taban putch, dichopsis obovata*.
gĕtang, = *kĕtang*.
gĕtar, = *kĕtar*.

getek, a loose gait or manner; *mĕnunjok g.*, to assume a "fast" manner; loose conduct.
gĕti-gĕti, a Malay cake.
gĕtil, pinching, nipping—cf. *kĕtip, kĕtam, gĕtu*, etc.
gĕtu, nipping between the fingernails; *mĕnggĕtu kuman*, to kill a louse or flea—cf. *gĕtil, kĕtip*, etc.
gewang, a large shell-fish (portions of which are constantly used in the Straits Settlements as paper-weights).
ghafur, Ar. very forgiving; all merciful (of God); *ya ghafur ur-rahim*, oh, most forgiving and merciful One!—a common superscription to letters.
ghaib, Ar. hidden, concealed, obscure; *ghaib-lah ia*, he vanished; *pĕrkataan yang ghaib*, mysterious words; *rijal ul-ghaib*, spirits presiding over good and evil fortune; also (colloquially) *raip*.
ghali, Eur. a galley.
ghalib, Ar. victorious, conquering.
ghalias, Eur. a galleass; a large galleon.
gharib, Ar. foreign, strange; a stranger.
ghulam, Ar. a slave.
gi, Hind. ghee; clarified butter.
gian, exhausted (of money); penniless.
giang, = *miang*.
giau, *pisau pĕnggiau*, a bill-hook.
gibas, = *kibas*, II.
gigi, tooth; the serrated or rippling edge of anything; *g. anjing* or *g. asu*, the canine teeth; *g. ayer*, the rippled surface of water; the edge of the sea (on the beach); *g. bĕrdukong*, overlapping teeth; *g. hutan*, the uneven fringes of the jungle; *g. jĕntĕra*, the teeth of a toothed wheel; *g. kapak*, large front teeth; *g. laut*, high-watermark; *g. manis*, the incisor teeth; *g. parang-parang*, small separated teeth; *g. sisir*, the teeth

of a rake or comb; *g. sulong*, the four front teeth; *g. tikus*, small regular teeth; *pĕnchungkil g.*, a toothpick—cf. *gigit, gĕrigi, gĕrigis*.

gigit, biting; to bite; *mĕnggigit*; to bite—cf. *gigi*.

gila, madness, insanity; *g. babi*, epilepsy; *g. bahasa*, cracked, eccentric; *g. bĕrahi*, madly in love; *anyam g.*, an apparently irregular pattern in *mĕngkuang* work; *murai g.*, a fantail flycatcher (*rhipadura*, spp.); *yu g.*, a fish (*chyloscillium indicum*); *gilakan*, or *mĕnggilakan*, to madden (with love)—cf. the Javanese form *edan*.

gilang, I. shining; *g. gĕmilang*, radiant, dazzling, resplendent—cf. *gilap*. II. a kind of toddy; a drink mentioned in old romances.

gilap, lustre from a polished surface; reflected light—cf. *gilang*.

gilau, = *kilau*.

giling, rolling into a spherical or cylindrical shape; rolling up a cigarette; grinding curry-stuff with a stone roller; *batu g.*, a roller for grinding curry-spices.

gilir, occurrence in succession; turn; *ia dudok sampai giliran tari-nya*, he sat down till it came to his turn to dance; *bĕngilir-gilir*, in succession; in turn.

gilis, a (Selangor) variant of *linggis*.

ginchah, = *kinchah*.

ginjat, on tiptoe; *tĕrginjat-ginjat*, moving about on tiptoe.

girap, to quicken the stroke when rowing.

giri, Skr. mountain—in compounds such as *Indĕra-giri*.

giring, I. *mĕnggiring*, to drive (wild animals). II. *giring-giring*, a sort of bell made out of sea-shell.

gisar, *mĕnggisar*, to twist; to give a twisting motion to anything—cf. *kisar*.

giwah, Pers. a shoe.

goa, I. a cave; *kĕlawar g.*, the bat (*chiromeles torquatus*); *kambing g.*,

a name sometimes given to the Malayan serow. II. Ch. I, me.

gobar, gloomy, sombre, overcast (as a sky when a storm is brewing).

gobek, an areca-nut pounder (used by men with bad teeth); *g. api*, a fire-syringe.

gochoh, striking with the fist; *gochohi*, to so strike (a blow); *mĕnggochoh*, to so strike (a person).

goda, spurring on; incitement; pursuing; following; goading; *mĕnggoda*, to urge on.

godak, *nasi g.*, a preparation of rice for use as medicine.

godam, a heavy pounding blow—e.g., with a club or mace; *mĕnggodam*, to strike such a blow; *pĕnggodam*, a club or knuckle-duster.

godok, *g. kĕpala*, the occipital bone.

gogoh, shivering with extreme cold.

gogol, a long-handled chisel used by braziers.

goha, = *goa*.

golak, *g.-galek*, topsy-turvey—cf. *bolak-balek*.

golang, *g.-golek*, to sway (of a spherical or cylindrical body).

golek, easily swaying; easily shaken or rolled; *golang-g.*, swaying or rocking; *hantu g.*, a sheeted ghost believed to propel itself by rolling along the ground; *sampan g.*, (Penang) the common Chinese sampan.

golok, a heavy chopper or bill-hook for clearing jungle.

golot, fussiness; hurry; over-work; *bĕrgolot-g.*, with fussy energy.

gomba, Skr. the frontlet of an elephant.

gombak, a tuft (of grass); a lock (of hair); also *gĕmbak*.

gombala, = *gĕmbala*.

gombang, an anchored purse-net; also *pompang*.

gomeng, = *komeng*.

gomol, *bĕrgomol*, to wrestle.

gonchang, to cause anything to

rock or sway; to shake; *gonchang-kan* and *mĕnggonchang*, id.
gondah, sorrow, sadness, despondency; *g. gulana*, id.; *gondahkan*, to sorrow after.
gondang, *siput gondang*, a generic name for several marine shells of the genus *dolium*; *g. bukit*, a land shell (*cyclophorus*, sp.)
gondok, squat; short and stout; *leher g.*, bull-necked.
gondol, bare; hairless; treeless.
gondong, an inflammation on the neck—a sort of goitre.
gong, a gong [this—the gong proper —has a hemispherical protuberance, while the *chanang* has not]; *pĕmukul g.*, the wooden striker of a gong.
gonggong, I. seizing and carrying off between the teeth (as a dog carries off a bone). II. a generic name for a number of shells (mostly of the genus *strombus*).
goni, = *guni*.
gonjak, to hint at.
gonjong, very sharp-ridged (of a Malay roof).
gonyeh, chewing between the gums; mouthing.
gonyoh, rubbing out impurities; scrubbing (when bathing).
gopoh, haste, hurry; *g. gapah* or *g. mamang*, extreme haste; hurry scurry.
gorap, Ar. an Arab dhow.
goreng, frying; cooking in a pan.
goris, a scratched line; *g. api*, matches.
gosok, friction, rubbing; *gosokkan*, to scrub; *mĕnggosok* and *mĕnggosokkan*, id.
gotis, to snap a link; to break the stalk of a flower.
goyang, a shaking or swaying motion; *bĕrgoyang*, to shake; to sway—cf. *gonchang*.
gu, a (double) yoke for bullocks; = *igu*—cf. *kok*.
gua, = *goa*.

guam, a disease attacking young children.
gubah, wearing in the hair (as a flower or jewelled ornament is worn).
gubal, the portion (of a tree-trunk) immediately under the bark; *nyior g.*, a coconut with the husk off.
gubang, I. a one-masted sea-going *pĕrahu* of a Bugis type. II. a notch cut in a tree-trunk to facilitate climbing.
guchi, a vessel of glazed earthenware.
gudang, a store-house; a godown.
gudu, *gudu-gudu*, a hookah, a hubble-bubble.
gugur, miscarriage; premature fall (of fruit); a sudden and unnatural fall; *g. pengsan*, to fall in a faint; *bintang g.*, a falling star.
gugus, patchy; *g. pulau-pulau*, an archipelago; *bĕrgugus-g.*, in patches, in clusters.
guit, a gentle sidelong push with the foot.
gula, sugar; sugary substances obtained from plants; *g. batu*, loaf sugar; *g. mĕlaka*, coconut sugar; *g. pasir*, granular sugar.
gulai, currying; curried food; *mĕng-gulai*, to prepare curry.
gulana, *gondah g.*, extreme depression; despondency; sadness.
guliga, a bezoar-stone; *batu g.*, id.
guling, rolling, revolving; *g. gantang*, rolling over and over; *g. garak*, rolling uneasily; *gulingkan*, to roll (a cylindrical object); *tĕrguling-g.*, rolling about.
gulita, *gĕlap g.*, pitchy darkness.
gulong, rolling up; *tikar dua g.*, two rolls of matting; two mats; *mĕng-gulong*, to roll up.
gumpal, rolling up anything into a ball or roughly spherical lump or clod; *bĕrgumpal g.*, clotted, coagulated.
gumpong, a thicket; a clump of thick jungle.
gun, (Kedah) gently rising ground.

guna, Skr. use, utility; magic art; *obat g.*, a philtre; *apa g.*, why; for what purpose; *gunakan*, to make use of; *bĕrguna*, useful.

gunawan, Skr. skilled in magic art —v. *guna*.

gundek, an inferior wife of a prince —i.e. a wife married formally to his *kĕris* or to his *bulang hulu*, but not to the prince himself.

gunggong, = *gonggong*.

guni, a sack; a "gunny-bag."

gunjai, a fringe or ornamental tassel at the end of a puggaree.

gunong, a mountain.

guntak, the rattle of pips in a dry fruit.

gunting, shearing; shears, scissors; *mĕnggunting*, to cut with a pair of scissors.

guntong, I. stumpiness through the removal of a projection; cutting short; *tiang g.*, a mast when the topmast has been removed. II. a creek.

guntur, thunder.

gurau, sporting, jesting, flirting; *g. jĕnaka*, quips and cranks; *sĕnda g.*, dalliance, flirtation; *bĕrgurau*, to jest.

gurdi, Tam. an auger; also *gĕrodi*.

guri, a small vessel of earthenware.

gurindam, Tam. a proverbial verse; a well-known saying appositely quoted.

guroh, thunder—cf. *gĕmuroh*.

guru, Skr. a teacher; *mak g.* or *siti g.*, a school-mistress; *Bĕtara G.*, Siva.

gus, together; all at a time; collectively; *di-tembak-nya tiga kali gus*, they all fired together three times—i.e. they fired three volleys.

gusar, taking offence; *jangan g.*, do not be offended, *gusari*, to become angry.

gusi, the gums.

gusti, I. Jav. a title of some distinction; master, lord. II. Pers. wrestling; *bĕrmain g.*, or *bĕrgusti*, to wrestle.

H

habat, way, manner.

habis, done, finished; entirely; the end of; *bĕlum h.*, not yet finished; *sa-habis-habis*, to the very end; to the very last; *habisi*, to come to an end of; *habiskan*, to put an end to; *pĕnghabisan*, termination, end.

hablok, Hind. piebald (of a horse).

hablur, = *abĕlur*.

habok, dust, chaff, powder; *h. yĕrgaji*, sawdust.

Habshi, Ar. Abyssinian, Ethiopian, Negro; *orang H.* a Negro.

hadap, position in front of; *raja di-hadap mantĕri-nya sakalian*, a prince with his ministers before him; *hadapan*, front; portion in front; *di-hadapan*, in the presence of, in front of—e.g. *raja di-hadapan mantĕri*, would be "a prince in the presence of his minister"—a discourteous expression compared with *raja di-hadap mantĕri*; *ka-hadapan*, to the front, forward; *hadapi* or *mĕnghadapi*, to face; *hadapkan* or *mĕnghadapkan*, to set in front, to place in front; *mĕnghadap* or *mĕngadap*, to enter the presence of (a prince); to have an audience of a sultan.

hadiah, Ar. a gift; a present.

hadis, Ar. the traditional sayings and deeds of the Prophet.

hadzir, Ar. presence; to be present; also pronounced *halir*.

hadzrat, Ar. presence; the royal presence; majesty.

hafal, Ar. well versed in the Koran; also *hapal*.

hai, oh—a vocative interjection; ho, there!

haibat, Ar. terrible, awe-inspiring, alarming; also *hebat*.
haidz, Ar. the menstrual flow.
hairan, Ar. astonishment; to wonder; wonderful; also *heran*.
haiwan, Ar. animals; living creatures.
hajat, Ar. wish, desire, intention.
haji, Ar. a man who has made the pilgrimage to Mecca; *naik h.*, to perform this pilgrimage.
hajrat, Ar. year of the Hegira; A.H.; also *hijrat*.
hak, Ar. truth; due, rightful claim; rights of property; description of property; *kaul-ul-hak*, the writing is true—a superscription to Malay epistles; *h. mana*, of what description?
hakikat, Ar. truth.
hakim, Ar. a judge; a judge of the supreme court.
hal, Ar. state, condition, position, case; *mĕngadukan, h.*, to lay one's case (before any person); *darihal*, concerning, regarding; *h. ahwal*, circumstances; facts of the case; things generally.
hala, direction, tendency; *ta'-tĕntu h.*, aimless, inapposite, irrelevant.
halai, confusing; *h. balai*, upsetting, confusing; confused, disorderly.
halal, Ar. legitimate; permissible according to divine law; food which is not forbidden—cf. *haram*.
halaman, a lawn before a palace or mansion.
halau, expulsion; driving away or driving out; *halaukan* or *mĕnghalaukan*, to drive away.
halba, Ar. an aromatic plant (*fœnum græcum*.)
halban, *kayu halban*, a plant (*vitex pubescens*); also *lĕban*.
halia, ginger, (*zingiber officinalis*).
halilintar, = *halintar*.
halimun, invisible or transparent through magic art; *halimunan*, the magic art of making oneself invisible.

halintah, a horse-leech; also *lintah*.
halintar, a thunderbolt; *panah h.*, id.; *batu h.*, fossil stone implements (believed to be bits of a thunderbolt); also *lintar*.
halipan, a centipede; *h. bara*, a centipede with a dark back and light legs; *h. laut*, a *nereis*; *h. pĕsan-pĕsan*, a black and yellow hairless spider-like animal; *jari h.*, a pattern made by cutting trailers diagonally from the midrib of a palm-leaf; also *lipan*.
halir, I. Ar. present; = *hadzir*. II. = *alir*.
halkah, a horse-collar.
halkum, Ar. throat, gullet.
haloba, covetousness; also *loba*.
haluan, the bows of a boat.
halun, = *alun*.
halus, fine in texture; delicate; *pisau h.*, a lancet-like knife; *tangan yang h.*, a delicately made hand; *pĕrkataan h.*, refined language.
halwa, a generic name for confectionery—preserves in sugar.
hama, a gnat; a very small insect.
hamak, disobliging; gruff and ill-tempered.
hamba, slave; your servant; I; *h. Allah*, God's poor; *h. Kompĕni*, Indian convicts, *h. sahaya*, slaves generally; *bĕrhamba*, (1) to be possessed of slaves; (2) to serve; *mĕmpĕrhambakan diri*, to give oneself to; to marry; *minta pĕrhamba*, to offer oneself in marriage.
hambal, = *ambal*, II.
hambar, = *ambar*.
hambat, pursuit, chasing; *bĕrhambat*, to pursue; in pursuit.
hambong, = *ambong*.
hambur, I. strewing about; scattering; *hambur-hambur*, largesse; *hamburkan*, to scatter; *bĕrhamburan*, strewn or scattered about. II. to curvet; to prance.
hamil, Ar. pregnant (with child)—a more polite expression than *bunting*.
hamis, = fish-scented; malodorous.

hampa, lacking contents; empty, idle, useless.

hampar, spreading out flat; extension in all directions; *batu h.,* bedrock; *h. khemah,* to pitch a tent; *hamparan,* a carpet; a mat; *hamparkan* or *mĕnghamparkan,* to spread out.

hampas, dregs, dross; the residuum or waste portion of anything; *h. tĕbu,* megass; *h. sutĕra,* silk dross.

hampir, proximity; near; nearly; *h. sa-rupa,* nearly identical; *hampir-hampir,* very nearly; *hampiri* or *mĕnghampiri,* to approach; *hampirkan,* to get close to; *bĕrhampiran,* in close touch with; in proximity to.

hampong, = *ampong.*
hampus, = *hapus.*
hamput, = *amput.*
hamun, indiscriminate abuse; reviling.

hamzah, Ar. the *spiritus lenis.*

hanching, rank, foul (of smell).

hanchur, melting, crushing, dissolving; *h. hati,* broken-hearted; *h. luloh,* utterly crushed; *mĕnghanchurkan,* to crush to pieces.

handai, companion, associate, comrade.

handak, = *hĕndak.*
handal, trusty, reliable.

hang, I. you, thou; a (Kedah) equivalent of *ĕngkau.* II. an obsolete Malay title.

hangat, hot; warmth; warm glow; *h. hati,* angry excitement.

hangit, scorching, singeing; *bau h.,* the smell of burning.

hangus, burning; being consumed by fire; *hanguskan,* to consume by burning.

Hanoman, Skr. the Hindu monkey-god; an evil dog-faced spirit (in Kedah); *sang sĕri H.,* the god Hanuman in romance.

hantap, = *antap.*

hantar, I. conveying, escorting, accompanying; sending in a person's charge; *hantarkan* or *mĕnghantarkan,* to accompany away; to escort. II. lying prostrate; lying spread out, *tĕrhantar,* stretched out.

hanti, = *anti.*

hantu, an evil spirit; a ghost or goblin; wild (of fruit—i.e. planted by ghosts not men); *h. bangkit,* the ordinary sheeted ghost risen from a grave and making its way by rolling along on its side as the fastenings of the winding-sheet prevent its walking; *h. bĕlian,* the tiger spirit; *h. bungkus,* = *h. bangkit; h. golek,* = *h. bangkit; h. jamuan,* a familiar spirit; *h. kochong* = *h. bangkit; h. orang mati di-bunoh,* the revengeful spirit of a murdered man; *h. pĕmburu,* the spectre huntsman; *h. rimba,* the demon of the woods that preys on lonely travellers; *h. tanah,* the gnomes of the soil; *burong h.,* an owl; *di-rasok h.,* to be attacked by an evil spirit; *jari h.;* the middle finger.

hanya, except, unless; only; *anak-ku hanya-lah sa-orang,* my child is an only child; *yang mĕngetahuï hanya-lah Allah,* who know that there is only one God.

hanyir, fishy; foul-smelling; musty.
hanyut, drifting along; floating; *hanyutkan,* to set adrift; *bĕrhanyut,* adrift; *bĕrhanyut-h.,* to be drifting about.

hapal, Ar. well versed in the Koran; also *hafal.*

hapek, = *apek,* I.
hapit, = *apit.*
hapus, expunging, wiping out.
hara, *huru-h.;* uproar; also *hiru-h.* and *haru-h.*

haram, Ar. unlawful, forbidden by religious law; a strong expression of negation; *h. zadah,* born out of wedlock; *h. ta'-dapat,* he utterly failed to get.

harang, = *arang.*

harap, hope, expectation, confidence,

trust; *harap-lah ěngkau kapada Allah*, put your trust in God; *harapan*, trusted, trusty; *harapi*, to confide in.

haras, = *aras*.

harbab, = *rěbab*.

hardek, strong reproof, scolding, censure.

harga, Skr. price, monetary value; *h.-nya tiga ringgit*, its price is three dollars; *hargakan*, to appraise; to price.

hari, day (both the day of 24 hours and the daylight hours by themselves); *siang h.*, daylight; *těngah h.*, midday; *malam h.*, night time; *sa-panjang h.*, all day; *kěesokan h.*, the morrow; *sělang sa-hari*, every alternate day; *lat sa-hari*, id.; *sahari-hari*, every day; *h. raya*, holiday; *h. běsar*, id.; *h. bulan*, day of the month.

harimau, tiger; leopard; any of the larger felidæ; a type of the strong and unscrupulous; also *rimau*; *h. akar*, the leopard-cat (*felis bengalensis*); *h. anjing*, the golden cat (*felis temminckii*); *h. bělang*, the tiger; *h. bělang chěchak*, the common wildcat—grey with black spots (*felis planiceps*); *h. bělang kasau*, the tiger (*felis tigris*); *h. bělang těbuan*, the common leopard, the "yellow" panther (*felis pardus*); *h. bintang*, = *h. bělang těbuan*; *h. burong*, a Pětani name for *felis planiceps*; *h. dahan*, the marbled cat (*felis marmorata*); *h. daun pinang*, a name given to the tiger when the black markings are not extensive; *h. jadi-jadian*, a were-tiger; *h. kumbang*, the black panther (*felis pardus*, var. *niger*); *h. lalat*, a jumping spider; *h. sipahi*, = *h. daun pinang*; *h. tarum*, a large black panther; *h. tělap*, the golden cat (*felis aurata*); *h. těrong kasau*, the royal tiger (*felis tigris*) when of very large size; *tulang h. měnangis*, the manubrium;

uban tahi h., the colour of the hair when either black or white largely predominates; also *rimau*.

harip, = *arip*.

haris, = *aris*.

harong, = *arong*.

harta, Skr. property, wealth; *hartanya banyak*, he had large possessions —cf. *hartawan*.

hartal, a yellow face-powder; saffron; also *rětal*.

hartawan, Skr. possessed of property; wealthy—cf. *harta*.

haru, confusion, uproar, disturbance; *h. hara*, a noisy disturbance; *h. biru*, id.; *di-haru shetan*, plagued by an evil spirit.

haruan, = *aruan*.

harum, fragrance, aroma, perfume.

harus, I. stream, current, freshet; *di-bawa oleh h.*, borne by the current; *songsong h.*, a shell (*murex ternispina*). II. proper, fitting, right.

hasad, Ar. envy, jealousy, spite.

hasil, Ar. outcome, return, rent, revenue; *h. tanah*, land-rent; *h. pokok*, land assessment; *měmbayar h.*, to pay land-rent to Government.

hasta, Skr. a Malay cubit (from the elbow to the finger-tips).

hasut, = *asut*.

hata, Ar. ? well then; next—an expression of common occurrence in commencing a new paragraph.

hatam, Ar. end, finish; termination; *sudah h.*, it is finished—used especially of the completion of studies.

hati, the heart and liver; the interior portion of anything; the seat of the feelings; *ambil di-h.*, to store up a grudge; *bacha didalam h.*, to read to oneself; *bakar h.*, wrath; *bělas h.*, compassion; *běrbalek h.*, a revulsion of feeling; *běrděbar h.*, a quicker beating of the heart; excitement, fear; *běrkata didalam h.*, to say to oneself; *běsar h.*, presumptuous pride; *buah h.*, heart—as a term of endearment; *chondong h.*, inclination towards; *gĕrak h.*, emotion; *hanchur h.*, heart-break; despair; *hulu h.*, the pit of the stomach; *tulang hulu h.*, the xiphoid process; *jantong h.*, the heart in its anatomical sense; *jauh h.*, alienation of affection or interest; *karat h.*, malice; *kĕchil h.*, spite, a grudge; *kĕras h.*, obstinacy; *kĕroh h.*, malice, ill-feeling; *kurang h.*, spiritless; *lĕbur h.*, crushed in spirit; *lĕmbut h.*, softer feelings; *makan h.*, to brood; *mata h.*, inward perception; *mĕmbawa h.*, to betake oneself anywhere in wrath; *mĕngambil h.*, to captivate; *panas h.*, zeal; *pilu h.*, melancholy; *puas h.*, satisfaction; *puteh h.*, sincerity; *putus h.*, heart-break, despair; *rawan h.*, rapture; *sakit h.*, anger; *sangkut h.*, loving attachment; *sayup h.*, melancholy; *sĕbal h.*, patience; *sĕdap h.*, pleasure; *sĕjok h.*, contented feelings; *suchi h.*, purity of motive; *susah h.*, sorrow, regret; *tawar h.*, disinclination; *tĕrang h.*, clearsightedness, calmness; *tinggi h.*, proud elation; *waswas h.*, annoyance; *mĕmpĕrhatikan*, to grasp, to understand, to realise.

hatta, = *hata.*
hatur, = *atur.*
haus, I. reducing by friction; wearing away. II. thirst.
hawa, I. Ar. breath, air; affection, lust, desire; *h. nafsu*, carnal lusts; *h. api*, the hot breath of a furnace. II. Ar. *Siti Hawa*, Eve.
hawar, a pestilence, an epidemic, a murrain.
hayak, = *ayak.*
hayam, = *ayam.*
hayat, Ar. life.
hayun, = *ayun.*
he, = *hai.*
hebat, Ar. terrible, awe-inspiring; also *haibat.*
heja, = *eja.*
hela, I. drawing over the ground; dragging; *mĕnghela*, to pull after one; *pĕnghela*, a puller, a drawer. II. aiming at, pointing to; *mĕnghelakan*, to aim (a weapon) at.
helah, = *elah.*
hĕlai, a numeral coefficient for tenuous objects such as sheets of papers, garments, leaves, blades of grass, etc.; also *lai.*
helat, = *elah.*
hĕlat, alternate, intervening; also *lat.*
heman, Jav. affection; interest; care; devotion to.
hemat, Ar. care, attention; *jaga dan hemat*, watchfulness and attentiveness.
hĕmbachang, = *ĕmbachang.*
hĕmbalau, = *ĕmbalau.*
hĕmbat, = *ĕmbat.*
hĕmbus, = *ĕmbus.*
hĕmpa, = *hampa.*
hĕmpas, dashing down violently; *hĕmpaskan*, to dash down; *mĕnghĕmpaskan*, id.
hĕmpĕdal, = *pĕdal.*
hĕmpĕdu, the gall; *pundi-pundi h.*, the gall-bladder.
hĕmpit, I. wedging or squeezing between two surfaces. II. *badak hĕmpit*, (Kedah) the two-horned rhinoceros (*rh. sumatrensis*).
hĕmpulur, = *ĕmpulur.*
hemul, = *emul.*
hĕndak, wish, desire, intention, purpose; *hĕndakkan*, to desire; *kĕhĕndak*, desire, wish; *sĕpĕrti kĕhĕndak tuan*, as you please; *bĕrkĕhĕndak*, to wish for, to be desirous of; *sa-kĕhĕndak*, in accordance with one's wishes.
hendel, = *endel.*
hengar, = *ingar.*
hĕning, limpid, pure, clear, transparent.
hĕnjal, = *ĕnjal.*
hĕntam, stamping with the foot.
hentek, = *entek.*
hĕnti, stopping; *bĕrhĕnti*, to come to a stop; *bĕrhĕntikan*, to put a stop to; *pĕrhĕntian*, an ending; a place to stop at.

hĕntimun, = *timun*.
hĕram, = *ram*.
heran, Ar. astonishment; to wonder; wonderful; also *hairan*.
herang, = *erang*, II.
herap, = *irap*.
hĕrat, = *rat*.
herau, = *erau*.
hĕrbab, = *rĕbab*.
hĕrdek, = *hardek*.
hĕrek, to shriek; to cry out with pain.
heret, = *eret*.
hĕrga, = *harga*.
hĕrta, = *harta*.
hĕrti, = *ĕrti*.
herut, = *erut*.
hĕsta, = *hasta*.
hetong, = *hitong*.
hias, adornment; ornamenting; *hiasi*, to adorn; *mĕnghiasi*, id.; *pĕrhiasan*, ornament, decoration.
hiba, = *iba*.
hiboh, noise, uproar (caused by traffic and not by noisily-disposed persons).
hibur, consoling, soothing; *mĕnghibur*, *hiburkan* or *mĕnghiburkan*, to allay sorrow; to calm; to console; *pĕnghibur*, a comforter.
hidam, = *idam*.
hidang, placing in a dish; a "portion" or plateful of food; *hidangan*, a plateful; *tĕrhidang*, served up.
hidayat, Ar. right guidance in religion.
hidong, the nose; *h. manchong*, a sharp-cut nose; *batang h.*, the ridge of the nose; *liang h.*, the nostril cavity.
hidu, to be on the scent of; to smell.
hidup, life; alive; *gajah h.*, a live elephant; *sa-umur h.*, as long as I live; *matahari h.*, the rising sun; *hidupi*, *hidupkan*, *mĕnghidupi* or *mĕnghidupkan*, to bring to life; (also) to keep alive; *kĕhidupan*, life; means of livelihood; *hal kĕhidupan*, condition of life.
higa, Jav. rib, side; = *rusok*.

higau, = *igau*.
hijau, green.
hijrat, Ar. the hegira; *tahun h.*, A.H.; also *hajrat*.
hikayat, Ar. a tale; a romance.
hikmat, Ar. wisdom; knowledge; magic art; *gĕmala h.*, a wonder-working talisman.
himat, = *hemat*.
himpit, = *hĕmpit*.
himpun, assembly, gathering together; *bĕrhimpun*, to meet together; *himpunkan*, or *mĕnghimpunkan*, to bring together; *pĕrhimpunan*, a gathering, a meeting.
hilai, = *ilai*.
hilam, = *ilam*.
hilang, loss, disappearance; death; *h. akal*, loss of self-restraint; *h. arwah*, or *h. sĕmangat*, loss of consciousness; *h.-lah ia*, he died; *hilangkan* or *mĕnghilangkan*, to drive away; to throw away; *kĕhilangan*, loss.
hilap, Ar. error; better *khilaf*.
hilat, = *elah*.
hilir, progress down stream; the lower waters of a river; *hulu-hilir*, top and bottom; beginning and end.
hina, Skr. mean, poor, contemptible; *h. dina*, the poor and lowly; *hinakan*, or *mĕnghinakan*, to disdain, to insult; to abase; *kĕhinaan*, degradation, abasement.
hinai, = *inai*.
hinchang, = *inchang*.
hinchit, departure, exit, quitting.
hinchut, = *inchut*.
hindek, = *indek*.
Hindi, Indian.
Hindu, Hindoo.
Hindustan, India.
hingga, up to; as far as; until; *h. pada masa ini*, up to the present time; *sa-hingga*, until; *pĕrhinggaan*, boundary, limit; also *pĕrenggan*; *tiada tĕrhingga*, boundless.
hinggap, perching, settling, alighting (of a bird); *h. api*, to catch fire.
hingus, = *ingus*.

hintai, = *intai*.
hira, *hiru-hira*, uproar; = *huru hara*.
hirap, = *irap*.
hirau, = *hiru*.
hirek, = *irek*.
hiri, = *iri*.
hiris, slicing, slitting, ripping up.
hiru, *hiru-hara*, a great disturbance; confusion; uproar; *h.-hira*, id.
hirup, = *irup*.
his, for shame! also *is*.
hisab, Ar. enumeration, calculation; *elmu h.*, accounts; commercial arithmetic; *tiada tĕrhisabkan banyak-nya*, innumerable.
hisap, = *isap*.
hitam, black; very dark in coloration; *h. bogot*, hideously black; *h. lĕgam*, pitch black; *h. manis*, dark brown; *h. muda*, deep blue.
hitong, calculation, reckoning; *elmu hitongan*, arithmetic.
hoe, Ch. a "hoey," a secret society.
hogoh, to mimic.
Hokian, Ch. appertaining to the Fuh-kien province (especially the Amoy and Chang-chow divisions, not Fuh-chau itself).
Holanda, Dutch; also *Bĕlanda*.
homa, = *huma*.
homam, Tam. a burnt offering, a sacrifice.
honar, Pers. discredit; a subject of reproach or censure; *khabar bĕrhonar*, a scandal; a tale to somebody's discredit.
hong, the Sanskrit and Buddhist "om," a word of mysterious import used by Malay medicine-men.
Hongkong, Hongkong; *kĕreta h.*, a jinrikisha.
horloji, Eur. a watch; a clock.
hormat, Ar. respect; reverence—especially with the idea of respectful behaviour; *mĕmbĕri h.*, to pay respect to.
hu, Ar. the possessive pronoun (third, singular, masculine) in its genitive and accusative forms.

Hua, Ar. He—i.e., God.
hubaya, entirely, in every way, altogether; *hubaya-hubaya*, above all things.
hubong, connection, linking; *hubongan*, link; *bĕrhubong*, united; *hubongkan* or *mĕnghubongkan*, to unite, to connect.
Hudai, *orang H.*, the name of a tribe of aborigines in the Malay Peninsula.
hudam, = *udam*.
hudang, = *udang*.
hudar, (Kedah) to run away; to bolt; to abscond.
hudhud, Ar. the hoopoe.
hudoh, = *hodoh*.
hui, an interjection of astonishment.
hujah, questioning, cross-examination.
hujan, rain; *h. dĕras*, pouring rain; *h. lĕbat*, rain in large drops; heavy rain; *h. rĕnyai*, drizzle; *h. rintek-rintek*, a few drops of rain only; *ayer h.*, rain-water; *musim h.*, the rainy season; *tĕdoh h.*, to stop raining; *hujani*, to rain down upon.
hujat, reviling; to abuse.
hujong, end, point, extremity; *h. tĕlunjok*, the tip of the index finger; *h. tanah*, a headland; *bĕrhujong*, pointed.
hukah, Ar. a hookah, a hubble-bubble; also *ogah*.
hukama, Ar. the plural of *hakim*; learned men, authorities on law and theology.
hukum, Ar. order, command; judicial decision, sentence; *bĕri h.*, to give an order; *jatoh h.*, to give a judicial decision; *kĕna h.*, to suffer a penalty; *hukuman*, punishment.
hukur, = *ukur*.
hukup, = *ukup*.
hulam, vegetable accessories to a dish; vegetable condiments.
hulat, = *ulat*.
hulkum, = *halkum*.
hulu, head, upper portion; beginning; hilt; handle; the **upper**

waters of a river; the interior of a country; *h. hati*, the pit of the stomach; *h. kĕris*, the handle of a *kĕris*; *gĕring h.*, head-ache (when speaking of a prince); *orang h.*, dwellers up-country; *dahulu*, before; *pĕnghulu*, headman, chief; Muhammad (as chief of Muhammadans).

hulubalang, a leader in war; a warrior in the first rank.

hulur, letting go, slacking; letting a rope become loose; paying out; *hulurkan*, to slacken, to pay out.

huma, "dry" or "hill" padi, (in contradistinction to *padi* planted on swampy soil); a padi-clearing on high ground; a "*ladang*"; *bĕrhuma*, to plant hill-padi.

human, = *uman*.

humbas, flight; *mĕnghumbas*, to "make oneself scarce."

hun, Ch. a Chinese measure of weight; one tenth of a mace (*chi*).

hunjam, = *unjam*.

hunjur, = *unjur*.

huntang, = *untang*.

hunus, unsheathing; drawing a sword from a scabbard, a finger from a ring, etc.; *di-hunus-nya kĕris-nya*, he drew his *kĕris*; *tĕrhunus*, bare, naked (of a weapon).

hurai, = *urai*.

hurmat, = *hormat*.

hurmuz, Ar. Ormus.

hurong, = *urong*.

huru, *huru-hara*, uproar, confusion, turmoil, tumult.

huruf, Ar. letters; an alphabetical symbol.

hurup, I. = *urup*. II. = *huruf*.

hurus, = *urus*.

hurut, = *urut*.

hutan, jungle, forest; wild; *anjing h.*, the wild dog (*cyon rutilans*); *ayam h.*, the jungle fowl (*gallus ferrugineus*); *babi h.*, the wild pig (*sus cristatus*); *orang h.*, a wild man; an aboriginal tribesman; a jungle-dweller; a boor.

hutang, debt; owing, due; *h. kĕpala*, a debt on the repayment of which one has staked one's life and liberty; *h. piutang*, debts; *bĕrhutang*, to owe; *orang bĕrhutang*, debtor; *orang hutangan*, the creditor.

huyong, = *uyong*.

I

ia, he, she, it; *ia-itu*, that is to say; namely.

iau, *mĕngiau*, to mew (of a cat).

iba, Ar. yearning, passionate regret, loving longing.

ibadat, Ar. service to God; pious duties.

ibar, *ibar-ibar*, a small river dug-out.

ibarat, Ar. metaphor, parallel; analogous case; *ambil i.*, to take a parallel case; to illustrate a point by a parable or fable.

ibau, an edible mussel.

Iblis, Ar. the devil; *di-haru i.*, harried by Satan.

ibni, Ar. son of; = *bin* [but *ibni* is used more politely or ceremonially than *bin*].

ibtida, Ar. exordium, beginning.

ibu, mother, dam (of animals); source, matrix; *saudara sa-ibu*, a uterine brother; *i. bapa*, parents; *i suri*, royal mother; *i. jari*, thumb; *i. kaki*, big toe; *i. pasir*, gravel; *i. tangan*, thumb; = *i. jari*.

ibul, a palm (unidentified).

ibur, = *hibur*.

ibus, a palm (unidentified).
idam, the longings of a pregnant woman; *i.-idaman*, the things so longed for; *idamkan*, to long for anything (when pregnant).
idang, = *hidang*.
idap, chronic (of sickness or melancholy); *mĕngidap*, to linger on in illness.
idar, revolution (as opposed to rotation); *idari* or *mĕngidari*, to wander round; *idarkan* or *mĕngidarkan*, to send round; to pass or hand round; *bĕridar*, in revolution; circulating; *bintang bĕridar*, a planet; *pĕridaran*, a revolution; a turn; *pĕridaran dunia*, the changes and chances of mortal life.
idong, = *hidong*.
idzin, Ar. permission; also *izin*.
iga, = *higa*.
igal, *mĕngigal*, to spread the tail (of a peacock).
igama, Skr. religion; *i. Islam*, Muhammadanism; also *agama* and *ugama*.
igau, wandering in delirium; talking or movement in sleep; *igau-igauan*, ravings, nightmare; muttering or crying in sleep; *tĕrigau-igau*, wandering, delirious.
igu, a double yoke (for oxen); also *gu*—cf. *kok*.
ihram, Ar. anathema; interdict.
ihsan, Ar. beneficence; kindness.
ihtiar, Ar. choice; elected action; *dĕngan ikhtiar-nya sĕndiri juga*, by his own choice; *mĕnchari i.*, to think out some plan to adopt; *pulangkan i.*, to leave the decision to another; *bagaimana i. kamu*, what conclusion have you come to; what do you think.
ihtimal, Ar. to endure; to bear.
ihwal, = *ahwal*.
ijabat, Ar. the hearing of prayer.
ijau, = *hijau*.
ijazat, Ar. diploma, certificate, license.

ijin, = *idzin*.
ijok, a fibrous vegetable substance resembling horse-hair; *tali i.*, rope made of this fibre.
ijtihad, Ar. zeal, solicitude, diligence.
ikal, curly (of the hair).
ikan, a generic name for fish; *ikan-ikan*, the log; *i. kĕring*, dried fish; *nyawa i.*, the life of a fish on shore; nearly lifeless; at the last gasp.
ikat, binding, fastening; *i. pĕrang*, the line of battle; *i. pinggang*, a belt; *i. rumah*, to build a house; *ikatan*, bonds, fastenings; *ikatkan* or *mĕngikatkan*, to fasten together; to put together; *tĕrikat*, in bonds; tied up.
ikhlas, Ar. sincerity; sincere; *surat ul-ikhlas*, the letter is sincere—a common exordium to an epistle.
ikhtiar, = *ihtiar*.
ikhtilaf, Ar. discord, inconsistency.
ikhtisar, Ar. definition.
ikut, following (in point of space, not time); coming after; *mĕngikut*, to follow.
Ilaha, Ar. God; *la Ilaha ila'llah*, there is no God but Allah.
Ilahat, Ar. Godhead.
ilahi, Ar. my God; oh God.
ilai, loud laughter; *mĕngilai*, to laugh loudly.
ilam, *ilam-ilam*, dimly or intermittently visible.
ilang, = *hilang*.
ilau, flickering (as light on water)— cf. *kilau*.
ilham, Ar. divine inspiration.
ilmu, Ar. knowledge, scholarship, science; magic art; also *elmu*.
imalat, Ar. joining two letters in pronunciation—e.g. *insha'llah* for *insha Allah*.
imam, Ar. "imam"; president of a mosque.
iman, Ar. faith, creed, belief, religion; the true faith; *mĕmbawa i.*, to accept the true faith; *bĕriman*, religious.

imbal, roundish (but not globular), as the rounded leg of a table.

imbang, hovering about, haunting, shadowing (as a ghost haunting a place or a thief shadowing a man).

imbas, the air immediately round a person (which he can be supposed to infect if diseased); *kĕna imbasan hantu*, to be slightly affected by a passing spirit of disease.

imbau, to throw a stick, not as one throws a spear but by seizing an extremity and hurling the stick boomerang-wise through the air— e.g. to knock fruit off a tree.

imboh, making up the balance; giving a small final payment.

impit, = *hĕmpit*.

inai, Ar. henna; a red dye obtained locally from a shrub (*lawsonia alba*); *i. batu*, a pink balsam (*impaticus griffithii*); *i. paya*, the water balsam (*hydrocera triflora*); *malɩm i.*, the night on which the bride's fingers are stained with henna—i.e. the commencement of the wedding festivities; *siput i.*, a shell (*mitra episcopalis*).

inang, a nurse, a duenna, a chamberwoman to a princess.

inangda, a more respectful variant of *inang*.

inas, I. the humming apparatus on a Malay humming-kite. II. *pĕkong inas*, a malignant tumour.

inchang, *inchang inchut*, awry, askew.

inchar, a drill bore.

inche', Mr.; an honorific prefix; better *ĕnche'*.

inchi, Eng. inch.

inchit, = *hinchit*.

inchut, *inchang-inchut*, awry, askew.

indah, beauty; attractiveness; precious, important, fine, handsome; *i. khabar dari rupa*, report is fairer than reality; *apa i.*, of what value is it (to me); what does it matter;

indahkan, to consider important; to care about.

indang, winnowing with a sidelong jerk or shake.

indar, = *idar*.

indek, leverage by pressure with the foot; *lĕsong i.*, a padi-pounder worked with the foot; *lang i.*, a large bird of prey (*nisaëtus limnaëtus*).

Indĕra, Skr. the Sanskrit divinity Indra; a name given to a class of minor divinities inhabiting Indra's heaven; a royal title; royal; *kĕ-indĕraan*, the heaven of Indra; *mĕng-indĕra*, royal.

inding, watching constantly; keeping an eye on anything.

indok, *indok kĕrbau*, a milch-buffalo; *pĕrindokan* or *pĕrindun*, a brood—cf. *indong*.

indong, mother (but this word is rarely used); *i. mutiara*, mother-of-pearl—cf. *indok*.

ing, Jav. of, for—cf. *yang*.

ingar, brawling, noisy disturbance; *i. bangar*, very great uproar.

ingat, attention, recollection, remembrance; *ingat-ingat*, take care, look out; *ingatan*, attention to one's surroundings; recollection; *ingati*, to remember; *ingatkan*, to remind; to call to mind.

ingau, *ingau-ingau*, dozing; half awake.

inggeh, Jav. yes.

Inggĕris, English.

inggu, Skr. asafœtida; *ikan i.*, a generic name given to a large number of fish of the genera *pempheris*, *pomacentrus*, *pterois*, *amphiphrion*, *stolocentrum*, *stolacanthus* and *pseudoscarus*.

ingin, lust, longing, strong desire.

ingkar, Ar. breaking a pledge, violating a promise.

ingsang, = *isang*.

ingu, = *inggu*.

ingus, mucus from the nose; *buang i.*, to blow one's nose.

ini, this, these; *aku i.*, I who stand here; I myself; *sěkarang i.*, at this very moment—cf. *sini*.

injap, the inturning spikes which permit entrance into a basket-trap for fish but stop the fish from getting out again.

injil, Ar. the gospel; *i. Lukas*, the gospel according to St. Luke.

insaf, Ar. justice, equity.

insan, Ar. a human being.

insang, = *isang*.

insha, Ar. *insha'llah* please God.

intai, *měngintai*, to peer, to peep, to spy on.

intan, a diamond.

inti, a name given to a number of Malay dishes.

inu, Jav. a title of distinction, princely.

ipar, brother-in-law; sister-in-law.

ipoh, the poison-tree or upas (*antiaris toxicaria*); the poison obtained from it; dart-poison generally.

ira, *ira-ira*, a fish (unidentified).

iradat, Ar. will; the will of God.

iram, I. *iram-iram*, the fringe round a State umbrella. II. change of colour; blushing.

irap, resemblance; *irap-irap*, very much alike.

iras, connection, similarity; *sa-iras*, alike; of the same material, blood or character; *kěris ganja iras*, a *kěris* of which the blade proper and the *aring* (or guard) are in one piece.

irau, = *hiru*.

irek, stamping on padi that is too short for threshing; *irekkan*, to so treat padi.

iri, *iri hati*, spite, malice.

iring, processional following; Indian file; one after another; *běriring-iringan*, in long succession; *měngiring*, to proceed in procession; *iringi* and *měngiringi*, to follow in procession; *di-iringkan*, to be followed by.

iris, = *hiris*.

irup, to suck up liquor from a spoon or cup.

is, for shame; also *his*.

Isa, Ar. *Nabi Isa*, Jesus Christ (in Muhammadan tradition).

isak, sobbing; sneezing; asthmatic coughing.

isang, the gills of a fish.

isap, sucking; drawing in one's breath; smoking; *měngisap*, to smoke.

isha, Ar. *sěmbahyang i.*, the evening prayer.

isharat, Ar. signal, sign; *měmběri i.*, to give the signal.

isi, contents; that which fills; *i. něgěri*, the inhabitants of a town; *i. rumah*, the household; *i. dunia*, mankind; *i. surat*, the contents of a letter; *i. kahwin*, the marriage settlements on a bride; *bagai kuku děngan isi*, like the nail and the flesh within it—inseparable except at great pain, prov.; *isikan* or *měngisikan*, to fill; *běrisi* filled with, containing.

Iskandar, Ar. Alexander; *I. dzu'l-karnain*, Alexander the Great.

Islam, Ar. salvation; peace in God; the Muhammadan world; the Muhammadan religion.

isnin, Ar. *hari isnin*, Monday.

Istambul, Constantinople.

istana, Pers. a palace.

istanggi, Skr. incense; also *sětanggi*.

istěri, Skr. wife (more respectful than *bini*); *běristěri*, to be married (of a man); *běristěrikan*, to marry (a woman); *měmpěristěrikan*, id.

istiadat, Ar. ceremonial custom.

istimewa, especially; more especially.

istinggar, Port. a match-lock.

istinja, Ar. ablutions prescribed by Muhammadan custom.

istirahat, Ar. repose, rest, peace, tranquillity.

istiwa, Ar. being parallel; *khattu'l-istiwa*, the equator.

istri, = *istěri*.

itam, = *hitam*.

itek, duck; *i. ayer*, the cotton-teal

(nettopus coromandelianus); *i. surati*, the Muscovy duck; *peler i.*, an auger; *ular i.*, a fabulous duck-billed snake (the finding of which brings luck in money matters).

itong, = hitong.
itu, that, those—cf. *situ*.
iu, = yu.
izin, Ar. permission; also *idzin*.
Izrael, Ar. Azrael.

J

jabal, Ar. mountain.
jabar, Ar. omnipotent; *Malik ul-jabar*; the King of Kings; God; *Khalik ul-jabar*, the Almighty Creator.
jabat, grasping in the hand, holding; *jabatan*, (1) the sense of touch; (2) occupation, profession, = *jawatan*; *bĕrjabat*, to hold.
jabu, rising in clouds (of smoke, dust, etc.)
jabur, much mixed up.
jadah, Pers. son, born of (but used in a bad sense—i.e. bastard, ill-begotten).
jadam, an extract of aloes used as medicine.
jadi, coming into existence; becoming; turning out satisfactorily; accomplishing its purpose; *aku pun jadi-lah*, I was born; *kĕrja itu ta'-jadi*, that work will not do; *jadi-jadian*, a supernatural creation; *harimau jadi-jadian*, a were-tiger; *mĕnjadi*, to become; *mĕnjadikan*, to create; *kĕjadian*, creation.
jadwal, Ar. a tabular statement.
jaga, Skr. to be awake; to be watchful; *orang j.*, a watchman; *j. daripada tidur*, to awake from sleep; *jagakan* or *mĕnjagakan*, to wake (a person); *bĕrjaga*, to be awake; *bĕrjaga-jaga*, to keep awake, to keep open house day and night (in marriage festivities); *mĕnjaga*, to watch.
jagat, Skr. the world; *j. buana*, id.
jago, Jav. a cock.
jagong, maize; Indian corn.

jaguni, Skr. spirits of good fortune.
jagur, massively built.
jagut, Jav. chin—cf. *dagu* and *janggut*.
jah, Pers. worth; greatness.
jahad, Ar. a holy war.
jahan, Pers. the world.
jahanam, Ar. gehenna, hell; destruction.
jahang, I. violent abuse. II. deep red (in colour).
jaharu, Hind. a pariah, a low scoundrel.
jahat, wicked, evil, immoral; *dĕngan j.*, with evil intent; *pĕrĕmpuan j.*, a prostitute; *kĕjahatan*, wickedness.
jahi, Jav. ginger.
jahil, Ar. ignorant of God's word.
jahiliat, Ar. the general ignorance of God's word that prevailed before Muhammad enlightened mankind with the Koran.
jahim, Ar. fiercely blazing (of hell-fire); *naraka j.*, the hottest hell.
jahit, sewing; *tukang j.* or *orang pĕnjahit*, a tailor.
jahudi, = *jaudi*.
jait, = *jahit*.
jaja, hawking about for sale; *bĕrjaja*, to hawk about; *mĕnjaja*, id.; *pĕnjaja*, a hawker.
jajahan, a district; a division of a country.
jajar, a row, a line; drawn up in a row, stretching out in a line—cf. *janjar* and *banjar*.
jajat, to mimic; taking off; ridiculing by mimicry.

jaka, Jav. a young unmarried man—cf. *bujangga*, II.

jakas, a kind of *mĕngkuang*.

jaksa, Jav. a Javanese title of inferior distinction.

Jakun, a name given to aboriginal tribesmen in the southern parts of the Malay Peninsula.

jala, I. a casting-net. II. Ar. great, illustrious (of God).

jalak, I. a one-masted or two-masted sailing vessel peculiar to Pahang. [It is built up fore and aft and is not decked except for a loose framework of split nibongs or planks]. II. licentious, loose.

jalan, road, way; movement in a definite direction; the course taken; *j. bahasa*, idiom; *j. ugama*, theology; *j. raya*, the main road; *mata j.*, an outpost; *mĕmbawa j.*, to lead the way; *bĕrjalan*, to be in motion; *bĕrjalan kaki*, to walk; *bĕrjalan kĕreta*, to travel by carriage; *jalani*, to travel over; *mĕnjalani*, id.; *jalankan* or *mĕnjalankan*, to set in motion; *pĕrjalanan*, journey.

jalang, a strumpet.

jalar, creeping; *mĕnjalar*, to creep (as a snake or creeping plant).

jali, Ar. *tĕrjali*, evident, clear, bright, distinguished.

jalin, tied parallel to one another by means of string or rattan (as the strips of bamboo in chicks or fish-screens are fastened).

jalis, Ar. *sa-jalis*, sitting together; in company.

jalma, = *jĕlma*.

jalu, the natural spur of a fighting-cock; *ikan j.*, a fish (*lutianus*, sp.)

jalur, a broad band or stripe of colour; broad stripes separated by lines; a strip of padi-field as marked by the lines of padi-stalks; a river-boat of very shallow draught (the ribs of which give it a striped appearance) —cf. *lajur*.

jam, Pers. a clock; an hour; *sa-tĕngah j.*, half-an-hour; *sa-jam dua*, an hour or two.

jamah, physical contact or handling; actual (even if temporary) possession; sexual intercourse; *jamah-jamahan*, an occasional mistress of a prince.

jamal, Ar. beauty, elegance.

jaman, Ar. time, age; = *zaman*.

jamang, a gold or silver frontlet worn by a woman.

jamar, = *chamar*.

jambak, a (double) handful; the contents of two hands held together.

jamban, a privy.

jambang, a flower-pot or stand for flower-pots; *jambangan*, id.

jambar, I. *sa-jambar*, a plateful. II. a rough temporary hut built by travellers camping in the jungle.

jambatan, a bridge; a pier; a way with a hand-rail; a variant of *jabatan* (from *jabat*).

jambiah, Pers. a broad-bladed curved dagger.

jambu, Skr. a generic name for a number of fruits of the rose-apple class; *j. ayer* (*eugenia aquea*); *j. bĕrsin* = *j. biji*; *j. biji*, the guava (*psidium guava*); *j. mawar* (*eugenia jambos*); *j. monyet*, the cashew (*anacardium occidentale*); *jambu-jambu*, the plume or crest on a helmet; the ornamental top of a standard; *punai j.*, a bird (*ptilopus jambu*).

jambua, a shaddock.

jambul, a tuft of hair or feathers rising from the head; the crest of a peacock; the queue of a Chinese; the tassel of a fez; *j. mĕrak*, the crest of a peacock; a plant (*poinciana pulche*); a common grass (unidentified, but not a *selaginella*).

jamin, Hind. bail, security; *orang j.*, a bailor; a surety.

jamjam, water (very poetically expressed); *j. durja*, complexion, expression; = *ayer muka*; *j. mas*, gold paint.

jamong, (Kedah) an extemporised torch.

jampal, a weight or coin of varying value.

jampi, Skr. incantation; magical formula; the practice of the black art; *mĕnjampi*, to practice magic.

jampok, I. a small owl. II. breaking into a conversation.

jamu, entertaining; providing food and lodging; a guest; *mĕnjamu*, to entertain (a guest); to keep (a familiar spirit); *hantu jamuan*, a familiar spirit; *pĕrjamuan*, entertainment, dinner; *jamu-jamu*, a plant (*aporosa microcalyx*).

janda, a widow; a divorced woman; *lenggang j.*, a small curved knife broadening and fretted at the point.

jandela, = *jĕndela*.

janek, radiation from a common centre; *ringgit j.*, the Mexican dollar so called from its depicting a rising or setting sun.

janela, = *jĕndela*.

jangak, abandoned; utterly profligate.

jangan, don't; lest; *j.-lah*, do not; *supaya j.*, lest; *jangankan*, so far from; not to mention.

jangat, a process of splitting rattans; *pisau pĕnjangat*, the knife used in this process; *pĕrĕkat j.*, glue.

jangga, a variant of *jaka*.

janggal, discordant, inharmonious.

Janggi, I. Pers. Zanzibari; African; *pauh j.*, a tree supposed to grow in the centre of the great ocean; *buah pauh j.*, shells of the coconut (*cocos maldiva*), believed to be the fruit of this tree. II. Pers. warrior-like.

janggus, *buah j.*, cashew (*anacardium occidentale*).

janggut, the beard; *bĕrjanggut*, bearded; *j. bauk*, a full beard; *j. bĕramus*, a matted beard; *j. di-urut*, a forked or pointed beard.

jangka, a pair of compasses.

jangkah, stepping over an obstacle.

jangkang, I. wide open (of the arms)-wide apart (of the legs). II. a generic name to a number of trees.

jangkar, I. Eur. a grapnel. II. spreading above ground (of the roots of a tree such as the mangrove).

jangkeh, *jangkeh-mangkeh*, helter-skelter.

jangki, a basket or wicker knapsack.

jangkil, morose, ill-tempered.

jangking, *jongkang-jangking*, rising and falling irregularly (as the points of the picks of a party of coolies).

jangkit, I. hidden dissemination; spreading without visible cause (as an infectious disease or as a fire which breaks out in several places at once); *sakit bĕrjangkit*, an infectious disease. II. pierced by a barbed thorn or point.

janjar, a row or line of people.

janji, contract, agreement; to agree; *minta j.*, to request the fulfilment of an agreement; *pĕgang j.*, to observe an agreement; *bĕrjanji*, to agree, to contract; *pĕrjanjian*, a contract.

jantan, male (usually of animals); masculine; *anak j.*, a manly person; *ĕmbun j.*, dew in heavy drops; *kĕtam j.*, a plane; *pahat j.*, a narrow deep chisel.

jantong, core, heart; *j. bĕtis*, the calf of the leg; *j. hati*, the heart, the seat of love; a term of endearment; *j. kalbu*, = *j. hati*; *j. paha*, the fleshy portion of the thigh; *j. tangan*, the triceps.

jantur, Jav. sorcery.

jap, come together, collected; *sudah j.*, it is complete; it is come about.

jara, an instrument for cleaning coarse cotton-wool; a churning instrument for milk; *kĕpala j.*, buttermilk.

jarah, I. prowling about as a plunderer; *jarahan*, a slave carried off by raiders. II. Ar. a mite; an atom. III. a pilgrimage; also *ziarah*.

jarak, I. interstice; intervening space. II. the castor-oil plant (*ricinus communis*); *minyak j.*, castor-oil; *padang j.*, a desolate place.

jaram, a cooling lotion for the head.

jarang, scarce, rare, separated by wide intervals.

jaras, I. a creel. II. a handful (when the stalks or strings only are held in the hand); a bunch.

jari, a finger; a toe; *j. hantu*, the middle finger; *j. kaki*, a toe; *j. kělingking*, the little finger; *j. manis*, the ring-finger; *j. tělunjok*, the index-finger; *anak j.*, a finger; *buku j.*, the knuckles; *chělah j.*, the cleft between two fingers; *ibu j.*, a thumb; *sarong j.*, a thimble.

jariah, I. Ar. *amal j.*, a charitable work of permanent utility. II. Ar. a slave-girl.

jaring, a wide-meshed drift-net.

jaru, *ikan jaru-jaru*, a fish (*caranx boops*); also *chěncharu*.

jarum, a needle; *j. chuchok*, a bodkin; *lobang j.*, the eye of a needle; *mata j.*, id.

jasa, Skr. meritorious service; deserts; loyalty; *měmbuat j.* or *běrjasa*, to do one's duty loyally; *lupakan j.*, to be remiss in one's duty.

jasad, the material and visible body (as opposed to the soul).

jati, true, real; *Mělayu j.*, a real Malay; *timur j.*, due east; *kayu j.*, teak (*tectonia grandis*).

jatoh, to (accidentally) fall; to happen; to occur; *j. sakit*, to fall sick; *j. hati*, to fall in love; *jatohkan* or *měnjatohkan*, to let drop; *kějatohan*, fall.

Jaudi, Ar. a Jew; Jewish.

jauh, distance; far; *dari j.*, from afar; *jauh-lah malam*, the night was far spent; *jauhi* or *měnjauhi*, to put a distance between; to keep off; *jauhkan* or *měnjauhkan*, id.

jauhar, Ar. gem, jewel, essence, embryo.

jauhari Ar. a jeweller.

jauk, a small tortoise (unidentified).

Jawa, Javanese; *tanah J.*, Java; *orang J.*, a Javanese; *asam J.*, tamarind.

jawab, Ar. answer; *minta j.*, to request a reply; *běri j.*, *běrjawab* or *měnjawab*, to reply.

jawat, *jawatan*, an office, a duty, a post.

Jawi, I. Ar. Malayan; Sumatran and Javan; *huruf J.*, the Arabic character. II. Jav. an ox. III. *jawi-jawi*, a large fig-tree (*ficus rhododendrifolia*).

jaya, Skr. victorious, successful; *měnjaya*, to succeed; to "come off."

jayeng, Jav. and Skr. victorious; = *jaya-ing*, *jayeng sětěru*; conquering all foes.

jěbah, broad and full (of the face); square-faced.

jebah, *běrjebah*, assorted (of merchandise).

jěbak, a snare for birds.

jěbang, an oblong shield.

jěbat, Ar. civet; *musang jěbat*, the Indian civet (*viverra zibetha*).

jěboh, a fish (unidentified).

jěbong, a fish (*balistes stellatus*).

jěda, Ar. pause, break; *ta'-běrjěda*, without a pause or break.

jěgel, prominent (of the eye-ball).

jěgong, stern-lockers.

jěhěnam, = *jahanam*.

jějahan, = *jajahan*.

jějak, = *jijak*.

jějal, *měnjějal*, to close a crack; to force food into a child's mouth.

jějamang, a variant of *jamang*.

jějamu, a variant of *jamu-jamu*.

jějas, abrasion, scratch, graze.

jějawi, a variant of *jawi-jawi*.

jějeh, slightly leaking or spilling.

jejer, row, line.

jěla, "gadding about" (of a woman).

jela, *běrjela*, trailing slackly or loosely; *běrjela-jela*, id.

jěladan, a bird (unidentified).
jělaga, soot.
jělah, clear, unobstructed (of the view).
jělai, a kind of millet (*aphania paucijuga*).
jělak, sated, glutted; *jěmu j.*, sick of.
jělanak, advancing under cover, wriggling through long grass.
jělantah, insufficiently cooked (of food); underdone.
jělapang, a padi-barn.
jělar, extended at full length (of a long-bodied animal).
jělas, clearing up; settling; winding up.
jělatang, the tree-nettle (*laportica crenulata*).
jělatek, the Java sparrow.
jělau, *jěngok j.*, to peer at anything.
jělěbut, = *kělěbut*.
jělek, (Batav.) pleasant, nice.
jělěma, = *jělma*.
jělěmpah, a general rotting of fruit on a tree.
jělěpak, (onom.) the sound of a book (or any similar body) falling on the ground; flopping.
jělěpang, cross-gashes; cross-cutting with a sabre.
jělěpok, (onom.) a variant of *jělěpak*; to flop.
jělimpat, *měnjělimpat*, to break a journey.
jělinap, *měnjělinap*, to shoot ahead (as a horse in a race).
jěling, a sidelong languishing look; *měnjěling*, to look at anyone through the corner of the eye.
jělingar, *měnjělingar*, to pay little attention to a fact; to half-remember, half-forget.
jělir, *měnjělir*, to project the tongue.
jělma, Skr. incarnation; the assumption of human form; a man; *měnjělma*, to assume human form; to be re-incarnated; *pěnjělmaan*, an incarnation.
jělojoh, = *gělojoh*.

jělok, deep (of a bowl).
jěluak, the noise before expectoration; hawking.
jěluang, tissue-paper.
jěluat, *jěling-j.*, to give a long sidelong look—cf. *jěling*.
jělujur, loose sewing, temporary stitching.
jělum, wetting without actual immersion; washing.
jělungkap, *měnjělungkap*, to bound back into position (of an elastic body released from strain).
jělutong, a leaf-monkey (especially *semnopithecus obscurus*).
jěmaat, = *jumaat*.
jěmah, proximate; nearest; very near; *kělak j.*, almost at once; *pagi j.*, this very morning.
jěmala, the crown of the head; the cranium.
jěmalang, = *jěmbalang*.
jěmawa, conceit, pride.
jěmba, a measure of length equal to about 12 feet.
jěmbak, *těrjěmbak-jěmbak*, flapping up and down as a child's locks when the child runs.
jěmbalang, an evil spirit of the soil; a gnome of disease.
jěmbangan, = *jambangan*.
jěmbatan, = *jambatan*.
jěmlah, = *jumlah*.
jěmpana, a state-litter for ladies of the court.
jěmpul, Jav. the cushion of the thumb.
jěmput, gripping between fore-finger and thumb; *sa-jěmput*, a pinch.
jěmu, satiety; weariness of; *j. jělak*, nauseated with anything; *j. daripada hidup*, sick of life.
jěmuan, shameless criminality; open villany.
jěmuas, besmeared; dirty.
jěmuju, caraway-seed.
jěmur, drying by exposure to the sun's rays; *měnjěmur*, to put a thing out to dry.

jěnak, a short space of time; a pause.
jěnaka, Hind. a farce, a practical joke; a wily, much-contriving setter of snares for others; *běrgurau běrjěnaka*, with quips and jokes.
jěnang, prop, support; aid, co-adjutor; the chief assistant to a batin or headman of Orang Laut; *j. pintu*, the uprights of a door.
jěnawi, a long sword or rapier; *pědang j.*, id.
jěnazah, Ar. a royal hearse; (by metaphor) the body of a deceased prince.
jěndala, Skr. scoundrelly, low, mean.
jěndela, Port. a window.
jěnděra = *chěnděra*.
jěndul, prominent (of the forehead or frontal bone).
jěnela, = *jěndela*.
jěngěla, = *jěnggala*.
jěnggal, *jěnggal-jěnggul*, uneven; all notched.
jěnggala, Skr. wild; untamed; appertaining to the forest.
jengger, Jav. the comb of a cock.
jěnggul, *jěnggal-jěnggul*, covered with notches.
jěngkal, a span (between thumb and finger); *j. tělunjok*, the span between the thumb and index-finger; *j. kělengkeng*, the span between the thumb and little finger.
jengkang, drawing out a leg; extending a leg.
jengkang, on its back with legs in the air (of a carcase or of a dead insect).
jěngkau, raising the hand to pluck or grasp an object above one; to erect its head (of a leech); *j. ulat*, finger-tips which stick out backwards.
jengkeng, moving about on tiptoe—cf. *jengket*.
jengket, walking on tiptoe—cf. *jengkeng*.
jěngking, raising the tail aloft; *kala j.*, the common house-scorpion.

jěngkit, walking on the heels.
jěngkolet, tilted to one side (as a man's head when he goes to sleep on a chair).
jěngkul, the span between the thumb and the joint of the bent index-finger.
jěngok, peeping at; watching through a crevice; peering after; *měnjěngok*, to peer, to peep.
jěngul, *měnjěngul*, to suddenly emerge above the surface (as the snout of a crocodile); to poke out.
jěnis, Ar. kind, species; *běrjěnis-jěnis*, of all kinds, various; *tiada běrjěnis*, confused, "at sea," bewildered.
jenjeng, = *jinjing*.
jenjet, = *jinjit*.
jěnoh, *makan jěnoh*, to eat one's fill.
jěntaka, Skr. ill-luck.
jěntat, *měnjěntat*, to leap (of a flea, or of any other creature with great jumping powers).
jěntayu, Skr. a fabulous bird believed to have the power of calling down rain and dew.
jěntek, a jerk by way of propulsion (as a boy throws a marble by a jerk with his thumb); a jerky or wriggling action.
jěntěra, Skr. a wheel; spinning-wheel; circling, wheeling; *běrjěntěra*, to rotate; to move in waves (of light); to be on wheels; *pěsawat běrjěntěra*, machinery; *tanglong běrjěntěra*, a rotating Chinese lantern.
jěpang, sea-weed jelly.
jěpit, = *sěpit*.
Jěpun, Japan.
jěput, = *jěmput*.
jěra, warned by experience; taught caution; *tiada j.*, he has not yet learnt by experience.
jěrabai, tattered; also *jěrambai*.
jěrabun, a (Kedah) variant of *jěrěmbun*.
jěragah, a (Kedah) variant of *chěranggah*.
jěragan, = *juragan*.

jĕrah, plentiful (of a crop); numerous (of cases of illness in an epidemic).
jĕrahak, given up as a bad job (of a work).
jĕrahap, falling prostrate (with limbs outstretched).
jĕrait, interlinked as the links of a chain.
jĕram, rapids in a stream.
jĕramah, seizure with claws and teeth; seizure by a tiger or by any similar beast; to fight (of a woman).
jĕrambah, a wooden platform outside a Malay house for supporting water-jars, etc.
jĕrambai, tattered; also *jĕrabai*.
jĕrambang, St. Elmo's light; an *ignis fatuus* taken by sea-faring Malays to be an evil spirit.
jĕrami, stubble.
jĕrang, warming at a fire.
jĕrangau, a medicinal plant (*acorus calamus*).
jĕrangkah, = *chĕranggah*.
jĕrangkang, the attitude of an animal lying on its back with its paws in the air.
jĕrap, saturation (till drops begin to fall); thoroughly steeping (as a wick is steeped in oil).
jĕrat, a running noose; a lasso; a noose-trap.
jĕrau, deep red.
jĕraus, agile, sprightly.
jĕrawat, pimples on the face.
jĕrbak, *mĕnjĕrbak*, to pervade; = *mĕnyĕrbak*.
jĕrbu, *laut jĕrbu*, the sea out of sight of land or when the land is only a dim haze on the horizon.
jĕreh, worn out; dispirited; exhausted; done up.
jĕrĕhak, = *jĕrahak*.
jĕrĕjak, = *jĕrjak*.
jĕreket, adhering rigidly together; so connected that independent movement is not possible.
jĕrĕlok, *mangkok jĕrĕlok*, a deep bowl or cup—v. *jĕlok*.

jĕrĕmal, = *jĕrmal*.
jĕrĕmang, = *jĕrmang*.
jĕrĕmba, meeting suddenly and unexpectedly.
jĕrĕmbap, *mĕnjĕrĕmbap*, to fall to earth in a sitting posture.
jĕrembet, interlinked, intertwined; = *jĕrait*.
jĕrĕmbun, heaped up all together.
jĕrĕnang, = *jĕrnang*.
jĕrengkah, swollen with milk (of the udders).
jĕrepet, interlinked but capable of independent movement (as two links in a chain).
jĕriah, = *jariah*.
jĕriat, = *sĕriat*.
jĕring, a tree with evil smelling pods (*pithecolobium lobatum*).
jĕringai, *mĕnjĕringai*, to grin; also *jĕringing*.
jĕringau, = *jĕrangau*.
jĕringing, *mĕnjĕringing*, to grin; also *jĕringai*.
jĕrit, *mĕnjĕrit*, to shriek; *bĕrjĕritan*, with shrieks; shrieking.
jĕrjak, thin perpendicular laths in Malay atap walls or partitions.
jĕrkah, menacing gesture.
jĕrmal, a marine fish-trap [in which fish are herded by converging rows of stakes into passing over a submerged screen where they are caught by the borders of the screen being raised.]
jĕrmang, short props or buttresses; propping with short props.
jĕrnang, the vegetable product known as "dragon's blood."
jĕrneh, clear, limpid, transparent, pure.
jĕrobong, an awning for deck-cargo or exposed cargo.
jĕroh, very steep and sloping (of a declivity—especially the slope of a roof).
jĕrohok, stumbling into a hole concealed by long grass.
jĕrojol, = *rojol*.

jěrok, a generic name for fruits of the citron class and for acid pickles preserved in salt.
jěrong, a man-eating shark (especially the ground shark).
jěrongkah, uneven, jagged (of a mouthful of teeth).
jěrongkis, gradually falling aslant.
jěrongkong, knocked on one's back.
jěrpak, *měnjěrpak*, to fall over.
jěruju, a flowering shrub (*acanthus ebracteatus*).
jěrukup, joining boughs overhead; over-arching—cf. *rungkup*.
jěrumat, darning.
jěrumbai, dangling of a tassel-fringe.
jěrumbong, a permanent awning in a Malay boat—cf. *jěrobong*.
jěrumbun, the lair of a wild boar.
jěrumun, a (Kedah) variant of *jěrumbun*.
jěrumus, a sprawling attitude; *jatoh těrjěrumus*, to fall sprawling.
jěrungkau, = *rungkau*.
jěrupeh, *měnjěrupeh*, to add a band or layer to the top of anything so as to increase its height.
jěrut, drawing a slip-knot or noose.
Jibrael, Ar. the Archangel Gabriel.
jidar, Ar. the "walls" within which type is confined on some printed pages.
jidwal, = *jadwal*.
jih, = *jir*.
jijak, step, tread; bearing; *běrjijak*, to step on, to touch (with the lower extremities).
jika, if; supposing that.
jikalau, if; supposing that; = *jika-lau* (*lau* being an Arabic equivalent of *jika*).
jilat, licking up; *měnjilat*, to lick up, to lap up.
jilid, Ar. a volume; binding, to bind; *měnjilid*, to bind; *tukang jilid*, a book-binder.
jilit, = *jilid*.
jima', Ar. sexual intercourse; *běrjima' děngan*, to have sexual relations with.

jimat, I. Ar. a talisman. II. Ar. care, attention, solicitude, forethought.
jimbit, lifting an object with the fingers (but not lifting it entirely off the floor).
jin, I. Ar. a wonder-working spirit; a genius; *j. islam*, a good genius; *j. kafir*, an evil genius. II. Hind. a saddle.
jinak, tame, docile, familiar; *j. hati*, familiarised.
jingga, dark yellow; yellow mixed with red.
jinggang, slender; thin.
jingkat, walking painfully on tiptoe or on the side of the foot.
jingkir, a platform on which a newly-confined woman is laid so that she may be warmed.
jinis, = *jěnis*.
jinjal, hardship, trouble.
jinjang, I. narrow and tapering, but not too long (of the neck). II. a native dance. III. the attachment of a spirit to a man; *hantu ta'-běr-jinjang*, a familiar spirit that has not found a master.
jinjing, carrying a light burden, using the fingers only.
jinjit, picking out, pinching out, pulling out (a loose body).
jintan, caraway-seed (*carum caru*); *j. hitam*, the seeds of *nigella sativa*; *j. manis*, anise seed (*pimpinella anisum*); *j. puteh*, cumin seed (*cuminum cyminum*).
jinteh, a generic name for several trees; *j. merah* (*baccaurea wallichii* and *baccaurea griffithii*); *j. puteh* (*urophyllum*, sp.)
jintek, *jintek-jintek*, the larvæ of the mosquito.
jir, target; the point aimed at in a game.
jirai, *sa-jirai*, a strip, a small quantity.
jirak, a tree (*eurya acuminata*).
jiran, Ar. relatives.
jirat, Ar. a non-Muhammadan grave.

jirjir, Ar. olives.
jirus, irrigating—cf. *dirus*.
jismani, Ar. bodily (as against spiritual).
jiwa, Skr. life; the spirit of life; *sĕrahkan, j.*, to give up one's life; *utama j.*, the breath of life; *ayer utama j.*, the water of life; *ayer mĕrta j.*, id.
jodo, = *jodoh*.
jodoh, match; a pair; a counterpart; *jodohan*, counterpart; twin-soul; *jodohkan*, to match.
jogan, Pers. a standard with metallic emblems like the Roman *signum*.
joget, a dancing-girl.
jogi, Skr. a yogi; a religious ascetic.
johan, Pers. a champion; *j. pahlawan*, a warrior champion; *j. arifin*, a champion of learning.
johong, a charm to counteract the machinations of others.
jojol, a bundle of cross-pointed sticks used in making barriers or chevaux-de-frise across a river.
jokong, a variant of *jongkong*.
jolok, poking with a stick at an object above one.
jolong, tip, point; a projecting prow, nose or snout; *buaya jolong-jolong*, the gavial (*tomistoma schlegeli*); *ikan jolong-jolong*, a sword-fish.
jong, a junk.
jongang, projecting, prominent (of the teeth).
jonggar, = *jongkar*.
jongit, curving up (of the upper lip).
jongkah, jagged and projecting (of a tooth).
jongkang, *jongkang-jangking*, raising and falling irregularly (as the points of the picks of a party of coolies).
jongkar, sticking out (as a long object amid short objects); *jongkar-jongkir*, bristling with projecting points.
jongkat, *jongkat-jongkit*, see-sawing, unsteady.

jongkir, *jongkar-jongkir*, bristling with points—v. *jongkar*.
jongkit, to tip up; *jongkat-jongkit*, see-sawing, unsteady.
jongkok, to squat; to stoop down to pick up something.
jongkol, a tin Trengganu coin.
jongkong, a dinghy; a short beamy boat; *sampan j.*, id.; *tampang j.*, a tin coin, or rather slab, cast roughly into the shape of a boat and formerly used as currency.
jongor, snout; nose; projection (such as the bowsprit of a ship or the sword of a sword-fish).
jongos, (Dutch) servant-boy.
jonjot, picking out (as a man picks hemp or oakum).
joran, a fishing-rod.
jorang, a narrow-channel, a water-course, a gully.
joreng, a shred or patch; *tanah sa-j.* a small patch of land.
jori, Hind. a pair of horses; *kuda j.*, id.; *kĕreta j.*, a carriage and pair.
jorong, I. a flat oval betel-nut tray. II. a section, a division, a corner. III. a conical funnel or tube.
jotor, a medicinal drug (unidentified).
jua, and yet; all the same; for all that; still; to some extent; also *juga*, q.v.
juadah, Pers. cakes, provisions.
juah, a heavy curl of the lower lip; *mulut yang j.*, coarse-mouthed—cf. *jueh*.
juai, = *chuai*.
juak, I. a raja's retainer; an attendant generally. II. stretching out a sail; spreading.
jual, selling; *j. janji*, a conditional sale; *bĕrjual-bĕli*, business, trade; *jualan*, a thing for sale; *mĕnjual*, to sell.
juang, the fighting of animals; *bĕrjuang*, to fight—of large animals (especially elephants); *biram bĕrjuang*, a fighting elephant.
juar, *kayu juar*, a black ebony-like

wood used for making plain furniture but not suitable for carving.

juara, a trainer of fighting cocks; *bujang j.*, id.; *ikan j.*, a fish (unidentified).

jubah, Ar. a long surtout worn by hajis.

jubin, *batu jubin*, floor-tiles.

jubong, a variant of *jĕrobong*.

jubur, Ar. the buttocks, the posterior; also *dubur*.

judi, gambling; *main j.* or *bĕrjudi*, to gamble.

jueh, a slight downward curl of the lower lip—cf. *juah*.

juga, and yet; all the same; for all that; still to some extent; *mahu ta'-mahu naik juga*, willing or not up they went all the same; *intan itu batu juga ada-nya*, a diamond is a stone for all that; *tuan ada baik?—baik juga*, are you well?—yes, fairly well.

juita, (Skr. and Kawi) a term of endearment; precious, of great price, rare; *ratna j.*, pearl of price; *mas j.*, gold of fineness; *tali j.*, an ornamental girdle.

jujat, Ar. *mulut jujat*, a slanderer.

jujoh, unbroken succession; continuous.

jujong, = *junjong*.

jujur, I. *wang jujur*, money paid to the parents of a bride by a bridegroom. II. *bĕrjujuran*, sticking out, projecting.

jujut, = *jonjot*.

julai, I. hanging down, heavily laden. II. *julai-julita*, neat, pretty, graceful.

julang, lifting up aloft; bearing up a prince on the shoulders of his vassals at his installation; *julangan*, a seat on the shoulders; *pĕnjulang*, a nurse.

julat, the range or reach of anything; *sa-pĕnjulat pĕluru mĕriam*, the distance a cannon can carry; *tikam mĕnjulat*, stabbing as far as one can reach.

julek, wrapped in a single petal (as a very young bud seems to be).

juli, Hind. a dhooly or litter.

juling, a cast in the eye; squinting.

julir, a fish-spear or harpoon with a detachable barbed head to which a long rope is attached.

julita, *julai-j.*, neat, pretty, graceful.

julong, = *jolong*.

julur, the emergence of a long body; the darting out of a snake's tongue; *mĕnjulur*, to dart out, to dart forward; *tĕrjulur*, hanging out (as the tongue of a corpse).

Jumaat, Ar. *hari Jumaat*, Friday.

jumbai, pendent, dangling—cf. *umbai, jĕrumbai*, etc.

jumhur, Ar. the righteous, the learned in God's way.

jumjumah, Ar. skull.

jumlah, Ar. sum total; *jumlahkan*, to add up.

jumpa, meeting, encountering, coming across; *bĕrjumpa*, to meet.

jumpong, *ikan jumpong*, a fish (*cheilissus chlorurus*).

jumpul, *ikan jumpul*, a fish (unidentified).

junam, downwards motion; diving head foremost; swooping.

junjong, carrying on the head; (by metaphor) obeying a raja's order or submitting oneself to his will; *mĕnjunjong*, to carry on the head; to obey; *j. sireh*, the post on which the *sireh* vine is trailed.

juntai, loose waving suspension; dangling; *bĕrjuntai*, to dangle; *dudok bĕrjuntai*, to sit with the feet dangling in the air.

juput, = *jĕmput*.

juragan, the master of a native *pĕrahu*.

jurai, hanging down loosely of thread-like bodies; forming a loose fringe; *sa-jurai*, a strip.

juram, = *churam*.

juri, = *jori*.

jurit, Jav. *pĕnjurit* or *pĕrjurit*, a warrior; a roving plunderer.

juru, I. a skilled workman other than a handicraftsman; *j. bahasa*, an interpreter; *j. batu* and *j. tinggi* petty officers on a ship; *j. masak*, a cook; *j. tulis*, a writer, a clerk. II. *pĕnjuru*, a corner, an angle.

jurus, I. a pause; a very brief interval of time; *sa-jurus lama-nya*, for a second or two. II. dragging; pulling; hustling. III. a variant of *dirus*. IV. a variant of *lurus*.

juta, Skr. a million.

juz, Ar. a section of the Koran (which is divided into thirty such).

K

ka, I. to; *ka-atas*, upwards; *ka-sana*, thither; *ka-dalam*, into; *ka-mana*, whither. II. Ar. thy (masculine).

kaabah, Ar. the Caaba or great mosque at Mecca.

kabab, Pers. small pieces of meat cooked on a spit.

kabir, I. Ar. great, mighty. II. drawing the paddle towards oneself so as to turn a boat.

kabong, I. the sugar-palm (*arenga saccharifera*); *kalam k.*, the ordinary Malay pen. II. a white band worn as a symbol of mourning.

kabu, *kabu-kabu*, a coarse tree-cotton; *pokok k.-k.*, the shrub (*trevesia sondaica*) from which this cotton is obtained.

kabul, Ar. approval, confirmation; *kabulkan*, to confirm.

kabur, dim-sightedness (as the result of age).

kabus, dimly visible (as distant mountains).

kabut, cloudy, misty, indistinct; mist; *hilang k.*, the clearing away of mist; *kĕlam k.*, extreme obscurity; *mata k.*, dim-sighted.

kacha, glass (the material); *roda k.*, a glass-wheel.

kachak, I. smart; dandified; got up. II. stepping gingerly along; walking quietly on tiptoe.

kachang, a generic name for beans; *k. bendi*, the okra or beni fruit (*hibiscus esculentus*); *k. bunchis*, French beans; *k. China*, the pea-nut (*arachis hypogœa*); also *k. goreng*; *k. chindai*, *phaseolus mungo*; *k. Jĕpun*, the soy bean (*soya hispida*); *k. kara*, *dolichos lablab*; *k. kayu*, the Indian dall (*cajanus indicus*); *k. puteh*, peas; *ikan kachang-kachang*, a fish (*sphyræna acutipinnis*).

kachapuri, the capital of a column; the heart or centre of a building; *durian k.*, a durian that has some flesh at its very centre.

kachar, I. *siput kachar*, a shell (*voluta pulchra*). II. fussy behaviour; running hither and thither.

kachau, confusing, mixing up, a mess; *k. birau*, extreme confusion; *kachaukan*, to upset; to throw into disorder.

kacheh, *kochah-kacheh*, fiddling about with things.

kachip, (Kedah) betel-nut scissors—cf. *kĕlati*.

kachit, = *kachip*.

kachong, Jav. "youngster" (a way of addressing a child).

kachu, (*terra japonica*), catechu.

kadal, Jav. the grass-lizard; = *bĕngkarong*.

kadam, Ar. the sole of the foot; *di-bawah k.*, below the sole of the (prince's) foot—the position of the subject.

kadang, I. *kadang-kadang*, at times; occasionally; *tĕrkadang* or *tĕrkadang-kadang*, id. II. *kadang kĕdayan*, followers or retainers of a Javanese chief; a prince's suite.

kadar, Ar. power, ability; *sa-k.*, as far as one can; as far as one's ability goes.

kadi, Ar. a "kali," a registrar of Muhammadan marriages and divorces to whom certain judicial powers are given; also *kali*.

kadir, Ar. mighty, powerful.

kadok, a vine the leaves of which resemble those of the *sireh* vine (by metaphor) an unworthy imitator; *pa' kadok*, a nickname for a man who poses as learned when he is not so.

kadut, *kain kadut*, a coarse sacking made of *rami* fibre.

kaf, Ar. *bukit kaf*, Mount Kaf (the king of mountains according to Muhammadan tradition).

kafan, = *kapan*.

kafilah, Ar. a caravan.

kafir, Ar. an unbeliever; a non-Muhammadan; also *kapir*.

kafsigar, Pers. a shoe-maker.

kah, an interrogative suffix; *sung-goh-kah*, is it true.

kahin, Ar. a pagan priest.

kahwa, Ar. coffee.

kahwin, = *kawin*.

kaifiat, Ar. manner, way, mode.

kail, line-fishing; *mata kail*, a fish-hook; *mĕngail*, to fish with a hook and line; *pĕngail*, a line-fisherman.

kain, cloth; a sarong; a generic name for patterns of sarongs and kinds of cloth; *k. baju*, sarong and baju; clothing generally; *k. basah* or *k. basahan*, old clothes used as bathing clothes; *k. Batek*, Javanese painted sarongs; *k. bĕlachu*, unbleached calico; *k. chita*, flowered chintz; *k. kadut*, *k. rami* or *k. rawa*, coarse sacking made of *rami* fibre; *k. mas tuli*, a heavy silk fabric; *k. songket*, a heavy silk fabric shot with gold thread; *k. tĕlĕpok*, a printed Malay sarong; *kĕpala k.*, a portion of the sarong differing in pattern from the rest.

kais, scratching up (as a fowl scratches up the earth); drawing anything towards one with a stick, crook, etc.

kait, hooking; catching (of thorns); *di-kait onak*, caught by thorns; *bĕrkait kĕlengkeng*, to sit with the little fingers interlinked (as a bride and bridegroom at the *bĕrsanding* ceremony).

kajai, *tali kajai*, a halter for a horse.

kajang, a kind of waterproof matting used as a protection against rain on boats and carts; *tĕrkajang*, in shelter, protected from the rain.

kaji, *mĕngaji*, to read the Koran; to study.

kakak, I. elder sister; *adek kakak*, younger and elder brothers and sisters; near relatives. [In some works *kakak* is used of elder brothers also, but *abang* is more common colloquially.] II. (onom) *mĕngakak*, to quack (of ducks).

kakaktua, the cockatoo; a nail-extractor (from its resemblance to a cockatoo's beak).

kakanda, elder brother or sister; a politer variant of *kakak*.

kakang, elder brother or sister (used especially in Javanese tales as an equivalent for *kakak*).

kakap, I. *pĕrahu kakap*, a river boat with a lofty prow and stern but a low waist. II. *ikan kakap*, a fish (*lates nobilis*); also *siakap*. III. *mata kakap*, a plug-hole in a boat's bottom.

kakas, *pĕrkakas*, instruments; appliances.

kaki, foot, leg, base, lower extremity, foundation, pedestal; *k. bukit*, the foot of a hill; *k. dian*, a candlestick; *k. langit*, the horizon; *k. tembok*, the foundations of a wall; *bĕkas k.*, footprint; *jalan k.*, to go on foot; *mata k.*, ankles; *tapak k.*, sole of the foot; *pĕkaki layar*, the boom (of a sail).

kaku, hard, stiff, tough; lockjaw.

kal, a measure of capacity; half a *chupak*.

kala, I. Skr. time, epoch, period, age; *apa k.*, when; *barang k.*, whenever; *dahulu k.*, past ages; the past; *pĕrba k.*, id.; *sĕdia k.*, the time that has just gone by; the immediate past; *sĕnja k.*, evening. II. a scorpion; *k. bangkang*, the black forest scorpion; also *k. kala* and *k. lotong*; *k. jĕngking*, the common house-scorpion; *k. lipan*, a name for the centipede—cf. *halipan*; *k. mayar*, a name for the luminous millipede; better *kĕlĕmayar*. III. Skr. the Hindu divinity (Kala); *bĕtara k.*, id.; Siva as the destroyer (usually represented as a maleficent deity).

kalah, I. defeat; being worsted—cf. *alah*. II. (Jalor) a bamboo gong.

kalai, a venomous insect; a sort of water-hornet.

kalak, *sungsang-kalak*, upside down, topsy-turvy.

kalakian, moreover; well then; to continue.

kalalawar, = *kĕlawar*.

kalam, I. Ar. a pen. II. a flaw in a gem; an impurity in a metal.

kalang, I. (Kedah) *kalang ayam*, a hen-roost. II. the name of a piratical tribe of Orang Laut. III. = *galang*.

kalas, I. a thole strap (of rattan). II. Ar. *habis kalas*, utterly exhausted, quite finished.

kalat, the portion of (*nipah*) leaf that is useless as a cigarette-wrapper.

kalau, if; supposing that—an abbreviation of *jikalau*.

kalbu, Ar. heart.

kaldai, Tam. donkey; ass.

kaldu, Port. chicken broth.

kaleh, shifting; change of position; = *aleh*.

kalek, *kolak-kalek*, up and down motion, or motion backwards and forwards.

kali, I. time, occasion, instance; *barang k.*, perhaps; on some possible occasion; *bĕrapa k.*, how often; *sa-kali*, (1) once; (2) altogether; very; *dĕngan sa-kali gus*, all at once; *baik sa-kali*, altogether good, excellent; *sa-kali-kali*, most exceedingly; *sa-kali-pun*, even; *sa-kalian*, all. II. Ar. a kali; a registrar of Muhammadan marriages and divorces who has some judicial powers.

kalikausar, Ar. a river of paradise.

kalimah, Ar. the creed; the attestation of the Muhammadan faith, = *kalimat as-shahadat*.

kaling, I. tinned iron sheeting; *tukang k.*, a tinker. II. *kolang-kaling*, topsy-turvy, upside down.

kalis, inadhesive; irreceptive; impermanent; *dĕndam ta'-kalis*, love that does not pass away; *kalis bagai ayer di-daun kĕladi*, non-permeating, as water on calladium leaf (rolling off like water on a duck's back).

kalok, hook-shaped; *tongkat bĕrkalok*, a walking stick with a crook for handle.

kalong, I. a fruit-bat; = *kĕluang*? II. a metallic ornamental collar. III. *akar kalong*, a wild pepper (*piper caninum*).

kaluar, see *luar* and *kĕluar*.

kama, Skr. *bĕtara kama jaya*, the victorious god of love.

kamar, I. (Dutch) room; a cabin in a ship. II. Ar. the moon.

kamat, Ar. the last call to prayer.

kambang, = *ambang*.

kambau, a turtle (unidentified).

kambĕli, rough woollen cloth such as blankets are made of.

kambi, a thin light planking; a partition; a sort of dado; *pintu k.*, a light door made of a wooden framework covered with cloth.

kambing, a sheep; a goat; *k. biri-biri*, or *k. Bĕlanda*, a sheep; *k. jati*, a goat; *k. Bĕnggala*, a large imported goat; *k. gĕrun*, *k. hutan*, *k. bukit*, *k. gua, k. burong* or *k. gunong*, the Malayan serow (*nemorhoedus swettenhami*); *k. pĕrahan*, a milch-goat; *k. randok*, a rank old he-goat; *kuku k.*, (1) the trotters of a sheep; (2) the feet of a salver; (3) a peculiar forked instrument for planting padi-shoots taken from the nursery.

kambu, the block at the end of a piston-rod; *kayu tiga sa-kambu*, a sort of crude "three-card-trick" based on guessing which of three sticks is the shortest.

kambus, choked up (of a channel or orifice).

kambut, a large padi-basket.

kameja, = *kĕmeja*.

kamek, *komak-kamek*, mouthing; the movement of the mouth when speaking or eating.

kamĕli, = *kambĕli*.

kamĕra, = *kamar*, I.

kami, we—the speaker's party and not including the person addressed; *nous autres*. [In some cases the word is used for I or me—cf. (in English) the royal or editorial "we."]

kamil, Ar. complete; fulfilled.

kamir, Ar. leaven; fermentation.

kamit, *komat-kamit*, the movements of the mouth in speaking or eating; mouthing.

kampil, I. a short heavy pointed sword; also *kampilan*; II. = *kampit*.

kampit, a small bag of plaited *mĕngkuang* work.

kampoh, I. a weapon now obsolete. II. a head-dress mentioned in romance; III. a numeral coefficient for pieces of *tĕrubok* roe, the Malay caviare.

kampong, assembling, grouping; a cluster of houses; a hamlet; the buildings (with out-houses, etc.) making up a dwelling; *kampongkan*, to collect (people) together; *bĕrkampong*, to come together (of people).

kamu, you (usually plural); *k. sakalian*, you all.

kamus, Ar. a dictionary, an encyclopædia.

kan, I. an abbreviation for *akan*. II. a causal suffix to verbs.

kana, Jav. *gĕlang kana*, large hollow armlets.

kanak, *kanak-kanak*, a child; a very young boy or girl.

kanan, the right-hand side; *tangan k.*, the right hand; *sa-bĕlah k.*, on the right.

kanchap, flush with; on an exact level; full to exactness.

kanchapuri, = *kachapuri*.

kanchil, a name given to the small chevrotin (*tragulus pygmæus*) on account of its size—cf. *kĕchil* and *pĕlandok*.

kanching, a bolt; a rivet; a buckle; *kanchingkan* or *mĕnganchingkan*, to bolt (a door); to buckle up; *tĕrkanching*, secure; fastened up.

kanchut, a worn piece of cloth used as a loin-cloth.

kanda, an abbreviation of *kakanda*.

kandang, an enclosure; a pen; a sty; *k. kuda*, a stall for a horse; *k. babi*, a sty; *k. kĕrbau*, a pen for buffaloes.

kandar, carrying on a pole (a burden being hung at each end).

kandas, running aground; being stopped by some obstacle.

kandi, a purse or small satchel; *kandi-kandi*, id.

kandil, Ar. lantern, lamp.

kandis, I. a tree with an edible fruit (*garcinia nigrolineata*). II. Jav. sweets; a type of sweetness.

kandong, carrying in a sack or enclosure; carrying in the womb; *mĕngandong*, to be pregnant.

kandul, folding up in a cloth, curtain or net.

kandut, stowing away in the lap; *kanduti*, to so stow away.

kang, I. the bridle and reins; *k. kuda*, id. II. *kang sĕnohong*, a Javanese title of the highest rank used in addressing royalty or divinity.

kangka, Ch. a gambier plantation (in Johor).

kangkang, wide apart (of the legs); *chĕlah k.*, the perineum; *mĕngangkang*, to step out; *tĕrkangkang*, extended wide apart (of the lower limbs).

kangkong, a white or pink flowered convolvulus—commonly used as a spinach (*ipomea aquatica*).

kangsa, I. = *angsa*. II. = *gangsa*.

kangsin, Ch. a mischief-maker.

kangsur, = *angsur*.

kanjar, I. Pers. a broad dagger. II. tearing at anything; tugging and running.

kanji, rice-gruel; "congee."

kanjus, [congee-house] the lock-up at a police-station; imprisonment; gaol.

kantan, a large wild ginger (*nicolaia imperialis*).

kantang, a mud-bank at a river mouth.

kantil, *kontal-kantil*, pendulous and swaying (of a short thick pendant) —cf. *anting, kanting*, etc.

kanting, *kontang-kanting*, dangling and swinging (of a long pendant)— cf. *anting, kantil*, etc.

Kantong, Ch. the Canton province; *Orang China Kantong*, Muhammadan Chinese from Yunnan.

kantu, cramped stiffness in the limbs.

kantur, (Dutch) a police court in the Dutch Indies.

kap, I. the roof of a palanquin; the hood of a carriage. II. *kain kap*, a kincob. III. to fix a cable.

kapa, nervous trembling; *tĕrkapa-kapa*, in a quiver.

kapada, to; = *ka-pada*.

kapah, = *kapa*.

kapai, *tĕrkapai-kapai*, nervously moving about the arms (as a bad swimmer; flapping (as a flag).

kapak, an axe; *bĕndera k.*, a broad ensign; *gigi k.*, large front teeth;

ular k., a generic name for viperine snakes, notably *k. bakau* (*lachesis purpureomaculatus*), *k. rimba* (*l. wagleri*) and *k. daun* (*l. gramineus*).

kapal, Tam. a ship; *k. api*, a steamer; *k. hantu*, see *lanchang*; *k. layar*, a sailing ship.

kapan, I. Ar. a shroud; a winding-sheet; *tĕrkapan*, shrouded, sheeted. II. (Batavia) when; = *bila*.

kapang, the *teredo navalis*.

kapar, lying strewn about without order or method; *bĕrkaparan*, scattered about.

kapas, cotton; a generic name for cultivated cottons (especially *gossypium herbaceum*); *limau k.*, the common lime (*citrus acida*).

kapek, I. *kopak-kapek*, very limp and pendulous (of the breasts). II. *kopak-kapek*, plucked to pieces, scattered, dispersed.

kapi, I. a pulley. II. Ar. accomplished, complete.

kapir, Ar. infidel; non-Muhammadan; also *kafir*.

kapis, a generic name for shells of the genus *pecten*.

kapit, support on each side; *pĕngapit*, a supporter, a second—cf. *apit*.

kapitan, Port. a headman of a racial division of the population.

kapok, I. tree-cotton; the cotton of *eriodendron anfractuosum*. II. to enfold in the arms and climb (as a tree-trunk or pillar is climbed).

kapong, = *apong*.

Kapri, Caffre, African, Negro.

kapur, camphor; chalk; the lime eaten with *sireh*; *sireh sa-k.*, a quid of betel; *k. barus*, camphor; *k. Bĕlanda*, chalk; *k. masak*, plaster; *k. tohor*, whitewash.

kapus, = *apus*.

kara, I. *kachang kara*, a plant (*dolichos lablab*). II. *udang kara*, a large crab or lobster.

karah, I. spotted, variegated; *kulit karah*, tortoise-shell; *pĕnyu k.*, the turtle yielding the best shell. II. *sa-batang karah*, alone; by oneself.

karam, I. to founder; to go down (of a ship); to be wrecked. II. Ar. term of abuse.

karang, I. a reef, a coral bank; coralline sponge; *kĕna k.*, to run on a reaf; *batu k.*, (1) coralline rock; (2) galena ore; *bunga k.*, a sponge; *isi k.*, shells, corals, etc. (picked up on the shore); also *karang-karangan*; *pĕnyakit karang-karang*, a form of syphilis; *bĕrkarang*, to go hunting for shells. II. order, arrangement; literary composition; an ordered garden; *karangan*, composition, setting; *karang-mĕngarang*, to do literary work; *karangkan*, to set in order; to compose; *pĕngarang*, an author.

karap, a weaver's comb.

karat, I. rust; deterioration; *k. di-hati*, malice; *bĕrkarat*, to rust. II. to fight with claws (as cats) or pincers (as crabs); *k. gigi*, to grind the teeth.

karau, stirring up, disturbing; stirring up the oil when frying.

kareh, stirring up rice with a spoon when boiling the rice.

karib, Ar. near (especially of near relations).

karim, Ar. merciful, generous.

karna, Skr. because; owing to.

karong, a coarse sack made of matting.

kartas, = *kĕrtas*.

Karun, Ar. Korah (the enemy of Moses), believed by Malays to have been a man of enormous wealth whose treasure is now buried in the earth for wizards to find.

karut, involved, self-contradictory, obscure, lying.

kasa, Ar. a rich cloth.

kasad, Ar. wish, intention, resolve.

kasai, a cosmetic face-powder, better known as *bĕdak*.

kasap, I. rough to the touch (as coarse paper or coarse wool). II. a sailor whose duty it is to attend to the lamps, flags, cordage, etc., of a ship.

kasar, coarse or rough in texture; coarse in manner.

kasau, a rafter, a cross-beam; *k. jantan*, the main rafters; *k. bĕtina*, the subsidiary rafters.

kaseh, affection, love, strong liking; *tĕrima k.*, " the receipt of favour "— a Malay equivalent of "thank you"; *kasehan*, kindness, favour; pity, an unfortunate thing; *kasehani*, *kasehankan* or *mĕngasehankan*, to show pity for; to pity; *kasehi* or *mĕngasehi*, to love; *mĕngaseh*, to be in love with; *pĕngaseh*, a creator of love— e.g. a love-philtre; *kĕkaseh*, the object of love; beloved; see also *kasi*.

kasek, *kosak-kasek*, the sound of a restless man fidgeting on a couch.

kasi, I. give (in "bazaar" Malay); = *bĕri*. [This word is possibly a variant of *kaseh*.] II. Hind. castration, gelding; *lĕmbu k.*, a bullock; *ayam k.*, a capon.

kasih, = *kaseh*.

kasrah, Ar. the name of one of the vowel-points; *e* or *i*.

kasut, shoes, boots; *pakai k.*, to wear boots; *k. kayu*, clogs; *tapak k.*, the sole of a shoe.

kata, saying, utterance; *bĕrkata*, to say, to speak; *bĕrkata-kata*, to have the power of speech; *mĕngatakan*, to utter, to mention; *pĕrkataan*, a saying.

katak, a frog, a toad; *k. bĕtong*, the bull-frog; *k. lempong*, a frog (*oxyglossus*, sp.); *k. pisang*, a green frog with great leaping powers (*rana erythræa* or *rhacophorus leucomystax*); *k. puru*, a toad; *buaya k.*, a broad-bodied variety of crocodile; *mĕriam k.*, a gun of few calibres, a howitzer.

katang, I. *katang-katang*, a small *mĕngkuang* pouch for drugs. II. *katang-katang*, runners; rattan rings allowing a pole to have free play up and down—e.g. the poles forcing down the submerged screen in a large fish-trap of the *jĕrmal* type. III. *ular katang tĕbu*, the banded karait (*bungarus fasciatus*).

katek, stunted, dwarf (of a cock).

kati, a measure of weight; a "catty" = 1¼ lb.

katib, Ar. writer.

katil, Tam. a bedstead.

katir, outrigger.

katlum, Tam. bastion.

katok, = *kĕtok*.

katong, I. a turtle (unidentified). II. = *atong*. III. = *kotong*.

katup, closing up tightly; *tĕrkatup*, closed; *mulut tĕrkatup*, silenced.

kau, thou; you; = *ĕngkau*.

kaul, Ar. *bĕrkaul*, to offer prayers—(e.g. at a shrine) with the object of bringing about some special event.

kaum, Ar. crowd, multitude, family, people; *k. kĕluarga*, family.

kaup, = *kaut*.

kaus, I. Ar. shoes; *di-bawah k.*, below the sovereign's foot; the position of a subject. II. Eng. couch.

kaut, scraping towards oneself; striking towards oneself.

kawah, a cauldron, a kettle, the crater of a volcano.

kawal, Tam. watching; the work of a sentry or watchman; *kĕras k.*, a rigorous watch; *kawalan*, a watch, a guard; *mĕngawal* or *bĕrkawal*, to be on the watch; *mĕngawali*, to be watching over.

kawan, a company, a party; a herd or flock; accompaniment; a companion; a friend; *k. gajah*, a herd of elephants; *k. pĕnyamun*, a band of robbers.

kawang, *minyak kawang*, the fat of the tree *diplocnemia sebifera*.

kawar, = *gawar*.

kawat, wire; *surat k.*, a telegram.

kawi, I. *bahasa kawi*, the old poetic language of Java; *kĕkawin*, a poetic narrative. II. *batu kawi*, cinnabar, manganese. III. Ar. *bĕsi kawi*, iron of supernatural hardness.

kawin, I. Pers. marriage, wedding; *mas k.*, the settlements on a bride. II. *tombak pĕngawinan*, a state halbert. III. *kĕkawin*, a poetic narrative—v. *kawi*, I.

kaya, I. wealth, power; *mĕnjadi k.*, to become rich; *orang k.*, (1) a rich man; (2) a Malay dignitary; *Tuhan Yang K.*, God Almighty; *kĕkayaan Tuhan*, the power of God. II. *buah sĕri kaya* or *buah sireh kaya*, the bullock's heart fruit (*anona squamosa*).

kayal, Ar. intoxicated, inebriated.

kayap, a dangerous eruptive disease.

kayau, I. Dyak head hunting. II. overflooding; inundation.

kayoh, a paddle; *bĕrkayoh*, to paddle (intransitive); *kayohkan*, to paddle (transitive); *pĕngayoh*, a paddle.

kayu, wood; wooden; *k. api*, firewood; *k. arang*, ebony; *k. gaharu*, camphor wood; *k. manis*, cinnamon; *akar k.*, a creeping or climbing plant; *ayer k.*, wood and water; ship's stores; *batang k.*, a log, a tree-trunk; *buah k.*, fruit; *daun k.*, a leaf; *kulit k.*, bark; *pokok k.*, a tree.

kayul, flavourless (of tobacco).

kĕbabal, the young half-grown *nangka* or *chĕmpĕdak* fruit.

kĕbah, I. breaking into perspiration during fever. II. rubbing quicksilver into the body (to render a man invulnerable).

kĕbahi, a Javanese village official.

kebak, gaping open (of a deep cut).

kĕbal, impenetrability of the flesh; invulnerability.

kĕbam, I. *kĕbam bibir*, to turn in the lips till they cease to be visible. II. leaden-coloured (of the sky).

keban, a work-basket (of *mĕngkuang* leaf) made at Malacca.

kĕbas, I. (onom.) shaking out a cloth vigorously; *kĕbas-kĕbus*, the sound of cloth being shaken. II. deadened,

paralysed temporarily (of a limb)—
e.g. by a blow on the funny-bone
or the attack of an electric ray.
kĕbat, = *bĕbat.*
kĕbaya, Port. a long outer garment
worn by Malay, Eurasian and Straits
Chinese women.
kĕbayan, Jav. an order; a village
regulation; a village headman;
nenek k., an old woman who plays a
great part in Malay romance as the
complaisant guardian of princesses.
kĕbek, having one's tongue in one's
cheek.
kĕbil, the blinking of an absent-
minded man; inattentiveness;
absent-mindedness.
kĕbin, = *kĕban.*
kĕbirah, = *kĕmbiri.*
kĕbiri, = *kĕmbiri.*
kĕbok, a hollow cylinder used in
making vermicelli.
kĕbun, a plantation; a garden; an
estate; *tukang k.*, a gardener.
kĕbur, to clean a well by agitating
the water.
kĕbus, (onom.) *kĕbas-kĕbus,* the rustling of stiff cloth when beaten or
shaken.
kĕchah, *kĕchoh-kĕchah,* fussing about,
always on the move.
kĕchambah, a seed bud.
kĕchap, (onom.) tasting; smacking
the lips; sobbing; the sound made
by a lizard; *mĕngĕchap,* to sob.
kĕchapi, Skr. a native lute with four
strings; *buah k.*, the fruit of *sandoricum radiatum.*
kechek, wheedling, worrying by importunity; *kĕna k.*, to be taken in
by plausible stories; to be talked into
a foolish bargain.
kecheng, having one eye closed.
kĕchewa, injured; put to shame.
kechi, Eng. a ketch; a sailing vessel
of small tonnage and light draft.
kĕchik, = *kĕchil.*
kĕchil, small; inferior; younger;
dari k., from youth up; *k. hati,*

malice, a grudge; *mĕngĕchilkan,* to
reduce in size.
kĕchoh, *kĕchoh-kĕchah,* fussing about;
fidgeting; always on the move.
kechoh, cheating at cards, swindling.
kechong, swindling by denying a
debt incurred; repudiating a fair
claim.
kĕchopong, = *kĕtopong.*
kĕchuak, Ch. a cockroach; = *lipas.*
kĕchuali, excepting; *k. kĕbanyakan,*
a number of—i.e. a certain minority.
kĕchubong, the datura (*datura metel*
and *datura fatuosa*); *mabok k.*, the
intoxication produced by datura
poisoning; *batu k.*, the amethyst.
kĕchundang, the relationship of the
conquered to the conqueror; a "conquest."
kĕchup, kissing with the lips (and
not in the Malay way—cf. *chium*);
kĕchupi, to kiss.
kĕchut, shrunken, shrivelled up.
kĕdadah, = *kĕdadak.*
kĕdadak, a choleraic attack [the
word is only used as a rule in the
expression *chĕkek k.*, an imprecation
calling down a horrible death upon
a person].
kĕdah, I. exposed, wide open; *mangkok k.*, a bowl with a wide mouth.
II. Kedah.
kĕdai, a shop; a selling booth; *bĕr-
kĕdai,* to keep a shop.
kĕdak, I. (onom.) *kĕdak-kĕdok,* the
noise made by a rickety cart on a
bad road. II. *lintang kĕdak,* lying
across each other confusedly.
kĕdal, a disease causing discoloration
of the skin.
kĕdali, = *kĕndali.*
kĕdang, stretched out; with limbs
extended.
kĕdangsa, *limau kĕdangsa,* a cultivated lime (*citrus acida*).
kĕdap, I. tight, close, almost waterproof in closeness. II. *sa-kĕdap,* a
handful (of stalks, especially padi-
stalks).

kĕdau, *mĕngĕdau*, to cry out loudly —e.g. for assistance.

kĕdaung, *pokok kĕdaung*, a large tree (*parkia roxburghii*).

kĕdayan, Jav. servants, followers of a prince.

kĕdek, a slight bend; *dudok tĕrkĕdek*, sitting with shoulders bent.

kĕdĕkek, a greenish medicinal compound resembling salt.

kĕdĕlai, *kachang kĕdĕlai*, a plant (*phaseolus mungo*).

kĕdĕmpong, I. worm-eaten (of fruit). II. a tobacco-pouch made of *mĕngkuang* leaf.

kĕdĕngkek, extreme emaciation.

kĕdĕpong, = *kĕdĕmpong*.

kĕdĕra, *ikan kĕdĕra*, a fish (unidentified).

kĕdewas, *bawal kĕdewas*, a fish (unidentified but probably *stromateus* sp.)

kĕdi, congenital impotence.

kĕdidi, a generic name for small sandpipers (*totanus*) and plovers (*ægialitis*).

kĕdit = *kĕndit*.

kĕdondong, a generic name for a number of trees mostly of the genus *canarium*.

kĕdu, a slight stoop (such as that of a writer at a desk).

kĕdudok, a generic name for a number of plants with showy pink flowers (*melastoma polyanthum* and allied species); also *sĕndudok*.

kĕdut, a crease, a wrinkle; *bĕrkĕdut*, crumpled (of a dress).

kehel, inharmonious, out of place; out of its course (of a ship).

kĕhĕndak, see *hĕndak*.

kĕjam, closing (the eye) for some time; keeping (the eye) shut; *kĕjamkan* or *mĕngĕjamkan*, to close (the eyes).

kĕjan, inciting, stimulating.

kĕjang, stretching out the limbs stiffly (as a man yawning or as a man in agony).

kĕjap, closing (the eye) for a moment; winking; *sa-kĕjap*, the time it takes to wink; an instant only— cf. *kĕjip*.

kĕjar, pursuit; *mĕngĕjar*, to pursue.

kĕjat, immovably imbedded; firmly stuck in a place; definitely settled.

kĕji, discreditable, disgraceful, infamous; *nama yang k.*, infamy.

kĕjip, a wink, = *kĕjap* (but even shorter in duration).

keju, Port. cheese.

kĕjur, stiff, unpliable, inelastic.

kĕjut, sudden alarm; nervous shock; *tĕrkĕjut*, startled.

kek, (onom.) the note of the argus pheasant.

kĕkah, a long-armed monkey—either a gibbon (*hylobates*) or a leaf-monkey (*semnopithecus*), but not the common *semnopithecus obscurus*.

kĕkal, enduring, lasting, eternal; *akhirat yany k.*, eternal life; *kĕkalkan*, to perpetuate.

kĕkandi, = *kandi-kandi*.

kĕkang, = *kang*.

kĕkar, to set things further apart.

kĕkaseh, see *kaseh*.

kĕkat, scum and drifting matter on the surface of water; *mati k.*, dead low water; *balek k.*, the turn of the tide.

kĕkau, starting out of sleep in terror.

kĕkawin, see *kawi*.

kekek, I. a gusset. II. (onom.) a giggling laugh.

kekel, extreme stinginess.

kĕkĕtua, = *kakaktua*.

kekok, awkward, blundering, clumsy.

kĕlabat, Ar. a seed (*foenum græcum*).

kĕlabu, grey or ash-coloured; *mata k.*, a film over the eye.

kĕladak, dregs, refuse; the last and worst of anything.

kĕladi, a common name for a number of aroids (notably *colocasia antiquorum*).

kĕlahi, fighting, disputing, quarrelling; *bĕrkĕlahi*, to be engaged in a quarrel, to quarrel.

kělak, an idiomatic adverbial expression indicative of future possibility; may; possibly; perhaps; *burong k.*, a bird (*macropygia assimilis*).

kělakar, joking, jesting.

kělam, darkness, gloom obscurity; *k. kabut*, profound gloom; cloudy gloom; *pěning k.*, dizziness affecting the optic nerve.

kělambit, the large fruit-bat (*pteropus edulis*); also *kěluang*.

kělambu, a mosquito-curtain.

kělambur, dimpled, wrinkled.

kělamin, a pair (male and female); a married couple.

kělamkari, a cloth-fabric; a climbing plant (unidentified).

kělana, I. wandering; a vagabond; *k. yang hina papa*, a miserable wandering wretch. II. a Bugis title given in Sungei Ujong to a ruling chief.

kelang, the rollers or crushers of a mill; a mill; *k. ubi*, a tapioca-mill.

kělangkang, the perineum; also *kělěngkang*.

kělanit, opening out a seam.

kělapa, the coconut (*cocos nucifera*); *k. hijau*, the young coconut, also *k. muda*. [But *nyiur* is the commoner word for coconut in the Northern States.]

kělar, a dent; a cut which does not altogether sever.

kělara, *ikan kělara*, a fish (unidentified).

kělarah, a maggot which eats into wood and fruit.

kělarai, a peculiar diamond-shaped pattern.

kělasa, a hard protuberant mass of flesh; a hump.

kělasak, I. a floor-mat. II. a long, light shield of leather or wood with a handle in the centre.

kělasi, I. Pers. a sailor. II. the long-nosed Borneo monkey (*hylobates leuciscus*).

kělat, I. acidity of taste setting the teeth on edge. II. *tali kělat*, the sheet of a small boat. III. a generic name for a number of trees (mostly of the genus *eugenia*).

kělati, I. betel-nut scissors. II. = *kěliti*.

kělau, *kělip-kělau*, glistening (as the surface of the sea); alternating brightness and darkness (as when shadows chase each other).

kělawar, a generic name for bats; *k. gua*, a name given to the bats *chiromeles torquatus* and *nycticeius kuhli*.

kělayu, *pokok kělayu*, a tree (*arytera littoralis*).

kěldu, = *kuldu*.

kěldai, = *kaldai*.

kělebet, *měngělebet*, to turn up the edge, tip or fold of anything to see what lies underneath.

kělěbok, (onom.) the sound of a heavy body falling on a flat surface.

kělěburan, a pit; a chasm.

kělěbut, a fez-rest.

kěledang, a large tree (*artocarpus lanceæfolia*).

kěledar, defensive measures or preparations.

kěledek, *ubi kěledek*, a common tuber (*convolvulus batatas?*) *lawyer k.*, a cheap lawyer.

kělědut, crumpled, ruffled—cf. *kědut*.

kěleh, seeing, noticing, glancing at.

kelek, carrying anything under the arm without using a cloth or sling.

kělěkati, = *kělěkatu*.

kělěkatu, the flying ant; the Malay equivalent for the proverbial moth which is attracted by flame and perishes in it.

kělěkian, = *kalakian*.

kělelut, *kata běrkělelut*, broken and inaccurate speech.

kělěmarin, = *kělmarin*.

kělěmayar, the luminous millipede.

kělěmbahang, a wild aroid [the leaves of which give a sort of itch to the hand that clasps them]; *anak k.*, a term of abuse.

kĕlĕmbai, *sang kĕlĕmbai*, the name of a wonder-working wizard in Malay folk-lore.

kĕlĕmbak, a fragrant wood (*radix rhei*)?

kĕlĕmbong, blown out with wind; a blister.

kĕlĕmoyang, a name given to a number of plants, including *homolomena coerulescens, h. rostrata* and others.

kĕlĕmping, flabby and pendulous (of the breasts).

kĕlĕmumur, scurf, dandruff.

kĕlĕmunting, = *kĕmunting*.

kĕlĕndara, the ring or fastening connecting a boom with the mast.

kĕlĕngar, swooning, fainting, loss of consciousness.

kĕlĕngkang, the perineum; also *kĕlangkang*.

kĕlengkang, a key-ring; also *gĕlang kunchi*.

kĕlengkeng, I. *burong kĕlengkeng*, the small pied hornbill (*anthracoceros albirostris*). II. *jari kĕlengkeng*, the little finger; *kurong k.*, the innermost chamber in a fish trap.

kĕlĕngkok, a (Kedah) variant of *kĕlongkong*.

kĕlĕnjar, *buah kĕlĕnjaran* or *biji kĕlĕnjaran*, the lymphatic glands; *sakit kĕlĕnjaran*, bubonic inflammation.

kĕlĕnong, (onom.) the booming of a gong.

kĕlĕntang, (onom.) the clanging of a gong.

kĕlentang, *buah kĕlentang*, the horseradish (obtained from the plant *moringa pterygosperma*).

kĕlĕnting, (onom.) the tinkling of a gong.

kĕlĕntit, the clitoris.

kĕlĕntong, (onom.) the booming of a gong.

kĕlentong, (onom.) a Chinese hawker (so called from the gonglike instrument he uses to draw attention to his passing presence).

kĕlĕnyar, scratching continually (of a man troubled with itch).

kĕlĕpai, broken and crooked (but not absolutely pendulous—as a broken twig)—cf. *kĕlepet*.

kĕlepak, heavy and pendulous (of the breasts)—cf. *kĕlepek*.

kĕlĕpat, caulking (a boat).

kĕlepek, light and pendulous (as the broken wing of a bird)—cf. *kĕlepak*.

kĕlepet, a turned down corner (of a page)—cf. *kĕlebet*.

kĕlĕpir, the testes.

kĕlĕpit, hanging down slightly (as a broken twig)—cf. *kĕlĕpai*.

kĕlesek, the thin skin or coating on an object (such as a banana-stem or aloe-leaf).

kĕlĕtak (onom.) continuous rapping —cf. *kĕtak*.

kĕlĕtang, (onom.) the clang of metal falling on the ground.

kĕlĕtar, quivering, trembling—cf. *kĕtar*.

kĕlĕtek, (onom.) the sound of continued ticking.

kĕlĕting, (onom.) the sound of continuous tinkling.

kĕlĕtok, (onom.) continuous rapping or knocking—cf. *kĕtok*.

kĕlĕtong, (onom.) a thumping sound.

kĕlewang, a heavy chopping broadsword used by Achehnese.

kĕlewer, (Dutch) a foresail.

kĕli, *ikan kĕli*, a cat-fish (*clarias majur*).

kĕlian, a surface mine; = *galian*.

kĕlibat, I. a double-bladed paddle. II. the wriggling movement with which a leech gets over the ground; *tĕrkĕlibat-kĕlibat*, wriggling on forward.

kĕlichi, a hard fruit (unidentified— used in playing some children's games).

kĕlichu, pilfering (stealing a little at a time).

kĕlikir, I. a loop of rattan; the thole-strap. II. *batu kĕlikir*, gravel.

kĕliling, position round; the part around; *bĕrkĕliling*, around, encircling; *mĕngĕliling* or *mĕngĕlilingi*, to encircle; to travel round; *kĕlilingkan* or *mĕngĕlilingkan*, to whirl round; to bear round.
kĕlim, a small seam; hemming.
kĕlinchir, = *gĕlinchir*.
kĕlindan, strong sewing thread.
Kĕling, "Kling," a name applied to all immigrants from the Coromandel coast (but sometimes limited to Muhammadan immigrants from that coast the others being called *Orang Hindu*); *orang K.*, a Tamil or Telugu; *nĕgĕri K.*, the Madras Presidency.
kĕlingsir, = *gĕlingsir* and *gĕlinchir*.
kĕlip, a twinkle; the appearance and disappearance of light; the peculiar radiance of the stars; *kĕlip-kĕlip*, fireflies; spangles; *kĕlip-kĕlau*, shimmering.
kĕliru, confusion of thought; muddle-headedness; *pikir k.*, id.; *barang k.*, a thing difficult to grasp (mentally).
kĕlisa, I. a church. II. *kachang kĕlisa*, a plant (unidentified).
kĕlit, dodging, avoiding, getting out of the way.
kĕlitah, manner, idiosyncracy; *banyak kĕlitah*, capricious, uncertain of temper.
kĕliti, a thole-pin.
kĕlmarin, yesterday; *k. dahulu*, the day before yesterday; also *kĕmarin*.
kĕlochah, broken (of water); choppy (of the sea).
kĕlodak, thunder—cf. *kĕlodan*.
kĕlodan, *panah kĕlodan*, a thunderbolt—cf. *kĕlodak*.
kĕloh, deep breathing, sighing; *k. kĕsah*, sighing and restless (as a lover); *mĕngĕloh*, to sigh.
kĕlok, a curve; an arc; a semicircle; *bĕrkĕlok-kĕlok*, cut in semi-circles (of a border)—cf. *lok*, *tĕlok*, etc.

kĕlola, I. management; superintendence of work. II. steel; also *kĕluli*.
kĕlompang, the broken egg-shell when the chicken has been hatched.
kĕlompok, a cluster; a collection of many objects in one place; a group.
kĕlonet, *sa-kĕlonet*, a little.
kĕlong, I. curved, arching, concave —cf. *kĕlok*. II. a wooden shield large enough to protect the whole body. III. *tikam kĕlong*, to turn on its keeper (of an elephant).
kelong, a large marine fish-trap used off the coast of Malacca and Selangor. [It consists of several compartments; fish are hustled from the outer into the inmost and smallest where the entrance is closed and the fish caught.]
kĕlongkong, the soft-shelled young coconut.
kĕlongsong, a very thin loose wrapper or covering such as the tissue-paper cover of a fez, the leaf enfolding the maize or the slough of a snake.
kĕlongsor, = *gĕlongsor*.
kĕlontang, a noisy scare-crow used for frightening away birds from the padi-fields.
kĕlopak, a sheath or covering (of leaf); the calyx of a flower; a similar covering though not of leaf; *k. mata*, the eye-lid; *k. salak*, the calyx of the *salak* (*zalacca edulis*).
kĕlorak, *rumput kĕlorak*, a grass (*lophaterium gracile*).
kĕlosok, = *gĕlosok*.
kĕloyak, tattered and torn—cf. *koyak*.
kĕlpat, = *kĕlĕpat*.
kĕlu, dump, speechless.
kĕluang, a large fruit-bat (*pteropus edulis*); *siku k.*, a very acute angle.
kĕluar, motion outwards, = *ka-luar*; to go out; *mĕngĕluar* or *mĕngĕluari*, to issue; *mĕngĕluarkan*, to drive out; to remove out.

kĕluarga, Skr. family; kinsfolk; circle of relation; *kaum k.*, id.

kĕlubi, *asam kĕlubi*, a plant (*zalacca conferta*).

kĕlubong, veiling; to veil—cf. *sĕlubong*.

kĕlueh, *mĕngĕlueh*, to empty (one's pockets, etc.) by turning them out.

kĕluli, steel; also *kĕlola*.

kĕlulus, a ship of an obsolete type mentioned in old romances.

kĕlulut, a small bee (*trigona*, sp.)

kĕlumbong, = *kĕlubong*.

kĕlumpong, = *kĕlompok*.

kĕlun, *bĕrkĕlun*, to raise in spirals (of smoke)—cf. *lok, tĕlok, kĕlong* I., etc.

kĕluna, a climber with green berries (*smilax megacarpa*).

kĕlupas, *mĕngĕlupas*, to keep peeling off; to waste away—cf. *kupas*.

kĕlupur, *mĕngĕlupur*, to struggle and sprawl (of a slaughtered fowl).

kĕlur, to call; = *panggil*.

kĕlurut, a gathering or sore near the finger-tip.

kĕlus, an edible sea-worm.

kĕmala, a talisman; a luminous bezoar; also *gĕmala*.

kĕmalai, *lĕmah kĕmalai*, extreme lassitude; also *lĕmah gĕmalai*.

kĕmam, mouthing but not swallowing—(e.g. as a quid of tobacco is held in the mouth).

kĕmamam, weakness after illness.

kĕmang, an evil spirit affecting newborn children.

kĕmangi, *mĕdang kĕmangi*, a tree (*cinnamomum parthenoxylon*).

kĕmarau, a drought; *musim k.*, the dry season.

kĕmarin, yesterday; *k. dahulu*, the day before yesterday; also *kĕlmarin*.

kĕmarok, ravenous hunger.

kĕmas, packing; storing away in limited space; *kĕmaskan*, to pack (anything) up.

kĕmayoh, = *pĕngayoh*, from *kayoh*.

kĕmbal, a pouch or basket made of *mĕngkuang* leaf.

kĕmbala, = *gĕmbala*.

kĕmbali, return; going back to the point of original departure; *hidop k.*, to come to life again; *k. karahmat Allah*, to return to God's mercy; to die; *kĕmbalikan*, to give (anything) back; to resume.

kĕmban, fastening the sarong round the breast.

kĕmbang, expansion; spreading out; opening out (of a flower); *kain k.*, a sarong worn without trowsers underneath; *k. hati*, exultation; *bĕrkĕmbang*, to blossom out; *tĕrkĕmbang*, expanded, spread out.

kĕmbar, twin; duplication; *anak k.*, twin children; *saudara sa-k.*, twin-brothers; *mĕngĕmbari*, to duplicate.

kĕmbara, *mĕngĕmbara*, to wander; to rove.

kĕmbayat, *kain kĕmbayat*, cloth from Cambay in India.

kĕmbili, a tuber (*coleus tuberosus*).

kĕmbiri, gelding, castration; *ayam k.*, a capon.

kĕmboja, the frangipanni (*plumiera acutifolia*).

kĕmbong, inflation, blowing out; *pĕrut k.*, inflation after meals; *tĕrkĕmbong*, swollen out, puffed out.

kĕmdian, = *kĕmudian*.

kĕmeh, *bĕrkĕmeh*, to pass urine.

kĕmeja, Port. a shirt.

kĕmĕjan, = *kĕmĕnyan*.

kĕmek, dented (but not perforated); *hidong k.*, a nose eaten into by disease; *kĕmok k.*, covered with dents.

kĕmĕlut, the crisis in a disease.

kĕmĕndalu, a mistletoe; a tree-parasite; also *bĕndalu*.

kĕmĕndikai, a water-melon; also *mĕndikai*.

kĕmĕndit, = *kĕndit*.

kĕmĕntam, (onom.) to keep stamping on the ground.

kĕmĕnyan, benzoin; *kayu k.*, the tree (*styrax benzoin*); *pokang k.* or *bakar*

k., to burn benzoin; *yu kĕmĕnyan*, a species of dog-fish (unidentified).
kĕmĕring, a were-tiger.
kĕmetut, dwarfed (of fruit).
kĕmi, = *gĕmi*.
kĕmiri, the candle-nut (*aleurites moluccanus*); also *buah kĕras*.
kĕmok, *kĕmok-kĕmek*, covered with dents—cf. *kĕmek*.
kĕmonchak, summit, top, crest.
kĕmpa, Pers. a seal of state; the great seal.
kĕmpang, a sort of dug-out used on rivers.
kĕmpas, a large tree (*cumpassia malaccensis*).
kĕmpek, restlessness aroused by curiosity.
kĕmpilur, a wicker-work case divided into compartments.
kĕmpis, shrinking; becoming smaller in bulk through the gradual withdrawal of contents.
kĕmpit, = *kĕpit*.
kĕmpong, shrunken about the cheeks (as a toothless man).
kĕmpu, a round box or case with a cover to it.
kĕmpul, *tĕrkĕmpul-kĕmpul*, slow and laborious (of progress).
kĕmpum, = *kĕmpong* and *kĕpum*.
kĕmput, = *kĕmpong* and *kĕpum*.
kĕmpunan, a dilemma, a fix.
kĕmudi, a rudder; *bĕrkĕmudi*, to have the rudder, to steer; *k. chawat*, a rudder of European type; *k. sepak*, a paddle-rudder of the Malay type —cf. *kĕmudian* and *mudek*.
kĕmudian, after, afterwards, subsequent to; *k. daripada itu*, subsequently; *hari yang k.*, days to come.
kĕmukus, = *kĕmungkus*.
kĕmukut, = *dĕmukut*.
kĕmunchup, = *chĕmuchup*.
kĕmungkus, I. cubebs. II. *tĕlor kĕmungkus*, addled egg.
kĕmuning, the name of a tree yielding a beautifully-veined yellow wood (*murraya exotica*).

kĕmunting, the rose-myrtle (*rhodomyrtus tomentosa*); also *kĕrmunting*.
kĕmut, gentle throbbing movement (such as that of the pulse or of the fontanel).
ken, Skr. a title of Javanese ladies; also *kin*.
kĕna, contact; to incur; to experience; to exactly touch or hit off; *k. denda*, to incur a fine; *k. sakit*, to fall ill; *kĕnakan* or *mĕngĕnakan*, to affix, to put on; to deceive; *tĕrkĕna*, deceived, taken in.
kĕnal, recognition; knowledge by sight; *kĕnali*, *mĕngĕnal* or *mĕngĕnali*, to recognise; *kĕnalan*, an acquaintance.
kĕnan, lying, approval; *bĕrkĕnan*, to take kindly to something; *mĕmpĕrkĕnankan*, to approve, to assent to.
kĕnang, recalling to mind; loving remembrance; *kĕnangan*, loving recollection; *kĕnangkan*, to regret; to affectionately recall.
kĕnanga, a tree with scented green flowers (*cananga odorata*).
kĕnantan, *ayam kĕnantan*, a white fowl (especially a white fighting-cock).
kĕnapa, why, for what reason; = *kĕna apa*.
kĕnari, Eng. canary-seed (*canarium commune*); *burong kĕnari*, the canary.
kĕnas, shell-fish preserved in brine (with rice, sago, etc.)
kĕnchana, Skr. gold (in literary language); = *mas* (in colloquial).
kĕnchang, stiff (of a breeze); steady and strong.
kencheng, I. a Chinese drill worked with a bow. II. a kettle.
kĕnching, passing urine; *sakit k.*, gonorrhoea.
kenchong, I. *kasut kenchong*, a kind of slipper with upturning toes. II. *akar k.*, a large climbing plant (*melodorum manubriatum*). III. = *kechong*.
kenchup, coming to a point (of the petals of a bud); budding.

këndak, sexual intrigue; a mistress or guilty lover; *bërkëndak*, to commit adultery or fornication.

këndala, = *gëndala*.

këndali, Jav. the bridle of a horse.

këndara, Skr. *këndɪraan*, a mount, a steed, a vehicle, a carriage; *mëngëndaraï*, to ride, to be mounted on, to be borne on.

këndati, desire, wish; = *këhëndak hati*.

këndëri, Tam. a measure of weight, a "candareen."

këndi, I. *burong këndi*, a name sometimes given to the curlew (*numenius arquata*), to the whimbrel (*n. phæopus*), and to the large sandpiper (*limosa limosa*) and sometimes limited to the *limosa*—cf. *burong changgai*. II. Skr. gem; *nila-këndi*, the sapphire.

këndiri, self, oneself; = *sëndiri*.

këndit, a narrow belt or girdle.

kendong, carrying in a small fold or wrapper—cf. *kandong* (which refers to carrying on a large scale).

këndur, loose, slack, not taut.

këndəri, Pers. a feast in honour of the dead.

kenek, shrunken, dwarfish.

kënëri, = *këndëri*.

kengkang, walking with the knees wide apart; the walk of a bowlegged man.

kengkeng, I. raising a foot or paw; resting one knee on the other. II. the whining of dogs.

këning, the brows; *bulu k.*, the hair on the eye-brows.

kënjang, *mëngënjang*, to dig.

kënjur, erect, stiff.

kënong, a small copper gong forming part of the *gamëlan*.

këntal, thick (of a fluid); only slightly viscous.

këntang, *ubi këntang*, the potato (*solanum tuberosum*).

këntara, = *këtara*.

këntong, *këntong-këntong*, a wooden sounding-block used at a private mosque.

këntut, *bërkëntut*, to break wind.

kënyal, pliable to the touch; resilient, elastic.

kënyam, tasting (by simply touching the lips); judging flavour.

kënyang, satisfied; sated with food; full after a meal.

kënyir, lusting after; = *ingin*.

kënyit, slight jerky movement of the lips or eyelids.

kënyut, sucking movement.

këpah, a generic name for a number of shells (especially of the genus *capsa*).

këpak, a pinion; *mëngëpak-ngëpak*, to flap the pinions (of a bird).

kepak, bent, warped or twisted (of an arm, branch or limb).

këpal, a lump; a clot; a coagulated mass.

këpala, head; (by metaphor) fountain, source; *k. angin*, empty-headed, frivolous; *k. bërat*, heavy-witted, dull; *k. kongsi*, the head of a secret society; *k. ringan*, intelligence; *k. surat*, the heading to a letter; *k. susu*, cream; *batu k.*, the cranium; *pëning k.*, dizziness; *sakit k.*, headache.

këpalang, of little account; ordinary; *bukan k.*, out of the common.

këparat, Ar. unbelieving, infidel (as a term of abuse).

këpari, *daun pokok këpari*, mint.

këpaya, *buah këpaya*, the papaya fruit; better *buah bëtek*.

këpayang, a tree (*pangium edule*).

kepeng, a small coin; a "cash" or fractional part of a cent.

kepet, unwashed (of the *abaimana*) —a term of abuse.

këpiah, = *kopiah*.

këpialu, *dëmam këpialu*, fever accompanied by delirium; a severe attack of fever.

këpil, adjoining, alongside; *bërkëpil-këpil*, in line side by side; *këpilkan*, to draw up alongside.

kĕping, a fragmentary portion, a piece; a numerical coefficient of foliaceous objects—e.g. as sheets of paper.

kĕpir, a jerk with the hand or finger.

kĕpit, I. pressure between connected surfaces—e.g. between the arm and the body; *mĕngĕpit*, to carry under the arm—cf. *apit*, *sĕpit*, etc. II. a a vessel resembling a *buyong*.

kĕpiting, an edible marine crab.

kĕpoh, full (as the sails of a ship); bulging out.

kĕpok, a large wooden bin for storing rice.

kĕpong, surrounding; enclosing; hemming in; *bĕrkĕpong*, to patrol round and round; *mĕngĕpong*, to invest, to besiege, to surround; *tĕrkĕpong*, invested, besieged, hemmed in.

kĕpudang, *burong kĕpudang*, a kind of thrush mentioned in romances.

kĕpul, closely packed; clotted.

kĕpulaga, = *pĕlaga*.

kĕpum, shrunken (of the cheeks); hollow and drawn; also *kĕmpong*.

kĕpurun, broth made from sago-meal.

kĕpuyoh, = *puyoh*.

kĕpuyu, = *puyu-puyu*.

kĕra, the common long-tailed monkey (*macacus cynomolgus*); *pĕriok k.*, the "monkey-cup" or pitcher plant (*nepenthes*); *k. duku*, the slow loris (*nycticebus tardigradus*); *gĕmbala k.*, a bird (*eupetes macrocercus*); *hamba k.*, the racquet-tailed drongo (*dissemurus platurus*).

kera, = *kira*.

kĕrabat, climbing up, swarming up, clinging to (as a climber clings to a tree); *ikat k.*, a knot in several coils.

kĕrabek, *kĕrobak-kĕrabek*, picking or plucking to pieces.

kĕrabu, I. a flat round ear ornament. II. a sort of salad made of fish, prawns and cucumber. III. a tree (*xanthophyllum rufum* or *lophopetallum fimbriatum*).

kĕrachak, ripples, "cat's-paws" on the water.

kĕrachang, = *kĕrajang*.

kĕrachap, a wooden musical instrument used in *mĕnora* performances.

kĕrah, to call people together for forced labour, mutual defence, etc.; *juru k.*, an official subordinate of the *batin* or chief of a tribe of Orang Laut; *gong pĕngĕrah*, a gong used for summoning people to meet.

kĕrai, I. *rotan kĕrai*, a valuable rattan (*dæmonorops geniculatus*). II. = *gĕrai*.

kĕrajang, *mas kĕrajang*, tinsel, gold foil.

kĕrak, I. the scorched bits of food adhering to the sides of the saucepan; refuse in cooking. II. (onom.) a cracking sound.

kĕrakah, I. = Eur. a carrack, an ancient type of sailing-ship. II. = *kĕkah*.

kĕrakap, *sireh kĕrakap*, the larger (and coarser) *sireh* leaves; inferior *sireh* leaf.

kĕrama, = *kĕrma*.

kĕramat, Ar. miracle-working; invested with supernatural power (of a place, object, or person); *wali k.* or *dato' k.*, the saint buried in a wonder-working shrine; a *genius loci*; *di-timpa k.*, slain by unseen powers for sacrilege at a sacred spot.

kĕrampang, the fork; the point of junction of the lower limbs.

kĕran, a small portable stove or brazier.

kĕrana, = *karna*.

kĕranchang, = *kĕrajang*.

kĕranda, Skr. a three-plank coffin.

kĕrang, I. a generic name for a number of shell-fish (*arca* spp.) II. (onom.) *kĕrong-kĕrang*, a clanging sound.

kerang, *kerang-keroh*, uneven, irregular (as writing on unruled paper).

kĕrangkang, = *kĕrampang*.

kĕrani, Hind. a clerk, a writer.

kĕranjang, a coarsely made basket or sack.
kĕranji, a generic name for a number of trees (*dialium* spp.)
kĕrap, repetition, frequency; *k. kali*, often, frequently; *kĕrapi*, to repeat —(e.g. a dose of medicine).
kerap, = *kirap*.
kĕrapis, *kĕropas-kĕrapis*, odds and ends.
kĕrapu, a generic name given to a number of fish (*serranus* spp.)
kĕras, hardness, stiffness; obstinate; rigid, inelastic; *k. hati*, obstinacy of disposition; *buah k.*, the candle-nut (*aleurites moluccanus*); *kĕrasi*, to press for, to insist on; *kĕraskan*, to stiffen; to harden.
kĕrat, I. severance, cutting off; *sa-kĕrat*, a portion; half; *kĕreta sa-k.*, a "shandrydan" in Province Wellesley; *kĕratan*, a severed piece, a fragment; *kĕrati*, to cut, to sever. II. a carat, a measure of weight for diamonds.
kĕratun, Jav. the abode of a prince (*ratu*); a palace.
kĕrawai, a kind of large wasp making its home in the ground.
kĕrawak, *tupai kĕrawak*, a squirrel (*sciurus bicolor*)?
kĕrawang, open-work, fret-work.
kĕrawat, a rattan fastening connecting the iron of an adze with the handle.
kĕrawit, *chaching kĕrawit*, intestinal worms.
kĕrbang, = *gĕrbang*.
kĕrbas, to shake vigorously; a frequentative of *kĕbas*.
kĕrbat, enfolding in many folds; winding round.
kĕrbau, a buffalo; *k. balar*, a pink buffalo.
kĕrbok, boring into; gnawing into; tapping.
kĕrchut, a common sedge used in mat-making (*scirpus mucronatus*).
kĕrda, a curry-comb; also *kĕrok*.

kĕrdam, (onom.) *kĕrdum-kĕrdam*, a continuous thumping sound.
kĕrdil, undersized; below the average.
kĕrdum, see *kĕrdam*.
kĕrdut, wringled, crumpled, creased.
kĕredak, dry flaky dirt; dirty.
kerek, the tire of a wheel; the small wheel inside a pulley.
kĕrekut, shrivelled up into a coil; curling (as paper when exposed to great heat); *orang k.*, a miser (who "coils round money" and will not let it go).
kĕremut, puckering up the face.
kĕrĕnchang, (onom.) c h i n k i n g; clinking; clanking.
kĕrĕnchat, dwarfed, undersized.
kĕrĕncheng, the triangle (musical instrument).
kĕrĕngga, the red ant or fire-ant (*oecophylla smaragdina*).
kĕrengkel, to spread (of a skin disease).
kĕrengseng, = *kĕreseng*.
kĕrĕntat, = *kĕrĕnchat*.
kĕrenting, = *kĕriting*.
kĕrepek, a round flat cake of sago-meal and sugar.
kĕrepes, feeling about for something (with the fingers only).
kĕrput, shrivelling up round a central point (as a boil).
kĕresek, sand, gravel.
kĕreseng, just revealing the interior (as parted lips or as a crack in a fruit).
kĕresut, puckering the forehead.
kĕreta, a carriage; a generic name for wheeled vehicles; *k. angin*, a switchback railway, (sometimes) a bicycle; *k. api*, a railway or steam tramway; *k. bechak*, a jinrikisha; *k. "engine,"* a motor-car, also *k. gas* and *k. hantu*; *k. hantu*, a bicycle; a motor-car; *k. Hongkong*, = *k. bechak*; *k. kĕrbau*, a buffalo-cart; *k. lĕmbu*, a bullock-cart; *k. lereng*, a bicycle; *k. sa-kĕrat*, a Province Wellesley

shandrydan; *k. sewa*, a hackney-carriage; *ikan k.*, the octopus; *naik k.*, to go for a drive; *pasang k.*, to harness the horses to a carriage.

kĕretut, uneven (of sewing).

kĕri, a small sickle for cutting out weeds from a field of growing *padi*.

kĕriat, (onom.) *kĕriat-kĕriut*, the creaking of rowlocks or of a door upon its hinges.

kĕriau, crying out; clamouring; creating an uproar.

kĕribas, shaking vigorously (as one shakes a fan or piece of cloth)—cf. *kibas*.

kĕrichal, the slave of a slave; a term of extreme self-abasement.

kĕridek, the mole-cricket.

kĕrikal, a large salver or tray.

kĕrikam, an Indian cloth.

kĕrikil, *batu kĕrikil*, flints; pebbles.

kĕring, dry, dryness; *batok k.*, consumption; phthisis; *ikan k.*, dried fish; *tulang k.*, the shin.

kĕrintil, abundant (of fruit on a tree.)

kĕrinting, shell-fish dried for preservation.

kĕrip, (onom.) *mĕngĕrip*, to gnaw (as mice).

kĕris, a "kris" or Malay dagger; *k. alang*, a straight kris of medium length; *k. chĕrita*, a long sinuous kris with some fifteen or seventeen curves in the blade; *k. choban*, a kris with a piece running down the centre of the blade; *k. lĕndayan*, a long kris with a sword-handle; *k. pandak*, a short straight-bladed kris; *k. panjang*, a kris with a long and narrow blade used for executing criminals; *k. pichit*, a kris of a type that is believed to have been worked by mere finger-pressure; *k. sa-pukal*, the common straight-bladed kris (intermediate in length between the *k. alang* and *k. pandak*); *k. sĕmpana*, the common sinuous-bladed kris (with three, five or seven curves in the blade); *k. silam upeh*, a kris like the *k. sa-pukal* but with a narrower blade; *k. sonak udang*, a Raman type of the *k. sĕmpana*; *k. tajang*, a straight-bladed Patani kris with the typical Patani "kingfisher's head" handle; *buntut k.*, the ferrule at the base of the kris-sheath : *hulu k.*, the kris-handle; *pamur k.*, the damascening on the blade of a kris; *sampir k.*, that portion of the kris-sheath which covers the guard of the kris; *sarong k.*, the kris-sheath; *ukas k.*, a shell (*malleus*) resembling a kris-sheath.

kĕrisi, *ikan kĕrisi*, a fish (*synagris notatus*); *ikan k. bali* (*scolopsis bilineatus*).

kĕrising, = *kĕreseng*.

kĕrisut, = *kĕresut*.

kĕrit, (onom.) a scraping or scratching sound; *kĕritan api*, matches—cf. *gĕrit*.

kĕriting, *rambut kĕriting*, woolly or frizzled hair; extremely curly hair.

kĕrja, Skr. work, occupation, business, profession; bringing about, effecting, carrying out; *pĕkĕrjaan*, work, business, occupation; *kĕrjakan*, to effect.

kĕrjang, I. kicking out with the hind-legs (of a horse)—cf. *rĕjang*. II. *kĕrajang*.

kĕrkah, = *kĕrkak*.

kĕrkak, (onom) crunching (of a wild animal crunching up a bone).

kĕrkap, = *kĕrkak*.

kĕrkau, clawing.

kĕrki, Tam. the blinds of a palanquin.

kĕrkup, = *kĕrkak*.

kĕrkut, a chain for closing a door.

kĕrlap, glittering, glistening; *mĕngĕrlap*, to glitter.

kĕrling, a side-glance; *mĕngĕrling*, to give a side glance at a person.

kĕrlip, flickering—cf. *kĕlip*.

kĕrma, I. Skr. a curse; *jatoh k.*, the falling of a curse; *papa kĕrma*, an accident. II. Skr. *bĕtara kĕrma* or *kĕrma wijaya*, the Hindu Cupid (*Kama*) or conquering god of love.

kĕrmah, *siput kĕrmah*, a shell (*oliva subulata* or *oliva nobilis*).

kĕrmak, a generic name for a number of plants.

kĕrmangka, a plant (*dracoena maingayi*).

kĕrmunting, the rose-myrtle (*rhodomyrtus tomentosa*); also *kĕmunting*.

kĕrna, = *karna*.

kĕrnai, cutting or slicing into small pieces.

kĕrnu, Port. a gun-powder horn.

kĕrnyam, restlessness; fidgeting motion.

kĕrnyau, harsh, grating (of the voice); querulous, quarrelsome.

kĕrnyeng, angry snarling.

kĕrnyit, knitting or raising the brows (as a signal or hint).

kĕrnyut, palsied shaking or quivering; nervous convulsions.

kĕrobak, *kĕrobak-kĕrabek*, picking or plucking to pieces.

kĕrobek, a pinch of anything; picking out a very small portion of anything.

kĕrobok, a provision-hamper.

kĕrochok, a sort of rattle used to attract the *parang-parang* fish (*pristis* sp.?)

kĕroh, I. turbid (of water); *k. hati*, malice, ill-feeling. II. (onom.) the sound of snoring; snoring.

keroh, *kerang-keroh*, uneven, irregular (as writing on unruled paper).

kĕrok, I. (onom.) a dull cracking sound; the croak of a frog. II. a curry-comb; also *kĕrda*. III. a fruit-fly; = *bari-bari*.

kĕromong, a series of gongs forming part of a Javanese orchestra.

kĕronchong, I. a large hollow anklet. II. a roughly-made bell or clapper.

kĕrong, a roundish cavity.

kerong, *kerong-kerong*, the orifice through which water escapes from the scuppers; *ikan kerong-kerong*, a fish (*sebastes stolizkœ*).

kĕrongkong, the gullet; *kĕrongkongan*, id.

kĕrongsang, = *kĕrosang*.

kĕrontang, parched, extremely dry; *kĕring k.*, id.

kĕropas, *kĕropas-kĕrapis*, odds and ends.

kĕropok, a dish of fish and flour eaten with rice.

kĕrosang, a Malay brooch; a "krosang."

kĕrosek, (onom.) to wash rice; to scrape the scales of fish—cf. *kosek*.

kĕrosok, (onom.) the rustling and crackling of dry leaves when trodden on.

kĕrpai, a powder-flask.

kĕrpak, (onom.) the sound of crackling.

kĕrpas, I. (onom.) rustling. II. dregs, sediment, lees.

kĕrpis, = *kĕrpas*, I.

kĕrpus, = *kĕrpas*, I.

kĕrsai, crispness (in cooked rice).

kĕrsang, I. dry and stiff (of the hair) arid (of the soil). II. = *kĕrosang*.

kĕrsani, *bĕsi kĕrsani*, Khorassan iron; iron of proof.

kĕrsek, I. (onom.) a rustling sound. II. gravel, coarse sand; also *gĕrsek*.

kĕrsul, = *kĕrsang*, I.

kĕrsut, = *kĕresut*.

kĕrtak, I. a bridge; also *gĕrtak*. II. (onom.) a dull cracking sound.

kĕrtang, I. covered with dirty sores. II. a fish (unidentified).

kĕrtap, (onom.) a sound such as that of a door being closed.

kĕrtas. I. Ar. paper; *k. kĕmbang* or *k. tĕkap*, blotting-paper; *mas k.*, gold leaf. II. (onom.) the rustle of crisp paper.

kĕrtau, I. a small insect destructive to cloth. II. an evil spirit.

kĕrtika, = *kĕtika*.

kĕrtok, (onom.) the sound of rapping.

kĕrtup, = *kĕrtap*.

kĕrtus, = *kĕrtas*, II.

kĕru, a (Kedah) variant of *kur*.

kĕruan, Jav. *tiada kĕruan*, indescribable; in utter confusion; = *ta'-kĕtahuan*.

kĕrubong, gathering together (of people); mobbing; = *kĕrumun*; *kĕrubongi* or *mĕngĕrubongi*, to mob, to overwhelm by numbers.

kĕrubut, a plant (*thottea grandiflora*).

kĕrudut, = *kĕrdut*.

kĕruing, a generic name for a number of trees yielding a special kind of oil (*dipterocarpus* spp.); *minyak k.*, the oil so yielded.

kĕruit, motion of the tip—(e.g. of the tip of a cat's tail).

kĕrukut, curling round; clinging to.

kĕrul, Eng. curl; *rambut k.*, curly hair.

kĕrumit, I. to gnaw. II. slow crawling progress; *jalan tĕrkĕrumit. kĕrumit*, id.

kĕrumun, assembling in crowds; mobbing; *bĕrkĕrumun*, to mass together; *kĕrumuni*, to mob.

kĕrumus, wild embracing; hugging and kissing.

kĕrunting, a wooden clapper.

kĕrup, (onom.) a sound such as that of a man munching pastry.

kĕruping, the scab over a healing wound—cf. *kuping*.

kĕrusi, Ar. a chair; *k. panjang*, a long chair; also *kursi*.

kĕrusut, very much entangled—cf. *kusut*.

kĕrut, I. creasing up; puckering up, frowning. II. (onom.) a rasping sound.

kĕrutu, wrinkled, lined, creased, rough to the touch.

kĕrutup, I. (onom.) a cracking sound. II. (Penang) assault by a gang.

kĕruyup, uxoriousness.

kĕsa, first, the first (from *sa*).

kĕsah, restlessness; *kĕloh k.*, sighing and restless (as a lover in the absence of his beloved).

kesah, Ar. story, narrative; *al-kesah*, " the story runs "—a common exordium to a paragraph; also *kisah*.

kĕsak, edging about, shifting uneasily in one's seat—cf. *kĕsah*.

kĕsal, Jav. regret, repentance, = *sĕsal*.

kĕsambi, a tree (*antidesma ghoesembilla*).

kĕsan, the footprint of an animal; a dent or mark left by pressure.

kĕsang, I. sneezing; = *ĕsang*. II. an insect very destructive to crops.

kĕsat, I. roughness to the touch; coarseness of surface-texture. II. wiping moisture off a smooth surface.

kĕsek, (onom.) *kĕsek-kĕsek*, rustling, whispering—cf. *kĕsu-kĕsi*.

kesek, rubbing or scraping a sharp edge against anything (used especially of playing the violin); also *gesek*.

kesel, = *gesel*.

kĕsi, (onom.) *kĕsu-kĕsi*, rustling, whispering—cf. *kĕsek*.

kĕsing, = *kĕsang*, I.

kĕsip, lacking a kernel (of fruit); lacking a slice or section; *buta k.*, blindness when the eye-ball is destroyed.

kĕskul, Pers. a beggar's bowl.

kĕsmak, a dried fruit imported from China.

kĕsmaran, Skr. and Jav. in love, love; = *bĕrahi*; *edan k.*, madly in love; = *gila bĕrahi* (from *asmara*).

Kĕsna, Skr. *bĕtara Kĕsna*, the Hindu divinity Krishna.

kĕsoma, Skr. a flower; (by metaphor) a beautiful woman or handsome youth.

kĕsturi, Skr. musk.

kĕsu, (onom.) *kĕsu-kĕsi*, the sound of whispering—cf. *kĕsek*.

kĕsuari, *burong kĕsuari*, a cassowary.

kĕsumba, Skr. the arnotto (*bixa orellana*); a red dye; red; dyed red.

kĕsup, (onom.) a sucking sound.

kĕsut, edging towards anything; making advances.

kĕta, = *gĕta*.

kĕtageh, see *tageh*.

kĕtai, crumbling to pieces.

kĕtak, a crease; a fold; a wrinkle.
kĕtam, I. a plane; planing; *tahi kĕtam*, shavings. II. harvesting; *pĕngĕtaman*, id.; *mĕngĕtam*, to harvest. III. a generic name for crabs.
kĕtan, Jav. dry *pulut* rice.
kĕtang, taut, astretch; *k. ka-dada*, drawn tight over the breast (of a sarong).
ketang, = *kitang*.
kĕtap, *mĕngĕtap bibir*, to bite the lips.
kĕtapang, the Indian almond (*terminalia catappa*).
kĕtar, quivering; nervous tremor; *tĕrkĕtar-kĕtar*, trembling all over.
kĕtara, visible; obvious; to appear.
kĕtat, tight-fitting (of a stopper or cork).
kĕtaya, a torch-holder.
kĕtayap, I. a small white skull-cap worn under a turban. II. = *kĕtiap*.
kĕtĕgar, obstinacy.
kĕtek, the long pair of legs in grasshoppers.
ketek, *bĕrjalan tĕrketek-ketek*, the strut of a short-legged person or animal.
kĕtĕki, = *tĕkak-tĕki*.
kĕtĕngga, *kayu kĕtĕngga*, a very pretty light-coloured veined ebony.
kĕti, I. hundred thousand; *sa-kĕti*, a hundred thousand; *bĕrkĕti-kĕti*, in hundreds of thousands. II. *anak kĕti*, a ball [used in playing certain obsolete games and usually mentioned in literature as a simile for the heads of the slain rolling about a battle field.]
kĕtiak, the armpit; *tongkat k.*, a crutch.
kĕtial, difficult to remove (as a cork buried in the mouth of a bottle).
kĕtiap, *pĕrahu kĕtiap*, a sort of houseboat used on rivers.
kĕtika, Skr. time; division of time; period; *pada k. itu*, at that time; *k. lima* and *k. tujoh*, the division of time into five or seven periods that

are lucky or unlucky as the case may be.
kĕtil, pinching, nipping.
kĕtimbal, a disorderly moving mass —(e.g. of maggots or dead flesh).
kĕtimpong, (onom.) a sound such as that of bathers splashing water about.
kĕtimun, = *timun*.
kĕting, the *tendon Achillis*.
kĕtip, I. the biting or stinging of a small and not very venomous insect; nipping slightly between the teeth as a man biting his lips. II. a very small silver coin; a five-cent piece.
kĕtirah, a plant (unidentified).
kĕtis, a sudden jerk intended to jerk off something adhering to a finger or limb.
kĕtitir, *burong kĕtitir*, the Malay turtle-dove (*turtur tigrinus*).
kĕtok, (onom.) tapping, rapping; the note of certain birds; a small sounding block.
kĕtola, a generic name for a number of pumpkins—e.g. *luffa cylindrica* and *trichosanthes anguina*.
kĕtong, I. (onom.) to give out the sound "tong"; the sound made by a drum. II. the stump left when a limb, tail or branch is cut off; *mĕngĕtong*, to cut *mĕngkuang*.
kĕtopong, a stiff peaked head-dress; a helmet or shako mentioned in old romances.
kĕtuat, a large wart.
kĕtubong, the swarming and stinging of hornets; *kĕna k.*, to be attacked by a swarm of hornets.
kĕtul, a thick piece; a clot; a hardish lump of anything; a loaf.
kĕtulul, a confederate in an offence; a thieves' spy; a go-between in dealings in stolen property; a procurer in offences against women.
kĕtumbar, Tam. coriander (*coriandrum sativum*).
kĕtumbit, I. a herb used in the treatment of skin-diseases (*leucas zeylanica*). II. a stye in the eye.

kětupat, rice cooked in a wrapper of leaf.
kětur, a spittoon used by betel-chewers.
kěyangan, see *yang*.
khabar, Ar. news; *apa k.*, what news; = how do you do; *kěrtas k.*, or *surat k.*, a newspaper; *tiada khabarkan diri-nya*, to be unconscious.
khair, Ar. good, excellent.
khalayak, Ar. the world of creation and created things; mankind.
khali, Ar. empty, void.
khalifah, Ar. caliph.
Khalik Ar. God the creator.
khalka, Ar. the creation (in the expression *Khalik-ul-khalka*, the Creator of created things); God.
khamir, Ar. yeast, leaven.
khamis, Ar. the fifth day of the week; Thursday.
khanjar, Pers. a cutlass; a chopper; a heavy cutting knife.
khasah, *kain k.*, gauze, muslin.
khatam, Ar. end, conclusion (used especially of the completion of studies).
khatan, Ar. circumcision.
khatib, Ar. the reader in a mosque; the chief mosque official after the imam.
khatifah, a rich cloth mentioned in old romances.
khayal, Ar. vision, trance.
khemah, Ar. a tent; *běrkhemah*, to encamp.
khidmat, Ar. service, obedience.
khilaf, Ar. error, mistake, blundering.
khiali, Ar. intoxicating.
khianat, Ar. deceit, treachery, abuse of confidence.
khizanah, Ar. treasury; strong-room.
khuatir, Ar. mind, soul, consciousness; also *kuatir*.
khula, Ar. divorce from a husband granted on a wife's application.
khurma, Ar. *buah k.*, a date (fruit); also *kurma*.
khusus, Ar. particular, special.

khutbah, Ar. the formula of a prayer; *k. nikah*, the marriage service.
kia, *yu kia-kia*, species of ray (*rhyncobatus*) which suggests a shark at one extremity of its body and a ray at the other; a type of a double-faced person.
kiah, *pěngiah*, a shoe-horn.
kiaï, Jav. a respectful title given to the venerable.
kial, *těrkial-kial*, making a supreme effort of exertion; putting out one's full strength.
kiamat, *hari kiamat*, the day of judgment.
kiambang, an aquatic plant (*pistia stratiotes*).
kian, "time" in such expressions as "five times," "ten times"; *sa-kian*, once; this much; so much; *děmikian*, to this extent; so; *ara-kian*, accordingly; *kala-kian*, next; afterwards; then.
kianat, = *khianat*.
kiani, Pers. royal.
kiap, the truck of a mast or flagstaff.
kias, Ar. analogy; parable.
kiat, out-of-joint; dislocated; not meeting exactly; *tulang k.*, a dislocated joint of a limb.
kibar, waving, flapping in the breeze; *běrkibaran*, to be waving (of flags, pennons, etc.); *kibarkan*, to wave (transitive).
kibas, I. holding (a fan or any similar object) in the hand and shaking that object vigorously. II. Ar. *kambing kibas*, the Arabian sheep.
kiblah, Ar. the direction in which Mecca lies.
kichak, (onom.) the note of the magpie-robin; also *chěrita*.
kichu, a swindle; a deceitful trick; *měngichu-ngichu orang*, to swindle people.
kida, *kida-kida*, thin lozenge-shaped spangles.
kidal, left; left-handed.
kidap, rubbish, dirt.

kidong, crooning; intoning; recitative; *mĕngidong*, to intone (an address or a tale).

kidul, Jav. the south.

kijai, *tĕrkijai-kijai*, quivering with pain (as a man stung by a venomous insect).

kijang, the barking deer (*cervulus muntjac*).

kijing, an edible marine mussel (species unidentified).

kikir, a file, a grater; (by metaphor) miserly.

kikis, a rough first scraping—e.g. scraping the paint off wood that is to be repainted.

kilan, Jav. the span of the hand; = *jĕngkal*.

kilang, = *kelang*.

kilas, a thong; a strap for pinioning.

kilat, scintillation; flashing; lightning; *pĕtir k.*, thunder and lightning; *bĕrkilat*, to flash.

kilau, brilliancy, glitter, radiance; *kilau-kilauan*, flashing at intervals.

kilek, = *kelek*.

kili. *kili-kili* the reel on a fishing-rod; the ring through a buffalo's nose.

kilir, sharpening, setting; *mĕngilir*, to sharpen.

kima, *siput k.*, a large shell (*tridacna squamosa*)?

kimbang, wheeling about in the air (as a hawk or eagle).

kimbul, the jakes (in a ship).

kimia, Ar. alchemy.

kin, Skr. a titular prefix to the names of Javanese ladies; also *ken*.

kinchah, cleaning by scraping or rubbing dirt off.

kinchak, *tĕrkinchak-kinchak*, pantomime accompanying singing; violent gesticulation.

kinchang, *kinchang-kinchang*, gadding about.

kinchar, a water-wheel turned by the pressure of the current against the paddles of the wheel [the revolving wheel raises water up in bamboo cylinders and pours it into a conduit at a higher level]; *k. ayer*, id.

kinchup, = *kenchup*.

kingkap, a "kincob" or piece of rich cloth.

kinyang, rock-crystal.

kiok, I. the cackling of a fowl. II. = *kiat*.

kiong, a marine shell-fish (unidentified).

kipai, besprinkling (by waving a wet cloth or aspergillus).

kipan, (Perak) the young tapir (showing striped markings and believed by Malays to be a different animal to the adult); also *badak k.*

kipas, a fan; *tingkap k.*, venetians; *kipasi*, to fan; *kipaskan*, id.

kira, estimating, calculation; *kira-kira*, accounts; *elmu kira-kira*, arithmetic; *sa-kira-kira*, about, approximately; *jikalau kira-nya*, if by any chance.

kirai, I. *bĕrkirai-kirai*, marbled (of markings). II. shaking out water from a wet cloth; shaking off moisture as a wet dog; shaking off dust; *kiraikan* and *mĕngiraikan*, to cleanse by shaking. III. *roti kirai*, a preparation resembling macaroni.

kirap, the flapping of a sail; the bustling of a man going at an unaccustomed pace; the movement of a fish darting along the surface of water.

kiri, left; left-hand side.

kirim, sending (things not persons); *di-kirim-nya surat*, he sent a letter; *kirimi*, *kirimkan* and *mĕngirimkan*, to send; *kiriman*, a thing sent.

kisa, a small drag-net or seine used by Malacca fishermen.

kisah, Ar. story, narrative; *al-kisah*, the story runs—a common exordium to a paragraph; also *kesah*.

kisar, revolution; motion round a central point; *kisaran*, anything that does its work by revolution—e.g. a lathe, grindstone, or mill-wheel; *pĕngisar*, id.

kisi, *kisi-kisi*, trelliswork.

kismis, Pers. raisins, currants.

kita, we, (sometimes) I; [*kita* includes the person addressed; *kami* does not].

kitab, Ar. a writing; a book (specially a religious book); scripture.

kitabi, Ar. "scriptural"—a name given by Muhammadans to Christians and Jews who accept biblical books revered as authorities but who do not accept the Koran.

kitang, a fish with a very poisonous dorsal fin (*holacanthus annularis*; also *scatophagus argus*).

kitar, motion in a circle—cf. *kisar*.

kiwi, a supercargo in a Malay *pĕrahu*.

kobah, Pers. a kettle-drum.

kobak, peeling, unhusking; *kobak-kan*, to peel.

kobok, a party, a group; *dudok bĕr-kobok-kobok*, to sit about in groups.

kochah, *kochah-kacheh*, fiddling about with things.

kochak, stirring up water so as to disturb the sediment at the bottom.

kochek, a pocket in a garment.

Kochi, I. Cochin-China. II. a water-jug.

kochoh, haste, hurry.

kochong, a long pyramidal cap; *hantu k.*, a sheeted ghost which progresses over the ground by rolling along sideways.

kodi, a score; twenty.

kodok, Jav. a frog or toad; = *katak*.

koe, you; the (Batavia) form of *kau*.

kohong, stinking; putrid.

koja, Ar. water-jug (with handles and a narrow neck but no spout).

kojah, Pers. a name given to the descendants of Indian traders by Javanese women.

kok, a single yoke—cf. *igu* (a double yoke).

kokoh, = *kukoh*.

kokok, I. (onom.) the crowing of a cock; *bĕrkokok*, to crow. II. to carry pick-a-back.

kokol, bent; bowed; curled up or huddled up.

kokong, very claw-shaped; claws that twist almost completely round.

kokop, = *kukup*.

kokot, shaped like a claw; clawing.

kolak, *kolak-kalek*, up and down motion, or motion backwards and forwards.

kolam, Tam. a pond; a reservoir; a tank.

kolang, *kolang-kaling*, topsy-turvy; upside down.

kolek. (Singapore) a Malay canoe.

koloh, *ayer koloh*, the coarse dye in which cloth is first steeped.

kolong, a hollow under anything—e.g. under a table or under a Malay house.

koma, Skr. *koma-koma*, saffron.

komak, *komak-kamek*, mouthing; the movement of the mouth when speaking or eating.

komat, *komat-kamit*, = *komak-kamek* —v. supra.

kombali, = *kĕmbali*.

komeng, small of its kind; dwarf; congenital impotence in the male.

Kompĕni, Eur. the Government; *hamba k.*, convicts (in the East India Company's days).

kompong, maimed (by the lopping off of a limb), if a stump is left.

kompot, maimed (by the lopping off of a limb), if no stump is left.

konang, = *kunang*.

konchah, choppy (of the sea); broken (of water).

konchak, the summit of a mound or heap—cf. *kĕmonchak*, *ponchak*, etc.

konchong, = *kochong*.

konchor, the young of the king-crab (*limulus moluccanus*).

kong, I. the rib of a boat. II. *siput kong*, a shell (*cassis cornuta*).

kongkang, a name given sometimes to the slow loris (*nycticebus tardigradus*) and sometimes to the *tarsius*.

kongkeng, altercation, wordy war, snarling.

kongkiak, a large black biting ant.

kongkong, I. the deep-toned bark of dogs. II. a block of any sort suspended from the neck to impede an animal's movements.

kongsi, Ch. an association; a society (especially a secret society); *kĕpala k.*, the head of a Chinese secret society.

konon, report; it is said; the story goes.

kontal, *kontal-kantil*, pendulous and swaying (of short thick objects).

kontan, (French) ready money.

kontang, *kontang-kanting*, dangling and swaying (of a long pendant).

kontol, short, stumpy and pendulous.

konyong, I. *sa-konyong-konyong*, all of a sudden, unexpectedly. II. *jalan tĕrkonyong-konyong*, to walk about stiffly erect.

kop, I. the cupola on the howdah of an elephant. II. a Siamese tical.

kopah, a mass, a lump, a clot, a quantity.

kopak, I. *kopak-kapek*, very limp and pendulous (of the breasts)—cf. *kopek*. II. plucking out a small piece of anything; *kopak-kapek*, pulled to pieces, scattered, dispersed. III. a case or box; *sĕnapang k.*, a breech-loading gun.

kopek, limp, long and pendulous (of the breasts).

kopi, I. Eng. copy. II. Eng. coffee.

kopiah, a cap; a hood.

kopok, an obsolete musical instrument mentioned in romances.

korang, = *kurang*.

korek, boring or digging a hole; *mĕngorek*, to dig; *ikan korek tĕlinga buaya*, a fish (*gastroteceus biaculeatus*).

koreng, a scurfy skin-disease.

koret, (Singapore) dregs, sediment.

kori, = *guri*.

koris, = *goris*.

korma, = *khurma*.

kosa, Skr. an ankus or elephant-goad; *kosaï*, to prod with the ankus; also *bĕsi kuasa*.

kosak, (onom.) *kosak-kasek*, fidgeting.

kosek, (onom.) the sound of washing rice or scraping the scales off fish.

kosel, to "keep hammering at" any task; to keep reverting to an argument, statement or work.

kosong, empty, idle, hollow.

kota, Skr. a fort; *kotaï*, to fortify; *kota maru*, the casement or breastwork protecting gunners (in a pirate ship), in contradistinction to the movable gun-shields (*apilan*).

kotah, *sa-kotah*, all, the whole.

kotai, I. *pinang kotai*, dried betel-nut. II. hanging by a thread; not quite severed.

kotak, a chest, a locker; *k. sorong-sorong*, a drawer; *sampan k.*, a Chinese shoe-boat with lockers in the stern.

kotek, tail, caudal projection; *tĕrkotek-kotek*, wagging the tail.

koteng, *parang koteng*, a chopper without a handle; *tĕrkoteng-koteng*, alone, solitary.

kotes, *sa-kotes*, a pinch, a very small quantity.

kotong, *baju kotong*, a jacket with short sleeves or no sleeves; *sĕluar k.* or *chĕlana k.*, short trousers like bathing drawers, but looser.

kotor, foul, dirty; filth; *kĕkotoran*, foulness.

koyak, tearing, rending; torn; *koyak-koyak*, much torn, ragged; *koyakkan*, to tear; *koyak-koyakkan*, to tear to pieces; to keep tearing up.

koyan, a measure of considerable weight or capacity; 40 *pikul* or about 800 *gantang*.

koyok, cur; pariah dog.
ku, I. I, me; = *aku*. II. "your highness;" an ejaculation made by a subject on hearing a prince's words; = *tĕngku* or *tuan-ku*.
kuah, sauce, gravy; *tuang k.*, to pour out the gravy; *makan bĕrkuah ayer mata*, to flavour one's food with tears (a life of sorrow, prov.)
kuak, to open a passage by pushing objects apart (as a man forcing his way through a crowd or opening out a pair of curtains). II. *mĕnguak*, to croak (as a bull-frog); to low; to bellow.
kual, the rolling of a ship.
kuala, the estuary of a river; the point where a main stream falls into the sea or a tributary into the main stream.
kuali, a cooking-pot.
kuang, a generic name for pheasants; *k. raya*, the argus-pheasant (*argusianus argus*); *k. ranggas* or *k. ranting*, the peacock-pheasant (*polyplectron bicalcaratum*)—cf. *kuau*.
kuantong, Ch. *orang China kuantong*, a name given to Muhammadan Chinese from Yunnan.
kuap, to yawn; to open the mouth wide and draw a long breath.
kuar, opening out a passage by swinging a long stick in front of one —cf. *kuak*.
kuarek, a (Bugis) gold ornament.
kuas, *kuas-kuis*, scratching up the earth (of a hen).
kuasa, I. Skr. power, strength, might; an attorney; a power of attorney; letters of administration to the estate of a deceased person; *bĕrkuasa*, possessed of power or authority. II. Skr. *bĕsi kuasa*, an ankus or goad; = *kosa*.
kuat, Ar. physical strength; vigorous; strong; *kuati*, to exert strength; to wrest by force.
kuatir, Ar. mind, soul, consciousness; also *khuatir*.

kuau, (onom.) the argus-pheasant, (*argusianus argus*); *k. chĕrmin*, the peacock-pheasant (*polyplectron bicalcaratum*)—cf. *kuang*.
kubal, = *gubal*.
kubang, a wallow; the act of wallowing in mud or water; *k. nadi*, the hollow at the base of the throat; *bĕrkubang*, to wallow.
kubis, Eng. cabbage.
kubong, the flying lemur (*galeopithecus volans*).
kubu, a stockade; a rough entrenchment of earth and wood; *k. gajah*, a large enclosure for catching elephants.
kubur, Ar. a tomb; *kuburkan*, to bury, to inter.
kuchai, Ch. a vegetable (*allium* sp.)
kuchil, slipping out of position (as a mast slipping out of a badly fitting truck).
kuching, a cat; a generic name for the smaller felidæ; *k. Bĕlanda*, the rabbit; *k. hutan*, the common wild-cat (*felis bengalensis*); *k. jalang*, a name sometimes given to the common wild-cat (*felis bengalensis*) and sometimes to domestic cats that have run wild; *k.-kuching*, the triceps muscle; *k. nĕgri*, the domestic cat; *k. pĕkak* a Chinese rat-trap; *k. tapai*, = *k. Bĕlanda*; *anak k.*, a kitten; *ekor k.*, a small plant with small spikes of flowers suggesting a cat's tail (*uraria crinita*); *mata k.*, a well-known fruit-tree (*nephelium malayense*); *damar mata k.*, the cat's-eye dammar (*hopea globosa* or *pachynocarpus wallichii*).
kuchir, a short queue such as that worn by a Tamil.
kuchup, a smacking kiss—cf. *kĕchup*.
kuda, Tam.? a horse; the knight in chess; an old Javanese title; *kĕreta k.*, a vehicle drawn by a horse (as opposed to a cart or jinrikisha); *k. ayer*, a tapir; *k. bĕraksa*, a pegasus; a magic steed; *k. kuda*, trestles; *k. laut*,

an insect that runs about on the surface of water; *k. sĕmbĕrani*, a pegasus, = *k. bĕraksa*; *k. tezi*, an Arab steed; *bangsal k.*, a stable; *gĕmbala k.*, a groom, a syce; *ikan kuda-kuḍa laut*, a fish (*hippocampus trimaculatus*); *kandang k.*, a horse-stall; a stable; *bĕrkuda*, mounted on a horse.

kudai, I. a pouch. II. the female of the *mawas*.

kudap, a snack; light refreshments.

kudis, skin-disease causing scurf; mange.

kudong, stumpy, maimed, docked—cf. *kotong*; *pĕrahu k.*, a vessel with a square stern; *sampan k.*, a boat with a broad stern and narrow bows.

kudrat, Ar. power, might (of God); *dĕngan k. ilahi rabbi*, by the power of our Lord God.

kudu, (Singapore) a Hindu idol.

kudus, Ar. holy (especially in the expression *roh-ul-k.*, the Holy Ghost).

kueh, a generic name for cakes.

kui, a brazier's mould.

kuini, the wild mango (*mangifera foetida*).

kujau, Ar. a jug; a water-jug (often used for a wash-hand jug).

kujong, = *kochong*.

kujur, a spear with a broad blade and long handle.

kujut, strangling, garrotting.

kukoh, firm, strong, stiff, steady; *k. sĕtia*, firm loyalty; *bĕrkukoh*, to adhere obstinately to; *kukohkan*, to strengthen, to fortify.

kukok, = *kokok*.

kuku, nail, claw, hoof, talon; *sapĕrti k. dĕngan isi*, like the nail and the quick—(separation causes intense pain, prov.); *bĕrgantong di-hujong k.*, hanging from the tip of the fingernail—(a very precarious position, prov.); *k. kambing*, a peculiar instrument for planting padi; *k. sauh*, the claw of an anchor; *bunga k.*, the light patch at the base of the fingernail; *pahat k.*, the round chisel; *pĕnyirat k.*, the skin covering the base of the finger-nail.

kukup, alluvial flats at the estuary of a river.

kukur, I. a rasper; to scrape, to rasp; *k. nyiur*, a coconut scraper; *nyiur tahan k.*, a young coconut just before the water begins to collect in it. II. (onom.) the murmuring note of the dove.

kukus, cooking by steaming; *kukusan*, a cauldron for steaming rice.

kula, I. Jav. I, me. II. Skr. race, people, family; *k. sĕntana*, id.

kulah, Pers. a helmet.

kulai, I. hanging down slackly (as a broken branch or limb). II. a shell (*turbo marmoratus*).

kulat, a fungus; a mushroom.

kuli, Hind. a coolie; an unskilled labourer.

kuliling, = *kĕliling*.

kulim, a large tree (*sorodocarpus borneensis*).

kulit, skin, peel, crust, shell, rind, husk, bark, leather; *k. babi*, pig-skin; (by metaphor) defilement, dishonour.

kulum, mastication, keeping in the mouth, mouthing; *mĕngulum*, to chew, to mouth.

kulun, Jav. the west.

kulup, Ar. foreskin; a name given to the young—i.e. "boy."

kulur, a cultivated variety of the breadfruit (*artocarpus incisa*).

kuma, = *koma*.

kumai, an ornamental line, either painted, inset, or in relief.

kumal, crumpled, ruffled, slightly soiled (as paper that has been written on).

kuman, a very small insect; a louse (as a type of the insignificant).

kumat, = *komat*.

kumba, Skr. a frontlet worn in the state-trappings of an elephant.

kumbah, washing; *bĕras k.*, wet (spoilt) rice; a type of the valueless.

kumbang, a generic name for humble-bees, coconut beetles, etc.; the bee as the assiduous lover of the flower; *bĕlat k.*, a peculiar Penang type of large fish-trap (a sub-variety of the *bĕlat kĕdah*); *harimau k.*, the black panther.

kumbar, a large and almost stemless palm (*zalacca wallichiana*).

kumbara, = *kĕmbara*,

kumbu, a basket used by anglers.

kumis, hair near the lips; the moustache and the hair under the under-lip.

kumkuma, = *koma-koma*.

kumpai, *rumput kumpai*, a swamp grass the pith of which is used as a wick (*panicum myurus*).

kumpal, a clot, a lump.

kumpul, assembly, gathering, meeting together; *sa-kumpul*, in one gathering, together; *kumpulan*, a gathering, an assembly; *kumpulkan*, to gather (people) together; to collect (objects).

kumur, to gargle, to rinse the mouth.

kun, I. Ar. be it so; = *jadi-lah*, in incantations. II. Ch. a border to a garment when that border is of a different colour.

kunang, *kunang-kunang*, a firefly; *k.-k. sa-kĕbun*, a garden of fireflies (a name given to a ring in which a large gem is set in a circle of smaller ones).

kuncha, a bale; a measure for straw, grass or anything easily made up into bales; = (approximately) ⅕ of a *koyan*.

kunchi, a lock; locking up; a key [but *anak k.* is more correct in this sense]; *tĕmu k.*, a ginger (*koempferia pandurata*); *kunchikan*, to lock (a door).

kunchit, = *kuchir*.

kunchup, closing up or folding up (of an umbrella or of any similar object which shrinks on itself but is not rolled round itself like a flag); *kĕmbang k.*, opening and shutting; expanding and contracting.

kundai, Tam. the short queue of a Tamil; *rambut anak k.*, the short hair at the top of the neck.

kundang, control, command, authority; (in magic) influence of the nature of hypnotic influence; *budak k.*, personal attendants or orderlies to a prince; *budak kundangan*, id.

kundur, the wax gourd (*benincasa cerifera*).

kungkum, elastic pressure or shrinkage round an object; *mĕngungkum*, to close in upon, to press in upon.

kuning, yellow; *puteh k.*, pale yellow; a much admired colour of the complexion (whence it has become a term of endearment "my fair one"); *mambang k.*, the sunset glow; *kĕkuningan*, the royal colour yellow.

kunjong, *mĕngunjong*, to visit.

kuntau, Ch. the fist; *bĕrkuntau*, to box.

kuntum, a bud, a blossom.

kunyah, chewing, ruminating.

kunyit, turmeric, saffron; *tĕmu k.*, turmeric (*curcuma longa*).

kupang, I. a coin or measure of value (equal in Penang to 10 cents). II. a marine mussel (*mytilus*).

kupas, shelling, peeling, skinning, removing the husk; *kupaskan*, to skin; *tĕrkupas*, skinned, shelled.

kupi, a flask.

kuping, I. Jav. the ear. II. the scab over a sore—cf. *kĕruping*.

kupu, I. Ar. equality of rank; parity. II. *kupu-kupu*, a butterfly.

kur, a cry for summoning fowls and birds; *k. sĕmangat*, the cry to summon the *sĕmangat*; a term of endearment.

kura, I. *kura-kura*, a generic name for a number of tortoises (other than *testudo emys*). II. *dĕmam kura*, low fever; ague fits.

kurai, straight broad lines in the veining of wood or the damascening of a *kĕris*.

Kuran, Ar. the Koran.

kurang, reduction; lessening; less; (by extension) a negative adverb; *k. hati*, lacking in spirit, spiritless; *kĕkurangan*, reduction; *kurangkan*, to reduce.

kurap, I. ringworm and similar parasitic skin diseases. II. a shell (*capsa deflorata*).

kurau, a fish (unidentified).

kurban, Ar. a sacrificial offering.

Kuripan, an old kingdom in Java, the home of Sira Panji.

kurma, Ar. the date-fruit; also *khurma*.

kurnia, Skr. favour, kindness, gift (from a superior to an inferior); *jikalau ada k. tuan-ku*, if your highness pleases; *kurniaï* or *mĕngurniaï*, to confer a favour or gift; to bestow.

kurong, enclosing; shutting off; an enclosure; the compartments of a large Malay fish-trap (*bĕlat* or *kelong*); a room; a cabin; *bĕrkurong*, to be enclosed or shut up; *tĕrkurong*, enclosed, shut up.

kursi, Ar. a chair; *k. panjang*, a long chair; also *kĕrusi*.

kurus, thin, lean, attenuated; *kurus k.*, withered and bony.

kus, a sound made to frighten away a cat.

kusa, = *kosa*.

kusal, rolling up by friction between the palms of the hands.

kusam, lustreless; dull.

kusar, = *gusar*.

kushkul, = *kĕskul*.

kusi, *rumput kusi*, a grass (*poa cynosuroides?*)

kusta, *sakit kusta*, leprosy.

kusu, a small group; *bĕrkusu-kusu*, in knots, in clusters. II. *kusu-kusu*, the vetiver or cuscus grass (*andropogon muricatus*).

kusut, tangled, matted, confused; *hati k.*, perplexity; *rambut k.*, tangled hair.

kut, (Penang) perhaps, possibly.

kutai, = *kotai*.

kutang, a thin bodice, = *choli*.

kuti, *kuti-kuti*, nagging, petty annoyance.

kutil, I. a wart. II. to pick or break off a small piece of anything.

kutip, picking up something that is below you; gathering, collecting.

kutok, a curse; accursed; *si-kutok*, a wretch, a scoundrel; *kutoki* or *mĕngutoki*, to curse.

kutu, I. a louse; *k. anjing*, a flea; *k. bidok*, the beetles infesting dirty lockers in boats; *k. busok*, a bug; *k. lĕmbu*, a tick; *tindas k.*, to kill lice (on the thumb-nail). II. Tam. an association; *sa-kutu*, a federation; *pĕrsakutuan*, id.; *bĕrsa-kutu*, federated; *Nĕgri Mĕlayu yang bĕrsa-kutu*, the Federated Malay States.

kutum, = *kuntum*.

kuyu, melancholy, rueful looking, out of sorts or ill.

kuyup, I. *basah kuyup*, sopping wet. II. = *kuyu*.

kuyut, = *kuyu*.

kyaï, = *kiaï*.

L

la, Ar. not, no.

laal, Ar. a ruby; ruby-red wine.

laanat, Ar. curse; *l. Allah*, the curse of God; *laanatan*, accursed.

laba, I. great profits, rich returns; *bĕroleh l.*, to profit greatly. II. *laba-laba*, a spider; *l.-l. bĕrok*, the large venomous bird-spiders; *l.-l. lotong*, a large black wall-spider.

labah, = *laba*, II.

labĕrang, a name given to some tackle in the rigging of a native ship.

labi, *labi-labi*, a name given to small soft-shelled turtles (*trionyx* *cartilagineus* and *pelochelys cantoris*); *siput labi-labi*, a large shell-fish with a peculiar yellow-spotted body.

laboh, letting down or lowering by means of a rope, string or cable; anchoring; letting down blinds or curtains; *labohan*, an anchorage; *labohkan*, to lower, to let down; *bĕrlaboh*, to moor, to anchor.

labu, a generic name for gourds and pumpkins; a calabash; a pipkin; an earthenware vessel resembling a bottle-gourd; *l. ayer*, a pumpkin (*cucurbita pepo*); *l. batu*, an earthenware pipkin; *l. jantong*, the bottle-gourd (*lagenaria vulgaris*); *l.-labu*, a calabash for holding water; *l. manis = l. ayer*; *l. merah*, a gourd (*cucurbita maxima*); *siput l.*, a shell (*murex haustellum*); *tampok l.*, the small stalk left on a gourd when it is plucked.

labur, I. smearing, daubing; *mĕlabur puteh*, to whitewash. II. *pĕlabur*, rations supplied to troops or labourers; *tauke labur*, the Chinese capitalist financing a tin-mine.

lachak, *bĕlachak* or *mĕlachak*, to be abundant.

lachi, (Dutch) a drawer; a chest of drawers.

lada, pepper; *pipis l.*, to grind pepper for cooking; *l. bĕrekur*, cubebs (*piper cubeba*); *l. China*, a pepper (*piper chaba*); *l. hantu*, a wild pepper (*piper canium*); *l. hitam*, black pepper (*piper nigrum*); *l. merah*, red pepper, capsicum (*capsicum annuum*).

ladan, *minyak ladan*, a strong oily preparation used in caulking native boats; *sĕtanggi l.*, joss-sticks.

ladang, planting on high dry ground in contradistinction to planting on low swampy ground (*sawah*); *l. padi*, "hill-padi"; *l. gambir*, a hill-clearing for planting gambier; *l. lada*, a pepper-clearing; *tikar l.*, a coarse type of mat; *bĕrladang*, to plant on dry soil.

ladeh, = *dadeh*.

lading, *parang lading*, a long cutter the blade of which tapers towards the handle; *pĕrahu l.*, a heavy cargo-boat.

ladong, stagnation, standing still; *batu l.*, a plummet; a lead on a fishing-line; *l. kail*, a lead on a fishing-line.

laga, the fighting of relatively large animals—such as buffaloes, bulls, rams and chevrotins; the fighting of quails (but not cocks or grass-hoppers).

lagam, Hind. the bit (of a horse).

lagang, the first steps in weaving a mat; starting to weave.

lagi, more; yet more; still, also, moreover; *dan-lagi*, furthermore, besides; *sa-lagi*, so long as; as long as; while.

lagu, tune; *mĕnurut l.*, in time with the music.

lah, a suffix sometimes having a preterite signification, and sometimes a quasi-demonstrative one emphasising the expression to which it is appended—e.g. *pĕrgi-lah ia*, he went; *orang itu-lah yang pĕrgi*, it was that man who went.

lahad, Ar. *liang lahad*, an excavation dug into the left side of the grave and used for the actual reception of the dead body.

lahap, *pĕlahap*, a glutton, a voracious eater.

lahar, a pool, a mere, a patch of water in the jungle; also *wilahar*.

lahir, Ar. clear, plain, visible.

lai, a numeral coefficient for tenuous objects—such as sheets of paper, garments, leaves, blades of grass, etc.; also *hĕlai*.

laichi, Ch. a well-known Chinese fruit (*nephelium litchi*).

laik, = *layak*.

lain, different; other than; exclusive (of); some...others...; *lain di-minum, lain di-sapu pĕrut*, some were potions, some were lotions; *lain orang lain hati*, different men have different hearts; *mĕnchari l.*, to seek a new love; *lain-lainkan*, to sort; *bĕrlainan*, differing from; apart from; *mĕlainkan*, but, nevertheless, except.

lais, I. *ikan lais*, a fish (unidentified). II. *mĕlais*, to back water.

laju, swiftness, speed, rapidity of motion; swift, fast.

lajur, a band, a broad line, a furrow —cf. *jalur*.

laka, *kayu laka*, a tree (*phyllanthus* sp.?)

laki, husband (less respectful than *suami*); *laki-laki*, male, masculine; manliness; *bĕrlaki*, to have a husband; to be married (of a woman); *bĕrlakikan*, to take as one's husband, to marry (of a woman marrying).

lakin, Ar. well, so, yet, but; *wa-lakin*, and yet; and still.

laksa, I. Skr. myriad; ten thousand; *sa-laksa*, a myriad; *bĕrlaksa*, in myriads; in countless numbers. II. Pers. a native vermicelli.

laksamana, Skr. a high native official corresponding in many respects to a minister of marine or admiral; *Dewa L.*, the hero Laksamana, the half-brother of Rama; *baris l.*, the double triangle; the magic figure drawn by the hero Laksamana to protect Sita, Rama's wife, from Rawana.

laksana, I. like; similar to; resemblance; = *sĕpĕrti* or *bagai*, but rather more literary in use; *laksana-kan*, to imitate, to equal, to compare with, to rival. II. *bijak laksana*, wise, prudent; = *bijaksana*.

laku, conduct, manner, behaviour; to act or behave; to take effect; to pass current; *rosak bangsa karna laku*, good birth is wasted by bad manners, prov.; *sĕpĕrti laku orang gila*, like the conduct of a madman; *ringgit ini tiada laku*, this dollar will not pass current; *tingkah l.*, general deportment; character; *lakukan*, to carry into effect; to cause to pass current; *mĕlakukan*, id.; *bĕrlaku*, to take effect, to prevail, to pass current; *kĕlakuan*, manner, bearing, behaviour.

lakum, a generic name for a number of wild vines—e.g. *vitis diffusa*, *v. mollisima* and *v. noremfolia*.

lakun, Jav. a staged play (especially a classical play in ancient Java); *lakunkan*, to represent (such a play) on the stage.

lala, I. *siput l.*, a salt-water bivalve resembling a mussel. II. *mĕlala*, to swim on one's back.

lalah, gluttonous eating.

lalai, I. careless, thoughtless, sleepy, listless; *lalaikan*, to forget, to lose interest in; *pĕlalai*, a spell to render people careless or forgetful. II. halliards.

lalak, the touch-hole of a cannon; *mĕlalak*, to flash in the pan; to miss fire.

lalang, I. the well-known "lalang" long-grass (*imperata cylindrica*); *gajah l.*, a tame elephant. II. *lalu lalang*, going and coming; passing backwards and forwards.

lalat, the common fly (*musca*); *l. hijau*, the "blue-bottle" fly; *l. kĕrbau*, the *oestrus*; *l. kuda*, the horsefly (*tabanus*); *bĕrani l.*, the courage of a fly (which flies away for a moment but returns)—courage that is discreet but persistent; *harimau l.*, the common small jumping spider; *tahi l.*, a freckle, a small mole; *tĕpok l.*, the peculiar flap used by Malays to catch grass-hoppers.

lalau, hindrance; *mĕlalau*, to warn off (trespassers); to prohibit (passage); *hikmat pĕlalau*, a charm to hinder a girl from marrying anyone.

lali, *buku lali*, the projecting portion of the ankle-bone.

lalu, past, after, afterwards; elapsing, traversing; moving past; *pada masa yang tĕlah lalu*, in the past; *tahun l.*, last year; *lalu-lah kami*, we passed by; *orang masok lalu dudok*, they entered and then sat down; *l. lalang*, passing to and fro; *sa-lalu*, always, continually; *laluï*, to traverse, to override, to disobey; *mĕlaluï*, id.; *tĕrlalu*, surpassingly, very, exceedingly.

lam, a marine worm from which an oil is obtained; *minyak l.*, the oil so obtained.

lama, duration of time; long; ancient; former; *orang l.*, the ancients; *bĕrapa l.*, how long; *rumah-nya yang l.*, his former house; *lama-lama*, in the end; in course of time; finally; *sa-lama*, while; as long as; *sa-lama-lama*, for ever.

laman, = *halaman*.

lamang, a heavy sword.

lamat, = *alamat*.

lambai, beckoning; *mĕlambai*, to wave, to beckon—(e.g., to a friend on a departing ship).

lambak, a confused heap, a pile; *mĕlambak*, to lie in heaps.

lambat, slow; behind time; *l. bĕlajar*, slow to learn; *l. sampai*, slow to arrive.

lambing, coming to a point; pricked up (of the ears).

lambok, I. *bubur lambok*, a soup of prawns, fish, ginger and other ingredients. II. = *lambur*.

lambong, I. side, flank; *roda l.*, a paddle-wheel. II. swelling up (as a wave); bouncing up (as an india-rubber ball); *mĕlambong*, to surge; to rebound.

lambur, a large jelly-fish.

lamin, *kĕlamin*, a pair (male and female); a married couple; *pĕlamin*, the bridal bed.

lamina, scale-armour.

lampai, slender, lissom, svelte; *mĕlampai*, to hang down—cf. *ampai*.

lampam, a fresh-water fish (*barbus jerdoni*).

lampan, washing for tin; an alluvial tin mine.

lampar, spread flat over, sprawling; *tidur bĕrlampar*, to sleep sprawling over the bed—cf. *hampar*.

lampas, polishing, smoothing.

lampau, excess; surpassing, exceeding; *tĕrlampau*, too much; *mĕlampau*, to go too far; *mĕlampauï*, to overdo.

lampin, a wrapper or swaddling-cloth for a newly-born child.

lampit, Jav. a sleeping-mat.

lampong, *pĕlampong* or *tĕlampong*, a float for a line or net—cf. *ampong*, *apong*, etc.

lampu, Port. a lamp.

lamun, if it be that; provided that; if only.

lanang, I. Jav. man, male, manly; = *laki-laki*. II. twining by twisting.

lanar, mud, slime (of the kind one meets on Malayan mudbanks).

lanchang, I. Port. a Malay war-vessel built for speed and fighting. [The word is now specially applied to the model ships (*kapal hantu*), laden with offerings, which are set adrift to propitiate the demons of the sea]. II. *mĕlanchang*, to push ahead, to outstrip.

lanchap, slipping down easy; smooth and slippery.

lanchar, quick-darting (as a snake); fluent (of speech); *l. mĕmbacha*, fluency in reading; *pĕrahu lancharan*, a swift cruiser; *mĕlanchar*, to dart along.

lanching, Jav. trousers (of the type worn by Javanese).

lanchok, a pool; a puddle.

lanchong, false, counterfeit, debased (of currency).

lanchur, gushing out violently; spurting out; emptying tin-bearing earth into a mining-washer; *mĕlanchur*, to spurt out—cf. *panchur*.

landa, I. *mĕlanda mas*, to wash for alluvial gold. II. *mĕlanda*, to force one's way into a house or room; to forcibly intrude.

landak, a porcupine; *l. raya*, the large porcupine (*hystrix longicauda*); *l. batu*, *l. kĕlubi* or *l. ubi*, the brush-tailed porcupine (*atherura macrura*).

landas, *landasan*, an anvil; *pĕlandas*, id.

landin, = *lĕndayan*.

landoh, *mĕlandoh*, increasing in breadth (as a cone).

landong, long (of a rope)—cf. *lanjar*.

lang, a generic name for hawks, kites and eagles; *l. bĕlalang* (*microhierax* spp.); *l. borek* (*pernis tweeddalii*); *l. hindek* (*nisaëtus limnaëtus*); *l. merah*, the Brahminy kite (*haliastur* spp.); *l. rajawali*, a generic name for small hawks—e.g. *tinnunculus alaudarius*; *l. rimba* (*spizaëtus* sp.); *l. siput*, the large sea-eagle (*haliaëtus leucogaster*); also (in Patani) the osprey; *l. tĕmbikar*, the young *haliastur*.

langau, a large stinging fly.

langgai, a triangular push-net worked by one man; *bĕlat l.*, a fixed (estuarine) purse-net (also known as *ambai*).

langgam, *bĕrlanggam*, to club together.

langgang, *tunggang langgang*, topsy-turvy; upside down.

langgar, I. knocking up against; attacking; *l. bahasa*, a breach of etiquette; *langgari*, to attack. II. Jav. a small private mosque; = *surau* or *bandarsah*.

langir, material used as soap for cleaning the person.

langit, the sky; the heavens; *tujoh pĕtala l.*, the seven folds of heaven; *kaki l.*, the horizon; *langit-langit*, a canopy; a ceiling; *kĕrongkongan l.-l.*, the roof of the mouth.

langkah, a step, a pace, a stride; *salah l.*, a false step; *langkahi*, to walk over; *langkahkan*, to put down the foot; to step; *mĕlangkah*, to travel, to set out.

langkan, Ch. a balcony; a balustraded terrace.

langkas, fiery (of a steed).

langkat, three days hence; the morrow of the day after to-morrow.

langkau, skipping; omitting a little and resuming further on.

langkup, *tĕlangkup*, capsized (of a boat); upside down (of a cup); face downwards.

langlang, Jav. travelling round; *l. buana*, wandering over the earth.

langsai, winding up; *habis l.*, quite finished.

langsar, long in proportion to width (as a flag-staff); tall and straight.

langsat, the well-known fruit (*lansium domesticum*).

langsi, I. shrill (of the voice); *mĕlangsi*, to give out a sharp shrill note. II. drapery, hangings.

langsing, = *langsi*, I.

langsong, moving on to; proceeding to; forthwith, next; *bĕrjalan-lah langsong ka-pĕkan*, they went straight to the market; *tĕrlangsong*, (1) gone forth; issued; (2) too much; *jangan tĕrlangsong*, do not go too far.

langun, = *lĕlangun*.

langut, *mĕlangut*, to look hungrily or longingly at anything.

lanjang, see *tĕrlanjang*.

lanjar, long (of a rope)—cf. *landong*.

lanjong, *tĕbu lanjong*, a long and thin variety of the sugar-cane.

lanjur, *tĕlanjur*, protracted; draging on—cf. *lanjut*, *anjur*, etc.

lanjut, long, lasting, lengthy, prolonged; *lanjutkan*, to lengthen; *mĕlanjutkan* or *mĕmpĕrlanjutkan*, id.

lantai, a floor (of laths or of strips of bamboo).

lantak, ramming down, hammering down; *luloh l.*, crushed under heavy blows or weights; *pĕlantak*, a ramrod.

lantang, clear, open, empty.
lantar, *pĕlantar*, a flooring without a roof; a piece of scaffolding; an open-air theatre-stage; *pĕlantaran*, id.; *tĕlantar*, lying stretched on the floor.
lantas, forthwith; thereupon; promptly; *sa-tĕlah datang lalu naik lantas ka-pĕraduan*, on arriving he went promptly to bed.
lantek, I. installing (a prince or very high dignitary); *mĕlantek*, to instal; to crown. II. *bĕlantek* or *pĕlantek*, a spring-gun or spring-bow.
lantong, strong (of a smell); putrid.
Lanun, Ilanun (the name of a piratical tribe from Mindanao); piratical.
lanyak, treading down (used especially of soil being trodden down by buffaloes as a rough way of preparing it for cultivation).
lanyau, mud with a hard crust or mud mixed with decayed vegetable matter.
lap, a dishcloth; *kĕrtas l.*, blotting-paper.
lapah, stripping, skinning (especially used of skinning a slaughtered animal for the market or kitchen).
lapang, empty space presenting an orifice or gap; vacuity; *l. hati*, loss of heart, despair.
lapar, hunger; *l. dahaga*, hunger and thirst; *l. susu*, hungering for milk (of a baby).
lapek, I. pedestal; base; the surface on which a thing rests; a rug, mat or doyly; *l. kaki*, sandles; *l. punggong*, a mat for sitting on. II. *lopak-lapek*, confused; in disorder; inconsistent.
lapis, fold, wrapping, stratum; *bĕrlapis*, double; in folds; in coats.
lapok, mould; *bĕrlapok*, mouldy.
lapun, converging rows of stakes used for trapping wild animals by leading them up to a snare.
lara, disquietude; anxiety; care; the solicitude of love; *orang yang l.,* the pining; *pĕnglipur l.*, a soother of cares; a story-teller.
larah, *bĕrlarah-larahan*, one after another; in succession.
larak, close together (as the seeds of a durian which has very little pulp in it).
larang, prohibition; *larangan*, a thing prohibited; *hutan larangan*, a forest reserve; *larangkan*, to forbid, to prohibit.
larap, I. readily saleable; = *laris*. II. multiplicity—i.e. *mĕlarapkan tali*, to separate the strands of a rope.
laras, smooth and cylindrical; the stem of a tree; the barrel of a gun; *sĕnapang dua l.*, a double-barrelled gun; *yu l.*, a fish (*mustelus manazo*).
larat, I. dragging on slowly; lengthy; difficult; *tahun-tahun larat ia mĕngatur dia*, he spent long years in arranging them. II. *tiada larat*, inability to manage; *ta'-larat*, id.
larau, annoyance; disturbance; *mĕmbalas l.*, to pay out a man for disturbing you.
larek, turning (with a lathe); polishing and rounding; *gading di-larek*, polished ivory.
lari, running (but not of liquids running); escaping; fleeing; *l. mĕngaji*, to play truant; *larikan*, to run from; to escape; *mĕlarikan*, id.; *bĕrlari*, to run.
laris, in demand; selling well (of goods); *pĕlaris*, a charm to secure good business.
larong, a coffin.
larut, to drag (of an anchor).
las, *batu las*, a hard mineral substance used as emery stone.
lasa, numbed; *anggota yang lasa mĕnjadi lagi rasa*, the numbed limbs regained the power of sensation.
lasah, striking, switching.
lasak, *pakaian pĕlasak*, every-day wear; working clothes.
lashkar, Per. soldiery.

lasu, staleness; mustiness of taste; overripeness.
lasum, Jav. *batek lasum,* a special make in painted sarongs.
lat, alternation; = *sĕlang; lat sa-pintu,* every alternate door; the next door but one; *lat sa-hari,* every other day.
lata, creeping, crawling; *mĕlata,* to creep.
latah, a nervous paroxysmal disease aroused by suggestion and often taking the form of hysterical mimicry.
latam, pressing or stamping down; rolling earth to harden its surface.
lateh, coherence, order; *mĕlateh mulut,* to speak coherently.
latok, *parang latok,* a long chopper the tip of which turns downwards.
lau, Ar. if; *wa-lau,* and if; although; *jika-lau,* if.
lauk, materials cooked for consumption with rice; *l. pauk,* all kinds of food (other than rice).
laun, protracted, dragging on; *jangan bĕrlaun,* do not spin it out too much.
laung, a resounding roar; a deep cry; *bĕrlaung* or *mĕlaung,* to cry out loudly.
laut, sea; *l. madu,* a sea of honey; *l. api,* hell; *barat l.,* the north-west; *utara barat l.,* N.N.W.; *timor l.,* N.E.; *ikan kuda-kuda l.,* a fish (*hippocampus trimaculatus*); *lautan,* the seas; the ocean; *mĕlaut,* to travel seawards; *mĕlauti,* to navigate.
lawa, a cross-bar in a fish-trap; *mĕlawa,* to stop the way; to intercept the passage of a bridal party pending the payment of a fee; *upah pĕmbuka lawa,* the fee so paid.
lawah, = *lawas,* I.
lawak, *lawak-lawak,* poking fun, jesting, teasing; *pĕlawak,* a tease.
lawan, opposition, rivalry, competition, contest; a rival, a foe; *lawani,* to contend against; *bĕrlawan,* to be engaged in a contest or competition; to be in rivalry or comparable.
lawang, I. *bunga l.,* mace; *kulit l.,* an aromatic bark (*cinnamomum culit lawan*). II. a great gate; a main entrance; *lawangan,* id.
lawar, a preparation of minced fish.
lawas, I. empty, clear, vacant (of ground); unobstructed (of a view). II. old, left over, survivals.
lawat, *mĕlawat,* to visit.
lawi, *bulu lawi,* the long feathers in a cock's tail; *l. ayam,* a name given to a curved dagger with a hole in the handle.
layah, I. *mĕlayah,* to bend over backwards; to sway about. II. a loose outer garment worn by women on the Mecca pilgrimage.
layak, I. Ar. right, suitable, proper, fitting, appropriate; *bukan layak kita mĕnakai dia,* it is not fitting that we should wear it. II. cutting open a fish (longitudinally) to preserve it.
layam, *bĕrlayam,* to dance a sword-dance.
layan, *layani* or *mĕlayani,* to wait on; to attend on.
layang, flying, soaring in the air; *mĕlayang,* to fly; *mĕlayangkan,* to fly away with; *l.-l.,* (1) a generic name for swallows and swifts; (2) a generic name for children's kites.
layap, *mĕlayap,* to skim the surface.
layar, sailing; a sail; *l. agong,* the main-sail; *l. apit,* a lug-sail; *l. dastur,* a studding-sail; *l. pĕnyorong,* a mizzen; *l. tupang,* a foresail; *ikan l.,* a fish (*histiophorus gladius*); *pasang l.,* to set the sails; *pĕbahu l.,* the yard; *pĕkaki l.,* the boom; *bĕlayar,* to sail; to travel by water; to set sail; *pĕlayaran,* a sea-voyage.
layu, faded, withered; to fade away (of a tree or flower).
layun, Jav. the dead body of a prince; *layunan,* id.

layur, I. parching, scorching up. II. *ikan layur-layur*, a fish (*trichiurus savala*).
lazat, Ar. delightful to the taste; delicious; pleasure-giving.
lazim, Ar. necessary; dependent on.
lazuardi, Pers. lapis-lazuli.
lĕbah, the honey-bee; *kawan l.*, a swarm of bees; *sarang l.*, a bees' nest.
lĕbai, a mosque official who attends to the order of the service; (Penang) the descendant of a family distinguished for piety.
lĕbak, (onom.) a thud.
lĕbam, I. livid (of a bruise). II. (onom.) a banging noise.
lĕban, a plant (*vitex pubescens*); also *halban*.
lĕbang, debility following on illness (especially on childbirth).
lĕbap, (onom.) a dull thud.
lebar, width; broad; *lebar-nya sadĕpa*, it was six feet broad.
lĕbat, dense (of foliage); close, thick; *hujan l.*, heavy rain; *bulu kĕningnya lĕbat*, having bushy eyebrows.
lĕbeh, more, superior, greater; *yang l.*, the most; the more; *l. kurang*, more or less; *lĕbehkan*, or *mĕlĕbehkan*, to augment; *bĕrlĕbeh-lĕbehan*, going on increasing; boasting; exaggerating; *tĕrlĕbeh*, much more, most, excessively.
lĕboh, a broad and busy street.
lĕbu, dust; *l. duli*, "dust below the royal feet"—a humble way of indirectly addressing a prince.
lĕbum, (onom.) a thumping noise.
lĕbun, fraud by adulteration or by specious appearances.
lĕbur, smelting; the molten state; solution, liquefaction, destruction; *hati l.*, a crushed spirit.
lĕchah, muddy (of the ground); wet (of walking).
lĕchak, (onom.) a splashing noise.
lĕchap, saturated; wet through (as a handkerchief).

lĕchat, extremely smooth and slippery.
lecheh, *mĕlecheh*, to coax, to cajole, to wheedle.
lechek, beating up with a spoon; hitting with the flat side of the foot.
lecher, *mĕlecher*, to be moist (as a sore or abrasion); to suppurate.
lechet, blistered, abraded—cf. *lecher*.
lĕchit, I. *mĕlĕchit*, to shoot out (as water from a leak)—cf. *lĕchut* and *lĕnchit*. II. (onom.) the twittering of birds; = *dĕchit*.
lĕchoh, steeping vegetables or rice in water.
lechok, a smooth oily or polished surface.
lĕchur, scalding, blistering.
lĕchut, *mĕlĕchut*, to ooze out (as the contents of some fruits when the fruit is squeezed).
ledang, light in colour; pale; shimmering.
lĕding, *mĕlĕding*, to warp; to slowly become convex—cf. *lĕdong*.
lĕdong, *mĕlĕdong*, to give (under a weight)—cf. *lĕding*.
lĕga, broad, wide; easy; *l. dada*, full chested; *ta'-lĕga*, disquieting, uncomfortable.
lĕgam, *hitam lĕgam*, coal-black; pitch-black.
legar, *mĕlegar*, to make the circuit of the rice-mill.
lĕgas, to "snick" off a projection.
lĕgat, keeping steadily on the same course (of a ship).
lĕgong, (onom.) the booming of a gong.
lĕgu, *mĕlĕgu*, to weave the selvage or border of a mat.
lĕgum, (onom.) thumping.
leher, the neck; *batang l.*, the column of the neck; *kĕrat l.*, to cut the throat; *panggal l.*, to behead.
leka, lingering over; dwelling on; dawdling over; *l. bĕrmain*, lingering over play; *l. mĕnangis*, continuous weeping.

lĕkah, = *rĕkah*.

lekak, *mĕlekak,* to whirl or buzz round and round a spot.

lĕkang, shelling (a fruit); *rambutan l.,* a variety of *rambutan* fruit [so called because the flesh is easily separable from the pip.]

lĕkap, cleaving to something; flattened on—cf. *lĕkat.*

lĕkar, a rattan frill for lifting pots off the fire without burning the fingers.

lĕkas, speed; speedily, quickly, soon; *nanti lĕkas rosak mata,* your eyesight will soon be spoilt.

lĕkat, adhering to, sticking to, pasted on; *lĕkatkan,* to stick (a thing) on; *mĕlĕkat,* to adhere to; *pĕlĕkat,* a bill (stuck on a wall); *tĕrlĕkat,* stuck on.

lekeh, low, mean, despicable.

lĕkir, *panau lĕkir,* a disease discolouring the skin; *ular sawa l.,* a snake with curious white markings suggesting the disease (*coluber melanurus*).

lĕkoh, (onom.) the sound of a cough.

lĕkok, low-lying ground; a hollow; a swampy patch.

lĕku, *bĕrtĕlĕku,* to lean on one's elbows.

lekur, a numeral which when occurring after the numbers one to nine signifies that twenty is added—i.e. *sa-lĕkur,* twenty-one; *dua lekur,* twenty-two, etc.

lela, I. a swivel-gun; II. beloved, darling (a term of endearment). III. *maharaja lela,* the title of a chamberlain or master of the ceremonies at a Malay court; *bĕrmaharaja lela,* to act as though the whole place belonged to you—as illustrated by a court chamberlain who possesses little real power but (at state ceremonies) orders about much greater personages than himself. IV. waving; to brandish; *mĕlela,* to wave. V. *bĕsi mĕlela,* steel; *kĕris mĕlela,* an undamascened *kĕris.*

lĕlah, weariness, exhaustion; *pĕnat l.,* extreme weariness; *batok l.,* whooping-cough.

lĕlak, to slip down (of clothing).

lĕlaki, = *laki-laki.*

lĕlakun, = *lakun.*

lĕlangun, Jav. a pleasure-garden; = *taman.*

lĕlap, deep (of sleep).

lĕlar, iteration, repetition; to keep doing an action.

lĕlas, *mĕlĕlas,* to trim (the comb of a cock).

leleh, *mĕleleh,* to trickle, to flow gently.

leler, careless, slovenly (of work).

lĕlewa, Jav. behaviour, conduct; *tingkah l.,* id.; = *tingkah laku.*

lelong, I. Port. sale by auction. II. a measure of length and area; a quarter of an orlong in area.

lĕmah, weak, soft; lack of firmness or rigidity; *l. lĕmbut,* gentleness; *lĕmahkan,* to enfeeble, to enervate.

lĕmak, fat, grease, *isi lĕmak dapat ka-orang, tulang bulu pulang ka-kita,* others get the flesh and fat, we get the bones and bristles.

leman, Jav. an elephant.

lĕmang, I. *mĕlĕmang,* to cook in a bamboo vessel lined with plantain leaves. II. *mĕlĕmang,* to bend over backwards and pick up a coin with the lips (as is done occasionally by Malay dancers).

lĕmari, = *almari.*

lĕmas, I. death by suffocation; drowning; stifling; *l. pikir,* confused thought. II. = *lĕmah.*

lĕmau, weak, sleepy, apathetic.

lĕmba, a plant (*pothomorpha subpeltata*).

lĕmbaga, embryo; beginnings; primeval (customs); *l. bisul,* the early stages of a boil; *adat l.,* customary laws handed down from prehistoric times.

lĕmbah, low-lying land, meadow, valley.

lembak, *mělembak*, to boil over.
lěmbang, soft-spokenness; blarney; compliment.
lěmbap, moist, clammy, wet.
lěmbar, a thread, a strand, a piece of string; a numeral coefficient, = *hělai*.
lěmbayong, a climber (unidentified, it has purple flowers).
lěmbega, a plant (*calotropis procera*).
lěmbek, pulpy; soft and moist.
lembek, an Arabian rug.
lěmbidang, a flat rim, brim or edge.
lěmbing, a spear; *l. buang-buangan*, a dart, a light javelin; *l. tikam pari*, a spear with three barbs.
lěmbong, *mělěmbong*, to be blown out or puffed out; to expand into globular shape.
lěmboyan, = *bunian*.
lěmbu, an ox; *l. jantan*, a bull; *l. kasi*, a bullock; *l. tanah*, a large beetle; *l. hutan*, the smaller wild ox (*bos sondaicus*); *ikan l.*, a fish (*triacanthus brevirostris*, also, perhaps, *ostracion cornutus*).
lěmbut, soft, delicate, weak, flexible; *l. hati*, softening of angry feelings; loss of resentment; *lěmah l.*, extremely soft or delicate; gentle; *lěmbuti*, *lěmbutkan* or *mělěmbutkan*, to soften.
lempah, overflowing; to flow out; *l. kurnia*, ever-flowing kindness; *mělempah*, to flow over; *mělempahkan*, to spill, to shed.
lěmpai, *mělěmpai*, to curl up at the edge (as a withering leaf).
lěmpang, lying athwart or across anything; *mělěmpang*, to lie outstretched.
lempar, throwing, casting; to throw; *lempari* or *mělempar*, to pelt; *lemparkan* or *mělemparkan*, to throw (anything).
lěmpědal, = *pědal*.
lěmpědu, = *hěmpědu*.
lempek, *běrlempek-lempek*, in coats or layers.

lěmping, a name given to light flat cakes.
lěmpok, I. sugared durian. II. a poultice; a plaster.
lěmpong, light (as wood, pumice, etc.); spongy; of little weight or value; *katak l.*, a frog (*oxyglossus* spp.)
lěmpoyan, a fishing-reel.
lěmpoyang, a ginger (*zingiber casumunaar*).
lěmuas, filth; *běrlěmuas*, smeared with dirt.
lěmukut, broken grains of husked rice; also *mělukut*.
lena, sound (of sleep); sleep; *tidur l.*, to sleep soundly; *lenakan*, to put to sleep.
lenang, = *linang*.
lenchah, = *linchah*.
lěnchit, springing forward (as a slippery body squeezed between the fingers—cf. *lěchit*).
lenchun, dripping; soaked; *l. basah*, soaking wet.
lěndayan, a full-sized handle; a sword-handle in contradistinction to a *kěris*-handle.
lěndeh, nestling up against, pressing up against.
lěndir, viscous secretions of all sorts; greasy matter; matter exuded from a boil; the runnings in certain diseases.
lěndong, *mělěndong*, to be dented or knocked in (of convex surfaces).
lěndut, "giving," as a plank under a heavy weight.
leng, a measure of capacity; half a *chupak*.
lěnga, *minyak lěnga*, sesamum oil.
lenga, dawdling; wasting time; *l. mata*, to droop with sleepiness (of the eyes).
lěngai, listlessness; carelessness.
lěngan, arm; *l. baju*, the sleeve of a garment; *pangkal l.*, the upper arm.
lěngang, sparse (of population or of the attendance at a festival).

lĕngar, dizziness (consequent on a blow); *tĕrlĕngar*, "knocked silly;" *si-kĕpala lĕngar*, a man of giddy conduct.

lĕngas, clamminess, greasiness, moisture; *mĕlĕngas*, to become clammy or moist.

lengas, *mĕlengas* or *bĕlengas*, to be averted (of an angry countenance).

lĕngat, cooking in a receptacle which is immersed in boiling water.

lĕnggak, leaning the head back and looking skyward.

lenggang, rocking, swaying; swinging the arms; *lenggok-l.*, id.; *l. yang lĕmah-lĕmbut*, a slow undulating motion; *l. janda*, a small curved knife broadening towards the point and fretted at the broad end.

lenggar, wide apart (of packages in a receptacle).

lenggoh, *mĕlenggoh*, to sit resting one's arms on a table, = *bĕrtĕlĕku*.

lenggok, swaying—e.g. as a dancer —cf. *lenggang*.

lĕnggundi, a small tree with violet flowers and aromatic leaves (*vitex trifolia*).

lĕngkai, *panjang lĕngkai*, tall and willowy (of the figure).

lengkang, ring-shaped; a numeral coefficient for bracelets, anklets, etc.

lĕngkap, I. complete; fully equipped; sufficiently supplied; *chukup l.* or *l. gĕnap*, id.; *dĕngan sa-lĕngkap-nya*, in full; *lĕngkapi*, *mĕlĕngkapi*, *lĕngkapkan* or *mĕlĕngkapkan*, to fit out; *kĕlĕngkapan*, equipment. II. a plant (*arenga obtusifolia*).

lengkar, = *lingkar*.

lĕngkara, Skr. miraculous, fabulous, wonderful.

lĕngkayan, a "crow's-nest" in a Malay stockade.

lĕngkiang, = *rĕngkiang*.

lengkok, *mĕlengkok*, to bend, wind or curve (as a river or road).

lengkong, bow-shaped, curved; circular; the rim of a wheel; encircling; *bĕlat l.*, a long movable line of screens laid so as to shut in a large portion of water between it and the shore; as the tide recedes the fish in that area are left high and dry.

lĕngkoyan, = *lĕmpoyan*.

lĕngkuas, an aromatic fruit used in making curries (*alpinia galanga*).

lĕngkur, *mĕlĕngkur*, to be slightly bowed or bent.

lĕngoh, *mĕlĕngoh*, to feel stiffness and pain in the joints.

lĕngong, *mĕlĕngong*, to be pensive; to be absent minded or taken up with one's thoughts; to doze.

lengsan, listless, idle, dawdling.

lengser, slipping or sliding aside; side-slip; slipping down.

lengset, *bĕlengset*, turned inside out; having the inside exposed.

lĕning, (onom.) the tinkling of a little bell.

lĕnja, I. running of the saliva; foam at the mouth; *sawan l.*, fits accompanied by foaming at the mouth; *mĕlĕnja*, to run (of the saliva). II. a coarse sack of netting [in which things are hung from the roof so as to protect them from mice.]

lenja, *mĕlenja*, to sulk.

lĕnjan, stamping down in unison (of coolies).

lĕnjar, *biji kĕlĕnjar*, the glands; *sakit kĕlĕnjaran*, glandular swellings.

lĕnjuang, the dracoena; *l. bukit* (*dracoena congesta*); *l. merah* (*cordyline terminalis*).

lĕnong, (onom.) the booming of a gong or big bell.

lĕntam, (onom.) the sound of stamping.

lĕntang, (onom.) a clanging sound.

lentang, = *lintang*.

lenteh, *pĕrlenteh*, lustful, lascivious.

lĕntek, curling back, curving concavely (used of wavy hair, of teeth filed so as to give a concave surface, of the curve of the eyebrow, etc.)

lĕnting, I. (onom.) a tinkling sound. II. *mĕlĕnting*, to warp (of fresh wood exposed to heat).
lĕntok, supple, flexible; = *lĕntur*.
lentok, to move the head to one side.
lĕntong, (onom.) a deep booming sound.
lĕntul, *mĕlĕntul*, to feel empty (of the stomach).
lĕntum, (onom.) a thumping sound.
lĕntur, flexible; yielding; bending (as a bough); *lĕnturi*, to give a twist or bend to anything; *mĕlĕntur*, to bend (intransitive).
lĕnyak, deep (of sleep).
lĕnyap, disappearing, vanishing; *mĕlĕnnyapkan*, to cause to vanish or disappear.
lĕnyau, = *lanyau*.
lĕpa, Skr. carelessness, negligence; also *alpa*.
lepa, I. *tĕrlepa*, thrown carelessly away, sprawling. II. *mĕlepa*, to plaster.
lĕpak, *puteh mĕlĕpak*, milk-white, snow-white.
lepak, beetling, overhanging.
lĕpang, a creeper (unidentified); *ombak bunga l.*, white-crested billows.
lĕpas, liberation, release, escape, quitting; past, ago, since; *l. sĕmbahyang*, after prayers; *tiada di-lĕpas pulang*, they did not let him go home; *kain l.*, a loose garment worn as a plaid; *lĕpasi*, to free from, to release; *lĕpaskan*, id.; *mĕlĕpaskan*, id.; *tĕrlĕpas*, having escaped.
lĕpat, *kueh lĕpat*, a generic name given to sweetmeats cooked in leaves.
lĕpau, a Malay verandah; = *sĕrambi*.
lĕpeh, the turning over or folding of a corner or small portion of anything —e.g. of the page of a book.
lĕpek, (onom.) a dull squelching sound.
leper, I. turned up vertically (of the edge of anything); *leper-leper*, the raised edge of a combing. II. provincial accent, brogue.
lĕpoh, *mĕlĕpoh*, to be blistered.
lepoh, crooked (of a limb); twisted, bent.
lĕpok, (onom.) *lĕpok-lĕpok*, a clapper.
lĕpong, (onom.) a thumping noise.
lĕpu, a generic name given to a number of fish—e.g. *antennarius mummifer, synnancidrum horridum* and (*l. panjang*) *pelor didactylum*.
lĕpur, *mati lĕpur*, death by suffocation in mud.
lĕrah, *tĕrlĕrah*, knocked out and injured (as fruit blown down by a storm or as a book knocked out of its binding).
lĕrak, *buah lĕrak*, a fruit (*sapindus rarak*).
lerang, strip; slip; the strips in a sail; *kain sa-l.*, a sarong woven in one piece and not in two.
lerap, a coin used for playing pitch-and-toss.
lerek, *mĕlerek*, to bore through.
lereng, contour; rounded brim; the castors under a piece of furniture; *kĕreta l.*, a bicycle.
leret, slipping away.
lĕsak, (onom.) *lĕsok-lĕsak*, to rustle.
lĕsap, disappearance; occultation; = *lĕnyap*.
leser, *mĕleser*, to drag along the ground (as a garment).
lĕsi, *puchat lĕsi*, extreme pallor.
lĕsing, (onom.) to whizz.
lĕsir, a sword-dance.
lĕsok, (onom.) *lĕsok-lĕsak*, to rustle.
lĕsong, a mortar (for rice-pounding); *l. indek*, a pounding-machine worked with the foot; *l. tangan*, a pounder worked by hand.
lĕsu, utterly tired out; completely exhausted; *lĕteh l.*, id.
lesut, I. shrunken, shrivelled. II. = *lĕsu*.
lĕta, mean, low, base, despicable, bad.

lĕtak, to set down; to put down; *lĕtakkan*, id.; *mĕlĕtakkan*, id.; *tĕrlĕtak*, laid down, set down.

letak, *mĕletak*, to lie prostrate (without a pillow).

lĕtam, (onom.) the sound of slamming.

lĕtang, (onom.) the sound of clanking.

lĕtap, (onom.) the sound of tapping or rapping.

lĕteh, weariness, lassitude, fatigue; tired.

lĕtek, (onom.) the sound of ticking.

leter, *mĕleter* or *bĕleter*, to chatter.

lĕting, (onom.) the sound of chinking.

lĕtis, (onom.) the sound of "whisking" along.

lĕtong, (onom.) the sound of thumping.

lĕtum, (onom.) a thumping or drumming sound.

lĕtup, (onom.) *mĕlĕtup*, to go off with a dull thud.

lewar, *mĕlewar*, to fly in coveys; to swim in shoals; to swarm.

lewat, I. past, after; *l. pikul ĕnam*, after six o'clock. II. hurry, speed, rapidity.

liang, I. aperture, orifice, hollow; *l. chinchin*, the hole in a ring; *l. luka*, the orifice of a wound; *l. mata*, the eye-socket; *l. roma*, the pores of the skin. II. *liang liok*, a rolling gait; swaying from side to side.

liar, wild, shy, unbroken, undomesticated; *orang liar*, wild aboriginal tribesmen.

lias, *pĕngĕlias*, *pĕlias* or *pĕngĕliasan*, invulnerability (taking the form that the enemy's weapons fail to touch).

liat, tough, leathery, lithe; *tanah l.*, clay.

liau, *mĕliau*, to fester, to run (of a sore).

lichau, glossy, shiny; oily-looking.

lichin, smooth, slippery, bare.

lidah, tongue; *l. api*, a tongue of fire; *l. badak*, rhinoceros-tongue, a name given to an aroid (*pothus latifolius*); *l. bĕrchabang*, a forked tongue; duplicity of speech; *l. biawak*, a monitor's (forked) tongue; = *l. bĕrchabang*; *l. buaya*, crocodile's tongue, a name given to the aloe (*aloe ferox*) [the crocodile itself is believed to have no tongue]; *l. gajah*, the elephant's tongue, a name given to a plant (*aglaonema oblongifolium*); *l. jin*, the "spirit's tongue," a plant (*hedyotis congesta*); *akar lidah jin* (*hedyotis capitellata*); *l. kĕrbau*, buffalo-tongue, a plant (*clerodendrum deflexus*); *l. kuching*, the cat's-tongue, a plant (*turneria ulmifolia*); *l. lĕmbu*, the ox-tongue, a plant (*aneilema nudiflorum*) *l. manis*, sweet-tongued; smooth-spoken; *l. panjang*, loquacity; *l. rusa*, deer's-tongue, a small tree (*fagroea racemosa*); *anak l.*, the uvula; *anak l. timbangan*, the tongue of a balance; *tatang di-anak l.*, to support on the uvula (a proverbial impossibility); *ikan l.* or *ikan l.-l.*, a generic name for flat fish—e.g. *l. l. baji* (*synaptura orientalis*); *l. l. barang* (*cynoglossus elongatus*); *l. l. lumpur* (*synaptura commersomana*).

lidal, Port. a thimble.

lidas, an acid smarting taste in the mouth.

lidi, the veins of a palm-leaf; *ular l.*, a small snake (*dendrophis pictus*)—(a type of the insignificant).

ligas, a canter or gallop.

ligat, whirling round and round; extremely rapid revolution.

lihat, seeing; to see; *lihati*, to inspect, to look over; *mĕlihati*, id.; *mĕlihat*, to see (intransitive); *kĕlihatan*, visibility; *pĕlihat*, the sense or power of sight; *pĕngĕlihatan*, the range of vision.

likas, a small wheel on which the skein is wound when weaving.

likat, sticky, adhesive, syrupy—cf. *lĕkat*.
liku, Jav. a royal title.
lilang, = *lilin*.
lilau, *mĕlilau*, to totter (of a stricken man).
lilin, wax; a taper; *l. lĕbah*, bee's-wax; *kain l.*, waxed sarongs; *burong l.*, the small pied hornbill (*anthracoceros albirostris*).
lilir, = *leler*.
lilit, twining round; coiling round; *mĕlilit*, to coil up.
lima, I. five (originally, the hand of five fingers); *buku l.*, the knuckles; *kĕlima*, all five; *yang kĕlima*, the fifth; *pĕnglima*, a leader in war. II. a generic name for a number of plants (*xanthophyllum* spp.)
liman, = *leman*.
limar, a rich cloth mentioned in romances.
limas, pyramidal; *atap l.*, a pyramidal roof.
limau, a generic name for oranges, limes, lemons, etc.; *l. kapas*, the common lime (*citrus acida*); also *l. kĕsturi* and *l. nipis*; *l. manis*, the orange (*citrus aurantium*); *bĕrlimau*, to use lime-juice in washing.
limbah, a cess-pool, a puddle; *limbahan* or *pĕlimbah*, id.
limbai, *mĕlimbai*, to wave about an object; to sway the arm; to brandish a whip or switch; *mĕmbuang limbai*, to let the arm sway out (of a dancer) when the swaying is intended to suggest a negative.
limbang, I. swampy or broken land. II. after; *l. tĕngah hari*, after midday.
limbok, a dove (unidentified).
limbong, *limbongan*, a dry dock.
limbur, *sambur-limbur*, appearing and disappearing; intermittent visibility.
limpah, = *lempah*.
limpat, fresh, jovial, genial.
limun, = *halimun*.

linang, falling in drops (as tears or as water percolating through porous stone).
linau, a red-stemmed palm (unidentified).
linchah, *tĕrlinchah-linchah*, fidgety, restless.
linchin, = *lichin*.
linchun, = *lenchun*.
lindong, protective cover, shelter; *lindongi*, *lindongkan*, *mĕlindongi*, or *mĕlindongkan*, to shelter, to protect, to hide by covering; *bĕrlindong*, to take shelter; *kĕlindongan*, shelter, hiding; *pĕrlindongan*, a place of shelter.
lindu, Jav. an earthquake.
lingar, *mĕlingar*, to look at anything with a sidelong look—cf. *jĕling*.
lingas, = *lengas*.
linggam, Tam. red; red-lead.
linggi, the covered or decked portions at the prow and stern of a boat.
linggis, *linggisan dayong*, the long pole fastened to the thole-pins and running parallel to the gunwale of a Malay boat.
lingkap, spent, destroyed, swallowed up, wasted.
lingkar, a coil (of a snake, rope, or anything similar); *bĕrlingkar*, in coils, rolled up.
lingkong, = *lengkong*.
lingkup, bundling to one side.
lingsir, = *lengser*.
lintah, a horse-leech; also *halintah*.
lintang, lying athwart or across; *l. bujur*, diagonal; *l. pukang*, sprawling; *balai l.*, a reception-hall built at right angles to the main building; *palas l.*, a sort of platform or bridge on a Malay ship; *lintangi*, to thwart, to cross; *lintangkan* or *mĕlintangkan*, to lay athwart; *mĕlintang*, to move across (a path); *tĕrbang mĕlintang*, to fly across the sky (in front of the spectator).
lintap, lying one on another (of flat objects—such as books).

lintar, a thunderbolt; *batu l.*, a prehistoric stone instrument—such as a spear-head or arrow-head; also *halintar*.

lintas, dashing past, flashing by; *mĕlintas*, to dart across; *jin lintasan*, an evil spirit darting like a comet or meteor in front of a man; a will of the wisp.

lintoh, dizziness, loss of consciousness; *ilmu pĕlintoh*, magic art to deprive a person of consciousness so as to facilitate theft or abduction.

lintup, = *litup*.

linyar, smooth-sailing (of a boat); gliding through the water.

liok, a twist or turn; the movements of a fencer or dancing-girl; *liang-liok*, a rolling gait.

liong, *tali liong*, a sort of belt for carrying a *kĕris*.

lipan, a centipede; see *halipan*.

lipas, a cockroach.

lipat, folding up (as one folds a piece of cloth or garment); *lipatan*, the folds of anything.

lipis, *pĕlipis* or *pĕlipisan*, the temples of the forehead.

lipit, a narrow fold (of thread, etc.); *kala l.*, the common slender-bodied house-scorpion.

lipur, calming, consoling, soothing; *pĕnglipur lara*, a "consoler of cares," a story-teller or story; *mĕlipurkan*, to soothe, to allay.

liput, flooding, swamping, permeating, overcoming; covering; *chahaya mĕliput sa-rata dunya*, her brightness permeates the world; *di-liputi oleh pĕmbujok*, overborne by endearments.

liring, = *lereng*.

liru, see *kĕliru*.

lis, I. (Dutch) a cord, a twist (of cord-like patterns in carving). II. Eng. list.

lisah, *mĕngĕlisah*, to fidget; = *mĕnggĕlisah*.

lisan, Ar. the tongue.

litah, *litah mulut*, loose-tongued.

litup, covering and concealing; completely overshadowing; *habis litup dunia ini banyak-nya*, their numbers were such as to hide the world under them.

liu, *liu-liu*, a stern-paddle.

liur, *ayer liur*, saliva.

liut, = *liok*.

liwat, Ar. sodomy.

loba, greed, covetousness; also *haloba*.

lobak, the Chinese radish (*raphanus caudatus*).

loban, Ar. *loban jawi*, gum benjamin.

lobang, hole, groove, hollow, aperture; *l. tikus*, a name given to the side-cavity in which the body rests in a Malay grave; *duit l.*, Sarawak cents.

lobok, a deep cavity in a river or in the sea; *galah l.*, the longest kind of punting-pole.

lochak, *mĕlochak*, to be abundant; to be plentiful.

locheng, Ch. a bell.

lochok, *mĕlochok*, to prod; to dig in the ribs.

lodan, *ikan lodan*, the whale or leviathan of Malay romance.

lodeh, *masak lodeh*, cooked to pulpiness—cf. *lodoh*.

lodoh, pulpy and rotten (of overripe fruit)—cf. *lodeh*.

loga, I. Skr. abode, place; *shurga-loga*, heaven; also *loka*. II. = *duga*.

logam, Tam. mineral (only in compound words); *pancha-logam*, an alloy of five minerals or a stone of five colours; *bĕrma-logam*, a red talismanic stone.

loh, Ar. slate; tablet.

loha, Ar. the forenoon.

lohok, rotten through and through.

lohor, Ar. midday, noon.

lok, a curve or bend in a *kĕris*.

loka, Skr. abode, place; *shurga-loka*, paradise, heaven; also *loga*.

lokah, = *lukah*.

lokan, an edible marine cockle.

lokek, stingy, mean, miserly.
loki, Ch. a Cantonese prostitute.
lokos, bedraggled.
lolak, a shell (*trochus niloticus*).
lo'lo', Ar. a pearl.
lolok, *mĕlolok*, to spy upon.
lolong, (onom.) *mĕlolong*, to howl.
lomak, oily, greasy.
lomba, billowy motion; cantering or galloping (in a horse); the play of a porpoise; *tĕmpat bĕrlomba kuda*, a race-course; *lomba-lomba*, a porpoise or dolphin; *l.-l. alur*, a porpoise (*arcella brevirostris* and *phocoena phocoenoides*); *l.-l. sungai*, the dolphin (*steno plumbeus* and, rarer, *delphinus delphis*).
lombong, a cavity in the surface of the ground; a surface mine; the chasm left after a volcanic explosion.
lomor, = *lumur*.
lomos, = *lumus*.
lompang, = *lumpang*.
lompat, jumping, leaping; *lompati*, to jump upon; *mĕlompat*, to spring.
lonak, = *lunak*.
lonchat, jumping with both feet together; leaping (as a fish out of water); *tĕrlonchat-lonchat*, hopping about, springing about.
lonchos, smooth and sharp as a spear point; bare and tapering; naked.
londang, a mud-hole.
londeh, insecurely fastened (of a sarong).
long, I. a native coffin. II. an abbreviation of *sulong*, q.v.
longgak, looking upwards with head bent right back; *hantu l.*, a name given to the spectre huntsman from his supposed appearance.
longgar, loose (as a *kĕris*); knocking against the sides of a receptacle; loose-fitting.
longgok, a mound or heap; *longgok-kan*, to stack; *bĕrlonggok-longgok*, in stacks.

longkah, loosened, strained (of a joint).
longkang, a ditch, a drain.
longlai, bent, bowed; *lĕmah l.*, swaying, willowy.
longsor, slipping or sliding forward; sliding down.
lonjak, *mĕlonjak*, to stand on tiptoe.
lonjong, tall, straight and slender (of a tree).
lonta, = *ronta*.
lontar, I. hurling, throwing with force; *lontarkan*, to throw; *pĕlontar*, a missile. II. a palm (*borassus flabelliformis*), the leaves of which were used as paper.
lonteh, Jav. a harlot.
lontok, short and thick; stumpy; *orang tua l.*, a broken-down old man.
lontos, smooth and cylindrical.
lonyah, = *lunyah*.
lonyai, slush; slushy.
lopak, I. a shallow puddle. II. *lopak-lopak*, a pouch of *mĕngkuang*. III. *lopak-lapek*, confused, in disorder, inconsistent.
lorah, a groove.
lorek, delicate graining or markings.
lorong, a lane; a narrow road or street.
loros, = *lurus*.
losong, a white scaly eruption; ichthyosis; *sakit l.* and *kurup l.*, id.
lot, = *lut*.
lota, Hind. a vessel for carrying water.
lotar, = *lontar*.
lotek, a kind of pitch for caulking boats.
loteng, Ch. upstairs; the upper floor or floors.
lotong, black; a name given to a number of varieties of monkeys of the genus *semnopithecus*; also *jĕlutong*; *ekur l.*, "monkey's tail," a name given to a long narrow swivel gun or jingal.
loya, squeamish; nausea.

loyak, soft (of overboiled rice).
loyang, bell-metal.
loyar, *Pinang loyar*, the palm of which the cudgels known as "Penang lawyers" are made. II. Eng. lawyer; *l. burok*, a hedge-lawyer or sea-lawyer; *l. këledek*, a qualified practitioner with a pettifogging practice.
loyong, *mëloyong*, to walk with tottering gait.
lu, Ch. you.
luah, spitting out (food, etc., but not saliva) from the mouth.
luak, I. *mëluak*, to feel nausea—cf. *loya*. II. an animal (unidentified).
luan, = *haluan*.
luar, outer portion; outer side; the part beyond or outside; *di-luar*, outside; *ka-luar*, outwards; *tanah l.*, foreign countries; *këluaran*, outer, strange, foreign, alien, common; see also *këluar*.
luas, spaciousness; extent; *dahi-nya l.*, his forehead was broad; *luaskan* or *mëluaskan*, to broaden, to extend.
luat, = *luak*, I.
lubok, = *lobok*.
lucha, Hind. obscene, low.
luchas, = *lunchas*.
luchu, bright, merry, sunny-tempered.
luchut, I. slipping off; slipping down or away; dropping and being lost. II. abrasion; scraping off skin.
ludah, spitting; expectoration; *ludahi*, to spit at; *mëludah*, to spit; *ludahkan*, to eject from the mouth; to spit out.
lughat, Ar. a vocabulary, a dictionary.
lugu, satisfied; *ta'-lugu*, insatiable.
luh, = *loh*.
lui, furthest from the goal; last in a race.
lujur, stringing roughly together; tacking.
luka, wounding; a wound; *mata l.*, or *liang l.*, the orifice of a wound; *lukaï* or *mëlukaï*, to wound.

lukah, a generic name for small portable fish-traps in the Riau-Johor districts, = *bubu*, in the Northern States.
lukis, writing, engraving, scratching; *pandai l.*, an engraver.
luku, *mëluku*, to scratch the head; to draw the fingers through the hair.
lukup, bottom upwards (of a cup, boat, etc.)
luloh, powder; crushing to powder; *hanchur l.*, crushed to pieces.
lulu, swallowing at a gulp; gulping down.
lulum, sucking at food (such as sweets, chocolate, etc.)
lulur, = *lulu*.
lulus, just slipping through; getting through; putting through; possible; *l. këhëndak*, to realize one's wish; *luluskan*, to put through (a task).
lulut, rubbing the body, shampooing.
lumang, *bëlumang*, smeared with mud; *mënggëlumang*, to wallow in mud.
lumat, fine, soft (of earth); crushed, ground, or chopped to pieces; *pipis lumat-lumat*, minced quite fine.
lumbong, = *lombong*.
lumpang, a pounder.
lumpoh, lameness (caused by oedema or peripheral neuritis).
lumpur, mud.
lumu, = *lumut*.
lumur, smearing; besmearing; *bërlumur*, smeared, polluted; *lumurkan*, to besmear; to defile.
lumus, smeared—cf. *lumur*.
lumut, moss, lichen; *bërlumut*, moss-covered.
lunak, fleshy (of stone-fruits).
lunas, the keel of a native boat.
lunchas, failing to hit; missing the mark.
lunchur, slipping forward or downward.
lundu, I. a generic name given to a number of fish (*bagrus gulioïdes*

and *arius* spp.) II. *pokok lundu*, a plant (*antidesma bunias*).
lunggok, = *longgok*.
lungkum, dome-shaped; covering like a dome.
lungkup, *tĕlungkup*, capsized, overturned; = *tĕlangkup*.
lungsur, = *longsor*.
lunjur, stretching; extending the limbs; *bĕlunjur*, to stretch; *bĕlunjur kaki*, to stretch the legs.
luntang, *pĕluntang*, a float (used with nets or lines).
luntok, = *lontok*.
luntur, *pĕluntur*, a purgative.
lunyah, treading down swampy soil (of buffaloes turned into a field so that they may give the soil a rough turning up).
lup, the rod through which the threads pass in weaving.
lupa, I. forgetting; *lupakan*, to forget; *pĕlupa*, a forgetful person. II. *lupa-lupa*, fish-maws.
lupas, see *kĕlupas*.
lupat, a shell-fish (*hippopus maculatus*).
lupi, *papan l.*, a piece of decking flush with the gunwale in a Malay boat.
lupoh, *mĕlupoh*, to hammer bamboo flat.
luput, slipping away from; escape, loss; *l. daripada kĕjahatan*, escape from evil; *hilang l*, lost and gone.
lurah, Jav. a district or division of a country; = *daerah*; *sa-lurah*, the entire divisions, all—usually pronounced *sĕluroh*.
luroh, I. falling, dropping; being shed (as leaves); *bĕrluroh*, to be falling (of leaves, flowers, etc.) II. see *lurah* and *sĕluroh*.
luru, *mĕluru*, to dash forward, to charge.
lurup, *susup-lurup*, helter-shelter (of running).
lurus, straight; smooth and straight; regular and straight; *luruskan*, to straighten.
lurut, I. passing the hand over a long body; running a chain through the fingers; drawing one's hand over a rope, a man's arm or any similar object—cf. *urut*. II. a whitlow.
lusa, the day after the morrow; the second day after.
lusoh, flexible through use (as boots that are stiff when new).
lut, penetration, effect; *tiada l.*, it did not penetrate (of an arrow or bullet).
luti, ruffled up; crumpled up; spoilt by use but not worn out.
lutong, = *lotong*.
lutu, striking out right and left; hitting out; *mĕlutu*, to rain blows.
lutut, the knee; *kĕpala l.*, the forepart of the knee; *pĕlipatan l.*, the intercondyloid fossa; *tĕmpurong l.*, the knee-pan; *bĕrlutut*, to be on one's knees.
luyu, *mata luyu*, drooping eyelids.

M

ma', mother (familiar).
maaf, Ar. pardon, forgiveness; *minta m.*, to ask for pardon; = *minta ampun*; *maafkan*, to forgive; also *mahap*.
maalim, = *malim*.
maalum, Ar. known, understood.
maamur, Ar. prosperous, populous, abounding.
maana, Ar. meaning, significance.
maashuk, Ar. the beloved one; mistress; loved.
mabok, intoxication, giddy sickness; *m. bĕrahi*, intoxicated with love; *m. darah*, faint from loss of blood or at the sight of blood; *m. kĕchubong*, dazed by datura poisoning; *m. ombak*, sea-sick.

macham, sort, type; as; *macham-macham*, of sorts, different kinds; *apa m.*, how? *m. ini*, this way, thus.
machan, Jav. a tiger.
machang, the horse-mango (*mangifera foetida*); also *ĕmbachang*.
madah, Ar. saying; utterance; *bĕr-madah*, to say, to speak. II. Ar. the name of the vowel point marking the long *alif*.
madam, I. depression, heaviness; oppression of spirit. II. Eur. a lady of rank.
madat, I. Hind. prepared opium; chandu. II. a turret, a watchtower; battlements.
madrasah, Ar. a school.
madu, I. Skr. sweetness, honey; *ayer m.*, honey; *laut m.*, an ocean of sweetness. II. rival (especially a rival in affections or a rival wife).
mafhum, Ar. understood, grasped, comprehended; *tiada mafhum akan maana bahasa Mĕlayu*, he had not grasped the true spirit of the Malay language.
magang, overripe (of fruit).
maghlub, Ar. conquered, overcome.
maghrib, Ar. the west.
magun, the steersman's compartment in a native ship.
maha, Skr. great (used in compounds only); *maha-bĕsar*, very great; *maha-mulia*, most illustrious; *maha-tinggi*, most exalted.
mahal, costly; difficult to get; rare; *mahal di-bĕli, sukar di-chari*, dear to buy and hard to get for oneself.
mahaligai, Tam. a palace; also *maligai*.
mahang, a generic name for a number of trees (*macaranga* spp.)
mahap, Ar. pardon, forgiveness; also *maaf*.
mahar, Ar. the settlement on a bride by the bridegroom; = *mas kawin*.
mahir, Ar. experienced; master of one's art.

mahisa, Skr. a buffalo; a title in ancient Java; also *misa*.
mahkamah, Ar. a court of justice.
mahkota, Skr. a crown; also *makota*.
mahu, = *mau*.
maidan, = *medan*.
maimun, Ar. lucky, fortunate.
main, sport, play, amusement; *m. judi*, gambling; *bĕrmain*, to play, to play at; *bĕrmain mata*, to cast amorous glances; *pĕrmainan*, an amusement.
maja, a generic name for a number of plants—e.g. *majakani, majapahit*, etc.
majakani, a medicinal plant (unidentified).
majal, short and broad (of a knife).
majapahit, a plant (unidentified); it gave its name to a famous Javanese city and empire.
majlis, Ar. assembly, gathering; *di-tĕngah m.*, in public.
majmu', Ar. sum total.
majoh, gluttonous in eating.
maju, progress, advance, prosperity.
Majuj, Ar. the giant Magog.
majum, oakum.
majusi, Pers. magian; connected with the Zoroastrian religion.
mak, mother; also *ma'*.
maka, then; and so; next; a short interval of time.
makam, Ar. a grave with a small pavilion over it; a grave-shrine.
makan, food; consumption; penetration or biting into; *m. nasi*, to dine; *m. jĕnoh*, to eat one's fill; *di-makan karat*, eaten into with rust; *m. suap*, to take bribes; *m. gaji*, to receive regular pay; *makanan*, food, things eaten; *pĕmakan*, a consumer.
makar, I. hard, stony (of fruit). II. Ar. trickiness; resourcefulness; wiliness.
makbul, Ar. confirmed, approved, agreed to.
makhluk, Ar. created things; mankind; humanity.

maki, I. abuse, reviling, bad language; *mĕmaki,* to revile. II. Ar. *sĕna maki,* "senna of Mecca" (*cassia angustifolia*).
makin, more, the more; *makin lama makin baik,* the longer the better.
makota, Skr. crown; also *mahkota.*
makroh, Ar. hateful, detestable.
maksud, Ar. wish, desire.
maktub, Ar. written; set down in writing.
mal, Ar. property; *bait-ul-mal,* the treasury.
mala, I. Skr. accursed; a curse; misfortune; *m. pĕstaka,* extreme ill-luck. II. faded, withered (of flowers).
malai, a flower worn in the hair; *sunting m.,* id.
malaikat, Ar. an angel.
malak, Ar. angel; *malak-ul-maut,* the angel of death—usually pronounced *malik-ul-maut.*
malam, night; the darkness of night; *tĕngah m.,* midnight; *siang m.,* day and night; *sa-malam,* last night; yesterday evening; *bĕrmalam,* to pass the night.
malan, drunk, mazed, confused, perplexed.
malang, I. adverse fortune; adversity; unlucky obstacles. II. a pinnacle-rock.
malap, flickering (of a light); dulled (of radiance).
malapari, a sea-shore tree (*fagræa fastigiata ?*)
malar, constantly, steadily; regularity; uniformity; *m. puchat kurus,* always pale and thin; *ayer malar dua dĕpa,* water with a constant depth of two fathoms.
malas, idleness, laziness, sluggishness.
malau, *malau gari,* (Kedah) sealing-wax [*malau* is a variant of *ĕmbalau*].
malaun, Ar. accursed, evil.
mali, I. *pĕmali,* tabooed, forbidden. II. *tali tĕmali,* cordage; *mĕmali,* to twine string. III., a generic name given to several plants, especially, (*mali-mali*) to *leea sambucina.*
maligai, Tam. a palace; also *mahaligai.*
malik, I. Ar. a king. II. see *malak.*
malim, Ar. a learned person (especially one learned in navigation); a navigating officer or first mate.
maling, Jav. a thief; thieving; *pintu m.,* a side or back entrance to a Malay house.
malis, faded, dulled (of bright colour).
malong, a large fish (*murænesox telabon*).
malu, shame; modesty; bashfulness; *mĕnaroh m.,* to feel shame; *mĕndapat m.,* to be put to shame; *dĕngan tiada m.,* shameless; *kĕmaluan,* feelings of modesty or shame; the pudenda.
mam, to suck at the breast.
mamah, chewing, masticating, crushing in the mouth; *m. biak,* to chew the cud.
mamai, talking in one's sleep.
mamak, uncle, aunt; uncle (as a form of address from a prince to an aged minister).
maman, a generic name given to some (unidentified) medicinal plants.
mamanda, uncle; a respectful variant of *mamak.*
mamang, I. a stony unnoticing stare; looking but not perceiving. II. *gopoh mamang,* extreme haste.
mambang, a spirit, the personification of the sunset-glow.
mambong, hollow, lacking in fleshy substance (of very young fruit).
mamek, slightly changed or gone off (of taste or flavour).
mamlakat, Ar. kingdom.
mamong, dull, unseeing (of the eyes) —cf. *mamang.*
mampat, I. tight; densely packed. II. *mampat-mampat,* a name given to some plants (*cratoxylon* spp.)
mampu, means, resources; = *upaya.*
mampus, to die (vulgarly expressed);

to be wiped out; to "kick the bucket," to "croak."
mamu, uncle; a variant of *mamak*.
mamun, obscure, involved (of accounts).
man, Hind. a measure of weight; a maund.
mana, I. where, which, what, how, why; *di-mana*, in what place, where; *ka-mana*, whither; *dari-mana*, whence. II. = *maana*.
manah, I. esteemed. II. heart, feelings.
manai, pale, anæmic; *puchat m.*, id.
manau, *rotan manau*, a long and flexible rattan (species unidentified).
manchit, to spout out or gush out.
manchong, clear-cut, sharp-angled (of the profile and especially the nose).
manda, = *mamanda*.
mandai, a tree (unidentified).
mandam, dizzy, intoxicated; *m. khiali*, id.
mandang, I. to see; to gaze at, = *mĕmandang*, from *pandang*. II. *tĕmandang*, aspect; imposing appearance.
mandarsah, = *bandarsah*.
mandi, bathing; to bathe; *batu m.*, a rock that is just awash; *tĕmpat m.*, a bathing-place; *mandikan* or *mĕmandikan*, to give a bath to.
mandong, a cock.
mandul, childless, unfruitful, barren.
mandur, Port. a "mandore"; a headman of coolies.
manek, Skr. a bead; *sa-utas manek-manek*, a string of beads.
manera, I, we, your servant; also *mĕndera*.
manfaat, Ar. profit, gain, success, advantage.
mangap, Jav. agape; with jaws wide open—cf. *mangau*.
mangau, agape (especially with astonishment); *mangap-m.*, wide-agape—cf. *mangap*.

mangga, Skr. the mango—usually *mĕmpĕlam*; *kunchi m.*, a padlock.
manggar, = *mangkar*.
manggis, the mangosteen (*garcinia manggostana*).
manggista, = *manggis*.
manggul, *tanah manggul*, high land.
manggustan, = *manggis*.
mangka, = *maka*.
mangkar, I. *mayang mangkar*, the opening blossom of the coconut (a simile for curly hair). II. unripe, hard; also *makar*.
mangkat, "to be borne aloft" (a euphemism for death when speaking of a prince).
mangkeh, sticking out in all directions; at sixes and sevens.
mangkin, = *makin*.
mangkok, a cup; *pinggan m.*, crockery.
mangkubumi, a regent (in literature), = *pĕmangku raja*.
mangsa, Skr. flesh; food; prey (of animals).
mangsi, Skr. a compound of burnt tamarind bast used for staining the teeth.
mangu, = *mangau*.
mani, Ar. the seminal fluid.
manikam, Tam. gem; essence; embryo; *jauhar juga yang mĕngĕnal m.*, it takes a jeweller to pronounce upon a gem, prov.
manira, = *manera*.
manis, I. sweetness; sweet; (in colour) lightness; *adas m.*, aniseed; *gigi m.*, incisor tooth; *kayu m.*, cinnamon; *kĕmanisan*, sweetness; *pĕ-manis*, a charm to render oneself attractive. II. *jari manis*, the ring-finger.
manja, = *maja*.
manjapada, Skr. the earth; the abode of mortals.
manjong, = *anjong*.
manok, bird; = *unggas*; *m. dewata*, the bird of paradise.
manora, = *mĕndora*.

mantega, = *měntega*.
mantěra, Skr. a magical formula.
manusia, Skr. mankind; man; *orang m.*, a human being; *nyawa m.*, the human soul; *lidah m.*, the human tongue.
manyan, = *kěměnyan*.
mapar, *gang mapar*, a flat-ended brazier's chisel—cf. *papar*.
mara, I. Skr. danger, misfortune; *mara-bahaya*, danger, risk, peril. II. *kota mara*, the breastwork protecting the gunners in the battery of a Malay pirate-ship.
marabahaya, see *mara*.
marah, anger, wrath; *m. angin*, idle threats; *měmarahkan*, to rouse to anger.
marak, to flare up (of a flame).
maras, = *marah*.
mardan, Pers. men.
mareka, = *měreka*.
marga, Skr. a wild animal; *marga-sětua*, wild animals generally.
marhum, Ar. that has found mercy; *al-marhum*, the late (prince).
mari, here; come here; *ka-mari*, hither; *bawa ka-mari*, bring; *pěrgi m.*, going and coming. [In the Straits, *mari* is often used for "come;" *mari sini*, come here; *dia sudah m.*, he has come].
marifat, Ar. perfect knowledge; true wisdom; the wisdom of holiness.
marika, = *měreka*.
marikh, Ar. (the planet) Mars.
maripat, = *marifat*.
markah, Port. the mark on a sounding line.
martabat, Ar. a rung of a ladder; a grade in the scale of rank.
martil, Port. a hammer.
marut, *charut-marut*, very vile (of swearing)—cf. *charut*.
mas, gold, golden; a term of endearment; a Javanese title; a weight = $\frac{1}{16}$ *tahil*; *m. kawin*, the settlements on a bride; *m. těmpawan*, hammered gold; a term of endearment; *m.*

urai, gold dust; *anak m.*, a born slave; *ayer m.*, gilding; *běnang m.*, gold thread; *kěrtas m.*, gold leaf.
masa, Skr. time, season, period, epoch; *pada m. itu*, at that time; *pada tiap-tiap m. dan kětika*, at all times and seasons; *m. mana*, when.
masaalah, Ar. a thesis'; a puzzling question; an enigma; an interrogatory.
masai, *kusut masai*, very much in disorder (of the hair).
masak, ripe, mature, cooked; to cook, to smelt; *m. měntah*, food cooked and raw—an offering to evil spirits; *juru m.*, a cook; *kapur m.*, plaster.
masakan, perhaps; what though; what if; supposing.
masalla, Ar. a prayer-mat.
masam, acid, sour; *m. muka*, sour-faced—cf. *asam*.
Maseh, I. Ar. *Al-maseh*, the Messiah, Jesus. II. = *masi*.
Masehi, Ar. Christian, Protestant.
mashghul, Ar. sad, sorrowful.
mashhur, Ar. famous, well-known; *mashhurkan*, to spread news.
mashrek, Ar. the east.
masi, still; while still; *m. lagi*, id. *di-lihat-nya masi ada lagi baginda sědang běrkata-kata děngan sa-orang těman-nya*, he saw that the king was still conversing with one of his companions.
Masih, = *Maseh*.
Masihi, = *Masehi*.
masin, salt, briny, brackish—cf. *asin*.
masing, separate, singly; *masing-masing*, each—cf. *asing*.
masiat, Ar. crime, treachery, wickedness.
masjid, Ar. a mosque; *masjid-ul-haram*, the great mosque at Mecca; also *měsěgit*.
masok, entering; progress inwards; *di-bawa m.*, carried in; *m. kěluar*, going in and out; *m. Islam* or *m. Mělayu*, to become a Muhammadan;

masoki or *mĕmasoki*, to enter into; *masokkan* or *mĕmasokkan*, to insert.

mastuli, *kain mastuli*, a heavy cloth of rich silk.

mat, Pers. mate (at chess) *shah-mat*, checkmate.

mata, I. eye, focus, centre; the blade or point of a weapon; a point of the compass; *m. ayer*, a spring; *m. bisul*, the head of a boil; *m. gobek*, the blade of a betel-nut pounder; *m. gunting*, the point of a pair of scissors; *m. hari*, the sun; *m. hati*, mental perception; the mind's eye; *m. jalan*, an outpost, a scout; *m. juling*, squint-eyed; *m. kail*, a fish-hook; *m. kakap*, the plug-hole; *m. kayu*, a knot in wood; *m. kĕris*, the blade of a *kĕris*; *m. kuching*, "cat's-eye," a well-known fruit (*nephelium malayense*); *damar m. kuching*, a valuable damar obtained from *hopea globosa*; *m. liar*, wild-eyed; *m. luka*, the orifice of a wound; *m.-mata*, (in independent Malaya), a satellite of the *shah-bandar* or harbour-master; (in Malacca) a *pĕnghulu's* assistant; (in British Malaya generally) a policeman; *m.-m. gĕlap*, a detective; *di-mata-mata*, openly; *sa-mata-mata*, obviously, clearly, plainly; *m. panah*, the point of an arrow; *m. pasak*, blue eyes; grey eyes; *m. pĕdang*, the blade of a sword; *m. pĕdoman*, the needle of a compass; *m. punai*, "green-pigeons' eyes"; the lozenge-shaped apertures in a grille or cross-grating; *m. sabun*, pale-eyed, white-eyed; *m. susu*, the nipple of the breast; *m. tong*, the bung-hole in a cask; *anak m.*, the pupil of the eye; *ayer m.*, tears; *bĕrmain m.*, eye-play, *biji m.*, the eyeball; *bulu m.*, eye-lashes; *chahaya m.*, light of the eyes; a term of endearment; *chĕrmin m.*, eye-glasses, spectacles; *ekur m.*, the corner of the eye; *kĕlopak m.*, the eyelid; *liang m.*, the eye-socket; *orang-orangan m.*, the image in the pupil of the eye; *puteh m.*, being put to shame; *silap m.*, false pretences; legerdemain; *tĕrus m.*, (1) clearness of vision; (2) second sight. II. Ar. things of value; gems, etc., which represent great value in small compass; *m. bĕnda* and *m. dagangan*, id.

matab, blue-lights; Roman candles.

matah, = *mĕntah*.

matahari, the sun—v. *mata* and *hari*.

matang, *pĕrmatang* or *pĕmatang*, a stretch of high sandy soil in a rice-swamp.

mateng, Jav. cooked, ripe, = *masak*.

mati, death; finality; ended; *m. di-bunoh*, death by violence; "a bad end"; *m. lĕmas*, death by suffocation or drowning; *m. puchok*, loss of virility; *bĕlanja m.*, fixed allowance; *grant m.*, a freehold grant of land; *hĕrga m.*, a fixed price; *simpul m.*, a knot which is not a slip-knot or running knot; *m. anak*, = *puntianak*, q.v.; *burong m. sa-kawan*, a bird (*anorrhinus galeritus*); *kĕmatian*, death, termination.

mau, wish, intention, will; a common but vulgar auxiliary for forming the future; *mau ta'-mau*, willy-nilly.

maulana, Ar. lord, master.

Maulia, Ar. O God; my lord.

maulud, Ar. birthday; *bulan M.*, the month containing the Prophet's birthday, the month *Rabi'i'l-awal*.

maung, unpleasant in taste; nasty (of flavour).

maut, Ar. death; the hour of death; *malak-ul-maut*, the angel of death.

mawa, a leaf-monkey (*semnopithecus* sp.)—believed by Malays to live on dew.

mawar, Ar. rose-water; *ayer m.*, id.; *bunga ayer m.*, the rose.

mawas, the Sumatran-Malay name for the mias or orang-outang (*simia satyrus*)—an animal only known to Peninsular Malays by tradition and

so endowed with miraculous attributes.
mawin, *kawin-mawin*, marriage-festivities generally; a frequentative of *kawin*.
maya, I. Skr. unsubstantial, illusory; *mayapada*, this transitory earth; = *manjapada*. II. *umur maya*, trickiness—a corruption of the name of *'Umar Ummaiya*, the Ulysses of the Hikayat Hamza.
mayam, a weight = $\frac{1}{16}$ of a *tahil* or *bongkal*.
mayang, the blossom of a palm; *sĕpĕrti m. mĕngurai*, or *sĕpĕrti m. mĕkar*, like the unfolding blossom of the palm—a symbol for beautiful curling hair.
mayapada, see *maya* and *manjapada*.
mayat, Ar. a dead body (expressed respectfully)—cf. *bangkai*.
mayau, absent-minded.
ma'yong, a theatrical performance met with in the Northern States of the Peninsula.
mazkur, Ar. mentioned, stated; *sĕpĕrti yang tĕrmazkur*, as stated.
medan, Pers. a plain, an open field, a field of battle.
mĕdang, I. a generic name given to a large number of trees of the order *laurineæ*, and to others which have a timber of similar appearance. II. *batu mĕdang sila*, a kind of gypsum used medicinally.
mĕdu, I. squeamishness, nausea. II. *mĕdu wangsa*, a complimentary epithet occurring in Malayo-Javanese romances.
meerat, Ar. to die; to fall in a trance; the admission of Muhammad to heaven; the golden stairs; *bulan M.*, a name given to the month *Rajab*.
mega, I. Skr. white fleecy clouds; cirrhus; *m. bĕrangkat*, rising white cirrhus; *m. bĕrarak*, white clouds chasing each other across the sky; *m. dadu*, a rosy-tinted sunset sky. II. you; = *ĕngkau*.

mĕgah, fame, glory; *pĕrkara yang mĕgah-mĕgah*, matters of weight—cf. *gah*.
mĕgak, disrespectful; taking liberties.
megan, a sweetmeat.
mĕgat, Skr. a (Kedah) title given to men of good birth (especially when of royal descent on the mother's side).
meja, Port. a tale.
mĕjam, rotation round a motionless centre; the rotation of a wheel in an engine-room.
mĕjĕlis, fair, pretty, handsome.
meka, = *mega*, II.
mĕkar, Jav. to open out (of a bud or blossom); *mayang m.*, the opening blossom of the palm—a simile for curling hair.
mĕkis, defiance; *mĕmĕkis*, to defy; also *mĕngkis*.
mĕlainkan, but, still, nevertheless; except; see *lain*.
mĕlaka, Skr. a plant (*phyllanthus pectinatus*), giving its name to the well-known town of Malacca; *gula m.*, syrup; coconut sugar; a well-known sweet eaten with coconut sugar; *buah m.*, a Malay dumpling—dough filled with sweets.
mĕlarat, I. difficulty, loss, injury. II. see *larat*.
mĕlas, badly fitting; not coinciding.
mĕlati, Skr. a name for the jasmine—usually *mĕlur* (*jasminum sambu*).
Mĕlayu, Malayan, Malay; Muhammadan; *anak M.*, a Malay; *orang M.*, id.; *masok M.*, to become a Muhammadan; *M. jati*, a true Malay.
mĕlela, see *lela*.
mĕlilin, = *mĕrlilin*.
mĕlimau, = *mĕrlimau*.
mĕlimun, = *halimun*.
mĕling, to turn away; to look in another direction.
mĕlit, inquisitiveness.
mĕlokan, = *mĕrlokan*.
mĕlong, over-developed; over-big for the age.

mĕlukut, broken grains of husked rice; also *lĕmukut*.
mĕlur, the Indian jasmine (*jasminum sambu*).
mem, Eng. a European lady.
mĕmali, = *mali-mali*—v. *mali*, III.
memang, permanently; definitely; for good; *memang tahu bahasa*, to know a language beyond the possibility of forgetting it.
mĕmar, bruised, crushed (of a fruit).
mĕmbachang, = *ĕmbachang*.
mĕmbalau, = *ĕmbalau*.
mĕmbĕrang, = *bĕrang-bĕrang*.
memek, whining, fretting (as a very young child).
mĕmĕrang, = *bĕrang-bĕrang*.
mĕmpas, = *mĕpas*.
mĕmpĕdal, = *pĕdal*.
mĕmpĕdu, = *hĕmpĕdu*.
mĕmpĕlai, Tam. a bridegroom; *naik m.*, to ascend the bridal dais; to be married.
mĕmpĕlam, the mango (*mangifera indica*).
mĕmpĕlas, a plant (*tetracera assa*).
mĕmpĕlasari, a name given to two plants (*alyxia stellata* and *alyxia lucida*).
mĕmpĕning, a generic name for several trees (*quercus* spp.)
mĕmpoyan, a plant (*rhodamnia trinervia*).
mĕna, I. calculation; = *kira*; *samĕna-mĕna*, about, approximately; *tidak bĕrsamĕna* or *tiada tĕpĕrmĕnaï*, incalculable. II. see *sĕmĕna*.
mĕnalu, = *bĕndalu*.
mĕnang, to win; to prevail; to be successful; *mĕnangkan*, to give victory to.
mĕnantu, son-in-law, daughter-in-law.
mĕnara, Ar. a minaret.
menat, coveting; desiring what is in another's possession.
mĕnatu, a laundryman.
mĕnchak, fencing (in a sort of sword-dance); = *main pĕnchak*.

mĕnching, at full stretch, fully distended.
mĕndam, = *mandam*.
mĕndĕleka, a tree yielding a kind of bread-fruit.
mĕndera, I, we; your servant.
mĕndĕrong, a sedge used in mat-making (*scirpus grossus*).
mĕndikai, a water-melon.
mĕndong, Jav. gloomy; overcast (of the weather).
mĕndora, a theatrical performance of Siamese or Buddhist origin.
mĕndusta, false, sham (of a chignon, etc.); see *dusta*.
mĕnera, = *mĕndera*.
mĕnĕrong, = *mĕndĕrong*.
mĕngah, = panting; puffing.
mĕngeh, drawing a quick breath (as a man after exercise).
mĕngĕrna, gay with colour; pretty —cf. *warna*.
mĕngkal, half-ripe (of fruit); just beginning to soften.
mĕngkarong, = *bĕngkarong*.
mĕngkawan, = *bĕngkawan*.
mĕngkĕlan, sticking in the throat; *tĕrmĕngkĕlan*, stuck in the throat (of food).
mĕngkis, defiance; also *mĕkis*.
mĕngkong, *chĕngkong-mĕngkong*, very hollow and emaciated (of the face).
mĕngkoyan, = *mĕmpoyan*.
mĕngkuang, the common screw-pine (*pandanus atrocarpus*). [The name is also given to some other species of *pandanus*.]
mĕngkudu, a generic name for a number of plants used in dyeing (especially *morinda tinctoria*).
mĕngkunyit, = *mĕrkunyit*.
mĕngsu, *bulu mĕngsu*, the fine hairs round the forehead.
mengut, ill-fitting, unsuitable, inharmonious.
mĕniaga, = *bĕrniaga*.
mĕnjak, see *sĕmĕnjak*.
mĕnjana, see *sĕmĕnjana*.

měnjangan, the barking-deer (*cervulus muntjac*); usually *kijang*.
měnjělai, = *jělai*.
měnjělis, = *mějělis*.
měnong, *těrměnong*, sunk in thought.
měnora, = *měndora*.
měnta, = *měta*.
měntah, raw, uncooked; *masak m.*, food cooked and uncooked—as an offering to evil spirits.
měntang, see *sěměntang*.
měntangur, = *běntangur*.
měntega, Port. butter.
měntělah, see *sěměntělah*.
měntěra, = *mantěra*.
měntěri, Skr. minister, vizier; *pěrdana m.*, prime minister.
měntigi, a plant (*thibaudia* sp.?)
měntimun, a generic name for gourds, pumpkins, passion-flowers, etc.; also *timun*, q.v.
měntua, father-in-law; mother-in-law.
měpas, fly-fishing.
měraga, = *marga*.
měragi, variegated in colouring—cf. *ragi*; *burong m.*, the painted snipe (*rostratula capensis*).
měrah, a Sumatran title of distinction.
merah, red; *m. tua*, dark red; *m. měrang*, bright red; *m. muda*, light red; *m. padam*, lotus-red, fiery red—as the face of an angry warrior.
měrak, a peacock (*pavo muticus*); *m. mas*, a "golden peacock," a type of a beautiful bird; *jambul m.*, "the peacock's crest," a name given to a plant (*poinciana pulcherrima*).
měrakap, Ar. *jahil měrakap*, ignorance added to ignorance; extreme ignorance.
měrang, *merah měrang*, bright red.
měrangu, an obsolete musical wind-instrument.
měranti, a name given to a number of trees (*shorea* spp.) which yield a good soft wood.

měrawan, I. a tree (*hopea mengarawan*). II. = *běrawan*, from *awan*, q.v.
měrbah, the yellow-vented bulbul (*pycnonotus analis*).
měrbak, see *sěměrbak*.
měrbatu, a generic name given to several trees (*parinarium* spp.)
měrbau, the well-known hard-wood tree (*afzelia palembanica*).
měrbaya, = *mara-bahaya*.
měrbok, the Malay turtle-dove (*turtur tigrinus*).
měrbulan, a tree (unidentified).
měrbuloh, a plant (*gynotroches axillaris*).
měrcha, Skr. to faint, to swoon.
měrchapada, Skr. the earth; = *manjapada*.
měrchu, summit, crest, highest pinnacle.
měrchun, crackers, fireworks, cartridges.
měrdangga, an ancient Javanese musical instrument.
měrděheka, Skr. freedom (in contradistinction to slavery); *měrdehekakan*, to liberate; also *měrdeka*.
měrdeka, see *měrděheka*.
měrdu, Skr. soft, sweet (of the voice or of music).
měreh, Ar. *urat měreh*, the windpipe.
měreka, they; *měreka-itu*, id.
měrěla, improperly suggestive (of behaviour).
měrělang, smooth-edged; without a rim or raised border.
mereng, to heel over (of a boat).
měrga, = *marga*.
měrgěstua, = *marga-sětua*.
měrgok, = *běrgok*.
měriam, a cannon; *pědati m.*, the gun-carriage; *ringgit m.*, the pillar-dollar.
měrikan, Tam. an honorific in use among Muhammadan settlers from Southern India.
měrinyu, Port. an overseer; an inspector of police; a municipal inspector; a land bailiff.

měrjagong, a plant (*ixonanthes obovata*).
měrjan, Ar. red coral beads.
měrkah, to crack, to split; *saga m.*, the cracking Indian pea—a simile for the mouth; *dělima m.*, the cracking pomegranate; another simile for a beautiful mouth.
měrkubang, a tree (*mezzetia herveyana*).
měrkunyit, *akar měrkunyit*, a plant (*coscinum blumeanum*).
měrlilin, a plant (unidentified).
měrlimau, *akar měrlimau*, a scandent thorny wild orange (*paramignya monophylla*).
měrlokan, a tree (unidentified).
měrombong, a small tree (*timonius jambosella*). [The name is also applied to *adina polycephala*, *vernonia arborea* and *vatica pallida*.]
měroyan, I. *sakit měroyan*, a disease of women. II. a generic name for a number of plants—e.g. *dissochoeta* spp.
měrpadi, a plant (*symplocos fasciculata*).
měrpati, Skr. a pigeon.
měrpisang, a palm (*polyalthia jenkinsii*).
měrpuing, a plant (*carallia integerrima*).
měrsek, sharp, shrill (of sound).
měrta, I. Skr. *ayer měrta-jiwa*, the water of life; = *ayer utama jiwa*. II. *sěrta-měrta*, and on that very moment; thereupon.
měrtajam, a tree (*erioglossum edule*).
měrtapal, a tree (unidentified).
měrtua, = *měntua*.
měruap, to boil over; to boil up.
měrunggai, the horse-radish (*moringa pterygosperma*); also *rěmunggai*.
mesa, = *misa*.
měsarong, a shell (*pinna*).
měsěgit, Ar. a mosque; also *masjid*.
mesem, grinning, smiling; *běrmesem-mesem*, to keep grinning.

měshuarat, Ar. counsel, conference; *běrměshuarat*, to take counsel.
měsirah, a name given to some small plants (*ilex cymosa* and *randia densiflora*).
měsiu, saltpetre.
měski, Port. although, even though; *m. běrbisek, sahaya pun tahu*, even though you speak in whispers, I can tell what you are saying.
měsra, Skr. complete assimilation or absorption through and through.
městěri, a master-workman; a "maistry."
městi, Jav. needs; needs must; must; certainly must.
městika, a bezoar; a talisman; a term of endearment.
Měsuara, Skr. Maheswara; Siva.
měsui, a tree with a fragrant bark used medicinally (*cortex* sp.)
měta, Skr. uncontrollable; mad (of an elephant); *gajah m.*, a rutting elephant.
mětapal, = *měrtapal*.
mětěrai, see *těra*.
mětu, = *mutu*.
mewah, excess, over-abundance, overflowing prosperity; *kěmewahan*, id.
mewek, pursing up the mouth to cry; pouting.
miang, the fine hair-like pieces of bamboo seen when a bamboo is split or broken; the smart created by them or by a nettle; ticklish; itchiness; lasciviousness; *m. gatal*, extreme itchiness or lustfulness.
miap, *miap-tiap*, every, each—cf. *tiap*.
midar, = *měngidar*, from *idar*, q.v.
mihrab, Ar. the niche in a mosque indicating the direction in which Mecca lies.
mika, = *mega*, II.
Mikael, Ar. the Archangel Michael.
milam, an old man or old woman.
milek, Ar. property, possession; *grant m.*, a freehold title.
mimbar, Ar. a sort of pulpit or lectern in a Malay mosque.

mimpi, dream, dreaming; *bĕrmimpi*, to dream.
mina, Skr. the sea; *gajah m.*, the sea-elephant or leviathan; the whale.
minat, = *menat*.
minggu, Port. week; *hari M.*, Sunday.
minta, requesting; applying for; asking for; *m. ampun*, to beg pardon; *m. tabek*, to ask to be excused; *m. doa*, to pray for any person or thing; *mĕminta*, to request; *pĕrmintaan*, a request—cf. *pinta*.
minum, drinking; *makan dan m.*, eating and drinking; *m. madat*, opium smoking; *m. rokok*, smoking; *minuman*, a drink; *mĕminum*, to drink; *pĕminum*, a man given to drink.
minyak, oil, fat, ointment, grease; *m. gas*, kerosene oil; *m. ikan*, train oil; *m. jarak*, castor-oil; *m. kachang*, ground-nut oil; *m. kĕlapa*, coconut oil; *m. sapi*, suet; *m. tanah*, crude petroleum; *m. zetun*, olive-oil.
mipis, = *nipis*.
mirah, *batu mirah*, a ruby, a carbuncle, a jacinth.
miring, = *mereng*.
misa, Skr. buffalo; an ancient Javanese title; = *mahisa*.
misai, moustache; *m. bĕrtaring*, a moustache with fiercely turned-up ends; *m. lĕbat*, a drooping moustache.
misal, Ar. example, instance; *misalnya*, for instance.
Misir, Ar. *nĕgĕri Misir*, Egypt.
miskal, Ar. a weight of about 1¼ drachms.
miskin, Ar. poor; poverty.
misoh, Jav. to abuse, to scold.
misru, shot with gold (of cloth); cloth shot with gold thread.
mistar, Ar. a ruled line; an instrument for ruling lines.
mithal, = *misal*.
modal, Tam. capital for working a business; *makan m.*, to live on one's capital.

modar, *mati modar*, to die choked—in imprecations of a violent end.
modin, Ar. a circumciser.
moga, *moga-moga*, would that; might it be; may it be.
mogah, adultery, fornication; also *mukah*.
moh, = *ĕmboh*.
mohon, *bĕrmohon*, to take one's leave; to depart—cf. *pohon*.
mohor, Pers. the stamp or die-mark on a coin.
mola, = *mula*.
molek, charming, pretty.
molong, *buah molong*, a sweetmeat resembling the *buah mĕlaka*.
mo'mit, the movements of the mouth in speaking or eating.
momok, blunt.
momong, = *mongmong*.
monchong, snout-shaped; a snout; *m. cherek*, the spout of a kettle.
mondok, short and thick; stumpy—cf. *montok*.
monggok, rising in the form of a dome; protuberant (as a small mound); *batu m.*, a cairn.
monggol, knotty, gnarled (of a tree).
monggor, = *mongkor*.
mongkok, = *monggok*.
mongkor, a litter or sedan-chair (mentioned in romances).
mongmong, (onom.) a small brass gong (laid on the ground and beaten).
montok, short in proportion to its length; stumpy—cf. *mondok*.
monyet, a monkey; "monkey" (as a term of abuse).
mopeng, pock-marked; also *bopeng*.
morah, = *murah*.
morang, = *murang*.
moreng, = *choreng-moreng*, streaked with dirt in all directions—cf. *choreng*.
morong, I. gloomy, despondent, despairing, miserable. II. a cooking-pot. III. a medicinal plant (*scirpus grossus*).
mota, a coarse sail-cloth.

mo'tabar, Ar. worthy, excellent, honourable.
moyang, great-grandfather or great-grandmother ; *nenek m.*, ancestors.
moyangda, a respectful form of *moyang*, great-grandfather.
mozah, Pers. shoes, boots (in literature only).
mu, you ; = *kamu*.
mua, disgust, abhorence ; also *muak*.
muafakat, Ar. agreement, arrangement, settled plan ; *bĕrmuafakat*, to meet in conference ; to settle by discussion ; to agree upon ; also *mupakat* and *pakat*.
muak, disgust, nausea ; also *mua*.
mual, to expand ; swelling out (of rice when boiled).
mualim, Ar. a learned man ; an expert ; a navigator—cf. *malim*.
muara, the estuary of a river ; = *kuala*.
muat, loading cargo ; *muatan*, cargo ; *bĕrmuat*, to be laden with ; *muatkan*, to load with.
muazam, Ar. awe-inspiring, majestic, sublime ; *sultan al-muazam*, the august sultan—i.e. the Sultan of Turkey.
mubarak, Ar. blessed.
mubut, fragile, weak.
muda, young, unripe, light (of colouring), much alloyed (of metals) ; *raja m.*, the heir-apparent ; *mas m.*, much-alloyed gold ; *merah m.*, light red.
mudah, easy, light, trivial ; *dĕngan mudah-nya*, easily ; *mudah-mudahan*, perhaps ; possibly ; would that ; *mudahkan* or *mĕmudahkan*, to render easy, painless, or light ; *pĕrmudahkan*, to treat as of little account, to slight.
mudek, travelling up stream.
mudĕli, an obsolete musical instrument.
mudi, rear, stern, rudder ; *juru m.*, the steersman ; *kĕmudi*, a rudder ; *kĕmudian*, after, subsequently.

mufti, Ar. a specialist in law and theology ; a doctor of Muhammadan law ; a sort of chief justice.
mugah, = *mogah*.
muhabat, Ar. love.
muhallil, Ar. an intermediate husband required by Muhammadan law to render the remarriage of fully divorced persons legal.
Muharram, Ar. the first month of the Muhammadan year.
mujarrab, Ar. tried ; tested by experience ; trusty.
mujur, fortunate ; good luck ; good fortune ; *kĕmujuran*, id.
muka, face, countenance, visage, front ; *m. papan*, brazen-faced impudence ; *m. manis*, pleasant look ; *m. surat*, a page ; *di-m. pintu*, in front of the door ; *ayer m.*, expression, look ; *chahaya m.*, id. ; *sĕri m.*, the charm of the countenance ; *muka-muka*, feigned feelings, hypocritical airs.
mukaddis, Ar. *bait-ul-mukaddis*, the heavenly city.
mukah, fornication, adultery ; also *mogah*.
mukim, Ar. a parish ; a territorial division ; the area served by one mosque of general assembly.
mukun, a bowl or cup.
mula, commencement, beginning, source ; *mula-mula*, to begin with ; firstly ; *sa-mula*, as at first ; *sa-bĕrmula*, in the first place ; *mulaï*, to commence, to begin ; *mĕmulaï*, id. ; *pĕrmulaan*, commencement, beginning.
mulas, *mulas pĕrut*, griping pains in the stomach—cf. *pulas*.
mulia, Skr. illustrious, glorious ; *kain yang m.*, a mantle of splendid appearance ; *maha-mulia*, most illustrious ; most exalted ; *pĕrmuliakan*, to honour ; to treat with distinction ; *kĕmuliaan*, a mark of honour or distinction.
mulut, mouth ; *manis m.*, soft-spoken ;

panjang m., loquacious; *sĕdap m.*, fair-spoken; *bawa m.*, tale-bearing.

mumbang, the young coconut; the nut in its early stages of development.

mumbong, loaded above the gunwale (of a ship or boat).

mumin, Ar. devout, religious, God-fearing; *Amir-ul-muminin*, Commander of the Faithful, Caliph.

mumut, beating (as the pulse or fontanel); throbbing.

munajat, Ar. private devotions.

munchong, = *monchong*.

mundam, a large wash-tub of earthenware.

mundu, a tree (*garcinia dulcis*).

mundur, to retreat; = *mĕngundur*, from *undur*.

mungkir, Ar. to deny, to repudiate a statement, to refuse.

mungkum, dome-shaped, covering like a dome.

mungut, to totter.

munshi, Hind. a teacher of languages.

muntah, vomiting; *muntahkan*, to vomit up; *muntahkan darah*, to vomit blood—believed to be the result of an evil spirit's work and consequently imprecated as a curse.

muntĕri, = *mĕntĕri*.

mupakat, Ar. agreement; decision after consultation; *bĕrmupakat*, to agree upon a course; also *muafakat* and *pakat*.

mura, *ular mura*, a venomous snake (*lachesis purpureomaculatus*, black variety, or *naia sputatrix*)—cf. *bura*.

murah, generous, good-hearted, liberal; cheap; *lagi murah, lagi ditawar*, the more I reduce, the more he bargains! *maha-murah*, all-generous (of God); *kĕmurahan*, generosity.

murai, *burong murai*, the magpie-robin (*copsychus saularis*); *m. batu*, the shama (*cittocincla macrura*); *m. gajah*, the fairy blue bird (*irena cyanaea*); *m. gila*, a name given to fantail fly-catchers (*rhipadura* spp.)

murang, Port. the match (applied to a cannon).

muri, I. Pers. a flute or clarionet of metal. II. moiré-cloth.

murid, Ar. pupil, disciple; *anak m.*, id.

murka, Skr. wrath, anger; the wrath of God or of a prince; *murkaï*, to be angered; *murkakan*, to be angry with (a person).

mursal, Ar. one sent; an apostle.

murtad, Ar. renegade; the abandonment of the true faith.

murup, fiery (of colouring); brilliant.

Musa, Ar. *nabi Musa*, Moses.

musafar, Ar. a traveller.

musang, a generic name for civets; *m. akar*, the small-toothed palm-civet (*arctogale leucotis*); *m. babi*, the water-mongoose (*herpestes brachyurus*); *m. batu*, the zebra civet-cat (*arctogale leucotis*); = *m. akar*; *m. buah*, the tiger-civet (*prionodon gracilis*); *m. bulan*, the white-whiskered palm-civet (*paradoxurus leucomystax*); *m. jĕbat*, the Indian civet (*viverra zibetha*); *m. mĕngkuang*, = *m. pandan*; *m. pandan* (the civet *paradoxurus hermaphroditus*); *m. tĕbĕrau*, a dark civet (probably *paradoxurus niger*); *m. tĕnggalong*, the Burmese civet (*viverra megaspila*); *Pa' Musang*, a legendary person, whose extraordinary good luck always got him out of the scrapes into which his impulsive and foolish disposition plunged him.

mushkil, Ar. difficult.

Mushtari, Ar. *bintang Mushtari*, Jupiter.

musim, Ar. season; monsoon; *m. hujan*, the rainy season; *m. kĕmarau*, the dry season; *m. utara*, the north-east monsoon.

muslihat, Ar. resource, stratagem, means; = *daya* or *upaya*.

Muslim, Ar. Moslem, Muhammadan.

musoh, a public enemy; a national foe; *bĕrmusoh dĕngan*, to be at war with; *pĕrmusohan*, a state of war.

mustaed, Ar. in working order; ready for use; ready.

mustahil, Ar. foolish, absurd, incredible, ridiculous.

mustajab, Ar. efficacious; sure to act (of a medicine).

mustakim, Ar. upright, sincere.

mutabir, = *mo' tabar*.

mutia, Skr. pearl; *siput m.*, mother-of-pearl shell; *intan m.*, diamonds and pearls—cf. *mutiara*.

mutiara, Skr. a pearl; *indong m.*, the pearl oyster; mother-of-pearl; *ayam m.*, a guinea-fowl.

mutu, I. sad, sorrowful, melancholy, brooding; *bĕrhati m.*, id. II. a pearl. III. Tam. a measure of the purity of gold; *mas sa-puloh m.*, 24 carat gold.

muyu, *buah muyu*, a black and sour fruit (species unidentified).

N, Ng, Ny

naam, Ar. yes; certainly; so it is.

nabi, Ar. prophet; *n. Ibrahim*, Abraham; *n. Idris*; Enoch; *n. Isa*, Jesus; *nabi-nabi*, the starfish of seven points—cf. *tapak sulaiman*.

nadar, = *nadzar*.

nadi, = Skr. the arterial pulse.

nadir, I. *pĕrahu nadir*, a large Malacca type of sea-going fishing-boat. II. Ar. inspector, supervisor, overseer; = *nadzir*.

nadzar, Ar. a vow; a promise made to God.

nadzir, Ar. an overseer, a superintendent, an inspector; also *nadir*.

nafas, Ar. breath, respiration; *mĕnarek n.*, to breathe; *bĕrnafas*, id.; also *napas*.

nafi, I. Ar. expulsion, banishment; *nafikan*, to expel. II. Ar. advantageous, profitable, spiritually useful.

nafiri, Pers. a long narrow trumpet solemnly blown at a coronation, and so one of the jealously guarded appurtenances of Malay royalty.

nafkah, Ar. means of livelihood; a living; *mĕnchari n.*, to seek a livelihood; *mĕndapat n.*, to earn a livelihood.

nafsu, Ar. lust, passion, the promptings of the flesh; *hawa n.*, id.; *mĕnahan n.*, to bridle one's passions.

naga, Skr. a dragon, a snake of supernatural size; *chula n.*, the horn of a dragon; *gĕmala n.*, the luminous bezoar with which a dragon lights its way; *n. balun*, a dragon that kills by lashing with its tail; *n. bĕrapi*, a fire-breathing dragon; *n. bura*, a snake that spits out venom on its foes (*naia sputatrix*?); *n. gĕntala*, a gigantic dragon that lies still and simply sucks its prey into its mouth—see also below: *n. umbang*, a huge marine dragon; *n. bĕrjuang*, *n. bĕrsĕru* and *n. gĕntala*, names of patterns (converging, diverging and parallel lines, respectively); *n. naga*, (1) a dragon-shaped figure-head; (2) the keelson; *pĕrahu kakap n.*, a boat with a dragon-shaped figure-head.

nagasari, a tree yielding a pretty flower (*messua ferra*).

nah, there!—an interjection.

nahak, *tĕrnahak*, excited (of appetite, lust, or desire).

nahas, Ar. ill-starred; foredoomed to misfortune; *saat yang n.*, an unlucky hour.

nahi, Ar. the forbidden; *n. Allah*, what God has forbidden.

nahu, Ar. grammar—i.e. Arabic inflexions.

naib, Ar. deputy; *n. kali*, a kali's deputy; *n. raja*, a viceroy.

naik, ascent, motion upwards; *n. raja* or *n. kĕrajaan*, to ascend the throne; *n. kĕreta*, to mount up into a carriage; *n. darat*, to go ashore; *n. haji*, to go on the pilgrimage to Mecca; *tĕngah n.*, half-grown; *kĕnaikan*, a mount; a steed or vehicle.

najis, Ar. filth; things which defile; *kĕna n.*, to incur pollution; *kĕlakuan yang n.*, filthy habits.

nak, = *hĕndak*.

naka, part-singing; singing in alternation.

nakal, perverse, mischievous; *bĕrnakal* or *mĕnakal*, to commit mischief in sheer wantonness.

nakhoda, Pers. the master of an Arab or Persian trading-ship.

nal, (Dutch) wad.

naleh a measure of capacity, = 16 *gantang*.

nali, I. a turn to play, an innings in a Malay game. II. = *naleh*.

nama, Skr. name, designation, renown; *nama-nya Muhammad*, he was named Muhammad; *bĕroleh n.*, to obtain renown; *namaï* and *namakan*, to name; *bĕrnama*, by name, named; *kĕnamaan*, reputation, renown; *tĕrnama*, famous.

nambi, an ulcerating disease of the feet.

namnam, a fruit tree (*cynometra cauliflora*).

nampak, to see; to be visible—cf. *tampak*.

nampal, marl; also *napal*.

nan, who, which, that—a poetic equivalent of *yang*.

nanah, matter, pus.

nanai, a monkey (in the language of magic).

nanar, giddy; silly (as the result of a blow); wild behaviour (as the result of illness).

nanas, the pine-apple (*ananassa* spp.)

nanda, = *anakanda*.

nandong, *tupai nandong*, the large squirrel (*sciurus bicolor*).

nang, = *nan* and *yang*.

nangak, a trunkless palm (unidentified).

nangka, the jack-fruit (*artocarpus integrifolia*).

nangui, dwarf; *babi n.*, a name given to the half-grown wild-pig; *anak n.*, a dwarf.

naning, a large wasp.

nanti, awaiting, to await; (in bazaar Malay) shall, will; *nantikan*, to await, to wait for; *mĕnanti*, to sit waiting.

napal, marl; also *nampal*.

napas, Ar. breath, respiration; also *nafas*.

napi, inability to notice; absent-mindedness; unconsciousness of one's surroundings.

napoh, the larger chevrotin (*tragulus napu*).

nara, Skr. hero, man (only occuring in titles).

naracha, = *nĕracha*.

naraka, Skr. hell; *api n.*, the fires of hell.

narwastu, spikenard; frankincense.

nasab, Ar. race, descent, family, origin.

nasar, Ar. *burong nasar*, the vulture.

nasek, *nasek-nasek*, a generic name for many plants (especially *eugenia zeylanica*).

nasi, boiled rice; *makan n.*, to dine; *n. hadap-hadap*, the rice consumed at a wedding feast [if the bride is a widow, it is called *nasi damai*]; *n. kabuli*, "pillau" rice; *n. kukus*, steamed rice; *n. kuning*, rice cooked with saffron; *n. lĕmak*, rice cooked in coconut water; *n. minyak*, rice cooked in oil or mutton-fat; *n. pĕlabur*, rations; *n. pulau*, = *n. kabuli*; *n. tambah*, a second helping of rice; *n. tanak*, plain boiled rice.

nasib, Ar. fortune, luck, destiny, lot in life; *sudah untong n.*, it is my destiny; *n. malang*, extreme bad luck; *mĕmbawa n.*, to trust to luck; to risk one's all.

nasihat, Ar. advice; the moral of a story; *mĕnasihat*, to advise.

naskah, Ar. original text (*editio princeps*).

Nasrani, Ar. "Nazarene"; Christian (especially Roman Catholic); also *Sĕrani*.

nata, Skr. lord, prince; *sang-n.*, the king.

natang, Siam. a French window.

natar, smooth, level; = *rata*; also *datar*.

nati, a fool, a blockhead.

nau, a palm (*arenga saccharifera*).

naung, shade; shelter from the sun; shelter generally; *naungi* or *mĕnaungi*, to give shelter to; *bĕrnaung*, to take shelter.

nayam, the blade of a ploughshare.

nazam, Ar. order, composition, arrangement; = *karangan*.

neemat, Ar. a delight; a pleasure; a joy; anything pleasant to the taste.

nega, = *neka*.

nĕgara, I. Skr. city, town—a poetic variant of *nĕgĕri*. II. Ar. a kettledrum (included among the insignia of Malay royalty).

nĕgĕri, Skr. town, city, state.

neka, Skr. kinds, species; *sĕrba n.*, various; also *aneka*.

nĕlayan, Tam. a fisherman.

nĕnas, = *nanas*.

nenda, a respectful variant of *nenek*, grandfather or grandmother.

nenek, grandfather, grandmother; *n. moyang*, ancestors.

nenenda, = *nenda*.

nenes, *bĕrnenes*, to ooze out (of pus).

nĕntiasa, Skr. *sa-nĕntiasa*, always, at all times [usually in the forms *sĕnĕntiasa* or *sĕntiasa*.]

nĕracha, a balance; a sensitive pair of scales.

nesan, Pers. a grave-stone.

nĕschaya, certain, sure, inevitable, must be, must come about.

nĕsta, = *nista*,

nĕstapa, Jav. and Skr. sorrow, misfortune, suffering.

nĕtiasa, = *nĕntiasa*.

ngada, *mĕnguda-ngada*, to be boastful or puffed up with conceit.

ngadah, *tĕngadah*, looking upwards.

nganga, open, agape (of the jaws).

ngangut, *mĕngangut*, to mutter to oneself.

ngap, (onom.) *ngap-ngap*, panting, catching at one's breath.

ngeh, (onom.) to blow the nose; also *nyeh*.

ngĕlu, aching (of the head).

ngĕngap, = *ngap-ngap*.

ngĕran, displeasure, annoyance, irritation, anger.

ngĕras, Jav. sour, rancid; unpleasant.

ngĕri, fear, alarm, panic; terrifying.

ngĕriap, *mĕngĕriap*, to swarm.

ngĕring, (onom.) the sound of ringing.

ngĕrong, (onom.) the sound of beating gongs.

ngiau, *mĕngiau*, to mew (of a cat).

ngilu, "on edge" (of the teeth).

ngungap, (onom.) to pant.

ngut-ngut, moping.

ni, an abbreviation of *ini*, q.v.

niaga, see *bĕrniaga*.

niat, Ar. desire, wish, longing, aspiration; *niatkan*, to will.

niaya, = *aniaya*.

nibong, the well-known palm (*oncosperma tigillaria*).

nika, = *neka*.

nikah, Ar. wedding; marriage ceremony; *nikahkan* or *mĕnikahkan*, to wed two other people together; *bĕrnikah*, to be married oneself.

nila, Skr. deep blue, sapphire, indigo; *pĕrmata n.* or *n. kĕndi*, the sapphire.

nilai, appraising, valuing; *nilaikan*, to appraise, to value; *tiada tĕrnilai*, invaluable.

nilam, I. the patchouli (*pogostemon patchouli*). II. Tam. the sapphire; *batu n.*, id.
nilau, a plant (*cupania pallidula*).
nilur, *pĕrisai nilur*, a long oval shield.
nin, this—a poetical variant of *ini*.
ning, = *ing*.
nipah, the well-known trunkless palm (*nipa fruticans*).
nipis, tenuous, thin; *limau n.*, the lime (*citrus acida*).
nira, the fresh juice of the palm (from which spirit is made by fermentation).
niru, a sieve; also *nyiru*.
nischaya, = *nĕschaya*.
nista, Skr. insult, abuse.
nobat, Pers. a hemispherical kettle-drum included in the appurtenances of royalty.
noga, a shell (*turbinella conigera*).
noja, a servant or caretaker in a mosque; *daun n.*, a herb used in dyeing (*peristrope montana*).
noktah, Ar. a diacritical mark, a vowel-point, a dot.
nona, I. Jav. an unmarried daughter of a European or Chinese. II. *buah nona*, the custard-apple (*anona squamosa*); *n. kapri*, the "bullock's heart" fruit (*anona reticulata*).
nonah, = *nona*.
nonam, a shell (*murex* sp.).
nong, a title given to distant descendants of a prince.
nonong, *mĕnonong*, to walk with uncertain feet.
nonya, a designation given to respectable Chinese and Eurasian married women; also *nyonya*.
no'reng, a vulture.
nu, that; = *itu*.
nugĕraha, = *anugĕrah*.
nujum, Ar. astrological tables; *ahlu-'n-ujum*, astrologers.
nuktah, = *noktah*.
nun, Ar. *ikan nun*, the "whale" that swallowed Jonah.
nur, Ar. light.

nuracha, = *nĕracha*.
nuraka, = *naraka*.
nurbisa, an antidote to venom.
nuri, a parrot, a lory.
nurmala, faded; = *mala*.
nus, the sepia or cuttle-fish.
nya, its, his, her—a possessive pronoun of the third person.
nyah, disappearance, vanishing.
nyaï, Jav. a term of endearment; (in Deli) a mistress.
nyala, shining, resplendent; *bĕrnyala*, to shine.
nyaman, feeling "fit"; healthful; a sense of personal enjoyment.
nyamok, a mosquito.
nyampang, *sa-nyampang*, the more.
nyanyi, singing; *bĕrnyanyi*, to sing; *mĕnyanyi*, id.
nyanyok, dull, in one's dotage.
nyapang, a friend, a companion.
nyarap, to plug or cork up anything.
nyaring, clear; distinct (of utterance); shrill (of the voice).
nyaris, nearly, all but, just short of.
nyata, Skr. clear, obvious, plain, manifest; *nyatakan* or *mĕnyatakan*, to make clear, to show.
nyatoh, a valuable timber-tree (*payena costata*).
nyawa, soul, life, spirit; "my life" (as a term of endearment).
nyĕdar, sound (of sleep).
nyĕdĕra, = *nyĕdar*.
nyeh, (onom.) to blow the nose; also *ngeh*.
nyĕnyai, coarsely woven (of cloth).
nyenyen, teasing, "badgering," worrying.
nyilu, = *ngilu*.
nyireh, a sea-shore tree (*carapa moluccana*).
nyiru, a sieve; also *niru*.
nyiur, a coconut; *pokok ny.*, a coconut-tree; *ny. ladeh*, a coconut, the water of which has coagulated into a pulp; *ny. di-makan bulan*, a coconut without water in it; *ny. mumbang*, the very young coconut; *ny.*

sĕmantan, the coconut when the water can be heard on the nut being shaken; *ny. sungkuran*, the nut before the shell has commenced to harden; *ny. tahan kukur*, the nut when the shell is hardening but the water cannot be heard.

nyolo, a brazier.

nyongkom, cuddling over.

nyonya, a designation given to Chinese and Eurasian married women; also *nonya*.

nyonyeh, old and toothless.

nyonyong, blown out; swollen up; inflamed.

nyonyot, pulling at the breast.

nyut, the throbbing of a boil or of the fontanel.

O

oak, = *kuak*, II.

obat, drug, medicine, chemical; a magical potion, philtre, or mixture; *o. sakit kĕpala*, a cure for headache; *o. bĕdil*, gunpowder; *o. guna*, a philtre; *tukang o.*, a vendor of magical simples; an apothecary; *obat-obatan*, drugs generally; *ĕbati*, to apply a remedy; *pĕngobat*, a remedy.

ochok, stirring up by teasing or tale-bearing; exciting; mischief-making.

odoh, ugly, unsightly, offensive to the eye.

ogah, Hind. a hookah, a hubble-bubble; also *hukah*.

ogak, *ogak-ogak*, a jester, a practical joker.

ogam, *pĕngogam*, a scraper; *pĕngogam mayang*, a borer or cutter for extracting palm sap; *pĕngogam sampah*, a sort of broom.

ogok, stinginess.

oh, an interjection of sudden recollection (oh! I have it!) or to call another's attention (ho, there!).

oja, *mĕngoja*, to excite cocks to attack each other.

olah, way of doing things, manner, method; excuse, attitude taken up; *banyak o.*, capricious, variable; *o.-elah*, duplicity *sa-olah-olah*, about the same as; similar to.

olak, an eddy or agitation on the water; *o.-alek*, backwards and forwards.

oleh, by means of, through the medium of, owing to; *oleh-nya*, by him; *bĕroleh*, to obtain—cf. *boleh*.

olek, = *ulit*.

oleng, the rocking or rolling of a boat.

olok, joking, jesting; *mĕngolok-olok*, to chaff; *burong o.-o.*, the booby (*sula leucogaster*).

olon, = *ulun*.

ombak, a wave, a billow; *bĕrombak*, to roll in waves; to surge; *mabok o.*, sea-sick.

omong, I. a mark to indicate that a place is reserved by a man for the erection of fishing-stakes. II. *mĕngomong*, to meet together; to gossip.

ompang, *ompang-ompang*, miscellaneous articles carried about by a trader (as gifts to chiefs, etc.)

ompok, I. a method of printing on cloth. II. a border sewn on to a piece of embroidery.

onak, barbed thorns; the "wait-a-bit" thorn—cf. *sonak* and *duri*.

onam, = *unam*.

onar, = *honar*.

ondeh, *ondeh-ondeh*, sweetened dumplings of dough rolled in coconut scrapings.

oneng, *oneng-oneng*, remote descendants.

ong, = *hong*.

onggal, *onggok-onggal*, swaying, rocking.

onggok, I. *onggok-onggal*, swaying, rocking. II. *bĕronggok-onggok*, in small heaps or clusters.

ongka = *ungka*.

ongkak, posts (in a boat's bows) to which the cable is secured.

ongkos, (Dutch) outlay, expenses, charges (especially travelling expenses).

onis, pallor, loss of colour; *puchat o.*, id.

onta, Hind. a camel; *burong o.*, an ostrich.

ontang, = *untang*.

onyak, *onyak-anyek*, vacillating, undecided; shaking (as a loose tooth).

opas, I. (Dutch) a watchman. II. = *upas*.

opau, Ch. a sort of purse-pouch attached to the waist-belt.

opor, Jav. cooking without vegetables or condiments; plain roasting or stewing.

orak, unloosing, unwinding, uncoiling, undoing; *mĕngorak*, to unfasten, to unfold.

orang, a human being; a man or woman; people generally (especially in the sense of other people); *o. Mĕlayu*, a Malay; *kata o.*, people say; it is said; *o. banyak*, the multitude, the people; *o. hutan*, *o. liar*, or *o. bukit*, aboriginal tribesmen.

ordi, Port. commands, instructions, orders; also *rodi*.

orloji, = *horloji*.

orlong, = *rĕlong*.

orok, (onom.) *orok-orok*, a number of perforated objects strung on a stick so as to rattle when the stick is shaken.

otak, brains, marrow; *o. tulang*, the marrow.

otar, = *utar*.

otek, an edible salt-water fish (*arius* sp).

P

pa', father (expressed very familiarly).

pachai, sandalwood dust sprinkled on a dead body to prepare it for the grave.

pachak, I, spitting; sticking a sharp-pointed stick through something else. II. accustomed to; experienced in; versed in.

pachal, slave of a slave; the humblest of the humble (a very self-depreciatory expression used as a pronoun of the first person).

pachar, a kind of carpet mentioned in old romances.

pachat, a leach.

pachau, a talisman hung on a tree to make the fruit of that tree disagree with anyone who steals and eats it.

pachu, goading on or spurring on (a horse); *mĕmachu*, to spur on.

pachul, squeezing or pressing out (as one presses matter out of a sore).

pada, I. Skr. *sĕri pada*, the holy feet of a prince; a royal title. II. sufficiency, adequacy, enough. III. by, at, near, in, according to; *kapada*, to; *dari-pada*, from; *pada akhir-nya*, finally.

padah, *mĕmadah*, to invite.

padam, I. extinguishing; putting out (a light); (by metaphor) putting an end to evil feelings. II. Skr. a lotus; *merah p.*, lotus-red.

padan, matching, fitting, harmonising; a match or peer.

padang, a plain; an open space; *p. saujana*, a stretch of open country; *p. jarak*, *p. tĕkukur*, a tract of waste land.

padat, cramming, crushing into a small space, stuffing.

padau, *layar padau*, a storm-sail.
padĕri, Port. a Christian priest; a clergyman.
padi, rice in the husk; *p. tĕnggala*, seed rice; *sĕmangat p.*, the spirit of life in the *padi*.
padok, a crease or starting line used in playing Malay games.
padong, a short shoot or projection from the stem of a creeper.
padu, I. welding together, hammering together. II. *bĕrpadu*, to sweep by each other (of birds on the wing).
paduka, Skr. a royal title derived from the fact that the subject addresses the raja's feet, being unworthy to address the prince himself; *paduka*, literally means "shoe."
paedah, = *faedah*.
pagan, solid; sturdy; strongly built.
pagar, a fence; a pallisading; a row of stakes or palings; *p. anak*, (1) the palings leading to an elephant corral; (2) a tree (*ixonanthes oborata*); *bunga p.*, the common lantana (*lantana camara*).
pagi, morning; in the morning; early.
pagu, a ceiling; *di-atas p.*, in the loft.
pagut, the peck of a bird, the bite of a small fish or snake; to peck out.
paha, the thigh of a man; the ham of an animal; a quarter or fourth part; *jantong p.*, the fleshy part of the thigh; *pangkal p.*, the upper portion of the thigh.
pahala, Skr. profit, gain, advantage.
paham, Ar. knowledge, acquaintance; to be well-versed in, to know well; *salah p.*, misunderstanding.
pahar, a large salver of metal resting on a stand or on legs.
pahat, a chisel; carving with a chisel; *p. jantan*, a chisel with a narrow deep blade; *p. kuku*, a gouge; *p. lebar*, a chisel with a flat broad and shallow blade.
pahit, bitter.

pahlawan, Pers. champion, leader in war; *johan p.*, world-champion.
pai, *bĕlum pai*, not yet, = *bĕlum sampai*.
pais, fish cooked in banana leaves.
pajak, (Dutch) farm, monopoly; *p. chandu*, the opium farm; *p. gadai*, the pawnbroking farm; a pawnshop.
pajar, = *fajar*.
pajoh, gluttonous eating; guzzling.
pak, father; = *pa'*.
pakai, using or wearing anything; assuming, adopting, employing; *mĕmakai*, to wear, to use; *pakaian*, clothes, garments.
pakak, *ulun pakak*, a name given to a class of imported shells from Celebes (*conus* spp.)
pakal, caulking.
pakan, I. the woof; *tirai yang bĕrpakankan mas*, curtains shot with gold. II. invulnerability caused by magical drugs.
pakat, Ar. arrangement by conference; agreement; settlement; *bĕrpakat*, to agree upon; to conspire to.
pakau, a cross-piece in a bucket or well.
pakir, Ar. a poor man; a mendicant; also *fakir*.
paksa, I. compulsion, force; *mĕmaksa*, to compel. II. auspicious, lucky, favourable.
paksi, I. Skr. a bird (expressed poetically). II. = *paksa*, II.
paksina, Jav. the north; *dari daksina datang ka-paksina*, from the south to the north.
paku, I. a spike, a nail; *tĕrpaku*, nailed; firmly affixed to. II. a generic name for the fern *filex*, and for plants resembling it.
pal, I. a tack (in sailing); *bĕrpal*, to beat about, to tack. II. (Dutch) the Dutch "pole" as a measure of length.
pala, I. Skr. *buah pala*, the nutmeg (*myristica fragrans*); *halwa p.*,

nutmegs in syrup. II. *pala-pala*, thoroughly, genuinely, properly; *sa-pala-pala*, as thoroughly as possible.

palam, plugging up the lower orifices of the body (*abaimana*) before burial.

palang, position across or athwart; *kayu p.*, the cross-bar on a buffalo's horns—cf. *alang*.

palar, grasping (as a prince who expects rich presents).

palas, a generic name for the fan-palms known as *licualas* (the leaves of which are used by Malays as cigarette-wrappers).

palat, an instrument for punishing schoolboys.

palau, a cicatrix or other prominent mark facilitating identification.

paling, looking or turning aside; *bĕrpaling*, to look aside—cf. *palis*.

palis, turning away the head—e.g. as a modest girl when compliments are paid her—cf. *paling*.

palit, smearing, smudging; *mĕmalit*, to smudge or smear.

palita, = *pĕlita*.

palkah, the hatch of a ship.

paloh, a hollow filled with stagnant water; a pool.

palong, a trough for watering or feeding animals.

palsu, Port. false, forged, counterfeit (of money, notes, etc.)

palu, striking with a stick or bar or other rigid cylindrical body.

palut, enwrapping, = *balut*.

pamah, low-lying (of ground).

paman, maternal uncle; a familiar form of address to persons a good deal older than oneself.

pampang, stretching out before the eye; *tĕrpampang*, extended.

pamur, the damascening on a *kĕris*.

pana, Ar. mortal, perishable; to die; also *fana*.

panah, a bow; the use of a bow; (better *anak p.*) an arrow; *panahan*, archery; the shooting of arrows; *mĕmanah*, to shoot with a bow.

panas, heat, warmth; *p. hati*, excitement; *hujan p.*, rain when the sun is shining; *roman p.*, prickly-heat.

panau, discoloured patches (usually white spots) on the skin.

pancha, Skr. five, multiple, varied; *pancha-indĕra*, the five senses; *p.-logam*, an alloy of several metals; *p.-pĕrsada*, a bathing place (usually a temporary structure) for the celebration of a bathing-ceremony; *p.-roba*, uncertain, fickle, changeable; *p.-rona*, or *p.-warna*, of many colours.

panchalogam, see *pancha*.

panchang, a long pole, pile, or stake driven into a river bottom (especially as a mooring-pole for light boats).

panchapĕrsada, see *pancha*.

panchar, flowing out violently; gushing out; pouring out; *kilat mĕmanchar*, the lightning flashing; *tĕrpanchar otak-nya*, his brains were blown out.

pancharoba, see *pancha*.

pancharona, see *pancha*.

panchawarna, see *pancha*.

panching, angling; fishing with hook and line; *p. ikan*, to fish.

panchit, to ooze out; to gush forth in a thin stream.

panchong, cutting off a projection; lopping; beheading; *mĕmanchong*, to lop off, to prune, to mutilate; *panchongkan kĕpala*, to behead.

panchur, flowing (of water in pipes and conduits); flowing from the end of a pipe; *panchuran ayer*, a conduit.

panchut, spouting or gushing out (of water).

pandai, skilled; versed in; a craftsman; a mechanic; a skilled artificer; industrial art; *p. bĕsi*, a blacksmith; *p. kayu*, a carpenter; *p. lukis*, an engraver; *p. mas*, a goldsmith; *kĕ-pandaian*, learning, knowledge, skill.

pandak, short (in a limited number of expressions, the usual word being *pendek*); *kĕris p.*, a short dagger.

pandam, fixing jewellery in resin to keep it steady when worked at.
pandan, a generic name given to the smaller screw-pines (*pandanaceæ*), the leaves of which are used in making mats.
pandang, gazing; looking fixedly at anything; seeing and observing (as opposed to merely glancing at); *pandangan*, observation, notice.
pandawa, = *pĕndawa*.
pandir, *pa' pandir*, the name of a legendary person who typifies a lucky fool.
pandita, = *pĕndita*.
pandu, a guide; a pilot; the leader of a dance.
pangan, extensive tracts of forests; *orang P.*, a name given to some aboriginal tribes.
pangeran, = *pĕngeran*.
panggal, cutting or chopping through, severing; *panggalkan*, to cut through, to decapitate, to sever; *panggal tiga*, cut into three pieces.
panggang, roasting, cooking, toasting; *pĕmanggang*, the roast.
panggar, a scaffolding.
panggau, a light raised framework used for drying fish—cf. *panggar*.
panggil, summoning, calling, sending for; *panggilkan*, to have a man summoned; to send for; *mĕmanggil*, to summon.
panggong, an erection on pillars; a stage; a raised flooring; *p. wayang*, the stage of a native theatre; *dudok bĕrsila panggong*, to cross one leg over the other—cf. *panggar* and *panggau*.
pangkah, I. cruciform; the mark of a cross; a caste-mark. II. Hind. a punkah.
pangkal, beginning; commencement; first stage or initial portion of anything; *p. bahu*, the shoulder; *p. lĕngan*, the upper arm; *pangkalan*, a landing place; the point where a traveller leaves the sea for a land journey, or vice-versa.

pangkas, to crop the ends of anything.
pangkat, grade, degree, rank, stage; *bĕrpangkat-pangkat*, in grades, in stages; *pangkatkan*, to confer rank on any person.
pangking, Ch. a bedroom, a sleeping-place.
pangkong, to pommel or pound with a heavy stick.
pangku, breast, bosom; holding between the breast and the fore-arm; nurturing; fostering; *pangkuan*, the upper portion of the lap; the breast; *mĕmangku*, to hold to the breast; to nurture; *pĕmangku*, a regent; *pĕmangku raja*, id.
pangkur, an instrument for scraping sago out of the tree-trunk.
panglema, = *pĕnglima*.
pangling, failing to recognise or notice; overlooking.
pangsa, a carpel of a durian; a natural "slice" of an orange; a natural division in fruit.
pangsi, the peg of a top.
pangus, to spout, to blow (of a porpoise).
panir, Pers. cheese.
panjak, a drummer at a *ma'yong*.
panjang, length; long, tall; *umur p.*, long life; *sa-panjang*, all along; *panjangkan*, to lengthen.
panjar, earnest-money; = *chĕngkĕram*.
panjat, to climb (tree-trunks, ropes, masts, etc., but not hills or ladders or walls or trees from bough to bough).
panji, I. *panji-panji*, a pennon, a long streamer. II. Jav. an ancient Javanese military grade; *Sira P.* the *nom de guerre* of the great Javanese hero *Radin Inu Kĕrtapati*, Prince of Kuripan.
panjut, tipped with white (a lucky marking)—of an animal's tail.
pantai, a beach; the sea-shore.
pantak, to drive a nail into a wall, a peg into a hole, etc.

pantang, prohibition; forbidding; the state of being forbidden; *p. pĕmali*, or *p. larangan*, tabooed.

pantas, swift, speedy; *p. mulut*, ready witted; *sĕpĕrti kilat pantasnya*, swift as lightning.

pantat, the base, the fundament, the buttocks.

pantau, *mĕmantau*, to look up a person; to visit.

pantek, striking together two hard substances; *pĕmantek api*, a flint and steel.

panting, *pontang-panting*, topsy-turvey, helter-skelter, scattered about.

pantis, a sligh smear; touching up with colour or rouge.

pantok, the combing on a Malay half-decked boat.

pantul, *pantul balek*, to rebound—cf. *antul*.

pantun, a quatrain, the first line of which rhymes with the third, and the second with the fourth; *bĕr-pantun*, to extemporise a quatrain; *sa-pantun*, like, similar to; = *sĕpĕrti*.

panus, a candle-bracket.

papa, Skr. poverty, pennilessness, destitution; *p. kĕlana*, a pauper vagabond; *p. kĕrma*, a pauper by misfortune.

papah, to totter along painfully and with support (as a sick or very aged man).

papak, I. flat, even, without cavities or prominences. II. Jav. *mĕmapak*, to receive, to welcome. III. = *pĕpat*. IV. crunching, mastication.

papakĕrma, see *papa*.

papan, a plank; a board; flooring; *p. batu*, a slate; *p. chatur*, a chess-board; *p. mistar*, a ruling-board; *muka p.*, brazen-faced; *tulang p.*, the lumnar vertebræ.

papar, flat, smooth; the blunt side; the back (as opposed to the edge) of a blade; the flat of a horn (as opposed to its point).

papas, removing or taking off objects —such as clothes, mats, *kajang* roofs, etc.; *mĕmapas khemah*, to furl up a tent.

para, I. a shelf, rack, attic or frame-work of any sort raised above the flooring; *arang p.*, soot. II. a collective prefix in expressions—such as *para-pĕnggawa*. III. sentry-go; *orang p.*, a sentry; a constable on duty at a door.

parah, severe, deadly (of a wound).

parak, Ar. separation, barrier (especially the barrier between the male and female guests at a wedding).

param, *param-param* (or *pĕparam*), a medicinal ointment used after a confinement.

parang, I. a chopper; chopping; cutting at; cleaving; *p. chandong*, a cleaver (the handle and blade of which are in one piece); *p. puting*, a very sharp chopper. II. *ikan parang-parang*, a fish (*pristis* sp.?)

parap, a blow struck hammer-wise with the side of the fist; *pĕmarap*, the lower part of the fist.

paras, I. appearance, looks (especially good looks). II. removing asperities; smoothing; *mĕmaras*, to trim.

parau, harshness or hoarseness of the voice—e.g. after much talking —cf. *garau*.

pareh, dealing (cards); casting (lots); throwing (dice).

parek, *porak-parek*, helter-skelter (in confusion).

pari, a generic name for fish of the skate and ray type; *p. bĕting* (*trygon* sp.); *p. daun* (*trygon sephen*); *p. dĕdap* (*eurogymnus asperrimus*); also *p. kĕlikir*; *p. lalat* (*trygon uarnak*); *p. lang* (*aetobatis narinari*); *p. pauh* (*dicerobatis* sp.); *p. tandok* (*ceratoptera* sp.); *kikir p.*, a skate-skin grater; *mĕnikam p.*, to spear the ray; *sĕngat p.*, the sting of the ray.

parit, a trench, a moat, a ditch, a drain, a canal for drainage.

paroh, I. the beak of a bird. II. *sa-paroh*, a half.

parong, I. *kĕris parong*, a *kĕris* with an exceptional number of curves. II. *pokok parong*, a plant (*dysoxylon cauliflorum*).

paru, I. the lungs; the gills of a fish. II. *paru-paru*, sweet fritters sold by street-hawkers.

parut, I. a scar, a cicatrix. II. the process of rasping; *mĕmarut*, to rasp.

pasah, Ar. *pasah nikah*, to dissolve a marriage.

pasak, I. a peg, nail, or wedge; *pasakkan sĕpatu kuda*, to shoe a horse. II. *mata pasak*, blue or grey eyes.

pasal, Ar. concerning; *apa p.*, why; *p. itu*, for that reason; therefore; also *fasal*, q.v.

pasang, I. pair; *sa-pasang*, a couple. II. the tidal flow; *ayer p.*, the rising tide; *pĕnoh p.*, the full rush of the tide. III. *sakit pasang-pasang*, hydrocele. IV. putting into working order, motion, or use; to light (a lamp); to harness (a horse to a carriage); to fire (a cannon); to hoist (a flag). V. to be effective (of a blow); to penetrate or produce the intended result; *kĕna p.*, hitting a vital spot or hitting "full."

pasar, Pers. a bazaar; a market-place; also *pĕkan*.

pasek, wrong-headed; unwilling to behave properly (of a child) or to listen to reason (of an adult).

pasiban, = *pĕseban*.

pasir, sand; the sands by a sea; the beach; *p. panjang*, a long stretch of sandy beach; *galah p.*, a short pole for punting over shallows; *gula p.*, sugar in minute grains; *ibu p.*, coarse-grained sand; *mas p.*, gold dust (better *mas urai*); *rumput p.*, a common weed (*adenostema viscosum*).

pasmen, (Dutch) a kind of lace-work; passementerie.

pasok, a troop, a body of men, a company; *pasokan*, a troop; a team; a side in a game; a gun-crew.

pasong, stocks, shackles, fetters; *pasongan*, id.; *rumah pasong*, a police station; also (Penang) *balai*.

paspa, = *puspa*.

pasu, a basin or bowl; a flower-pot; a wash-pot; a tub; *p. bunga*, a flower-pot.

patah, I. fracture, breakage, snapping asunder (used of rigid objects only being broken); *p. arang*, irreconcilable; *kayu p. tulang*, a plant (*euphorbia tirucalli* or *moesa ramentacea*); *patahan*, a broken fragment; *patahan bĕngkarong*, cramp; *mĕmatahkan*, to break. II. a numeral coefficient for sayings, pieces of advice, etc.; *tutur sa-patah*, a single saying; *pĕmatah* a piece of warning or advice.

patar, a wooden rasp.

patek, "humble slave," a term of self-depreciation used as a pronoun of the first person when addressing a prince.

patĕri, solder.

pati, I. Skr. a high officer of state; a term used as a component part of many old names and dignities—e.g. *adipati*. II. essence; extract; finest portion; "cream" of anything. III. death—the old root of *mati*.

patil, I. a small adze for roughly planing what has been rough-hewn with a hatchet. II. The feeler or antenna of an insect.

patin, an edible fish (unidentified).

pating, I. a stone-hewer's chisel. II. a peg [used especially of pegs driven into a tree to facilitate climbing or into the gunwale of a boat so as to allow of a temporary gunwale (*rubing*) being affixed to them].

patok, the peck (of a bird); the bite (of a snake); *mĕmatok*, to bite, to peck.

patong, I. a puppet, an image, a doll; *wayang p.*, a puppet-show; *ĕmpama p.*, statuesque; *ringgit p.*, the pillar-dollar. II. *ikan patong*, a fish (*selundia sykesii*).

patut, right, fitting, proper, suitable; *ta'-p.*, unfair, improper; *patutan*, harmony, suitability; *mĕmatutkan*, to settle, to put right.

pauh, I. a species of wild-mango; *p. janggi*, a tree (*cocos maldiva*) [believed by Malays to grow in the centre of the great ocean upon a bank which represents all that is left of a submerged continent]; *buah p. janggi*, a fruit (the shell of which is used as a beggar's bowl by Hindu mendicants); *tasek p. janggi*, the great ocean round the sunken bank above referred to; *p. kijang*, a large tree (*irvingia malayana*); *pauh-pauh*, a name sometimes given to trees of the *evodia* class. II. a quarter; a quarter-*chupak* as a measure for milk.

pauk, *lauk-pauk*, all kinds of food (other than rice)—v. *lauk*.

paung, Port. bread (but especially applied to Chinese bread or native-made biscuits, the usual word for ordinary bread being *roti*).

paus, the whale; also *ikan paus*.

paut, drawing (anything) towards oneself; hauling in; to be drawn to anything; to be attached, or attracted, or bound; *bĕrpaut*, to cling to (as a drowning or struggling man clutches and clings).

pawah, pay (especially pay according to profits or by piece-work and not as a daily wage, *upah*).

pawai, the suite or train of a *raja*; the followers in a bridal procession.

pawang, a man who practises some primitive industry (such as hunting, fishing or agriculture) by the aid of the black art; a witch-doctor; a man who combines magic and skill in the exercise of his profession; *p. bĕlat, p. jĕrmal, p. kelong*, and *p. pukat*, practitioners of magic in connection with various kinds of fishing; *p. gaharu* and *p. kapur*, collectors of scented woods and camphor; *p. gajah*, an elephant-trapper.

paya, a swamp, a marsh, a morass.

payah, difficult (of work); serious (of illness); hard times.

payang, a large sea-going fishing-boat or small trading-boat.

payar, *pĕrahu payar*, a small warship (such as a revenue-cutter or port-guard-ship.

payau, brackish (of water); insipid, tasteless.

payong, an umbrella; the head of a nail; shelter under an umbrella; *p. ubur-ubur*, a heavy-fringed umbrella; *p. bĕrapit*, two small umbrellas borne side by side in the train of a prince; *p. chĕtĕra*, a canopy.

payu, price, sale-price, precious; *tiada tĕrpayu*, priceless, invaluable.

pĕbean, see *bea*.

pĕchah, breakage into fragments; breaking open; breaking out; bursting; breaking up; spreading (of news); *p. pĕrang*, the breaking of a line of battle; *p. pĕloh*, breaking out into perspiration; *p. khabar*, the news spread; *pĕchahkan* or *mĕmĕchahkan*, to break anything up.

pechak, crushed flat or sunken in (of roundish objects).

pĕchat, to remove from office; to get rid off; to dismiss; to deprive; *di-pĕchatkan Allah makanan-mu*, may God deprive you of food.

pĕchut, a whip; whipping on.

pĕda, preserved fish, = *budu*.

pĕdada, a tree (*sonneratia acida*); also *bĕrĕmbang*.

pĕdah, a hint, a suggestion, a premonition.

pĕdaka, Skr. a collar with pendants attached to it as ornaments.
pĕdal, the gizzard.
pĕdang, a sword; a sabre; *p. kĕra-jaan*, a sword of state.
pĕdap, sucking up moisture; *kĕrtas p.*, blotting-paper.
pĕdar, rancid (of taste).
pĕdas, pungent (of taste); biting, acrid.
pĕdati, a wheeled vehicle; a car or waggon of any sort; *p. mĕriam*, a gun-carriage; *p. kĕrbau*, a buffalo-cart.
pĕdeh, smarting (in the eyes, or nose, or ears); *hati p.*, an angry feeling.
pĕdĕna, a large wide-mouthed jar or tub (usually of earthenware).
pĕdĕndang, I. *kain pĕdĕndang*, braid. II. *burong pĕdĕndang*, a bird (*heliopais personata*)—cf. *dĕndang*.
pĕdewakan, a Bugis trading ship.
pĕdiah, Ar. a fine; = *diat*.
pĕdoman, a compass.
pĕdukang, a fish (unidentified).
pĕduli, Ar. to care, to concern oneself; *sahaya tiada p.*, I do not care.
pedur, lameness caused by a bent shinbone.
pĕgaga, = *pĕnggaga*.
pĕgan, *tĕrpĕgan*, silent in meditation; also *tĕrpĕgun*.
pĕgang, holding, grasping, controlling; *di-pĕgang-nya tangan*, his hand was grasped; *kata tidak di-pĕgang-nya*, he does not keep to his promises; *pĕgangan*, hold, control, occupation; *bĕrpĕgang*, attached to, adhering to; *mĕmĕgang*, to hold, to grasp.
pĕgar, *ayam pĕgar*, the fireback pheasant (*lophura rufa*).
pĕgas, to beat its wings (of a bird).
pĕgawai, an officer in charge; a district officer or government agent.
pĕgi, = *pĕrgi*.
pĕgun, *tĕrpĕgun*, silent in meditation; also *tĕrpĕgan*.
pehak, = *pihak*.
pĕhala, = *pahala*.

pĕjal, firm (of flesh); not easily pressed or pinched.
pĕjam, closing the eye.
pĕjĕra, the sighting-bead of a gun.
pĕka, noticing, regarding, attaching importance to.
pĕkacha, *ratna pĕkacha*, a term of endearment; = gem of purity?
pĕkak, hard of hearing, deaf.
pĕkaka, a generic name for kingfishers, and also (*pĕkaka hutan* or *p. rimba*) for barbets. [The kingfisher is also called *raja udang* in the south.]
pĕkakas, = *pĕrkakas*.
pĕkan, I. a market; an emporium; *bunga p.*, a flower (*jasminum grandiflorum*). II. = *pĕgun*.
pĕkasam, a strong-smelling preserve of fish.
pĕkat, sticky and thick (of liquids); strong (of coffee).
pĕkau, a (meaningless) cry of excitement.
pĕkek, a shrill cry or scream; *jĕrit p.*, screams and shrieks; *mĕmĕkek*, to scream out.
pĕkĕrti, Skr. nature, disposition, character; *budi p.*, id., especially of good disposition.
pĕkin, pondering; puzzling a thing out—cf. *pĕkan* II, or *pĕgan*.
pĕkok, twisted (of the arm).
pĕkong, a name for a class of foul-smelling ulcers.
pekong, Ch. a joss.
pĕkur, *tĕrpĕkur*, = *tĕfĕkur*, q.v.
pĕlabur, see *labur*.
pĕlaga, *buah pĕlaga*, the cardamom (*amomum cardamomum*).
pĕlahap, gluttonous, voracious.
pĕlamin, see *lamin*.
pĕlampong, a floating mark; the floats of a net; a float marking the position of an anchor.
pĕlana, Pers. a saddle; *alas p.*, a saddle-cloth; a numnah.
pĕlanchar, a joist or cross-beam joining together the foundation-pillars of a house.

pělandok, the smaller chevrotin (*tragulus kanchil*); also *kanchil*.
pělang, coloration in stripes; *běndera běrpělang tiga*, a tricolour.
pelang, a native galley or barge.
pělangi, a rainbow.
pělangking, a palanquin.
pělantar, flooring, staging.
pělantek, see *lantek*.
pělanting, *běrpělantingan*, rolling over and over, falling and rebounding.
pělasari, a medicinal shrub (*alyxia* sp.)
pělasoh, a ne'er-do-weel, a worthless idler.
pelat, peculiarities of intonation; provincial accent; brogue.
pělata, *ikan pělata*, a fish (unidentified).
pělatok, a generic name for woodpeckers; also *bělatok*.
pělawas, *akar pělawas*, a plant (*calycopteris floribunda*).
pělbagai, varied (of different sorts) —cf. *bagai*.
pělěbaya, an executioner; = *pěrtanda*.
pělecheh, wheedling, cozening with fair words, flattering.
pělechok, a strain caused by a false step.
pělek, I. curious; out of the common; valuable; *barang yang p.*, curios. II. lacking in breeding; deficiencies in character.
pělěkat, I. (Dutch), a placard. II. to caulk a ship.
pělekat, *kain pělekat*, an Indian cloth-fabric.
pělěkoh, I. bowed or bent (of the neck). II. a term of abuse.
pělěmbaya, = *pělěbaya*.
pělěmpap, *sa-pělěmpap*, a hand's-breadth (as a unit of measurement); also *sa-tělěmpap*.
pělenchet, *těrpělenchet*, forced out by pressure (as matter from a boil).

pělěpah, a frond; the branch-leaf of the trees of the palm type.
pěler, = *pělir*.
pěleset, gumming on; sticking on.
pělěsit, a familiar spirit. [It is believed to be usually met with in the form of a cricket.]
pelet, = *pelat*.
pělěting, a piece of bamboo on which the thread is rolled up when weaving.
pělias, see *lias*.
pělihara, Skr. cherishing; nurturing; bringing up; protecting; guarding; *měměliharakan*, to nurture, to protect, to look after.
pělinggam, marble or stone the veining of which offers a contrast of colour with the rest.
pělipis, the temples of the forehead; also *pělipisan*.
pělir, *batang pělir*, the penis; *buah p.*, the testes; *p. itek*; a screw.
pělita, Pers. a lamp.
pěloh, perspiration, sweat; *běrpěloh*, to perspire; *pěchah pěloh*, to burst into a perspiration.
pělohong, gaping open.
pělok, folding in the arms; embracing; *běrpělok*, *měmělok*, or *pělokkan*, to embrace; *sa-pěmělok*, an armful; as much as the arms can encompass.
pelong, bent, warped.
pěluang, still, calm (of wind and weather).
pělupoh, to hammer out; to beat into a pulp; to flatten under a beating.
pělupok, *pělupok mata*, the eyelid; = *kělopak mata*.
pěluru, Port. shot, bullets, cannon-balls; *p. běsi lantai*, cylindrical shot; *p. bolang-baling*, chain shot; *p. jantong*, shot with a cylindrical body but rounded or pointed at the end.
pěmajangan, a state-bed (especially a bridal couch).

pĕmalam, to fill up a crack or crevice by pushing cloth or paper into it with a knife.

pĕmalap, to lower a wick; to lessen a flame.

pĕmali, forbidden, tabooed; a prohibition; *pantang p.*, id.

pĕmatang, a long stretch of high sandy soil in a rice-swamp; see also *matang*.

pĕmidang, a frame for embroidery.

pĕmuras, a blunderbuss.

pĕnaga, a generic name for a number of trees (especially *calophyllum inophyllum*).

pĕnah, = *pĕrnah*.

pĕnaka, so to speak; as it were; if by any chance.

pĕnakan, = *pĕranakan* from *anak*.

pĕnanggah, see *tanggah*.

pĕnaram, Malay pastry containing meat or prawns.

pĕnat, weariness, exhaustion, labour, fatigue.

pĕnchak, a sword-dance; *silat p.*, id.; *mĕmĕnchak*, to dance this dance (fencing with an imaginary opponent).

pĕnchalang, a sea-going type of ship used by Bugis traders.

penchang, = *pinchang*.

pĕnchil, detaching, separating from the main body; *tĕrpĕnchil*, separated, detached.

penchong, out of line; swerved; crooked.

pĕnda, amending, improving.

pĕndahan, a javelin; a dart hurled by hand.

pĕndam, *tĕrpĕndam*, concealed.

pĕndap, I. a plant (unidentified). II. *ikan pĕndap*, fish preserved in salt.

pĕndar, phosphorescence; luminosity in the sea; the glow of a firefly or luminous millipede.

Pĕndawa, Skr. a hero of the Mahabharata; any one of the five sons of Pandu; a pattern of sword named after these heroes.

pendek, short; *panjang p.*, tall and short; *bĕrkĕrja panjang p.*, to work intermittently—cf. *pandak*.

pĕndekar, a master of fence; a champion; a leader of a charge.

pĕndiat, a corral for elephants.

pĕnding, a waist-buckle; *tali p.*, a girdle for use with a buckle.

pĕndita, Skr. a sage; a learned man; a savant.

pĕndok, a wrapper of thin metal round the sheath of a *kĕris*.

pĕndomah, see *domah*.

pĕndongkok, a metal ferrule between the blade and handle of a *kĕris*.

pĕngampoh, = *pĕngapoh*.

pĕnganan, a cake; a sweetmeat.

pĕngantin, I. a party to a marriage; a bride or bridegroom; *sĕnapang p.*, a double-barrelled gun. II. the player of the viol (*rĕbab*) at a *ma'yong* performance.

pĕngap, covering up; sealing from intrusion; hermetically closing.

pĕngapoh, *layar pĕngapoh*, a topsail or top-gallant-sail.

pĕngar, heavy-witted (as a drugged man).

pĕngat, a sweetmeat made of fruit cooked in coconut milk and sugar.

pĕngawinan, *tombak pĕngawinan*, a spear of state.

pĕngeran, a title of nobility in use in Java and Borneo.

pĕngĕreh, a fish-trap of the *lukah* type.

penget, = *pingit*.

pĕngga, deep (of a bowl or dish).

pĕnggaga, a creeping herb (*hydrocotyle asiatica*).

pĕnggawa, an officer in charge of a district.

pĕnghulu, a headman; a local chief. [The term is also sometimes used of Muhammad as the head of Islam.]

pĕngkalan, = *pangkalan*; see *pangkal*.

pengkar, bow-legged.
pĕnglima, an executive officer; a leader in war.
pengsan, swooning; fainting; loss of consciousness.
pĕngulu, = *pĕnghulu*.
pĕning, dizziness; faintness; a rush of blood to the head; *p. kĕpala*, vertigo; *p. kĕlam*, id.
pĕninggir, the confines of a country; the outlying portions—cf. *pinggir*.
pĕniti, Port. a pin.
pĕnjajap, an ancient Malay type of fighting-ship.
pĕnjara, Skr. prison; *pĕnjarakan* or *mĕmpĕnjarakan*, to imprison; *tĕrpĕnjara*, imprisoned.
pĕnjurit, Jav. a warrior; a plunderer; a robber; see *jurit*.
pĕnjuru, an angle, a corner.
pĕnoh, fullness; full; *p. sĕsak* or *p. pĕpak*, chock-full; crowded; *pĕnohi* or *mĕmĕnohi*, to fill up; to complete; to accomplish; to fulfil; *dĕngan sapĕnoh-pĕnoh*, with full; with all; with every.
pĕnta, *bĕrpĕnta-pĕnta*, in crowds, in groups, in quantities.
pĕntas, a sleeping platform.
pĕnting, worth, soundness, value.
pĕntong, to club or cudgel.
pĕnyap, hidden, vanished, out of sight—cf. *lĕnyap*.
pĕnyĕngat, see *sĕngat*.
pĕnyu, the green turtle (*chelone mydas*).
pĕpah, striking with a long stick or pole.
pĕpak, I. complete; in full; fully attended; in full state; *pĕnoh p.*, quite full; chock-full. II. *papak* IV.
pĕpaku, *burong pĕpaku*, a bird (*sarcogrammus atrinuchalis*).
pĕparam, see *param*.
pĕparu, = *paru-paru*.
pĕpat, smooth; offering no inequalities of surface.
pĕpatil, = *patil*.

peper, motion sideways; edging; to be driven aside as a boat with a heavy sea on its beam.
pĕpuah, frizzled (of the hair).
pĕpuyu, = *puyu-puyu*.
pĕrabu, = *pĕrbu*.
pĕrada, Port. gold or silver leaf cut into patterns; tinsel; gold plate.
pĕrah, pressure in the hand; expressing; wringing out; milking; *kambing pĕrahan*, a milch-goat; *pĕrahkan*, to press out.
pĕrahu, a Malay sea-going boat or ship; *awak p.* or *anak p.*, the crew; *galang p*, the rollers on which a boat rests when hauled ashore; *tupai galang p.*, a descriptive name given to Raffles' squirrel (*sciurus raflesi*).
pĕrai, I. *bĕrpĕrai-pĕrai*, breaking up (of a crowd); scattering—cf. *bĕrai*. II. *kain pĕrai*, a black silk cloth of Siamese origin. III. turning about, from one side to another; *mĕmbuang p.*, to tack.
perak, silver.
pĕrak, a nervous start; a hasty glance to right and left.
pĕraksi, see *raksi*.
pĕram, I. storing fruit while still unripe with a view to its ripening in the store. II. *mĕmĕram*, to coo.
pĕrambut, invulnerability against weapons.
pĕran, a clown in a *ma'yong*.
pĕranchah, the wooden framework of a house.
Pĕranchis, Port. French.
pĕranchit, to splash up in all directions (as water or mud when a stone is dashed into it).
pĕranda, *porak-pĕranda*, helter-skelter; in confusion.
pĕrang, war, battle; *ikat p.*, the line of battle; *pĕnglima p.*, a leader in war; *gĕndang p.*, a war-drum; *bĕrpĕrang*, to go to war; to be at war; *pĕpĕrangan*, a state of war.
perang, *perang-perus*, very pale; very wan.

pĕrangai, nature; disposition; innate character.

pĕranggu, *sa-pĕrangguan,* a set—e.g. of buttons; a suit (of clothes).

pĕrangkap, a cage-trap for birds or mice.

pĕranja, a scaffolding in successive tiers; the seating arrangements in an amphitheatre; a dove-cote or pigeon-house.

pĕranjat, *tĕrpĕranjat,* startled; suddenly alarmed.

pĕrap, to fly at an enemy (of a fowl); to be touchy (of a disposition); to be anxious to always have the last word (of women).

perap, to quicken the stroke when rowing.

pĕras, (onom.) *pĕras-pĕras,* the rustling of garments or of paper.

pĕrat, acrid, sour; *tĕrong p.,* a small brinjal (*solanum aculeatissimum*).

pĕrawan, a maiden.

pĕrawas, a medicinal plant (*lindera* sp.)

pĕrawis, ingredients, factors, materials.

pĕrba, Skr. ancient, former; *p. kala,* days of old; also *purba.*

pĕrbani, extreme of the tide; at its highest or lowest point.

pĕrbu, Jav. a prince; *p. jaya,* the conquering prince (Panji).

percha, I. a rag; a piece of cloth. II. *Pulau P.,* Sumatra.

pĕrchaya, trusting; believing in; *harap ada, pĕrchaya tidak,* there is ground for hope but not for confident expectation; *pĕrchaya dĕngan tiada di-chuba,* trust without testing; faith; *kĕpĕrchayaan,* trust; trusty; *orang yang kĕpĕrchayaan,* a man who can be trusted.

perchit, squirting out (of water).

pĕrdah, the handle of a chopper or hatchet.

pĕrdana, Skr. surpassing; excelling; supreme in merit; *p. mĕntĕri,* prime minister.

pĕrdu, the base of a tree-trunk; the visible part of the root.

pĕrduli, = *pĕduli.*

pereh, worn out by a struggle or sustained effort; exhausted (as a fighting cock or fencer).

pĕrĕkat, lime, mortar, gum, cement, glue; any sticky compound for holding materials together—cf. *lĕkat.*

pĕreksa, Skr. investigation; enquiry; examination; *pĕreksaï,* to enquire into, to examine.

pĕrĕmpuan, a woman.

pĕreng, a repulsive smell.

pĕrenggan, a boundary; = *pĕrhinggaan.*

pĕrentah, rule, government, sway; command, order; *datang-lah p.,* an order came; *p. Inggĕris,* British rule; *mĕmĕrentah,* to govern; *pĕmĕrentah,* a governor, a ruler.

pĕrĕpat, a tree (unidentified) closely resembling *sonneratia acida;* *p. bukit* (*cupania lessertiana*).

pĕret, I. a ticklish or tingling feeling about the body. II. = *pĕreng.*

pĕrgam, the well-known large wood-pigeons (*carpophaga ænea* and *c. badia*).

pĕrgi, to proceed; to go; *pĕrgi-lah ia ka-Riau,* he went to Riau.

pĕrgul, (Dutch) gilt; gilding.

pĕri, I. Pers. a fairy; *dewa shah pĕri,* the king of the fairies; *dewa pĕri mambang,* fairies of all sorts—i.e. Indian, Persian, Indonesian. II. way, manner, matter; *p. hal,* matters, details, circumstances.

pĕria, a cultivated pumpkin with a proverbially bitter taste (*momordica charantia*).

pĕriaï, Jav. a minor noble; a local notable.

pĕriang, the proper moment for doing anything; the most auspicious time.

pĕridi, prolific; fast growing; fertile.

pĕrigi, a well, a spring.

pĕrindun, a brood (of chickens).

Pěringgi, Pers. Frank, European, Portuguese.

pěriok, a cooking-pot; *p. api*, a bombshell; a hand-grenade; *p. kěra*, the pitcher-plant (*nepenthes*).

pěrisai, a shield, a buckler.

pěrkakas, instrument; machine; appliance for doing anything; *p. chap*, apparatus for printing; *p. pěrang*, war-material.

pěrkara, Skr. a matter; an affair; a concern or business; *habis-lah p.*, there is an end of the business.

pěrkasa, Skr. brave; gallant; distinguished for valour.

pěrkasam, = *pěkasam*.

pěrkutut, Jav. the dove; = *těkukur*.

pěrlahan, slow, quiet, tranquil; *běr-kata děngan p.*, to speak quietly; *běrjalan děngan p.*, to move slowly.

pěrlang, glittering, flashing.

pěrlenteh, = *lenteh*.

pěrlu, Ar. compulsory; obligatory.

pěrlus, *těpěrlus*, putting one's foot into a hole or place where the soil gives way.

pěrmadani, Jav. a rug.

pěrmai, I. fair, pretty, lovely, beautiful. II. = *pěrmaisuri*.

pěrmaisuri, Skr. a queen.

pěrman, Ar. a command (of God); the word of God; *p. Allah taala didalam Kuran*, the word of God revealed in the Koran; also *firman*.

pěrmana, Skr. *tiada těpěrmanai lagi*, innumerable, incalculable.

pěrmata, Skr. a gem; a precious stone.

pěrmatang, see *matang*.

pěrmisi, (Dutch) a permit, a pass.

pěrnah, ever; *bělum p.* or *tiada p.*, never.

pěrnama, Skr. full of the moon; a full moon as a measure of time; a month.

pěrni, a bowl for gold-fish.

pěrohong, gaping wide open.

pěrok, putting aside carelessly; stowing casually.

pěronyok, to crumple up (paper or stiff cloth) in the hand; *těrpěronyok*, crumpled, ruffled.

pěrosok, to thrust into; to be thrust into; to stumble into; *barang-siapa měnggali lubang, ia juga těrpěrosok ka-dalam-nya*, who so diggeth a pit, the same shall fall into it.

pěrsada, see *pancha*.

pěrsangga, Pers. a parasang as a measure of length.

pěrseh, clean, clear, pure, bright, frank—cf. *běrseh*.

pěrsětua, Skr. *sa-kali pěrsětua*, "once upon a time,"—a common exordium to a story.

pěrtama, Skr. first; van; *yang p.*, the first.

pěrtewi, Skr. the earth (deified); *dewi p.*, id.

pěruan, the yard of a ship.

pěruang, *ilmu pěruang*, a magic art [by which the magician is believed to protect himself from drowning by creating an air-cavity around himself]—cf. *ruang*.

pěruï, crumbling (as earth or rotten wood).

pěrum, the sounding-lead.

pěrunggu, bell-metal.

pěrunjong, a measure of depth; the length of a man with arms raised as far above his head as possible.

pěrupok, a plant (*hemigyrosa longifolia*).

pěrus, gruff, unfriendly.

perus, *perang-perus*, very pale, very wan.

pěrusah, headstrong, wilful, domineering.

pěrut, the stomach; the uterine cavity; *bawa p.*, to cadge for a meal.

pěrwara, Skr. the damsels of a court (spoken of collectively); the retinue of a princess.

pěrwira, Skr. a hero; a warrior; heroic.

pěsa, a roller or rod on which cloth is wound up as it is woven.

pĕsah, = *pisah*.

pĕsai, *bĕrpĕsai-pĕsai*, crumbling away (as the mortar on an old wall).

pesak, a gore; a piece of cloth let in under the arm in making a coat.

pĕsaka, heirloom; family property (especially quasi-entailed property); *adat p.*, Malay customary law regulating succession; also *pusaka*.

pĕsan, order, instruction, command, direction; *pĕsani*, to give instructions; *bĕrpĕsan*, id.

pĕsara, Pers. bazaar; a variant of *pasar*.

pĕsawat, an instrument; a machine; a tool; *p. bĕrjĕntĕra*, machinery.

pĕseban, a broad gangway round the *sĕri balai*.

pĕsiar, = *bĕrsiar*—v. *siar*.

pĕsing, (onom.) the whizz of a projectile through the air.

pĕsirah, a district official (in Palembang).

pĕsok, perforated; broken through; broken down; knocked in; *pĕsok-pĕsok*, full of holes.

pĕsona, Pers. a spell; a magical incantation; the effects of a spell; witchcraft.

pesong, *tĕrpesong*, altered (of a course); change of direction in motion.

pĕspa, = *puspa*.

pesta, Port. a festival; a celebration; *p. mĕnari*, a ball, a dance.

pĕstaka, Skr. a book of divination or sorcery; the black art; injury as the result of the black art; *mala p.*, evil from hostile sorcerers or malignant supernatural powers.

pĕsti, certain, sure, positive, reliable; *khabar yang p.*, reliable information.

pĕta, a plan, map, sketch, drawing or design; *pĕtakan*, to make a picture or sketch-plan of anything.

pĕtai, a tree yielding a pod which is very offensive in smell (*parkia biglandulosa*); *p. bĕlalang* (*pithecolobium microcarpum*); *p. laut* (*desmodium umbellatum*).

petak, a square compartment; a division of a *padi* field; a locker in a boat; the hold in a ship.

pĕtaka, = *pĕstaka*.

pĕtala, Skr. a fold; a layer; a stratum.

pĕtaling, a tree yielding a good timber (*ochanostachys amentacea*).

pĕtam, a frontlet or browband worn by a bride.

pĕtang, evening, afternoon; *p. hari*, late in the day.

petar, taking a true aim; training a gun on to anything.

pĕtaram, a small knife.

pĕtarang, *pukat pĕtarang*, a deep-sea net used on the east coast of the Peninsula.

pĕtas, I. crackers, noisy fireworks. II. *bĕras pĕtas*, all kinds of rice; stores generally.

pĕtek, plucking, picking, gathering; playing on a stringed instrument; *mĕmĕtek*, to pluck, to pick, to play on a stringed instrument.

pĕtĕnah, Ar. calumny, slander; also *fitnah*.

pĕtĕra, = *putĕra*.

pĕtĕrana, Skr. a seat near the throne (used by princes of [the blood); the seat of the bride and bridegroom at a Malay wedding.

pĕtĕri, = *putĕri*.

pĕtĕrum, *ubat pĕtĕrum*, powder in packages or cartridges for use with artillery.

pĕti, Tam. a box, a case, a chest.

pĕting, a jerk with the thumb and finger.

pĕtir, a clap of thunder; thunder; *bunyi p.*, the sound of thunder.

pĕtola, a generic name given to a class of pumpkins; also *kĕtola*; *p. hutan* (*luffa acutangula*); *p. manis* (*luffa cylindrica*); *p. ular* (*trichosanthes anguina*).

pĕtua, Ar. a precept; a traditional rule; an authoritative ruling; advice by one who knows.

petur, Port. a factor, a minor official.

pĕtutu, a tree (*hibiscus floccosus*).

pi, *main pi*, to gamble on credit, an account being kept for settlement.

piah, a very small coin.

piak, a quid of betel-leaf; a fold; a strip.

pial, the wattles on the comb of a cock.

piala, Pers. a cup or goblet; a small beaker; a phial.

pialang, buying on credit.

pialing, a bird (unidentified).

piama, the rainy season (in Kedah).

piang, mother (in Boyanese).

pianggang, a green bug destructive to the crops.

pianggu, a tree yielding a red fruit (*clerodendron nutans*).

piara, to bring up; to nurture; to support; = *pĕlihara*.

piarit, a fish-spear with a double barb.

pias, a strip (of a sail).

piat, I. twisted, oblique, out of line. II. a remote descendant.

piatu, desolate; having no relatives; *anak p.*, an orphan.

pichek, narrow, confined, limited.

pichit, pinching; pressure between finger and thumb.

pichu, the trigger of a gun.

pihak, side; *p. kĕpala*, the side of the head; *p. igama*, on the side of religion; in the matter of faith.

pijak, treading on, stepping on; *mĕmijak*, to step on.

pijar, a resinous substance used by goldsmiths in their work.

pijat, a bed-bug.

pikat, I. a horse-fly. II. the snaring of birds; *mĕmikat*, to snare; *pĕmikat*, a fowler.

pikau, mental confusion; dullness; *burong p.*, the blue-breasted quail (*excalfactoria chinensis*).

pikir, Ar. to think; *pikiran*, consideration; *bĕrpikir*, to ponder; to meditate; also *fikir*.

pikul, to carry a heavy load slung on a shoulder; to lift a heavy weight; to weigh; a weight equal to about 133 pounds; *mĕmikul*, to carry.

pilau, a ship of a type now obsolete.

pileh, selection, choice; *pilehan*, id.; *orang pilehan*, picked men.

pili, *pili ayer*, a water-tap.

pilin, twining; plaiting; making a rope of several strands.

pilis, a mark traced on the forehead as a protection against evil spirits.

pilu, tender feeling, sympathy, sensibility, melancholy, regret; *mĕmbĕri p.*, to inspire tenderness.

pimpin, leading by the hand, conducting, guiding; *pĕmimpin*, a guide.

pina, *siput pina-pina*, a shell (*pinna?*)

pinak, *anak pinak*, descendants, family.

pinang, the areca-nut (*areca catechu*); the use of the areca-nut in a proposal of marriage; a proposal of marriage; *p. raja*, the red-stemmed palm (*cyrtostachys lacca*); *pinangkan*, to betroth one's daughter; *mĕminang*, to ask in marriage.

pinchang, *pinchang-pinchut*, zigzag, irregular.

pinchok, slicing sour fruits and vegetables and cooking them in sugar.

pinchut, *pinchang-pinchut*, zigzag, irregular.

pindah, transition, movement from one place to another; transference; *pindahkan*, to transfer; *bĕrpindah*, to move.

pindang, fish cooked with a piquante sauce containing *asam gelugur* and other ingredients.

pinggan, a plate, a tray, a saucer.

pinggang, waist; middle of the body; amidships; *p. ramping*, a slender waist; *p. gĕnting*, wasp-waisted; *ikat p.* or *tali p.*, a girdle;

pĕminggang, the midmost portion; *dayong pĕminggang*, the oars amidships.

pinggir, edge, border, boundary, limit; *pinggiran nĕgĕri*, frontier.

pingit, confined to the house; kept under lock and key; jealously shutting up and guarding.

pinjam, a transaction of the nature of a loan; borrowing, lending; *pinjaman*, a loan; *bĕri pinjam*, giving in loan; lending; *minta pinjam*, borrowing; *mĕminjam* or *pinjamkan*, to borrow.

pinta, asking; applying for; requesting; *pintaï*, to ask for; also *minta*.

pintal, twining (as in making rope); *awan p.*, a rope-like spiral pattern.

pintang, *hilang pintang*, lost for ever; altogether gone; wholly disappeared.

pintar, clever, wily, sharp.

pintas, cutting across; taking a short cut; intercepting by cutting across.

pintu, a door; a gate; an entrance; *di-muka p.*, in front of the gate; *pĕnunggu p.*, a porter; *p. ambang*, a light screen-door not touching the ground; *p. ayer*, a water-gate; *p. gĕrbang*, a main-gate or door; *p. kambi*, a light screen-door reaching down to the ground; *p. lawang*, an outer gate; *p. maling*, a side-door or back-door; *p. mati*, a door nailed up or permanently closed; *jĕnang p.*, the door-posts.

pioh, *tĕrpioh*, knotted (of roots or branches); involved or complicated (of a business).

pipa, Eur. a barrel.

pipeh, flatness; flat; *chaching p.*, the tapeworm.

pipi, the cheek; *kĕdua p.*, both cheeks; *mĕmerahkan p.*, to rouge the cheeks.

pipis, pounding between two hard substances; mashing; grinding down curry-stuff with a heavy pounder or roller.

pipit, a generic name for small sparrows and finches.

pirai, *pĕnyakit pirai*, a rheumatic or gouty complaint causing pain in the joints.

pirasat, Ar. a horoscope; astrological or magical fore-knowledge; also *firasat*.

pirek, to crush small; to grind to atoms.

piring, plate, saucer.

pirus, Pers. *pĕrmata pirus*, a turquoise.

pisah, putting asunder; severing; divorcing; *bĕrpisah*, to be separated.

pisang, a banana (*musa sapientum*); *p. karok*, the wild banana (*musa malaccensis*); *p.-pisang*, a generic name given to a number of wild anonaceous plants (especially *uvaria purpurea*); *bĕronok p.*, a sea-worm (*colochyrus anceps*); *gamat p.*, a sea-worm (*stichopus variegatus*); *ikan buntal p.*, a fish (*tetrodon lunaris*); *jantong p.*, the blossom of the banana; *katak p.*, a frog with great leaping-powers (*rana erythrœa* or *rhacophorus leucomystax*); *sa-pĕrpisang*, as much time as it takes to eat a banana.

pisau, a generic name for knives of all sorts; *p. chukur, p. pĕnchukur*, or *pĕnyukur*, a razor; *p. daun padi*, a lancet; *p. lidah ayam*, an office-knife (with a small blade which does not fold); *p. lidah ayam lipat*, a penknife; also *p. lipat*; *p. raut*, a small knife for cutting off excrescences on a stick and giving the stick a smooth surface; *mata p.*, the blade of a knife; *punggong p.*, the blunt side of a knife-blade.

piskal, (Dutch) a procurator-fiscal.

pistaka, = *pĕstaka*.

pita, Port. tape, ribbon.

pitah, eloquent, soft-spoken, gracious.

pitam, a rush of blood to the head causing dizziness.

pitis, a very small denomination of coin something like a Chinese cash.

pitu, seven; a rare equivalent of *tujoh*.

piut, a descendant in the fourth or fifth generation.

po, Ch. a sort of die-box used by Chinese gamblers; *main po*, to gamble by guessing at the position of the hidden die.

podak, *pandan podak*, the plant *pandanus inermis*.

podi, Tam. the dust of gems; very small gems mounted in large numbers to make a glittering show.

pohon, I. a tree; *p. kayu*, id.; *p. kĕlapa*, a coconut tree. II. begging, requesting; asking for leave to depart; *pohonkan* or *mĕmohonkan*, to apply for (anything); *bĕrmohon*, to ask leave to depart—cf. *mohon*.

pokah, to become bent; to give way.

pokok, a tree, a bush, a plant; the nucleus of a storm; the capital for working an undertaking; *p. kĕlapa*, a coconut tree; *p. angin*, a gathering cloud presaging wind; *p. ribut*, a storm-cloud.

polan, Ar. *si-polan*, so-and-so.

polis, Eng. a police court.

polok, swallowing a large mouthful.

polong, a familiar spirit.

pompa, (Dutch) a pump, spout, or hose; = *bomba*.

pompang, an anchored purse-net; also called *gombang China*.

pondok, a shed; a lean to; a temporary shelter; *kĕpala p.*, (Singapore) a Boyanese headman.

pondong, carrying in the folds of a scarf slung over the back.

pongkis, a shallow rubbish-basket.

pongsu, a hillock or mound; an anthill—cf. *busut*; *mĕrak p.*, the peacock-pheasant (*polyplectrum bicalcaratum*).

ponok, a fleshy bump or protuberance; a hump.

pontang, *pontang-panting*, topsyturvy; helter-skelter; scattered about.

pontianak, = *puntianak*.

porak, *porak parek*, helter-skelter; in confusion; *p. pĕranda*, id.

porok, a native game resembling quoits.

poros, the vertex of a cone; the top of a mast; the point of a spear.

po'ta, matchless; excellent.

potong, cutting off; a piece cut off; *sa-potong tanah*, a piece of land; *mĕmotong*, to cut off.

poyang, a Sumatran word sometimes meaning "ancestor"—(cf. *moyang*); and sometimes a magician (= *pawang*).

puadai, Tam. cloth laid down for a procession to pass over.

puah, *bĕrpuah*, to perform certain old-world ceremonies so as to drive away ill-luck from a district.

puak, an assembly, a troop; *bĕrpuak*, to gather together.

puaka, a spirit of the earth; a genius loci.

pualam, Tam. marble.

puan, I. a betel-box. II. = *pĕrĕmpuan* (in certain titles).

puar, *pokok puar*, a plant (*amomum cardamomum*).

puas, satisfied, sated; *p. hati*, id.

puasa, Skr. a fast; fasting; *bulan P.*, the fasting-month *Ramadzan*.

puchat, pallor, pale; *p. lĕsi*, pale through anæmia; *p. perang*, pale-red; the pallor of a dark skin; *p. pudar*, pale and tired-looking.

puchok, a sprouting branch; a shoot; *p. api*, a darting point of flame; *p. rĕbong*, (1) the edible young shoots of the bamboo; (2) chevrons (in art); *ular p.*, the common green tree-snake (*dryophis prasinus*).

puchong, a generic name given to bitterns—e.g. to *dupetor flavicollis*, *ardetta cinnamomea*, *ardetta sinensis* and *butorides javanica*.

pudak, = *podak*.

pudar, faded, dim, "washed out"; *puchat p.*, pale and tired-looking.

pudat, stowing or stuffing away anything in a casual or careless manner.
pudi, = *podi*.
puding, a common cultivated plant, the garden croton (*codiæum variegatum*); *p. hutan* (*tabernæmontana malaccensis*).
pugar, complete repair, restoration, renewal, doing up.
puih, *rĕput puih*, crumbling to pieces; rotting.
puja, Skr. prayer, adoration—but used of Hindoo rites and of the prayers to spirits of the jungle, and not of service in a mosque.
puji, praise, laudation; *puji-pujian*, praises, the complimentary phrases at the beginning of a letter; *mĕmuji*, to praise; to declare praiseworthy; *tĕrpuji*, belauded.
pujok, coaxing, flattery; *pujokkan* or *mĕmujok*, to coax, to flatter; also *bujok*.
pukal, a lump or clod of anything; *kĕris sa-p.*, the common straight-bladed *kĕris*.
pukang, the fork; the junction of the lower limbs; *lintang p.*, sprawling.
pukas, *bĕrpukas* or *bĕrpukas-pukasan*, in a state of nudity.
pukat, a generic name for large nets (especially drift-nets and seines); *p. tarek*, the common seine; *p. hanyut*, the common drift-net. [Many more specialised names are also in use.]
pukau, a narcotic (used by thieves to drug their victims to sleep).
puki, the female genitals.
pukul, beating, striking, knocking, hammering; *p. lima*, five o'clock; *p. chap*, printing; *p. bĕsi*, shoeing a horse.
pula, also; likewise; again; too; furthermore; *dĕmikian p.*, and so once more; *siapa p.*, who then; *mĕngapa p.*, why then.
pulaga, = *pĕlaga*.
pulai, a large tree (*alstonia scholaris*).

pulan, crisp (of cooked rice); well-cooked.
pulang, return to the point of original departure—e.g. to one's country, to one's home, etc.; *pĕnyakit-ku pulang-lah*, my illness returned; *bĕrjalan p.*, to return.
pulas, twisting, wringing, wringing out; *p. leher*, to wring the neck; *mĕmulas*, to twist (used of griping pains in the stomach); *pĕmulas*, a twister, a screw-driver.
pulasan, I. a fruit—closely resembling the *rambutan* (*nephelium mutabile*). II. a name given to the Malay weasel (*putorius nudipes*).
pulasari, = *pĕlasari*.
pulau, I. an island; an isolated piece of rising ground in a sea, river, or swamp. II. *nasi pulau*, pillau rice.
puleh, return, revival, renewal, reaction; *pulang p.*, restoration to an original state; *simpul p.*, a fastening which is easily undone; *pulehkan*, to bring back; to restore.
pulun, gathering up in folds; *bĕrpulun-pulun*, gathered up on one side (of a *sarong*).
pulur, = *ĕmpulur*.
pulut, adhesiveness, stickiness; glutinous varieties of rice; a generic name for cakes made out of glutinous rice; *pulut-pulut*, a generic name given to a number of plants—e.g. *mallotus* spp. and *urena lobata*.
pumpun, a harmless sea-millipede much used as bait.
pun, an inseparable particle suffixed to a word that it is intended to particularly emphasise in the sentence; *itu pun*, that also; *sa-kali pun*, yet; *ada-pun*, furthermore there are; *ia-pun pĕrgi*, he too went.
punah, *habis-lah punah*, utterly destroyed—a strong form of *habis*.
punai, a generic name for many green pigeons; *burong p.*, the common green pigeon (*osmotreron*

vernans); *p. daun* (*osmotreron nipalensis*); *p. gading* or *p. jambu* (*ptilopus jambu*); *p. rimba*, the cuckoo-dove (*micropygia ruficeps*); *p. siul* (*osmotreron olax*); *p. tanah*, the bronzewing - dove (*chalcophaps indica*).

punat, the core of a boil.

puncha, the loose end or fag end of anything—such as a piece of rope or cloth; the pendent extremity.

punchak, top, summit, crown; the knob on a flagstaff; *p. gunong*, the summit of a mountain.

pundi, *pundi-pundi*, a satchel, a bag, a purse; *p.-p. hĕmpĕdu*, the gall-bladder.

punding, to twist or ravel up (of a rope or thread).

pungah, arrogance, pride, self-conceit.

punggah, unloading, discharging; removing goods from one place to another; *p. angkat*, to pick up and remove; to transport.

punggawa, = *pĕnggawa*.

punggok, *burong punggok*, a small owl (*glaucidium brodii*); a proverbial simile for a despairing lover, as this owl is believed to pine for the moon.

punggong, the fundament; the buttocks; the seat; *p. pĕdang*, the dull side of a sword.

punggur, a fallen tree-trunk.

pungkah, a fragment; a large piece of anything.

pungkur, the posterior; the fundament; *p. siput*, the heart of the whorl in finger impressions; *tulang p.*, the pubic bones.

pungut, picking up, gathering, collecting; *mĕmungut*, to gather.

punjong, an arched framework on which plants are trailed.

punjut, to tie up sack-wise; to fold up.

puntal, to coil rope round the hand so as to get a good grip of it; to wring.

punti, *ular punti*, a name given to the snake *dipsadomorphus dendrophilus*; also called *ular tiong*.

puntianak, an evil spirit attacking women at the time of childbirth.

puntoh, a broad armlet of a type worn by heroes of romance.

puntong, a stump; a half-burnt log; the fag-end of a cigar.

punya, possession; (in bazaar Malay) a word used to form a possessive or genitive—e.g. *sahaya punya rumah*, my house; *baik punya orang*, good men; men of worth. [This use of *punya* is not literary.]

pupoh, to fly at each other (of fighting cocks); to fight gamely; *bĕr-pupoh ayam*, to set cocks on to each other (without artificial spurs)—cf. *sabong*.

pupok, the application of plasters and poultices to the body.

pupu, a grade or degree of relationship; a generation; *saudara sa-p.*, a first cousin; *saudara dua p.*, a second cousin.

pupur, a face-powder made of rice-meal scented with herbs; *pupuran* or *tĕpong pupur*, id.; *bĕrpupur*, to apply such powder to the face.

pupus, blighted (of plants); left desolate (of human beings).

puput, blowing; swaying (anything) of the wind; *di-puput bayu*, swayed about by the breeze.

pura, I. Skr. a city (only in compounds—such as *Singa-pura*). II. *pura-pura*, feigning, pretence; *mĕ-nangis p.-p.*, shedding crocodile's tears. III. *pura pĕranda*, = *porak pĕranda*; see *porak*.

purba, Skr. ancient, former; *p. kala*, days of old; also *pĕrba*.

puri, Skr. the residential portions of a palace.

purnama, = *pĕrnama*.

puru, a skin-disease (*frambosia indica*); *katak p.*, a toad.

pusaka, heir-loom; family property

(especially quasi-entailed property); also *pěsaka*.

pusar, a spiral motion; *pusaran ayer*, a whirlpool; *pusaran angin*, a whirlwind.

pusat, the navel, the centre; *p. bulat*, the centre of a circle; *p. tasek*, the centre of the great ocean; the navel of the seas; *tali p.*, the umbilical cord.

pusi, *bulu pusi*, a kind of lint used for dressing wounds.

pusing, revolution, rotation; *p. kěpala*, vertigo; *běrpusing-pusing*, revolving; [*pusing* is often used metaphorically for "to cheat"].

puspa, Skr. a flower; flowery; variegated.

pusu, *běrpusu-pusu*, surging to and fro (of a crowd of people).

putar, rotation, motion on an axis; *putaran*, a windlass.

putarwali, Jav. *akar putarwali*, a medicinal creeper (*lepidagathis longifolia* ?)

putat, a generic name for a number of plants (*barringtonia* spp.)

puteh, white; *p. kuning*, "white-yellow"—a much-admired complexion-tint; *p. mata*, being put to shame; "scored off"; *p. tulang*, the whitening of the bones—death; *kayu p.*, kajeput; *orang P.*, a white man; a European (especially an Englishman); *měmuteh*, to become white.

putek, the fruit as it appears immediately after the falling of the blossom.

putěra, Skr. a prince; the child of a prince; *běrputěra*, to bear a child.

putěri, Skr. a princess; the daughter of a prince; a fairy; *p. malu*, a name given to the sensitive plant; *burong sěpah p.*, a bird (*dicæum cruentatum*).

puting, the part of a knife-blade which is buried in the handle; a pointed projection; a fag end or stump; *p. běliong*, a waterspout; *p. chěpu-chěpu*, the foot of a mast; *p. susu*, the nipple; *parang p.*, a very sharp kind of chopper.

putu, a generic name given to a number of cakes.

putus, severance; splitting or breaking off; (by metaphor) to settle, to decide, to put an end to; *p. asa*, hopeless; despair; *p. harga*, to settle a bill; to pay a price; *p. hati*, heartbreak; *p. makan*, to exhaust one's supplies; *p. nyawa*, to die; *putuskan*, to settle, to terminate, to break; *kěputusan*, severance, termination, settlement; *yang tiada běrkěputusan*, endless.

puyoh, the bustard quail (*turnix pugnax*).

puyu, *puyu-puyu*, a small fresh-water fish (unidentified).

R

raba, groping or feeling about with the hands; *měraba*, to grope; to fondle.

rabak, gashed, rent, torn.

raban, *měraban*, to talk incoherently.

Rabbi, Ar. Lord (of God); *Ilahi R.*, the Lord God.

rabek, *robak-rabek*, tattered and torn.

rabi, Ar. *Rabi-ul-awal* and *Rabi-ul-akhir*, names of months.

rabit, I. a gash or rent at the edge of a cloth, mat, etc.; *bibir r.*, a harelip. II. *měrabit*, to drag third parties into a suit.

rabok, tinder, touchwood.

rabong, the double row of *atap* protecting the ridge of a roof; *pasang r.*, spring-tides.

rabu, I. the lungs; *kěmbang r.*, exaltation. II. Ar. *hari Rabu*, Wednesday.

rabun, fumigation; *mĕrabun*, to send smoke into a house so as to drive away mosquitoes or evil spirits.

rabut, tearing out, pulling out, forcibly extracting; *mĕrabut*, to tear out.

rachau, delirious utterance, raving.

rachek, I. a snare of hanging nooses for catching birds; *mĕrachek*, to snare birds. II. slicing up areca-nut.

rachun, poison (especially stomach poisons in contradistinction to blood poisons—*bisa*).

radak, thrusting or stabbing upwards; *mĕradak*, to spear or stab from below a person in a house.

radang, *mĕradang*, to become heated or excited.

radif, Ar. the burden of a song; the rhyme.

radin, Jav. a princely title.

radzi, Ar. may (God) bestow favour—in the expression *radzi Allah an-hu* (may God show him favour)—an exclamatory remark when the names of the early Caliphs are mentioned.

raga, I. a coarsely-plaited basket or creel of bamboo; *buah r.*, a sort of football of basket-work; *main r.* or *sepak r.*, a primitive Malay football. II. Jav. the body (in opposition to the soul). III. display; *mĕraga*, to show off; *pĕraga*, a dandy.

ragam, Hind. modes in music; variety in sound, colouring, or disposition; *banyak orang, banyak ragam-nya*, there are as many temperaments as there are men, prov.

ragang, *mĕragang*, to scale a wall; to climb a tree.

ragas, *mĕragas*, to pull at or tear at (but not to tear out).

ragi, essence, alloy, colouring matter, leaven, yeast; *buta r.*, with the pattern washed out (of cloth); *burong mĕragi*, the painted snipe (*rostratula capensis*).

ragong, *tĕragong-ragong*, knocking against one another (of heavy bodies hanging in a bunch).

ragu, uncertainty; "chopping and changing."

ragum, a vice or clip worked with a screw.

ragup, snatching and carrying away.

ragus, greed, gluttony; also *rakus*.

ragut, *mĕragut*, to tear out with violence (especially of tearing out hair).

rahang, the jaw; *tulang r.*, the jawbone.

rahap, *kain rahap*, a sort of pall cast over a body at a funeral but not buried with it.

rahasia, = *rahsia*.

rahat, I. a native boom. II. *gugur rahat*, a sudden and general (but untimely) fall of durians. III. Ar. rest, tranquillity, peace.

rahi, = *bĕrahi*.

rahim, I. Ar. merciful, compassionate. II. Ar. the uterus.

rahman, Ar. merciful, compassionate.

rahmat, Ar. mercy (especially the mercy of God).

rahsia, Skr. a secret; *mĕmbuka r.*, to reveal a secret; *mĕnaroh r.*, to keep a secret.

rahu, Skr. the dragon which is believed to attempt to swallow the moon (at eclipses); *bulan di-makan r.*, an eclipse.

raih, drawing towards oneself; taking (as opposed to giving).

raip, Ar. disappearance, vanishing; = *ghaib*.

rais, to sweep off (as one sweeps crumbs off a table).

raja, Skr. prince, ruler, governor; the king (in chess); *r. bĕrasal*, a prince by descent; *r. bintang*, the principal heavenly bodies; *r. digĕlar*, a prince by virtue of office; *r. muda*, a title given to the heir-apparent; *r. sari* or *r. sa-hari*, a bridegroom; *r. udang*, (Southern Malaya) a kingfisher; (North Malaya) a large sandpiper; *anak r.*, a prince; *budak r.*, (East Coast) courtiers; retainers at the court of a prince; *hamba r.*, servants or menials about a court; *pěnyakit r.*, a malignant ulcer on the neck or shoulders; *pinang r.*, the red-stemmed palm (*cyrtostachys lacca*); *kěrajaan*, rule, dominion, empire; *alat kěrajaan*, regalia.

Rajab, Ar. the name of a Malay month.

rajah, probing; groping for anything with a stick; tattooing; a design scratched on anything.

rajawali, Skr. an eagle; *lang r.*, a name given to small hawks—e.g. *tinnunculus alaudarius*.

rajin, persistent, frequent, diligent; frequency, assiduity; *r. běrbuat jahat*, persistence in doing wrong; *r. dan usaha*, assiduity and diligence.

rajok, *měrajok*, to sulk, *pěrajok*, sullen.

rajut, knitting, worsted work.

raka, fragility, brittleness.

rakaat, Ar. the bowing of the body in prayer.

rakam, Ar. painting or gilding cloth.

rakan, associate, companion, comrade, partner; *rakanan*, a partner in business.

rakap, creeping at a snail's pace; crawling; *měrakap*, to creep, to crawl—e.g. *orang hina měrakap*, a beggar crawling from door to door.

rakat, Hind. a scarlet pea, better known as *buah saga*.

rakit, arrangement side by side; the construction of a raft or of the framework of a house; a raft; *sa-rakit*, a pair—e.g. two *sirch* leaves one over the other.

rakna, = *ratna*.

raksa, Skr. mercury, quicksilver.

raksamala, a tree (*altingiana*) yielding a perfumed gum.

raksasa, Skr. an ogre; a goblin; an evil spirit.

raksi, I. yielding fragrance; *měraksi*, to perfume; *pěraksi*, flower petals and scented leaves used for perfuming a bed. II. union, commingling, affinity; *sa-r.*, harmonising; affinities.

rakus, greed, gluttony; also *ragus*.

rakut, *měrakut*, to deceive, to set a snare, to weave a web (of a spider).

ralat, Ar. error, miscalculation.

ralip, I. sleepy, tired. II. custom, habit.

ram, I. brooding, sitting on eggs (of a hen). II. *tingkap ram*, venetian blinds.

Rama, I. Skr. *Sěri Rama*, the Hindu demi-god Rama. II. *rama-rama*, a butterfly; *ringgit rama-rama*, the Mexican dollar. III. Jav. father—especially in the expression *rama aji*, princely father; sire.

Ramadzan, Ar. the fasting-month or *bulan Puasa*.

ramah, over-familiarity, effusive friendliness, courtesy over-done or forced; *pěramah mulut*, impertinent familiarities; taking liberties.

ramai, crowded, populous; numerously attended (of a festival); festive; joyous; *běramai-ramaian*, attended by a large following; with very many others; *měramaikan*, to give population and prosperity to a place.

ramal, I. Ar. soothsaying; horoscopic calculations. II. Pers. a scarf, a kerchief.

ramas, pressure between the fingers and the flat of the hand; kneading; massage; *měramas*, to knead; to massage.

rambah, moist, damp (of the ground).

rambai, I. a common fruit-tree (*baccaurea motleyana*). II. *bulu rambai*, short feathers on either side of the tail of a fowl.

rambaian, hairy.

rambak, extending in every direction (as a creeper); flourishing; prosperous.

rambang, extensive, wide, broad; *jala r.*, a casting-net for general fishing; *lela r.*, a wide-mouthed swivel-gun; *mulut r.*, erratic talk.

rambat, a dais for a prince or for a bridegroom.

rambeh, *bĕrambeh* or *mĕrambeh*, to go on an excursion with one's family.

rambu, I. a thick post. II. a hanging fringe; *rambu-rambu*, id.; *tombak r.*, a spear with a hanging fringe under the spear-head.

rambun, tangled undergrowth; roots, climbers and creepers.

rambut, I. hair; *r. ikal*, curly hair; *r. kĕriting*, frizzled hair; *r. tĕrurai*, dishevelled hair; *anak r.*, short hair round the central growth; *gigi r.*, the hair just at its junction with the forehead; *kaki r.*, the hair on the neck; *suak r.*, the parting; *rambutan*, a tree yielding a fruit with a hairy integument (*nephelium lappæum*); *rambuti*, woollen cloth; *pĕrambut*, the gut at the end of a fishing-line. II. *pĕrambut*, invulnerability to weapons; *p. sĕnjata*, id.

rambutan, the well-known fruit *nephelium lappæum*—v. *rambut*.

rambuti, woollen cloth—v. *rambut*.

rami, the rhea or China grass (*boehmeria nivea*); *kain r.*, a coarse sacking made of *rami* fibre.

rampai, miscellaneous; of a mixed character; varied; *bunga r.*, a fragrant preparation made by scenting *pandan* and other leaves; *rampaikan*, to scatter (*bunga rampai*), to spread news, etc.

rampak, spreading horizontally (of a tree); umbrageous.

rampas, plundering, seizing, carrying off; *rampasan*, booty, plunder; *mĕrampas*, to take by force.

rampat, sweeping about a long pole (or any similar object) so as to strike anyone approaching within a certain radius; giving sweeping blows instead of deliberately aimed blows; *mĕmaki mĕrampat papan*, abusing everybody who comes near; indiscriminate abuse.

ramping, I. slender; lissom (of the waist). II. *rompang-ramping*, tattered and torn.

rampus, *mĕrampus*, to use foul language.

ramput, *mĕramput*, to tell foolish lies.

ramu, picking up odds and ends; *mĕramu*, to collect materials of all sorts; *pĕramu kayu*, a wood-gatherer.

ramus, excessive hairiness; *bĕramus*, over-hairy (of the face); *buang ramus*, to get rid of superfluous hair.

rana, I. *mĕrana*, to pine; *sakit mĕrana*, a wasting disease. II. = *ratna*.

ranak, *bĕranak-ranak*, to play in a swift tremolo.

ranap, I. *mĕranap*, to crumple under great pressure. II. just visible above the ground; low-lying.

ranchah, to mark a track by cutting down an occasional sapling.

ranchak, gay; continuous and lively (of music, dancing, etc.)

ranchang, pointing upwards; a pointed stake stuck in the ground as a rude caltrop.

ranchap, giving a cylindrical form to anything; passing one's hands up and down a cylinder.

ranchong, sharp cut; cutting at a sharp angle (used of sharpening a pencil or native pen).

randa, *mĕranda*, to wander about capriciously; going here and there; see also *pĕranda*.

randai, *mĕrandai*, to wade through shallow water.

randeh, *rondah-randeh*, in disorder, dishevelled, in confusion.

randi, a silk fabric of Chinese or Siamese make.

randok, I. *kambing randok*, a rank old he-goat. II. treading down, treading underfoot.

randong, treading down—cf. *randok* and *sĕrandong*.

randu, the action of the arm when thrust into liquid and worked round and round.

rang, *tanah rang*, a rice-field (banked and previously cultivated, but temporarily lying fallow).

rangah, haughty, supercilious; *mĕrangah*, to swagger.

rangai, I. obstinate or chronic (of a disagreeable, but not dangerous disease). II. *mĕrangai*, to forage about.

rangak, a generic name for shells of the genus *pteroceras*.

rangga, I. pointed projections; sticking up in points (as the tine of a deer). II. Jav. a title of inferior distinction.

ranggah, I. *mĕranggah*, to strip a tree of fruit. II. To stab upwards, = *radak*.

ranggak, hauling a boat ashore.

ranggam, a thorny shrub or small tree (unidentified).

ranggas, a mass of twigs or fallen branches; *bĕranggas-ranggas*, spiky.

ranggi, spruce; neat in dressing.

ranggong, walking stiffly with long legs held wide apart; squatting; *burong r.*, a long-legged water-bird; *kail r.*, fishing when two sticks project from the lead, a hook being suspended from the extremity of each stick; *mĕranggong*, to crawl painfully or laboriously along (as a wounded man or very young child); to squat with the knees wide apart.

ranggu, see *pĕranggu*.

ranggul, *mĕranggul*, to dip (of a boat's bows).

rangin, Jav. a shield.

rangka, skeleton, framework; *bĕrangka*, possessing or serving as a framework.

rangkai, strung or fastened together; a string of; a combination; *rangkaian*, connecting, stringing together; *bĕrangkai-rangkai*, in strings or clusters.

rangkak, *mĕrangkak*, to walk on hands and knees; to crawl along; to make slow progress.

rangkap, I. pair, couple, set of two. II. to catch by covering; *pĕrangkap*, a falling trap.

rangkas, = *ranggas*.

rangkek, a generic name for shells of the genus *conus*.

rangkong, = *ranggong*.

rangkum, grasping between the hands; *sa-r.*, as much as one can so grasp.

rangkup, the formation of a cavity or channel between two sides which slope to meet each other.

rangsang, *mĕrangsang*, to get inflamed or excited; *pĕrangsang*, an exciting drug; a stimulant; *mĕmbĕri bĕrangsang*, to excite to passion.

rangup, crisp and brittle (as a biscuit).

rangum, snatching excitedly; grabbing at.

rani, Hind. the wife of a prince or governor.

ranjang, a large bedstead or double-bed.

ranjau, a caltrop; *r. chachak*, pointed stakes driven into the ground with the points uppermost; *r. mata parut*, a plank with nails projecting out of it; *r. mata satu*, a caltrop consisting of a plank and a spike; *r. mata tiga*, the common caltrop.

Ranjuna, Skr. Arjuna.

rantai, a chain; *baju r.*, a coat of chain-mail; *rantaikan*, to put in chains.

rantam, clubbing together for a common purchase—e.g. of villagers combining to purchase a buffalo to slaughter.

rantang, I. a basket or hamper for provisions, crockery, etc. II. penetrability to sight; *r. mata* *měmandang*, letting the eye see right through.

rantau, a reach of a river or of the sea-coast; *tělok r.*, bights and reaches; the entire territory; *měrantau*, to go wandering.

ranting, a minor branch, a twig; *bělalang r.*, a stick insect; *kuang r.*, the peacock pheasant (*polyplectron bicalcaratum*).

ranum, *masak ranum*, fully ripe (of fruit).

ranyah, *měranyah*, to pick small pieces of food here and there out of a dish.

rap, I. *tanah rap*, land that has been cleared, weeded and banked, and is ready for cultivation. II. (onom.) the sound of rapping or stamping.

rapah, to walk roughly over anything.

rapai, *měrapai*, to fumble with—cf. *gěrapai*.

rapang, *ikan rapang*, a fish (*mugil bleckeri*).

rapat, contiguity, close connection; *sahabat yang r.*, close friends; *měrapat*, to fit two things together; to work as a joiner.

rapeh, drawing in; pulling or hauling in; drawing towards oneself.

rapek, *měrapek*, to talk nonsense—cf. *apek*.

rapoh, brittle, fragile; *r. mulut*, inability to control one's tongue.

rapu, *měrapu*, to pick up ill-considered trifles—cf. *ramu*; *měrapu dana*, to beg.

ras, I. Hind. the reins. II. (onom.) a rustle.

rasa, I. taste, flavour, perception, sensation, feeling; *r. hati*, perception; *rasa-nya*, it seems; it appears; as it were; *putus r.*, forgetfulness, loss of sympathy; *sa-r.*, resemblance (in taste); like; *timpa r.*, to bear the brunt of anything; *rasai* or *měrasai*, to feel; *běrasa*, feeling; *pěrasaan*, perception. II. Skr. mercury, quicksilver; also *raksa*.

rasamala, = *raksamala*.

rasau, I. a screw-pine (*pandanus russow*). II. *měrasau*, to make a swishing noise (of branches moved by the wind).

rashid, Ar. orthodox.

rashwah, Ar. bribe; an illegal gratification.

rasi, = *raksi*, II.

rasmi, Ar. disposition, temperament.

rasok, I. the attack of an evil spirit; *di-r.*, *kěna r.*, or *di-rasok hantu*, to be possessed of a devil; to be afflicted by some spirit of disease. II. cross-beams from pillar to pillar.

rasul, Ar. apostle; one sent by God; *r. Allah*, God's apostle, Muhammad.

rat, I. constriction; *sa-gěnggam r.*, a tight handful; *měngěrat*, to squeeze. II. (Kawi) the earth; *jaya ning-rat*, victorious in the land; conqueror of the world.

rata, I. (1) level, evenness, flatness of surface; *sama r.*, on the same level; on a footing of equality; *ratakan* or *měratakan*, to smooth; (2) on the level of the ground; prostrate; *jatoh-lah rata ka-bumi*, he fell flat on the earth; (3) bringing everything to the same level; completing; "rounding off"; *rata-rata*, everywhere; *sa-rata*, all over; *měrata*, to spread over. II. Skr. a chariot (especially the winged chariots of the gods).

ratah, plain (of food when eaten without rice or vegetables); *měratah*, to eat food without rice.

ratap, prolonged lamentation; passionate exclamations of grief; loud mourning; *ratapkan*, to lament over.

ratib, Ar. the constant repetition of the name of *Allah* creating a sort of ecstatic trance; wild devotional cries accompanied by shaking of the body.

ratna, Skr. a jewel, a gem, a princess.

ratu, Jav. a prince, a princess; *sang-r.*, the king; *r. Kuripan*, the Prince of Kuripan, Panji.

ratus, hundred; *sa-ratus*, one hundred; *bĕratus-ratus*, in hundreds.
rau, (onom.) a sound—such as that of rushing water; *rau-rau*, a clapper-rattle or sistrum.
rauh, = *rahu*.
raum, (onom.) a deep crooning or moaning sound; *mĕraum dan mĕratap*, to moan and lament.
raung, (onom.) a cry of pain; a roar of agony; *mĕraung*, to cry out in pain.
raup, *mĕraup*, to scoop up with both hands; *bĕraup*, in double handfuls.
raut, smoothing, cutting off asperities; *pisau r.*, a small sharp knife for smoothing a stick.
rawa, I. *burong rawa*, the pied imperial pigeon (*myristicivora bicolor*). II. marshy ground. III. a large tree (unidentified.) IV. a shrimp-net also known as *sungkur*; *kain r.*, coarse sacking.
rawah, a partnership [where one man supplies labour and the other capital].
rawai, a line of unbaited hooks intended to foul-hook fish; *mĕrawai*, to fish with this contrivance.
rawak, see *dĕrawa*.
rawan, I. emotion (especially tenderness); *mĕmbĕri r.*, to stir the emotions. II. a numeral coefficient for articles made of cordage or string. III. *tulang rawan*, the sternum. IV. *mĕrawan*, in the clouds, = *bĕrawan*. V. Pers. *takhta rawan*, a vehicle mentioned in romance.
rawang, I. a hole or orifice; a gap; *kĕrawang*, fretwork. II. a morass. III. *mĕrawang*, to wash a body for burial.
rawat, I. *mĕrawati*, to visit. II. *mĕrawat*, to resume one's original form after a transformation.
rawi, Ar. a narrator, a story-teller; the author.
rawit, I. *mĕrawit*, to drag fresh people into a scandal—cf. *babit*. II. *chabai r.*, a capsicum (*capsicum fastigiatum*).
raya, great, large; *badak r.*, the large variety of rhinoceros (*rhinoceros sondaicus*); *bulan pĕrnama r.*, the full moon at its brightest; *bunga r.*, the cultivated hibiscus; *dewata mulia r.*, the most high god; *hari r.*, a holiday; *bĕrhari r.*, to make a holiday of an event; to have a good time; *hantu r.*, an evil spirit of great power and savagery; *jalan r.*, the high road; *landak r.*, the large porcupine (*hystrix longicauda*); *rimba r.*, primeval jungle; *tanah r.*, the mainland; the continent.
rayang, dizziness, light-headedness.
rayap, I. crawling, creeping (of insects). II. the white ant, = *anai-anai*.
rayat, Ar. subject; the common people; the rank and file of an army; troops.
rayau, *mĕrayau*, to wander along at random.
rayu, plantive, melancholy, stirring the emotions, rousing pity or allaying wrath; *mĕrayu*, to influence, to affect (as notes of music affect the hearer).
rĕba, fallen timber; felled masses of brushwood and undergrowth; an abattis.
rĕbab, a Malay viol; *tĕmpurong r.*, the drum of a viol.
rĕbah, falling (through weakness not violence); *r. pengsan*, falling in a faint.
rĕbak, *mĕrĕbak*, to spread (of a perfume).
rebak, a deep clean cut or wound; a rent.
rĕban, the empty space under a house when used as a fowl-house; *r. ayam*, id.
rĕbana, a Malay tambourine.
rĕbas, falling into decay (of a wooden building).

rĕbat, closing to traffic, barring, barricading.
rebeh, injured on one side only (as a bird with a broken wing).
rĕbok, *mĕrĕbok*, to fester (of a sore).
rĕbong, the edible young bamboo shoot; *puchok r.*, chevrons (as a design in art).
rĕbus, boiling in and with water (as distinct from boiling by immersion in boiling water); *ayam r.*, boiled fowl.
rĕbut, snatching, tearing away; *bĕ-rĕbut*, to snatch, to struggle for anything.
rĕchak, *rĕchak-rĕchak*, slightly pock-pitted.
rĕchek, *mĕrĕchek*, to splash up; to show drops of water or mud (as one who has been splashed); *jamjam mĕrĕchek*, a euphemism for perspiration; *pĕrĕchek*, splashed, dotted, speckled.
rĕchup, to appear just above the surface; to begin to sprout up.
rĕda, abating, lessening.
rĕdah, cutting a trace through the jungle.
rĕdam, I. faint visibility; just a sign of something. II. *rĕmok r.*, crushed to atoms; *r. padam*, completely extinguished.
redan, a tree (*nephelium maingayi*).
rĕdap, I. a small hand-drum or tabor. II. *mĕrĕdap*, to spring up plentifully (of pustules).
rĕdas, making straight for a point.
rĕdek, *mĕrĕdek*, to threaten or scold a child—cf. *hĕrdek*.
redi, a sort of hammock-litter (much used in the past by Straits-born Chinese women).
rĕdum, I. obscurity, gloom; the darkness that precedes a storm—cf. *rĕdup*. II. closing a road to traffic —cf. *rĕbat*.
rĕdup, dimmed, obscured (of the rays of the sun); overcast; gloomy weather—cf. *rĕdum*.

rĕgang, stretching to full length; racking; astretch, taut; *mĕrĕgang layar*, to boom out a sail to its full stretch.
rĕgat, = *rĕdas*.
reja, scraps left over; leavings; *r.-r. kain*, the bits of cloth left over when garments are made.
rĕjah, *pĕrĕjah*, unmannerly and self-assertive.
rĕjam, Ar. stoning; thrusting down and suffocating under mud, water, etc.
rĕjan, pain in evacuations; painful straining.
rĕjang, I. a spring forward; *sa-rĕjang kuda bĕrlari*, as far as a horse can gallop at a stretch. II. a name given to a series of symbols, one for each day of the month. [These symbols are believed to affect the "luck" of the day]. III. a tree (*alstonia scholaris* or *acronychia laurifolia*).
rejeh, blood-shot; filled with mucus (of the eye).
rĕjĕki, Ar. daily bread; means of livelihood; sustenance; also *rĕzĕki*.
rĕjok, a standing jump (as opposed to the running jump); *mĕrĕjok*, to spring or leap in this way.
reka, Skr. composition, stringing together, = *karang*; *rekaan*, a narrative, a tale.
rĕkah, splitting, cracking.
rĕkan, = *rakan*.
rĕkat, adhesion, cleaving, sticking; see also *pĕrĕkat*.
rĕla, voluptuous, sensual—a term of abuse.
rĕlah, ripping, splitting along a seam.
rĕlai, crumbling to pieces (of very rotten wood); *rĕput r.*, id.
rĕlang, a ring of rattan; a collar for a dog.
rĕlap, I. a flash; *mĕrĕlap*, to flash. II. *tali rĕlap*, a thick black rope hung with rushes and used for

driving fish towards a trap of the *bĕlat* type.

rĕlas, the scraping off of skin; abrasion.

rĕlau, a smelting-furnace.

rĕloh, (onom.) a low grunting sound.

rĕlong, I. a Malay measure of length and area; 1½ acre (as a measure of superficies). II. *mĕrĕlong*, to overarch; to cover like a dome.

rĕmaja, adolescent; just ripening into full maturity; *putĕra r.*, a prince just before he attains a marriageable age; *putĕri r.*, a princess at a similar age.

rĕmak, liefer, better, it were better that; *rĕmak mati haram ta'-lari*, better die; never, never run away!

rĕmang, I. thick cloudy weather. II. stiff, stiffly erect (of coarse hair).

rĕmba, *jalan bĕrĕmba-rĕmba*, walking in pairs.

rĕmbah, *rĕmbah-rĕmbeh*, improperly adjusted (of the *sarong*).

rĕmbang, the meridian or zenith; *matahari sĕdang-nya r.*, the sun at its zenith.

rĕmbas, utter disappearance or destruction; *habis r.*, completely gone — a strong form of *habis*.

rembat, a cross bar; the bars across a fence or gate in contradistinction to the uprights; the bar holding together the upright stakes in a fish-trap; a long pole fixed parallel to the gunwale of a boat; *rembati*, to strengthen with a cross-piece.

rĕmbega, = *lĕmbega*.

rĕmbeh, *rĕmbah-rĕmbeh*, improperly adjusted (of the *sarong*).

rembet, encumbrance, obstruction; anything which impedes or interferes with motion.

rĕmbunai, average height; fair or medium size.

rĕmis, a shell-fish (unidentified).

rĕmok, smashed or dashed to pieces; *r. rĕdam*, crushed to atoms.

rĕmpah, drug, spice, ingredient; curry-stuff; *ini-lah rĕmpah-nya*, these are the ingredients; this is the recipe or prescription.

rempah, *rĕbah rempah*, stumbling along.

rĕmpak, *sa-rĕmpak*, in unison, in harmony.

rempak, split down the side.

rĕmpang, *rĕmpang bahasa*, slightly mad; eccentric.

rempang, stretching out in long streamers.

rempat, blown aside (e.g. on a lee shore) by bad weather.

rĕmpĕnai, a tree (*ardisia coriacea* ?)

rĕmpoh, knocking over, upsetting.

rempong, pinioning (a man); tying the legs (of a fowl) together.

rempus, lifting bodily off the ground.

rĕmudu, a (Kedah) variant of *bĕrudu*.

rĕmunia, a fruit-tree (*bouea macrophylla*).

rĕmunggai, the horse-radish (*moringa ptergosperma*); also *mĕrunggai*.

rĕnang, *bĕrĕnang*, to swim.

rĕnchah, I. *mĕrĕnchah*, to plough through thick and thin; to travel through jungle and swamp without stopping to choose the easiest way.

rĕnchak, a large kind of cauldron.

rĕncham, confusing by number and minuteness or by variety; puzzling to the eye.

rĕnchana, narrative; transcription; account; *rĕnchanakan*, to relate.

renchong, a heavy Achehnese sword.

renda, Port. lace (especially gold lace and silver lace).

rĕndah, I. low; short; of limited height; humble; *mĕrĕndahkan diri*, to assume a humble tone; to abuse oneself. II. *rioh-rĕndah*, uproar, tumultuous noise—a stronger expression than *rioh*.

rĕndam, immersion in water or mud; *ular sawa r.*, the reticulate python when aquatic in its habits; *bĕrĕndam*, to wallow (of a buffalo); to plunge into water; *měrěndamkan*, to immerse, to submerge.

rěndang, baking or frying; *měrěndang*, to bake, to fry.

rendang, shady; umbrageous; leafiness; *pohon kayu r.*, a shady tree.

renek, tremulous (of the voice).

reng, *burong reng*, a vulture (of which three varieties are known in Northern Malaya).

rěnga, *běrěnga*, breeding maggots.

rěngang, throbbing pains in the head.

rěngap, (onom.) *běrěngap*, to puff out (a flame).

rěngas, a generic name given to some trees which yield a very fine timber, the sap of these trees is virulently poisonous (*melanorhæa curtisii, melanorhæa wallichii* and *gluta rengas*).

rěngat, griping pain, colic; *r. hati*, intense anger—a stronger expression than *sakit hati*.

rěngau, opening wide; *pěrěngau*, wide open.

rengek, *měrengek*, to whine or cry for something (of a child).

rěngga, a (Kedah) variant of *rěngka*.

rěnggam, (Kedah) a sickle.

rěnggang, wide separation; distance apart; *rěnggangkan*, to open out; to create a gap between.

renggek, *měrenggek*, to be protracted; to drag on.

rěnggis, thin; with few branches and leaves (of a tree).

rěnggut, wrenching or tearing away (some object that is actually attached to another); *rěnggutkan* or *měrěnggutkan*, to tear down or tear away.

rěngit, a small insect pest.

rěngka, the peculiar saddle used with elephants; the seat on which the howdah proper rests.

rěngkam, a growth (unidentified) found on coral rock.

rengkas, brevity; cutting short; conciseness; *rengkasan*, a summary, a précis; *rengkaskan*, to summarise, to cut short.

rengkat, *kaki rengkat*, one leg shorter than the other; inequality in length of legs; the halting gait caused thereby.

rengkeh, *měrengkeh*, to bow or stoop under a burden.

rěngkiang, a granary, a store, a barn.

rěngkoh, roughness in pulling or twisting; ill-regulated force.

rěngkong, = *kěrongkong*.

rengsa, obstinate (of a sore or disease); *měrengsa*, to refuse to heal.

rěngus, gruff, surly.

rěngut, *měrěngut*, to murmur; to grumble.

rěnjak, *měrěnjak*, to walk along springily.

rěnjis, *rěnjiskan* or *měrěnjiskan*, to besprinkle; to dash drops of water over.

rěnong, a fixed and steady look at anything; a searching look.

rěnta, *měrěnta*, to speak angrily or in high tones.

renta, *tua renta*, old and weak; decrepit.

rěntak, stamping the feet in anger.

rentak, hauling at a rope; tugging at a chain.

rěntaka, a small swivel-gun.

rěntan, a weak state of health predisposing to disease (but not actual disease); low vitality.

rěntang, I. stretching out or extending (used of objects like nets when in use and not of things like mats which are simply spread out and lie open on the ground)—cf. *běntang*. II. a "round" in cock-fighting.

rěntap, pulling, hauling, tugging.

rěntas, cutting a trace through jungle; clearing a path.

rěnti, = *hěnti*.

rěnut, *tali rěnut*, the belly-band in the harness of an elephant.

rĕnyah, *bĕrĕnyah* or *mĕrĕnyah*, to bestir oneself; to busy oneself.

rĕnyai, thin and continuous (of drizzling rain).

rĕnyak, *mĕrĕnyak*, to strike a tender spot; to tread on a corn.

renyeh, *mĕrenyeh*, to behave in an ill-humoured way.

rĕnyok, crushed; pounded to pieces; = *rĕmok*.

rĕnyut, = *dĕnyut*.

rĕpak, (onom.) a " slapping " noise.

rĕpang, smoothed; cut, trimmed or filed to the same level; levelled; *mĕrĕpang*, to trim.

rĕpas, fragile, crumbling; *rĕpas layu*, withered to fragility (of a flower).

rĕpeh, *mĕrĕpeh*, to pluck a little at a time; to pick away.

repek, = *repet*.

repes, slow and languid motion; *mĕrepes*, to fidget.

repet, *mĕrepet*, to chatter inconsequently.

rĕpis, *sa-rĕpis*, a chip.

rĕpoh, slightly overgrown; weedy; neglected.

rĕpui, crumbling at the least touch; extreme decay.

rĕput, rotten; crumbling—cf. *rĕpui* (which is a stronger expression).

rĕsa, internal motions—such as digestive motions, motions in childbirth, etc.

rĕsah, restlessness; fidgeting.

rĕsak, a generic name given to several timbers used in boat-building —e.g. *shorea barbata, castanopsis nephelioides*, and other woods.

rĕsam, I. a common fern used in making Malay pens (*gleichenia linearis*). II. Ar. order, arrangement, constitution, nature, bent.

rĕsan, taking as personal; taking offence.

rĕsap, *mĕrĕsap*, to vanish away; to disappear.

rĕsek, shrill, piercing; *mĕrĕsek*, id.

rĕsĕmi, Ar. nature, disposition; = *rĕsam*.

rĕsi, Skr. a " rishi "; a sage.

rĕstong, syphilitic ulceration of the nose.

rĕstu, *rĕstui*, to lay a spell upon (anyone).

reta, *mĕreta-reta*, to chatter inconsequently, = *mĕrepet*.

rĕtak, a crack; a line the result of a crack; the lines on the hand.

rĕtal, saffron; also *hartal*.

rĕtas, breaking or giving way at a slight blow.

rĕteh, *mĕrĕteh*, to form little watery vesicles (as certain festering sores).

rĕtna, = *ratna*.

rĕtok, *mĕrĕtok*, to shirk one's share of work.

rewak, having news to give; having something to say.

rewang, *mĕrewang*, to yaw (of a ship).

rĕzĕki, Ar. food, daily bread, livelihood, source of income; also *rĕjĕki*.

ria, I. joy, pleasure, noisy enjoyment. II. Ar. pride, arrogance.

riak, ripples of water.

rial, Port. a dollar.

riam, a waterfall or rapid.

rian, a measure of thread; a group of skeins.

riang, I. *riang-riang*, a cicada. II. dizzy with excitement; light-headed or feverish with pleasure. III. a motion on the surface of a stream caused by the presence of a snag or rock.

riap, *mĕriap*, to spread; to sprout up.

rias, the soft trunk of trees—such as the banana.

riba, I. taking on one's lap or breast; *mĕriba*, to support on one's lap. II. Ar. usury.

ribu, I. thousand; *sa-r.*, a thousand; *bĕribu*, in thousands. II. *ribu-ribu*, a plant (*lygodium scandens*).

richau, indistinct utterance—such as that of a child or talking-bird.

ridan, a tree (*nephelium maingayi*).
riding, I. toils for large game; thick rope netting. II. *mĕriding*, to just appear above the surface.
rihal, Ar. a Koran-stand or lectern.
rijal, Ar. *rijal-ul-ghaib*, spirits presiding over good or evil fortune.
rimah, crumbs of bread left on the table after a meal.
rimas, just breaking out into perspiration.
rimau, a tiger; see *harimau*.
rimba, primeval jungle; *r. raya*, the great forests; *ular kapak r.*, the viper*(lachesis wagleri)*.
rimbas, an agricultural instrument resembling the adze (*bĕliong*).
rimbun, lofty and spreading (as the foliage of a tree or the sails of a ship).
rimpi, dried banana.
rimping, *pĕrimping*, the last of a row.
rinah, *mĕrinah*, to shed drops of water.
rincheh, balance paid in small change.
rinchek, slicing, cutting into minute portions.
rindu, loving longing; affectionate regret; pining; *r. dĕndam*, id.; *rindukan* or *mĕrindukan*, to pine for.
ringan, light; of little weight or of little account; *mĕringankan*, to lighten; to ease.
ringgi, *pĕringgi*, baked young padi.
ringgit, milling; a dollar; *r. bĕsar*, a Spanish dollar; *r. burong, r. janek, r. lang* or *r. rama-rama*, the Mexican dollar; *r. kĕpala* or *r. tĕngkorak*, the 2½ guilder piece; *r. mĕriam*, the pillar dollar; *r. patong*, id.; *r. tongkat* or *r. orang bĕrtongkat*, the British dollar; *bĕringgit-ringgit*, crenelated, milled, serrated.
ringin, *sapu-sapu ringin*, the name of a game for children.
ringkai, emaciated; thin and withered.
ringkek, the neighing of a horse.

rinoh, *rinoh-rayu*, coaxing, cozening —a strong form of *rayu*.
rintas, taking the shortest course; cutting across from cape to cape.
rintek, a speck; speckled markings; *bĕrintek*, speckled; *hujan rintek-rintek*, drops of rain just sufficient to make a few specks on the ground.
rintis, cutting a thin line or trace from point to point—cf. *rintas*.
rioh, noise, clamour; *r. rĕndah*, uproar, tumult.
riok, *patah riok*, a compound fracture.
riong, a very tall grass (*antistiria gigantea*).
ris, a bolt-rope.
risa, a painless wen or bump.
risau, noisy and disorderly behaviour.
risek, making private enquiries; feeling one's way to a proposition so as to avoid the risk of a snub.
riwayat, Ar. a narrative; a story.
roba, *pancha-roba*, varied; uncertain; fickle.
robak, *robak-rabek*, in tatters.
robek, worn through; perforated.
roboh, falling (of heavy or massive bodies); *robohkan* or *mĕrobohkan*, to overthrow; *batu roboh*, a landslip.
robok, (onom.) *mĕrobok*, to give out a bubbling sound.
rochah, dirty and untidy-looking.
rochoh, prodding.
roda, Port. a wheel; *r. lambong*, a paddle-wheel.
rodan, injury in a tender spot; very painful.
rodi, Port. order, command, instructions; also *ordi*.
rodok, *mĕrodok*, to stab from below; = *mĕradak*.
rodong, doubtful or uncertain wandering.
rogol, Jav. rape; *mĕrogol*, to ravish.
roh, Ar. spirit, soul, life; *Roh-ul-kudus*, the Holy Ghost.
rojak, fruit or vegetables served up with vinegar and flavoured with spices.

roji, Pers. daily bread.
rojok, Ar. return to a divorced wife; making up a quarrel with an estranged friend.
rojol, *mĕrojol* to emerge from a hole; to stick out.
rokok, a (Malay) cigarette; *r. kĕrtas*, a European cigarette; *dua batang r.*, two cigarettes; *mĕngisap r.* to smoke a cigarette.
roma, Skr. *bulu roma*, the down on the human skin; *liang r.*, the pores.
roman, I. appearance, shape, figure, look, the body; *dagangan bĕrbagai r.*, goods of various types; *pĕroman*, general appearance. II. padi-straw. III. Eng. *Mĕlayu roman*, romanised Malay.
romba, a mark placed in the sea to guide fishermen in the erection of stakes.
rombak, taking down, taking to pieces, unravelling; *mĕrombakkan*, to unloose, to undo, to untie; *tĕrombak*, undone, solved, loosened.
rombong, I. piling or heaping up; *pĕnoh mĕrombong*, full till the contents appear over the top—(e.g. of clothes in a box, rice in a measure, etc.) II. a rice-bin or store.
romok, physical depression; *mĕromok*, to feel out of sorts.
rompak, piracy; *pĕrompak*, a pirate.
rompang, *rompang-ramping*, tattered and torn.
rompeng, defective; partly eaten away or destroyed.
rompis, chipped at the tip or at the edge.
rompong, destroyed or eaten away (of a prominent feature—such as a nose or ear); *rompongkan*, to cut off (a nose, an ear, or other feature); to mutilate.
rona, Skr. colour; = *warna*; *pancharona*, of many colours; gay, bright with colouring.
ronchet, *bĕronchet-ronchet*, in instalments.

ronda, Port. military rounds.
rondah, *rondah-randeh*, in disorder, dishevelled, in confusion.
rondeng, calculation by figures; accounts; bills; *rondengan*, id.
rong, *balai rong*, = *balairong*, q.v.
rongak, broken by gaps; *gigi r.*, gap-toothed; *pagar r.*, a fence from which palings are missing here and there.
rongga, hole, cavity, hollow; *bĕrongga*, hollow.
ronggang, broken by gaps; = *rongak*.
ronggeng, a dancing-girl; one of a pair of dancing girls who dance certain Javanese dances together.
rongkal, *tĕrongkal*, loose, come to pieces; unloosed (as a shoe-lace).
rongkas, taking to pieces (with a view to reconstruction and not destruction).
rongkol, a cluster of clusters; *bĕrongkol-rongkol*, in large clusters.
rongkong, see *kĕrongkong*.
rongos, *mĕrongos*, to be short-tempered; *pĕrongos*, peevish.
rongot, *mĕrongot*, to grumble, to murmur.
rongseng, *mĕrongseng*, to be querulous or peevish.
ronta, *mĕronta*, to struggle (to free oneself from the clasp of someone else or from bonds).
rontah, = *ronta*.
rontak, = *ronta*.
ronyeh, *mĕronyeh*, to talk indistinctly (as a toothless man).
ronyok, much dented; knocked in.
rosak, spoiling; violating; rendering futile; *r. mata*, injury to the eyesight; *r. iman*, corrupting religion; *r. hati*, heart-break.
rosok, see *pĕrosok*.
rot, = *rut*.
rotan, a generic name for rattans—i.e. plants belonging to the genera *calamus* and *dæmonorops*; among the best-known varieties are *r. kĕrai*

(*dæmonorops geniculatus*); *r. sĕga* (*calamus ornatus*); *r. sĕmambu*, the "Malacca cane" (*calamus scipionum*).

roti, Hind. bread; *tukang r.*, a baker; *r. kirai*, a preparation of dough resembling macaroni.

rotok, *mĕrotok*, to mutter angrily.

royak, *mĕroyak*, to spread (as an ulcer or skin disease).

royat, Ar. aspect, vision.

ru, the casuarina-tree (*casuarina equisetifolia*); *r. bukit*, a tree resembling the casuarina in general appearance (*dacrydium elatum*).

rua, *mĕrua*, to expand, to open out (as the neck of a cobra).

ruadat, Ar. ceremonial etiquette.

ruah, I. *mĕruah*, to call a person from a distance; *kĕruah*, as far as the sound of a cry can carry. II. *tumpah ruah*, poured out *en masse*. III. Ar. *bulan Ruah*, a popular name for the month *Shaaban*.

ruai, disproportionate length causing weakness; over-tall.

ruak, I. *mĕruak*, to spread (as the contents of an egg when the shell is broken). II. *burong ruak-ruak*, a bird (unidentified).

ruam, prickly-heat; pimples.

ruan = *aruan*.

ruang, hollow space; well; cavity; *r. bĕlakang*, the hollow of the back; *r. susu*, the hollow between the breasts.

ruap, *mĕruap*, to seethe up; to boil up; to foam up.

ruas, interspace; the portion between the rings of a bamboo, etc.; *sa-ruas jari*, a section of the finger from joint to joint.

ruat, I. the fall of anything that is not broken before or by the fall. II. *mĕruat*, to resume human shape (of a were-tiger or *hantu jadi-jadian*).

rubah, Pers. a jackal.

ruban, *ayer ruban*, the watery scum in the preparation of coconut oil; *mĕruban*, to purify oil.

rubin, = *ubin*.

rubing, a temporary light gunwale to increase the freeboard of a Malay boat.

rubong, see *kĕrubong*.

rudu, pendulous and heavy (of the upper eye-lid).

rudul, a (Kedah) variant of *rudu*.

rudus, a heavy cutting-weapon used in Sumatra.

rugi, Skr. loss, injury (other than physical injury); *kĕrugian*, id.

rugul, = *rogol*.

ruh, = *roh*.

ruing, a large winder used in spinning.

ruit, bent but not broken (of a branch); *chapek r.*, lameness through a bent limb.

rujah, stabbing at something below; thrusting a spear downwards at a foe under the house.

rukam, a name given to a number of trees (*flacourtia cataphracta* and other species).

rukh, Pers. the rook at chess.

ruku, a generic name for a number of plants, especially (*ruku-ruku*) the basil (*ocimum basilicum* and *ocimum album*).

rukun, Ar. fundamental doctrine; essential part of a religion.

Rum, Ar. "Rome" (a name given to the regions ruled by the Byzantine emperors).

rumah, a dwelling-house; *r. monyet*, a sentry-box; *r. tangga*, a homestead; *bĕrumah*, to have a house (and wife) of one's own; to be married.

rumal, = *ramal*.

rumbai, tassel, tuft, pendant.

rumbia, the sago-palm.

rumĕnia, a fruit-tree (*bouea macrophylla*); also *rĕmunia*.

rumpun, the stem of a grass; a numeral coefficient for grasses; *sa-rumpun sĕrai*, a sprig of lemon-grass.

rumput, grass; *mĕrumput*, to weed.

runding, = *rondeng*.

rundok, lowering the head—cf. *tundok*; *mĕrundok*, to bend one's course to a point.

rundong, "cadging" on a person; attaching oneself to another; "sponging"; *di-rundong malang*, to be continually dogged by ill-luck.

rundu, *rundu-randa*, erratic, capricious.

runggu, *runggu-rangga*, bristling with points.

rungkap, *mĕrungkap*, to speak in a surly tone.

rungkau, *mĕrungkau*, to hang down over the face (of hair).

rungkul, = *rongkol*.

rungkup, overarching; overspreading.

rungut, = *rongot*.

runjang, I. a kind of crowbar. II. *mĕrunjang*, to thrust blindly at what we cannot see.

runjau, lankiness.

runjong, *mĕrunjong*, to be piled up (of rice on a plate); *pĕrunjong*, a measure of depth—a man's length (with arms raised above his head).

runtai, dangling loosely.

runtas, breaking by a sudden pull or jerk.

runti, rubbing asperities off the common rattan of commerce (*rotan sĕga*).

runtoh, a heavy fall, a crash; *tĕbing r.*, the "sunken bank," the Malay Atlantis; *runtohkan*, to overthrow.

runtun, dragging off (by the hand or by a chain or rope).

runut, *mĕrunut*, to worry, to importune.

rupa, Skr. appearance, form, looks; *indah khabar dari rupa*, the report is fairer than the reality—not up to expectations; *rupa-nya*, it appears.

rupawan, Skr. handsome, beautiful.

rupiah, Hind. a rupee, a guilder.

rusa, the sambhur deer (*cervus unicolor*) [many varieties of this one deer are distinguished by Malays according to the shade of colour, the condition of the horns, etc.]; *r. bintang*, the (imported) deer (*cervus axis*); *r. sĕnggirek*, the unicorn; *babi r.*, the well-known "deer-hog" of the Celebes (*babirusa alfurus*).

rusing, = *rongseng*.

rusoh, a row; a tumult; a disturbance.

rusok, side, flank, rib; *r. surat*, the marginal space in a Malay letter; *tulang r.*, the rib-bone; *tumbok r.*, a "dig in the ribs," a quiet bribe.

rut, I. capability; endurance; *tiada r.*, inability to stand. II. pressure, squeezing, crushing.

S

sa, a prefix expressing or suggesting unity; one; a; forming or constituting one—i.e. making up a whole; forming one in some particular—i.e. alike in some one respect; *sa-umur-ku*, in all my life; as long as I live—life being considered as a single item though made up of many years; *sa-rasa*, forming one in taste; alike in taste; *sa-bagai*, one in type, of one type, like; *sa-bĕlah*, one side; on one side; in the direction of; towards; *sa-bĕlah-mĕnyabĕlah*, on both sides; *sa-bĕlum*, while as yet not; before; previous to; *sa-hingga*, until; *sa-kali*, at one time; all at one time; altogether; *sa-kali-kali*, altogether; *sa-kali-pun*, although; *sa-kian*, this much; so; thus; *sa-kian jauh*, thus far; *sa-kian lama*, so long; *sa-lagi*, while still; *sa-lalu*, always; *sa-mana-mana*, in any way; *sa-mata-mata*, clearly, obviously; *sa-orang*, one man; alone; *sa-orang-orang*, quite alone; *sa-saorang*, each person; *sa-suatu*, each; *sa-tĕlah*, when (a thing) was over; after; *sa-tĕlah ia pĕrgi*, when he had gone; *sa-tuju*, in harmony; harmonious.

saadat, Ar. fortune, happiness; highness, majesty (as a title); *Baginda s.*, H.M. the King.

saat, Ar. time, moment; *dĕngan sa-saat ini juga*, at this very moment.

sabak, I. boiling palm-sap (in the making of certain sugars). II. *mĕratap bĕrbiji sabak*, to weep copiously.

saban, Jav. every; *s. hari*, daily.

sabang, to muzzle (a dog).

sabar, Ar. patience, forbearance; *sabar-lah dahulu*, be patient awhile.

sabas, Pers. bravo, excellent, capital!

sabda, Skr. saying, utterance (used especially of words of the prophets). [The word also occurs in literature as the equivalent of *titah* (the word of a prince); and in some districts *sabda* is used of a chief—(e.g. the Pĕnghulu of Rĕmbau), while *titah* is used of the suzerain (the *yam tuan*).]

sabĕlah, see *sa*.

sabĕrang, = *sĕbĕrang*.

sabil, Ar. way, road; *pĕrang s. Allah*, a war in God's cause; a holy war.

sabit, I. a native sickle; *mĕnyabit*, to reap with a sickle. II. Ar. revealed as certain; truth revealed.

sabok, a sort of kerchief or plaid worn over the shoulder.

sabong, darting at each other (of cocks); cock-fighting; the apparently conflicting flashes of forked lightning; *ayam sabongan*, a fighting-cock; *mĕnyabong*, to fight (of a cock); *sabong mĕnyabong*, the zigzag flashes of forked lightning.

Sabtu, Ar. *hari Sabtu*, Saturday.

sabun, Ar. soap.

sabur, I. a confused *mêlée*; wild scurrying; *didalam sabur itu*, in the crush; *sĕmut s.*, a stinging ant (*sima rufonigra*). II. *layar sabur*, a top-gallant-sail.

sabut, the fibrous part or wrapper forming the outer portion of a fruit like the coconut; coconut fibre; *tali s.*, a rope of common fibre.

sadai, prone; extended at full length.

sadak, sloping (of masts).

sadap, a kind of pruning-knife; to use this knife.

sadau, rowing with long sweeps.

sadia, = *sĕdia*.

sadik, Ar. upright, true (of friendship).

sadikit, see *dikit*.

sadong, to get one's foot caught in a creeper—cf. *sĕradong*.

sadu, Skr. excelling; *s. pĕrdana*, first, foremost.

sadur, plating; overlaying with shining metal.

saeng, travelling in company; *bĕrsaeng* or *bĕrsaengan*, id.

saf, Ar. row, rank, file of soldiers; *bĕrsaf-saf*, in rows.

Safar, Ar. the name of a month in the Muhammadan calendar.

saga, the Indian pea, the seed of *adenanthera pavonina*; *biji s.*, id.; (by metaphor) red, bloodshot (of the eyes). [The pea was also used as a small measure of weight.]

sagai, = *sakai*.

sagang, propping up or buttressing (used when the prop is at an angle with the ground.)

sagar, Pers. sugar; also *sakar*.

sagi, = *sĕgi*.

sagu, sago; *s. Bĕlanda*, arrowroot.

sagun, a Malay dish made of rice-flour, rasped coconut and salt; also *sagun-sagun*.

sagur, a river dug-out; *pĕrahu s.*, id.

sah, I. Pers. check!—in playing chess. II. approved; in order;

admissible; made out (of a case); *tiada s.*, the charge has not been substantiated properly.

sahabat, Ar. friend, comrade; *s. beta* or *s. kita*, "my friend;" the person written to (in a formal official letter).

sahaja, I. only; *bahasa itu sahaja*, that language only. II. = *sěngaja*.

sahaya, Skr. slave; humble servant; I; *s. sěmua*, we all; *hamba s.*, slaves and chattels.

saheh, Ar. true, clear, correct.

sahib, Ar. master; owner of; *sahib-ul-hikayat*, the author of the story; the author's "we."

sahut, replying; answering back; response; *sahut-sahutan*, in continual response (as salutes after salutes); *sahuti*, to make reply; to answer.

said, Ar. a title given to descendants of the Prophet.

Saidi, Lord (God); *ya S.*, Lord!

saif, Ar. sword.

sais, Hind. a syce; a groom.

saja, = *sahaja*.

sajadah, Ar. a prayer-mat.

sajahtěra, = *sějahtěra*.

sajak, Ar. assonance, harmony, cadence; rhyme; *sajak-nya janggal*, harsh sounding; faulty rhythm.

saji, serving up (a dish); dressing food; *tudong s.*, a dish-cover; *běr-saji*, to dress food; to serve up food.

saka, I. the pillars of a house. II. = *pěsaka*.

sakai, dependents, retainers, subjects; *orang S.*, a name given to "subject" aboriginal tribes by Malays.

sakal, knocking against; knocking back; *angin s.*, a contrary wind.

sakalian, see *kali*.

sakar, Pers. sugar; also *sagar*.

sakat, I. vexation, trouble, annoyance. II. a generic name given to many epiphytes, especially aroids and ferns. III. *suku sakat*, a genealogical table showing all the ramifications of a family.

sakhlat, Pers. broad-cloth.

sakit, sickness, disease, pain; *měn-dapat s.*, to fall ill; *s. hati*, resentment, anger; *s. hidup*, illness without apparent cause (attributed by Malays to evil spirits); *s. orang baik*, a euphemism for small-pox; *s. payah*, serious illness; *měnyakiti*, to injure; to afflict with pain or sickness; *pěnyakit*, a disease.

saksama, Skr. diligent enquiry, investigation.

saksi, Skr. witness, evidence, testimony; *měmanggil s.*, to call witnesses (in a case).

sakti, Skr. supernatural power; *dewa yang s.*, a wonder-working divinity; *kěsaktian*, supernatural power; a talisman.

saku, Eur. a small canvas bag; a satchel; a pocket.

sal, Hind. a shawl.

salah, fault, error, flaw, discrepancy; being out of place or going wrong; *s. kěna*, tactless words; *s. sa-orang*, one or the other (person); *s. suatu*, one or the other (thing); *s. urat*, dislocation or straining of a sinew; *orang s.*, a defendant; *sěrba s.*, puzzled, confused, at a loss; *salahi* or *měnyalahi*, to vitiate, to render useless; *kěsalahan*, an error, a fault, a mistake.

salai, heating over the fire; smoking; fumigation or curative heating; *měn-yalai*, to heat in this way.

salak, I. a stemless thorny palm (*zalacca edulis*). II. the barking of a dog; *měnyalak*, to bark.

salam, Ar. a greeting; "Peace be unto you"; *měmběri s.*, to greet.

salamat, = *sělamat*.

salang, execution by the *kěris*.

salatin, Ar. sultans—the plural of *sultan*.

saleh, motion, approach; *s. kěmbali*, to return.

sali, strength, power, might; *sama s.*, of equal might.

salib, Ar. a cross; crucifixion.
salin, change of garb or of food or outward form; *salinan*, a translation; *salini*, to bestow garments upon anyone; *bĕrsalin*, to be confined (of a woman); to put on other clothes; to assume a different form by metamorphosis; *pĕrsalin* or *pĕrsalinan*, a change of clothing.
salla, Ar. *salla Allahu alaihi wa's-salam*, God give him peace!
salur, *saluran*, a channel, a gully.
salut, enwrapping, enfolding—cf. *balut*.
sama, Skr. identity, sameness, companionship, parity; *s. sĕndiri-nya*, one another; *s. bĕsar*, of equal size; *s. tĕngah*, in the very centre; *samakan*, to rank as equal; *bĕrsama*, along with; *bĕrsamaan*, similar, identical. [In bazaar Malay *sama* is used to mean "to," "with," or to form an accusative; *bilang sama sahaya*, tell me; *pukul sama dia*, hit him.]
samak, tanning; bark for tanning; a generic name for trees the bark of which is used for tanning.
saman, I. Ar. *ratib saman*, the name given to a peculiar *ratib* or mystical incoherent religious performance. II. Eng. summons.
samar, concealment; hiding one's identity; personating someone else; *s. muka*, change of aspect; *samarkan*, to pretend, to affect.
sambal, a generic name for highly spiced and other condiments used in small quantities to flavour curries.
sambang, I. an abandoned nest of the honey-bee. II. a patrol, a round; *bĕrsambang*, to patrol.
sambar, carrying off in the talons (used especially of a bird of prey swooping and carrying off its victims); *yu sambaran*, a man-eating shark.
sambat, to splice together.
sambau, a grass (unidentified) [it sometimes grows on thoroughfares, and is taken in such cases as a type of a difficult existence].
sambil, with, together with, simultaneously with.
sambilan, = *sĕmbilan*.
sambok, Pers. a dinghy.
sambong, adding in prolongation; joining on; *ada sambongan-nya lagi*, "more to follow"; "to be continued in our next."
sambur, *sambur-limbur*, intermittent visibility; appearing and disappearing.
sambut, to receive (used of a person standing to receive a person coming to him, and not of a person going to meet his guest); *gigi s.*, overlapping teeth; *sambuti* or *mĕnyambut*, to stand and receive.
sami, I. [Pali?] a Buddhist priest. II. Tam. a Hindu idol.
samir, the natural undried leaves of the *nipah* (used as a rough protection against rain).
samista, = *sĕmĕsta*.
sampah, rubbish, dry dirt, filth; *sampah itu ka-tĕpi juga*, rubbish always finds its way to the side; the poor are always shoved aside.
sampai, I. attaining to; reaching; as far as; *sampaikan*, to cause to attain to, or to cause to extend to—e.g. *sampaikan khabar*, to convey news. II. hanging loosely over anything (as a garment hanging on a clothes-line); *sampaian kain*, a sort of towel-horse or clothes-line.
sampak, I. the metal ring or band at the base of the shaft of a weapon [it serves to keep the haft (*puting*) from splitting the shaft]. II. *main sampak*, heads or tails. III. *sĕluar sampak*, trousers worn by Malays in padi-fields and swamps.
sampan, Ch. a generic name for a large number of types of boats (especially the Chinese shoe-boat); *s. chedok ikan*, a boat in use with large fish-traps; *s. golek*, (Penang)

the common Chinese sampan; *s. kotak*, the Chinese sampan with stern lockers (much used in Singapore); *s. kudong*, a heavy beamy Chinese sampan; *s. mĕngail*, the canoe-like boat in which fishermen visit their traps; *s. panjang*, a long narrow canoe-like passenger-boat used in Singapore harbour; *s. tunda*, a dinghy.

sampang, I. paddling. II. a Malay varnish.

sampean, Jav. a title used in addressing a prince.

sampil, the bast or husk at the lower end of a palm-branch.

samping, an obsolete drum.

sampir, I. the upper portion of a *kĕris*-sheath—the part that covers the *ganja*; *sampiran kĕris*, id. II. *pĕtiban sampir*, a tribute of respect to a prince. III. *sampiran kain*, = *sampaian kain*.

sampok, intrusion; interference (in other people's affairs).

sampu, decline, wasting away, emaciation; *dĕmam s.*, a wasting feverish disease.

sampul, a covering or wrapper—such as a pillow-case; a caul (but *tĕmbuni* is more technical in this sense).

Samsam, a name given to a mixed half-Siamese race inhabiting the northern parts of the Peninsula.

samsir, Pers. a scimetar

samsu, I. Ch. Chinese alcoholic spirit. II. = *shamsu*.

samun, I. robbing; theft accompanied by violence; *mĕnyamun*, to rob; *pĕnyamun*, a robber. II. *sĕmaksamun*, very tangled undergrowth or scrub.

sana, yonder; the further, in contradistinction to the nearer; there; *di-sana*, in that place; *di-sĕbĕrang s.*, on the opposite side.

sanak, kindred; blood relations; one's whole family; *s. saudara*, id.

Sanat, Ar. year of the Hegira.

sandang, wearing a band over the shoulder and across the body (as the cordon of a knightly order is worn); *mĕnyandang, mĕnyandangkan*, or *mĕmpĕrsandangkan*, to carry (a sword or *kĕris* suspended from a cross-belt or a gun slung over the back by a strap); *sayap sandang*, a sort of cross-belt.

sandar, resting the back against any surface; leaning back; *tĕrsandar*, leaning back upon, resting against.

sandarmalam, a name given to the tuberose; also *sundal malam*.

sanding, I. position adjacent; sitting next; *bĕrsanding*, to be set next to one another (as a bride and bridegroom). II. a corner; a projection; *ta'-bĕrsanding*, smooth, globular.

sandong, stumbling against—cf. *sĕrandong* and *sadong*.

sang, an honorific prefix applied, (1) to the names of heroes and minor divinities—such as Darmadewa, Kĕlĕmbai, Nila Utama (the founder of Singapore), Arjuna, and others; (2) to the titles of kings— e.g. *sang-nata*, *sang-aji*, *sang-ratu*, etc.; (3) in the expression *sang-yang* only, to the names of major divinities—e.g. *sang-yang Guru*, *sang-yang Maha-bisnu*, *sang-yang Tunggal*; (4) to the names of animals in fables—e.g. *sang-tupai*, *sang-kanchil*, *sang-nyamok*.

sanga, the scum or dross in smelting.

sangai, a rough dish-cover of *nipah* or *mĕngkuang* leaf.

sangaji, see *sang* and *aji*.

sangat, extremely; very; excess; *amat s.*, id.; *kĕsangatan*, excess; *tĕrsangat*, surpassingly.

sangga, holding up; propping up; sustaining; shielding from a downward blow; *s. buana*, "prop of the universe"; a Javanese title; *s. layar*, small props for holding up the boom; *s. mara*, a projecting knob or guard on a blade.

sanggan, a metal bowl with a rough milled edge.
sanggang, = *sagang*.
sanggat, running aground (of a boat).
sanggit, rubbing two hard bodies against one another.
sanggul, the binding up and dressing of the hair; *chuchok s.*, hair-pins.
sanggup, accepting responsibility for; acknowledging; *s. měmbayar wang*, accepting responsibility for a payment; *pa' s.*, a putative father.
sangka, I. Skr. thinking, suspecting, fearing; anxious thought, suspicion; *sangkakan*, to suspect or think anything. II. Skr. a triton shell (*chama gigas*); a conch-shell used as a trumpet; *sangka-kala*, the last trump.
sangkak, hindrance, resistance; *raja di-s.*, a ruler who should be risen against; *sangkaki*, to obstruct, hinder, or resist.
sangkakala, Skr. the last trump—v. *sangka*, II.
sangkal, disavowing, repudiating; *sangkali*, to deny (one's faith); to repudiate knowledge of.
sangkar, I. a coop; a cage (especially a bird-cage); *sangkaran*, id. II. *sungkur-sangkar*, sprawling.
sangkil, immersion to the load-line (of a ship); fulfilling a purpose satisfactorily; to achieve the end in view.
sangku, a large metal bowl or basin.
sangkur, a bayonet.
sangkut, stopping; not getting past; adhering to or remaining in; *s. di-dalam hati*, a thing that sticks in the memory.
sangsara, = *sěngsara*.
sangu, Jav. stores, provisions, supplies.
sangulun, Jav. a royal title.
sangyang, see *sang*.
santak, *měnyantak*, to strike with the fist or knuckles.
santan, the milk of the coconut; *kěpala s.*, the best of the milk; the thick creamy portion near the flesh of the fruit; (by metaphor) virginity.
santap, to eat, to consume, to dine—in court language; *s. sireh*, to chew *sireh* (of a prince chewing *sireh*); *santapan* or *pěrsantapan*, a royal repast.
santěri, = *sěntěri*.
santok, to knock against—cf. *antok*.
santun, slow, sedate, dignified, imposing.
sanya, of a truth; = *sa-sunggoh-nya*; *bahwa sanya*, verily, verily.
sap, I. a name given to a piece of cloth or fibrous material placed in an inkstand. II. = *saf*.
sapa, mode of address, courtesy; *těgur s.*, id.; *měnyapa*, to accost politely.
sapar, = *safar*.
sapau, a lean-to; a shelter for the night in the jungle.
sapěrti, = *sěpěrti*.
sapi, an ox; a bull or cow; *minyak s.*, suet; *s. hutan*, a name given to the anoa of Celebes (*anoa depressicornis*) [which is well-known to maritime Malays]; also, in the interior of the Malay Peninsula, to a local wild ox, either a small *bos gaurus* or a separate species (*bos sondaicus*).
sapir, I. Ar. a traveller; *běrsapir*, to encamp (of travellers). II. Eng. a sapper; a soldier of engineers; a gaol-official at Malacca.
sapu, wiping; sweeping off; smearing off or on; *s. chat*, painting; *s. minyak*, varnishing; *s. kapur*, whitewashing; *s. tangan*, a handkerchief; *sapukan*, to sweep; to pass a cloth or broom over; *pěnyapu*, a broom.
saput, a thin fleecy or cloth-like covering; a film; clouding over; *di-saput awan*, clouded over (as a mountain).
sara, I. *běrsara*, to join in an undertaking; to "chip in." II. *sara-bara*,

in confusion; helter-skelter; topsy-turvy.

sarak, severance, separation.

sarang, a nest; *s. lĕbah*, a bees' nest; *s. unam*, the shell of a hermit crab; *s. tĕbuan*, a hornets' nest; *s. burong*, the nest of a bird; *bĕrsarang*, to nest; *bĕrsarang-sarang*, full of cobwebs, mason-bees' nests, etc. (as a deserted house).

sarap, dust, fine dirt; *pĕnyapu s.*, a sweeper; *s. sampah*, sweepings, refuse generally.

sarat, heavily laden; of full burden; *bunting s.*, the last stage of pregnancy; *s. dĕngan muatan*, full of cargo (of a ship).

sarau, I. the groove between two parallel bones—for instance, along the *tibia*. II. a creel used by collectors of *agar-agar*.

sardi, Hind. glanders.

sari, Jav. a flower; the beauty, or delicacy, or charm of anything; a very common expression in the names of fair ladies—e.g. *Bidasari, Puspa-sari, Tunjong-sari*, etc.

sarip, = *sharif*.

saripah, Ar. a title given to female descendants of the Prophet; a sort of feminine of *said*.

sarok, putting one's foot into a noose, or trap, or hole; being tripped up—cf. *sadong*.

sarong, sheath, covering; *s. jari*, a thimble; *s. kaki*, socks; *s. kĕris*, a *kĕris*-sheath; *s. tangan*, gloves; *mĕnyarong* or *mĕnyarongkan*, to sheathe; *tĕrsarong*, sheathed.

sarun, Jav. a musical instrument.

sarut, scraping up against anything.

sarwa, Skr. all; usually pronounced *sĕru*, q.v.

sarwal, Ar. trousers.

sas, the crupper (in harness.)

sasa, Skr. strong, sturdy.

sasak, wattles; *pagar s.*, a wattled fence.

sasap, *susup-sasap*, up and down;

over and under; *lari susup-sasap*, rushing frantically over all obstacles.

sasar, I. dazed, confused; *anak kĕsasar*, a muddle-headed fool. II. *sasaran*, a target.

sasau, = *sasar* I.

sastĕra, Skr. the sacred books; astrological tables, divination.

sastĕrawan, Skr. one versed in the sacred books; an astrologer.

sat, I. measure of capacity; = 5 gantangs. II. = *saat*.

satai, Jav. kebabs; pieces of flesh or fish cooked on a skewer.

satar, Ar. a writing; a stroke; a line.

satu, one; = *suatu*.

satwa, = *sĕtua*.

sau, (onom.) a rustling sound; soughing.

saudagar, Pers. a merchant; a trader; a wholesale dealer.

saudara, Skr. brother, sister; cousin; an intimate friend whom one calls a brother or sister; *saudara sa-pupu*, a cousin; *s. sa-jalan sa-jadi*; a full brother or sister; *mĕngambil akan s.*, to break off a love-affair amicably by agreeing to be "brother and sister."

sauh, I. an anchor; *champak s.*, to cast anchor; *bongkar s.*, to haul up the anchor; *s. chĕmat*, an anchor fastened ashore for mooring a boat to; *s. larat*, anchor that is dragging; *s. tĕrbang*, a light grapnel used for scaling a wall; *batang s.*, the shaft of an anchor; *batu s.*, the stone or weight in it; *kuku s.*, the blade. II. a fruit-tree (*mimusops kauki*).

saujana, Skr. an expression suggesting "extent" or "distance"; *s. mata mĕmandang*, as far as the eye can see; *padang s.*, a wide plain.

sauk, I. catching with a noose. II. the lid of a pot. III. scooping up with the hands. IV. (onom.) sighing; *dĕngan s. tangis*, with sighs and tears.

sawa, a generic name for snakes considered by Malays to belong to the python class; *ular s. batu*, the reticulate python when living on rocky soil; *ular s. burong*, the long snake (*dipsadomorphus cynodon*); *ular s. chindai*, the reticulate python when its coloration is very brilliant; *ular s. lĕkir* (*coluber melanurus*); *ular s. rĕndam*, the reticulate python when dull in colouring and aquatic in habits; *ular s. tĕkukur*, a name for *coluber melanurus*.

sawab, Ar. the exact truth; *w'Allahu aalam bi's-sawab*, God knoweth what the real truth is!

sawah, a swamp padi-field; *s. bĕndang*, a stretch of padi-fields; *mĕmbuat s.*, to plant rice (on swampy ground).

sawan, convulsions, epilepsy, violent fits accompanied by foaming at the mouth; *s. babi*, epilepsy; *s. bangkai*, apoplexy.

sawang, a plant (unidentified) used as a remedy for skin-disease.

sawar, a fence, a row of stakes to stop the escape of small animals.

sawat, I. a sort of plaid; *s. sandang*, a sort of cross-belt. II. *pĕsawat*, a tool; an implement or appliance.

sawi, I. *sawi-sawi*, mustard (*brassica nigra*). II. = *sĕnawi*.

saya, = *sahaya*.

sayang, I. regret, pity, sorrow for; affectionate pining; love; *mĕnaroh s.*, to be in love; *sayangkan*, to regret, to love. II. *tombak sayang*, a sort of gaff used with a sail.

sayap, wing, pinion; *s. kumbang*, a humble-bee's (shiny black) wing; *baju bĕrsayap*, a coat with pendulous sleeves.

sayat, slicing off the skin, top, or cover of anything, or any projecting portion—such as a nose or ear.

sayong, cutting into parts of unequal length.

sayu, sadness, melancholy.

sayup, faintly visible or audible; just noticeable; *s. mata mĕmandang*, so far as to be only indistinctly seen; *s. piama*, (Kedah) the close of the rainy season.

sayur, vegetables in general; green food; *sayurkan*, to cook as a vegetable; to serve up as a vegetable; *sayur-mayur* or *sayur-sayuran*, all kinds of vegetables.

sĕbab, Ar. cause, reason; (better *dari sĕbab*) because; *s. itu-lah*, therefore; for that reason; *apa s.*, why.

sĕbahat, Ar. league, pact, conspiracy.

sĕbai, a kind of scarf passing behind the neck and with the ends hanging down over the chest.

sĕbak, *ayer sĕbak*, an inundation; water lying on ground usually dry.

sĕbal, mournful, sad, sorrowful; *s. hati*, id.

sĕbam, losing brightness of colour; growing duller.

sĕbar, a rush of warm blood through the body.

sĕbarau, a fish (*lalleo boggu*).

sĕbasah, a generic name given to a number of trees or shrubs of the order *euphorbiaceæ*—e.g. *glochidium desmocarpum*.

sĕbat, I. a blow with a switch. II. a shiver caused by the taste of something extremely acid. III. choked (of the nostril).

sĕbeh, a plant (*canna indica*).

sĕbek, to purse up the lips.

sĕbĕkah, *ikan sĕbĕkah*, a fish (unidentified).

sĕbĕrang, the opposite side; *di-sĕbĕrang sana sungai Singapura*, on the opposite bank of the Singapore river; *S. Pĕrai*, Province Wellesley (from Penang); *sĕbĕrangkan*, to ferry over; *mĕnyĕbĕrang*, to cross over.

sĕbĕrhana, Skr. full (of full dress); *mĕmakai sĕbĕrhana pĕrhiasan*, to wear all one's jewellery or decorations.

sĕbit, a dish of buffalo meat and vermicelli.

sĕbong, a single division (from node to node) of the bamboo.

sĕbu, filled up, choked up (of a well or cutting).

sĕbun, protracted (of labour); refusing to come to a head (of a boil).

sĕburut, a plant (*thottea grandiflora*).

sĕbut, saying, stating; utterance; *sĕbutan*, the thing said; the drift or tenor of remarks; *sĕbutkan*, to utter; to repeat; *tĕrsĕbut*, said; *sĕpĕrti yang tĕrsĕbut di-bawah ini*, as follows.

sĕdak, a choking hiccough.

sedak, the rattan fastening round a tambourine (*rĕbana*).

sĕdal, drying clothes on a line inside a house.

sĕdan, a catch in the breath; *tĕrsĕdan-sĕdan*, sobbing; hiccoughing.

sĕdang, medium; intermediate; during; while; *s. masak*, just ripening; *bunga s.*, a flower at its best; *sĕdangkan*, although; even though.

sĕdap, pleasant, agreeable; *s. hati*, satisfaction; *s. mulut*, pleasant words.

sĕdar, alive to; awake to; conscious; *tiada s.*, to be unconscious (of a fact); *s. daripada bius*, to recover consciousness after being drugged; *sĕdarkan*, to be conscious of; *tiada sĕdarkan diri*, to be unconscious; *tĕrsĕdar*, to be roused to consciousness.

sĕdawi, *akar sĕdawi*, a plant (*smilax calophylla*).

sĕdeh, the desire to weep; having tears in one's eyes; mournful regret; *mĕnahani s.*, to control one's feelings.

sĕdĕkah, Ar. alms, charity.

sĕdĕkala, Skr. always; at all times; immemorial; *adat s.*, immemorial usage; also *sĕdia-kala*.

sĕdĕlinggam, Tam. minium; red-lead.

sĕdĕrhana, Skr. the even mean; the proper average; *tuboh-nya s.*, he was of average height and build.

sĕdia, I. Skr. ready; in readiness; prepared; *sĕdiakan*, to get (things) ready; to prepare. II. Skr. former, ancient, original; *rupa-nya yang s.*, his original form; *s. kala*, days of old; also *sĕdĕkala*.

sĕdikit, see *dikit*.

sĕdingin, a common succulent herb (*bryophyllum calycinum*).

sĕdoh, *mĕnyĕdoh*, to soak; to infuse in water.

sĕdu, short broken sobs; hiccoughing or sobbing; *tĕrsĕdu-sĕdu*, id.; *sĕdu katak*, short quick breathing after violent exertion.

sĕduayah, a medicinal plant (unidentified).

sĕdut, vexation of feeling, suppressed anger; *hati tĕrsĕdut*, id.

sĕga, smooth; shining on the surface; *rotan s.*, the common rattan of commerce.

sĕgah, fullness after meals; a sense of distension.

segak, gorgeously got up; dressy.

sĕgala, all, every; the whole of; *s. tuboh*, the whole body.

sĕgan, slow to move; slow, sluggish, idle; *pĕnyĕgan*, a sluggard; *burong sĕgan*, the night-jar (*caprimulgus macrurus*).

sĕganda, Skr. a name, or introductory name, of several fragrant plants — e.g. *sĕganda-puri*, *sĕganda-mala*.

sĕgar, feeling fit; healthy and strong; well; *bĕrasa s.*, to feel fit.

sĕgara, I. Skr. the ocean. II. Pers. sugar; = *sagar*. III. Jav. a flower; = *sĕkara*.

segel, a Malay basket of rattan or wood for keeping captured animals in.

sĕgĕra, Skr. speedily, promptly; *mĕnyĕgĕrakan*, to expedite, to hurry up.

sĕgi, side, corner, angle; *ĕmpat sĕgi* or *ĕmpat pĕrsĕgi*, four-sided, square.

segok, bad (of work that offends the eye).

sĕhaja, = *sahaja*.

sehat, Ar. health; *s. dan afiat*, id.

sĕhaya, = *sahaya*.
seher, Ar. *ilmu s.*, the black art.
sĕjahtĕra, Skr. peace, tranquillity, ease; *sĕlamat s.*, id.
sĕjak, since; = *sĕmĕnjak*.
sĕjarah, Ar. family annals; pedigree history.
sĕjat, getting rid of water (by filtration or evaporation); rinsing or steaming out.
sĕjok, cold, cool; *s. hati*, calmness; *jawa s.*, a name given to the anthropomorphic pattern of the ordinary *kĕris*-handle.
sĕkah, broken but not broken off; fractured but not severed.
sekah, I. activity, nimbleness. II. Ar. the mint-impression; the "guinea-stamp" on a coin.
sĕkam, rice-husk, chaff.
sĕkanda, = *sĕganda*.
sĕkar, Jav. a flower.
sĕkara, Jav. a flower; a poetic variant of *sĕkar*.
sĕkarang, now; at present; *s. ini*, now at this very time; just now.
sĕkat, I. opposing, intercepting, obstructing, blocking, barring; *sĕkatan*, a bar; an obstruction; *mĕnyĕkati*, to hinder; to obstruct. II. a clod (of earth).
sĕkati, an obsolete musical instrument.
sĕkĕdudok, = *sĕndudok*.
sĕkĕdup, Ar. the litter-like saddle on a camel's back.
sĕkĕlian, = *sakalian*, from *kali*.
sĕkĕrba, I. Skr. full brother. II. Skr. the name of a nymph of heaven.
sĕkĕrup, (Dutch) screw.
sĕkhalat, = *sakhlat*.
sĕkian, see *kian*.
sĕkin, Ar. a knife, a dagger.
sĕkochi, (Dutch) a ship's cutter; a gig.
sĕkoï, Italian millet (*panicum italicum*).
sĕkopong, (Dutch) the suit "spades" in playing cards.

seksa, Skr. punishment, tribulation, suffering; *seksakan* or *mĕnyeksakan*, to torment; to torture; to pain.
sĕksama, = *saksama*.
sĕkul, Pers. a vessel made of coconut shell.
sĕkup, (Dutch) a spade; a shovel.
sĕkut, a narcotic drug used by thieves to stupefy people they intend to rob.
sĕkutu, see *kutu*.
sĕla, interval between; interstice; *tiada bĕrsĕla*, continuous, unbroken; *s. batu*, a shell (*pholas*)—cf. *chĕlah, sĕlang*, etc.
sela, Port. a saddle.
sĕlada, Port. salad.
sĕladang, the large wild ox of the Peninsula (*bos gaurus*).
sĕladĕri, = *sĕldĕri*.
sĕlah, = *sĕla*.
sĕlak, the bolt fastening a door; any sort of cross-bar.
selak, lifting up or drawing aside a curtain or garment; *kain tĕrselak*, with the *sarong* drawn up high (exposing too much of the person); *selakkan kain*, to pull aside a garment.
sĕlaka, I. a bamboo frame on which garments are placed to be perfumed by burning fragrant wood inside the frame. II. Jav. silver.
sĕlalu, see *sa* or *lalu*.
sĕlam, diving; *juru s.*, a diver; *sĕlamkan*, to give (a person) a ducking; *mĕnyĕlam*, to dive.
sĕlamat, Ar. peace, security, safety; *s. sampai* or *s. jalan*, bon voyage; *s. tinggal*, good-bye (from a traveller to those who stay behind); *raja pun sĕlamat-lah sampai ka-Mĕlaka*, the governor reached Malacca safely.
sĕlampai, wearing a thing loosely suspended over the shoulder; *mĕnyĕlampai*, to wear in this way.
sĕlampit, (Kedah) a travelling storyteller or rhapsodist.
Sĕlampuri, *kain Sĕlampuri*, Serampore-made cloth.

Selan, Ceylon; *batu S.*, the sapphire.
sĕlang, I. alternation; at intervals; *s. dua pintu,* every third door; *s. tiga ĕmpat bulan,* every three or four months; *s. sĕli,* pointing alternately in one direction and in the other; *sĕlangi,* to alternate; *bĕrsĕlang,* alternating. II. *sĕlangkan,* a variant of *sĕdangkan*—v. *sĕdang.*
selang, = *silang.*
sĕlangat, a fish (*clupalosa bulan*?)
sĕlangin, = *sĕnangin.*
sĕlangka, *tulang sĕlangka,* the collarbone; *kĕna s.,* to be executed (with the *kĕris*).
sĕlap, loss of sensation; unconsciousness.
sĕlaput, a film, a gauzy covering; *s. mata,* the film in cataract.
sĕlar, I. branding; *s. dĕngan bĕsi,* id. II. creeping along the ground like a snake; *ular tĕdong s.,* the hamadryad (*naia bungarus*); *mĕnyĕlar,* to creep. III. *ikan sĕlar,* a generic name given to a number of fish—e.g. *caranx cambon* and *caranx gymnostochrides.*
sĕlara, I. fine thorns like thistledown found on the skin of some plants. II. *anak sĕlara,* a fish (unidentified).
sĕlarong, a wild-beast track.
Sĕlasa, Ar. *hari Sĕlasa,* Tuesday.
sĕlasar, a side-gallery or verandah in a house.
sĕlaseh, Skr. the basil (*ocymum basilicum*); *s. dandi,* a little shrub (*stachytarpheta indica*); *mabok bunga s.,* an expression signifying that a person is very drunk indeed.
sĕlasĕma, = *sĕlĕsĕma.*
sĕlat, a strait; *s. Singapura,* the straits of Singapore; *s. tĕbĕrau,* the Johor straits.
sĕlatan, the south; *jauh ka-sĕlatan,* far away to the south.
sĕlayun, a scarecrow which frightens birds by the noise it makes—cf. *sĕlayut*
sĕlayur, *ikan sĕlayur,* a fish (*trichiurus savala*?)

sĕlayut, a scarecrow which frightens away birds by its appearance—cf. *sĕlayun.*
sĕldĕri, (Dutch) celery.
sĕlĕbu, *laut sĕlĕbu,* the open sea.
sĕleder, Jav. negligent, careless, slovenly.
sĕlĕguri, a shrub (*clerodendron disparifolium*); *s. padang,* a small shrub (*sida rhombifolia*).
sĕlekeh, a stain, a splash of dirt; *bĕrsĕlekeh,* bespattered.
sĕlekoh, a bend or twist in direction; a turn in a road.
sĕlekur, I. a fish (unidentified). II. = *sa-lekur;* see *lekur.*
sĕlĕmbana, *mĕnyĕlĕmbana,* to lay to (of a ship).
sĕlĕmbayong, an arm or yard from which decorative streamers are suspended.
sĕlĕmbubu, *angin sĕlĕmbubu,* an eddying wind.
sĕlempang, cross-wise; *sĕlempangkan,* to wear a garment cross-wise over the chest—cf. *sĕlepang.*
sĕlendang, a sort of shawl worn by woman over the head and shoulders.
sĕlĕpa, a small receptacle for *sireh;* a *sireh*-box.
sĕlepang, thrown carelessly on and over the shoulder (as a coolie carries a gunny-bag)—cf. *sĕlempang.*
sĕlĕpat, besmeared, bedaubed.
sĕlĕpong, *bĕrsĕlĕpong,* dirtied.
sĕlera, I. Skr. body; a very poetical equivalent of *badan.* II. appetite, enjoyment of eating; *s. tiada,* to have lost one's appetite.
sĕlesa, uncramped; spacious; with ample accommodation.
sĕlĕsai, settlement, termination; *satĕlah sĕlĕsai daripada bĕlajar,* when his education was finished; *sĕlĕsaikan,* to wind up; to terminate.
sĕlĕsĕma, a cold in the head; also *sĕma-sĕma.*
sĕleweng, a gossip.

sěli, *sělang-sěli*, pointing alternately in one direction and in the other.

sěliap, a fish (*chorinemus moadetta*).

sělidek, making diligent enquiry or investigation—cf. *sidek*.

sěligi, a sharp light bamboo, or wooden dart, or pointed stick.

sěligut, winding in and out (as persons making their way through a crowd).

sělimbar, a large wild gambier (*uncaria sclerophylla*).

sělimpat, plaited work; wicker; *s. ayer*, a small aroid (*aglaonema minus*); *ular s.*, a generic name for sea-snakes owing to their flattened tails [the name is applied especially to *enhydris hardwickii*]; *ular s. katang těbu*, a name for broad-banded sea-snakes—e.g. *distira stokesii* and *chersydrus granulatus*; *ular s. sungai*, a small sea-snake without distinctive markings (*enhydrina valakadyen*).

sělimut, sheeting, enfolding; *kain s.*, a sheet, a rug; *sělimuti*, to wrap up in a sheet; *sělimutkan*, to use as a sheet.

sělinap, tearing off the skin of anything—e.g. tearing off the skin of a fowl to avoid the trouble of plucking off the feathers.

sělindong, hiding, veiling—cf. *lindong*.

sěling, Jav. glazed earthenware; china-ware; porcelain.

sělira, = *sělera*.

sělirat, mesh-work; ordered entanglement—cf. *sirat*.

sěliri, a seat or stool mentioned in old romances.

sěliseh, want of harmony; discordant; disagreeing; disputing; *běrsěliseh*, to quarrel; *pěrsělisehan*, a dispute.

sělisek, picking out fleas or lice from the hair; preening the feathers (of a bird); *měnyělisek*, to cleanse the hair or feathers.

sělisir, walking round the edge of anything.

sělit, I. thrusting in between; *těrsělit*, stuck or jammed between two surfaces. II. (Dutch) end, conclusion, termination.

sělitar, all round, = *kěliling*; *s. alam*, all over the world; (by extension) a ruler or spirit whose power is felt all over the earth.

sělok, groping after something hidden—e.g. as a man gropes about in his pocket for a coin; *měnyělok*, to grope about with the hand.

sěloka, Skr. verses; rhyme, especially when humorous; ironical or satirical poetry when not in the form of the *pantun*.

sělomor, the slough of a snake.

sělongkar, *měnyělongkar*, to search a man's belongings—e.g. for stolen property.

sěloroh, farcical, droll.

sěluang, a fish (unidentified).

sěluar, Pers. trousers, breeches; *sahělai s.*, a pair of trousers; *s. bulat*, pyjama trousers; *s. China*, Chinese trousers; *s. kotong*, short trousers —such as those worn by 'rikisha coolies; *s. sampak*, trousers worn by Malays in the rice fields.

sělubong, veiling, covering; *sělubongkan diri*, to cover oneself with a veil.

sěludang, the sheath or outer covering of a palm blossom; *s. mayang*, id.

sěludip, the sheath or outer covering of a young palm.

sěludu, a fish (*arius gagora*).

sělukat, a musical instrument forming part of the *gamělan* or Javanese orchestra.

sělumar, a tree (*mussændopsis beccariana*).

sělumbar, long thorns—such as those of the *nibong*.

sělumput, touchy; ill-tempered.

sělupat, a natural thin filmy covering, such as the almost transparent skin under the shell of an egg—cf. *sělaput*.

sĕlurai, a kind of vermicelli.
sĕluroh, see *lurah*.
sĕlusoh, a generic name for all drugs, medicines and charms used for facilitating delivery in childbirth; *s. bĕranak*, id.; *s. uri*, a drug for getting rid of the afterbirth.
sĕlut, mud, slush; clammy as mud.
sĕma, *sĕma-sĕma*, a cold in the head; also *sĕlĕsĕma*.
semah, a propitiatory offering to evil spirits; a sacrifice; *jin yang kurang s.*, a hungry ghost; *pĕnyemah*, a sacrifice.
sĕmai, a nursery for young rice-plants.
sĕmaja, but, only; = *sahaja*.
sĕmak, thick undergrowth, scrub; *jalan yang s.*, a road that has become overgrown; *s. samun*, extremely overgrown.
sĕmambu, *rotan sĕmambu*, the Malacca cane (*calamus scipionum*); *s. bangkut*, a Malacca cane of which two or more joints occur exceptionally close to one another [this peculiarity is believed to bring luck].
sĕmampai, loosely lashed together (as the component parts of a raft).
seman, fruitless; abortive; coming to nothing.
Sĕmang, a name given to Negrito aborigines in the country near the headwaters of the Perak river.
sĕmangat, the spirit of life; the soul in the ancient Indonesian sense; a term of endearment; *ambil s.*, to capture another person's *sĕmangat* and so render that person subject to your will; *buah s.*, special *padi*-stalks used as an offering at the harvest rites; *hilang s., kurang s.*, or *lĕmas s.*, faintness, lassitude; *kur s.*, an expression used in invoking a *sĕmangat*, because of its bird-like character; a term of endearment; *tĕrbang s.*, the flight of the spirit of life, resulting in temporary unconsciousness; *s. padi*, the spirit of life in the *padi*.

sĕmanggi, water-cress.
sĕmangka, the water-melon (*citrullus edulis*).
sĕmangkok, a plant (*croton argyratus*).
sĕmanja, a variant of *sĕmaja* and *sahaja*.
sĕmantan, *nyiur sĕmantan*, a coconut at the stage when the water inside can just begin to be heard on the nut being shaken.
sĕmar, I. a clown or comic character in a Javanese play. II. as far as, up to, until.
sĕmat, a sort of lath used for pinning pieces of *atap* together in making roofing.
sĕmata, Skr. likeness; just like; almost exactly like; often *sa-mata*.
sĕmawang, a (Kedah) variant of *sĕmbawang*.
sĕmayam, sitting enthroned; *bĕrsĕmayam*, (literally) to sit on the throne in state; (metaphorically) to reside (of a prince).
sĕmbah, a salutation suggestive of deep respect or homage; (by metaphor) the speech of a subject to a prince; an offering by a subject to a prince; *dĕmikian-lah sĕmbah-nya*, thus he (the subject) spake; *mĕmbawa sĕmbah daripada buah-buahan*, bringing offerings of fruit; *sĕmbahkan*, to convey (a message or offering) to a prince; to represent (facts) to a prince; *mĕmpĕrsĕmbahkan*, id.; *mĕnyĕmbah*, to perform the salutation of homage; to do obeisance; *pĕrsĕmbahan*, an offering.
sĕmbahyang, the worship of God; prayer; ritual—cf. *sĕmbah* and *yang*; *ayer s.*, water for ceremonial ablution at a mosque.
sĕmbam, falling face foremost; *sungkur s.*, id.
sĕmbat, casting with a peculiar backward jerk (as one casts a net to make it open out).
sembat, I. a snare for rats and mice.

II. *mĕnyembat*, to whip (anything) forcibly up one's sleeve.

sĕmbawang, a tree (*kayea ferruginea*).

sĕmbawarna, a (Kedah) variant of *sĕmburna*.

sĕmbĕleh, slaughtering by cutting the throat; killing.

sĕmbĕlit, costiveness; constipation.

sĕmbĕrani, *kuda s.*, a Pegasus; a steed of supernatural power; *bĕsi bĕsĕmbĕrani*, magnetic iron.

sĕmbĕrap, a hexagonal *sireh*-box.

sĕmbĕrip, a brass salver with a foot to it.

sĕmbeta, props to keep a boat upright when hauled ashore or steady in a surf on a shallow.

sĕmbilan, nine; one taken from ten (*sa-ambilan*); *Nĕgĕri S.*, the Nine States (a name given to a confederacy of Menangkabau States).

sĕmbilang, *ikan s.*, a generic name for some fish with very poisonous fins (*plotosus canias, p. unicolor, p. lineatus* and, perhaps, *p. horridus*).

sĕmbilu, a bamboo knife; a sharpened splinter of bamboo.

sĕmbir, I. the edge or rim of a plate. II. to "show wrong" (of the compass).

sĕmboh, healing, getting well, recovering; *sĕmbohkan*, to heal; to cause an illness to end in recovery.

sĕmbong, a strongly scented herb (*blumea balsamifera*).

sĕmboyan, anything used to give the alarm; a tocsin; an alarm-gun, or alarm-bell, or gong.

sĕmbuang, I. an offering cast away in the jungle for evil spirits. II. a mooring-post or winning-post.

sĕmbul, protuberant, prominent (of the breasts).

sĕmbulu, rough-hewn, unplaned, in the rough (of timber).

sĕmbuni, = *sĕmbunyi*.

sĕmbunyi, concealment; *sĕmbunyikan*, to conceal; *bĕrsĕmbunyi*, in hiding; *tĕrsĕmbunyi*, hidden.

sĕmbur, ejecting forcibly from the mouth; spitting out [the word is not used of actual spitting (*ludah*), but of a snake spitting out venom or of a man spitting out a mouthful of water]; *sĕmburkan*, to spit out.

sĕmburit, sodomy.

sĕmburna, Skr. gold-coloured; aureate.

sĕmĕjak, = *sĕmĕnjak*.

sĕmĕjana, = *sĕmĕnjana*.

sĕmĕlit, = *sĕmbĕlit*.

sĕmemeh, besmeared, befouled, dirty (as the face after chewing betel carelessly).

sĕmĕna, *tiada s.*, without reason; often written *tiada sa-mana-mana*.

sĕmĕnda, the transference of a man's residence to the home of his wife's family; the husband going to live with the wife.

sĕmĕndal, mica.

sĕmĕndĕrasa, Jav. a name for the *chĕmpaka* flower.

sĕmĕnggah, harmonious, fitting, proper; *ta'-s.*, unbecoming.

sĕmĕnjak, since; *s. pĕrang China*, since the war in China.

sĕmĕnjana, mediocre, middling.

sĕmĕntang, although; granting that; while; = *sunggoh-pun*.

sĕmĕntara, while, during, for a time, temporary; *s. dia lagi kĕchil*, while he was still young; *hal nĕgĕri ini sĕmĕntara sahaja tiada akan kĕkal*, the status of this settlement is purely temporary; it will not endure.

sĕmĕntĕlah, the more.

sĕmĕntong, blunt, simple, dull-witted.

sĕmĕrbak, spreading, diffusive, all-permeating (of a perfume).

sĕmĕrbok, = *sĕmĕrbak*.

sĕmĕrdanta, Skr. white pearly teeth; often written *asmara danta*.

sĕmĕsta, Skr. all, entire; *alam s.*, the whole world; *sĕru sĕmĕsta sakalian*, the universe; all and everything.

sĕmilir, *silir-sĕmilir,* waving (as the loose end of a garment).
sĕmista, = *sĕmĕsta.*
sĕmpada, *kĕtam s.,* a kind of crab.
sĕmpadan, a boundary (especially a well-defined boundary—such as a stream or fence).
sempak, chipped, notched, injured along the edge.
sĕmpal, jutting out; *mĕnyĕmpal,* to jut out; *tĕrsĕmpal,* prominent.
sĕmpana, fortunate, lucky, blessed.
sempang, crossing; cutting across each other (of roads); cross roads; *s. siur,* zigzag; *mĕnyempang,* to turn off in another direction (of a man on a journey).
sĕmpat, ability to do anything; to "manage"; *aku tiada sĕmpat lari,* I could not manage to get away.
sĕmpĕlah, accursed, good for nothing; *anak s.,* a term of abuse;
sĕmpĕlat, soiled, dirty.
sĕmpĕna, a lucky mark on a *kĕris*—cf. *sĕmpana.*
sĕmpĕrna, = *sĕmpurna.*
sĕmpit, narrow; confined (of space); *kĕsĕmpitan bĕlanja,* narrowness of means; poverty.
sempok, *mĕnyempok,* to come into conflict with; to run up against.
sĕmporna, = *sĕmpurna.*
sĕmpuras, dirty, unwashed (of the face).
sĕmpurna, Skr. completion, realisation, perfection; *s. kĕtahuan-nya,* his knowledge is perfect; *s. pĕkĕrjaan,* the perfection of work; *sĕmpurnakan,* to complete, to perfect.
sĕmu, deceit by false representations or a false appearance; "taking in"; *tĕrsĕmu,* "taken in."
sĕmua, Skr. all; the whole; every one of; *kĕsĕmua-nya,* all of them.
sĕmudĕra, Skr. the ocean.
sĕmugut, = *sĕnggugut.*
sĕmurup, (Perak) a lean-to.
sĕmut, a generic name for ants other than the white ant (*anai-anai*) and the fire-ant (*kĕrĕngga*); *s. api,* a long black ant which stings badly (*nobopelta distinguenda*); *s. sabong,* a black and red ant found in boats and sandy places (*sima rufonigra*), it also stings badly.
sĕna, I. Ar. *sĕna maki,* "mecca senna"; the true senna obtained from the tree *cassia angustifolia.* II. *pokok sĕna,* the angsana tree (*pterocarpus indicus*); also *angsana.*
sena, Skr. an army; infantry.
sĕnak, griping pains in the stomach.
sĕnam, I. the dark colour visible when plated ware is scratched; the cheap background; *nampak s.,* he is seen in his true colours. II. *bĕrsĕnam,* to stretch oneself on waking.
sĕnang, comfort, ease, peace of mind; *s. mĕnipu dia,* it is an easy matter to deceive him; *kĕsĕnangan,* a feeling of comfort.
sĕnangin, a fish (*otholithus maculatus*).
sĕnantiasa, = *sĕnĕntiasa.*
sĕnapang, (Dutch) a musket, a gun; *s. batu,* a flint-lock; *s.* "*cap,*" a muzzle-loader; *s. kĕmbar,* a double-barrelled gun; *s. kopak,* a breech-loader; *s. tĕrkul,* a rifled gun; *mĕngisi s.,* to load a gun.
sĕnawi, a passenger who works his passage.
Sĕnayan, Ar. *hari Sĕnayan,* Monday; also *hari Isnin.*
sĕnda, I. a joke; a jest; flirtation; *gurau s.,* id.; *bĕrsĕnda-gurau* or *bĕrgurau-sĕnda,* to interchange jests. II. Skr. I, myself; = *sahaya'nda.*
sĕndal, I. fixing by filling up interstices. II. surreptitious theft; picking a pocket.
sĕndalu, *angin sĕndalu,* a moderate breeze.
sĕndar, to snore.
sĕndat, wedged in; nipped.
sĕndawa, Skr. saltpetre.
sendel, leaning against; *bĕrsendel bahu,* shoulder to shoulder.

sendeng, heeling over to one side; laid against anything at an angle; *těrsendeng-sendeng*, leaning first to one side, then to another.

sěnděrong, a marine mollusc (unidentified).

sěndi, Skr. muscle, sinew, joint; *těrchabut-lah sěndi bahu-nya*, his shoulder was put out of joint; *běrsěndi*, with a hinge or fastening; mounted in.

sěndiri, self; *sahaya s.*, I myself—cf. *diri*.

sěndochong, a fresh-water fish (unidentified).

sěndok, a spoon, a ladle; *siput s.*, a shell (*patella* sp.); *měnyěndok*, to eat anything with a spoon.

sěndong, a narrow pen or stall to confine a buffalo for milking.

sěndu, depressed, serious, melancholy—cf. *sědu*.

sěndudok, a rhododendron-like shrub (*melastoma polyanthum*).

sěněntiasa, Skr. always, perpetually; also *sěntiasa*.

sěngaja, intentionally, deliberately; *tiada sahaya s.*, I did not do it intentionally.

sěngal, rheumatic or gouty twinges of pain.

sěngam, *měnyěngam*, to gorge; to eat gluttonously.

sěngap, quiet (of a child).

sěngarat, a fish (unidentified).

sěngat, a sting; the venomous "bite" of an insect; *měnyěngat*, to sting; *pěnyěngat*, a wasp.

sěngau, talking through the nose.

senget, inclining to one side; heeling or leaning over; *těrsenget*, set at an angle, inclined.

sěnggama, Skr. union; federation.

sěnggau, rising on tiptoe and stretching out the hand to pick or draw something towards oneself.

sěnggayut, dangling in the air (of a man hanging by his hands).

sěnggirek, an auger; *rusa s.*, the unicorn.

sěnggok, nodding; tapping with the head; *sěnggokkan kěpala*, to bump the head (against the ground or wall).

sěnggugut, a generic name for a number of diseases of women; dysmenorrhœa.

sěnggulong, a millipede that rolls itself up into a ball when touched.

sěnggut, a sidelong blow with the head; a butt with the horn—cf. *sěnggok*.

sěngit, pungent (of odour).

sěngkak, nausea from overfeeding.

sěngkalan, a wooden slab on which curry-stuff is pounded.

sěngkang, thwart; position across; cross-bar; *těrsěngkang*, jammed across.

sengkang, *jalan měnyengkang*, to walk unevenly.

sěngkar, a crossbar or thwart in a boat.

sěngkarut, interlacing; *běrsěngkarut*, in a tangle; very much involved (of a story).

sěngkat, succinct; too short; limited.

sěngkayan, a waterspout.

sěngkěla, Skr. shackles, fetters, hobbles.

sěngkělang, crossed (of the arms or legs).

sěngkelang, a slanting cross; an irregular figure; bad work.

sěngkělat, = *sakhlat*.

sěngkelat, filthy; unwashed (of the *abaimana*)—a term of abuse.

sěngkěling, crossing the legs slightly by laying one just over the other.

sěngkělit, a sort of band or strap into which the feet are placed when climbing a tree.

sěngkěnit, a tick.

sěngkuang, the yam-bean (*pachyrrhizus angulatus*).

sěngkuap, a canopy.

sengkul, difficulty in swallowing (due to an inflamed or sore throat).

sĕngongot, a fish (unidentified).

sĕngsara, Skr. pain, agony, torture; *azab s., seksa s.,* or *susah s.,* id.

sengsat, bound up (of a *sarong*) so as to give freer play to the limbs.

sengseng, = *singsing*.

sĕni, delicate of texture; distinct or clear in tone; thin and fine; *intan yang s.,* diamonds of fine water; *ayer s.,* urine.

sĕnja, Skr. evenfall; *s. kala,* id.; *awal s.,* the early part of the evening.

sĕnjak, since, = *sĕmĕnjak*.

sĕnjakala, see *sĕnja*.

sĕnjata, Skr. instrument of warfare; weapon; *alat s.,* war-material.

sĕnjolong, having a long projecting snout—a descriptive name given to the gavial (*tomistoma schlegeli*), to small sword fish, and to certain types of boats—cf. *jolong*.

sĕnjong, the bar of a pair of scales.

sĕnohong, a salt-water fish (unidentified).

sĕnonoh, becoming; fitting; suitable; *tiada s.,* improper (especially of conduct).

sĕnta, the long timbers used in the construction of a boat; the timbers stretching from stem to stern as distinct from the ribs.

sĕntada, I. a species of ant. II. a tree resembling the yew (*podocarpus neglectus*).

sĕntadu, *ulat sĕntadu,* a large green caterpillar.

sĕntak, a jerk; a sudden pull; *sĕntakkan* or *mĕnyĕntakkan,* to give a sudden tug at anything—e.g. at one's *kĕris*.

sĕntal, rubbing vigorously with a hard surface; scrubbing.

sĕntana, Jav. family, kindred; *kula-sĕntana,* id.

senteng, = *sinting*.

sĕntĕri, Tam. a wandering student; a wanderer; a stranger generally; *dagang s.,* id.

sĕntiasa, Skr. always; also *sĕnĕntiasa*.

sĕntil, sticking anything into a hole or opening so that it is partly in and partly out.

sĕntoh, forcible contact; collision; knocking up against.

sentok, = *sintok*.

sĕntolar, plaiting or twisting an extra strand into a rope; adding a lash to a whip.

sĕntong, a ring, a circle, a circular enclosure; *kain s.,* a *sarong* that has been sewn so as to be ready for use; *baju s.,* a jacket that does not open the whole way down in front.

sĕntosa, Skr. rest, peace, tranquillity; *kĕsĕntosaan,* id.; *sĕnang sĕntosa,* "peace and happiness."

sĕntul, a fruit tree (*sandoricum indicum*).

sĕnuhun, Jav. a royal title; a monarch; *sang s.,* his majesty.

sĕnyak, = *sĕnyap*.

sĕnyampang, see *nyampang*.

sĕnyap, I. *sunyi sĕnyap,* extremely lonely; deserted—a strong form of *sunyi.* II. = *lĕnyap*.

sĕnyar, the tingling sensation caused by a blow on the funny-bone.

sĕnyum, smiling, a smile; *s. simpul,* a smile accompanied by a blush; *s. raja,* a hypocritical smile; *tĕrsĕnyum,* with a smile on the face; smiling.

sĕnyur, Port. senhor; Mr.; Sir.

sĕpah, a quid (of betel); *s. bulan,* a hazel-worm or filbert-worm; *s. putĕri,* a name given (1) to a pretty bird (*dicæum cruentatum*); (2) to a large tree (*pentace triptera*); *s. raja,* a name sometimes given to the bird of paradise.

sepah, littering about; *tĕrsepah,* littered about.

sĕpai, scattered about.

sĕpak, a blow with the flat of the hand; a slap; a blow with a racquet; *mĕnyĕpak,* to slap.

sepak, a kick with the side of the foot; spurning; *s. raga*, the Malay football; *kĕmudi s.*, a paddle-rudder in contradistinction to a hinged rudder of European type.

sĕpam, a large wild mango (*mangifera maingayi*).

sĕpan, a tree (*dialium patens*).

sĕpang, the "sappan" tree (*asalpinia sappan*).

sĕparoh, see *paroh*.

sĕpat, *ikan sĕpat*, a fish (*colera vulgaris*).

sĕpatu, Port. shoes.

sĕpegoh, a marine mussel yielding pearls of little value.

seper, = *sipir*.

sĕpĕrai, (Dutch) a counterpane or coverlet.

Sĕpĕrba, Skr. the name of a nymph of heaven; *Sang S.*, the legendary founder of the Malayan empires.

sĕpĕrti, like; similar to; as to; according to; *dĕngan sĕpĕrti-nya*, as a thing should be; appropriately; *sĕpĕrtikan*, as though about to.

sepet, half-closed (of the eyes); with the lids close together; *buta s.*, blindness—such that the eyes become closed up as well as sightless.

sĕpi, Jav. still, quiet, calm.

sĕpit, nipped, confined, squeezed or pressed between two surfaces; *kueh s.*, a wafer-like cake or biscuit much favoured by Chinese; *bĕrsĕpit*, possessing claws or nippers (as a crab).

sĕpoh, gloss, glaze, polish; *mas yang sudah tĕrsĕpoh*, burnished gold.

sĕpok, casting carelessly aside.

sĕpui, gently blowing (of the zephyrs); soft (of the breeze).

sĕpuleh, *akar sĕpuleh*, a plant (*fagræa racemosa* or *ophioxylon serpentinum*).

seput, dull (of colours).

sĕra, I. wild disorderly movement; *tĕrsĕra - sĕra*, rushing frantically about. II. bright, glowing. III. a midge.

sĕrabai, a cake made of flour and coconut milk.

sĕrabut, shaggy, fibrous—cf. *sabut*.

sĕradong, tripping over anything; *tĕrsĕradong kaki*, to have one's foot caught in anything.

sĕraga, *bantal sĕraga*, a flat square-sided state cushion.

sĕrah, surrendering; handing over possession; delivering; making over; *sĕrahkan* or *mĕnyĕrahkan*, to hand over; *sĕrahkan diri*, to submit absolutely to another's control; *bĕrsĕrah*, in submission to; *tĕrsĕrah*, given over to.

serah, glowing red; fiery red.

sĕrahi, Ar. a wine-bottle or decanter.

sĕrai, lemon grass (*andropogon schœnanthus*).

sĕrak, I. hoarseness; mucus in the throat and nostrils; *tĕrtawa sampai s.*, to laugh oneself hoarse. II. a little loose (of a fastening).

serak, scattering in disorder; *serak-serakkan*, to disperse.

sĕram, to stiffen (of the muscles); to stand on end (of the hair).

seram, = *siram*.

sĕrama, Skr. in time, in measure, rhythmical; *gĕndang s.*, a drum (one side of which is beaten by the hand, the other by a drum-stick); *mĕnyĕrama*, to beat time.

sĕrambi, a Malay verandah.

sĕrampang, a barbed trident used for spearing fish.

sĕrana, I. Skr. style, fashion; general effect. II. *mĕnyĕrana*, to pine away; also *mĕrana*.

sĕranah, curse, cursing; imprecations; *sumpah s.*, id.

sĕrandang, a prop formed by crossing two sticks.

Sĕrandib, Pers. *pulau Sĕrandib*, Ceylon.

sĕrandong, tripping or stumbling over.

sĕrang, I. assault, attack, charging, onslaught; *mĕnyĕrang*, to assail.

II. a "serang" or petty officer on a ship; a quarter-master. III. wavy (of colouring); changing tint according to light.

serang, wide-meshed (of baskets, nets, etc.)

sĕranggong, *mĕnyĕranggong*, to sit with one's elbows on the table; to squat with the knees wide apart—cf. *ranggong*.

sĕrangkak, a girdle of thorns put round the trunk of a tree to prevent thieves climbing it.

Sĕrani, Ar. "Nazarene"; Christian (especially Roman Catholic); Eurasian; also *Nasrani*.

sĕranta, advertising a fact; letting everyone know.

sĕrap, absorption, sponging up, sucking up; *ĕmbun di-sĕrap panas*, dew sucked up by heat.

serap, I. a sort of wooden dado or planking along the base of a wall. II. a Javanese sleep-producing spell.

sĕrapah, Skr. a curse; an imprecation.

sĕrapeh, *kĕna sĕrapeh*, to be chipped by a blow.

sĕrasa, a name for *sireh*.

sĕrasi, = *sa-raksi*.

sĕrat, jammed; held fast in an aperture.

sĕratong, a small tree (*tabernæmontana corymbosa*).

sĕrau, I. noisy; creating a disturbance. II. celluloid tissue; net-like stuff.

sĕrawa, a fritter made of banana and flour.

Sĕrawak, Sarawak.

sĕrawan, = *sĕriawan*.

sĕraya, I. with, while, along with, during, as; *bĕrtanya sĕraya tĕrsĕnyum*, to ask with a smile. II. a generic name for a number of timbers obtained from trees of the genera *shorea* and *hopea*. III. Skr. appealing to; invoking assistance of.

sĕrba, Skr. all; of all sorts; various; all kinds of; *s. neka* or *s. sĕrbi*, id.; *s. salah*, puzzled; in doubt; *s. sadikit*, some small smattering of.

sĕrbah, *sĕrbah-sĕrbeh*, shaking out a *sarong*.

sĕrbak, *mĕnyĕrbak*, to spread; to be diffused (of an odour).

sĕrban, I. Pers. a turban. II. numbed.

sĕrbat, Ar. a cooling drink of any sort; also *sharbat*.

sĕrbeh, *sĕrbah-sĕrbeh*, shaking out the *sarong*.

sĕrbet, (Dutch) serviette, napkin.

sĕrbi, *sĕrba-sĕrbi*, all sorts; various.

sĕrbok, powder, fine dust; *s. kikir*, filings.

sĕrbu, impetuous onslaught, dashing forward, charging; *mĕnyĕrbukan diri*, to throw oneself impetuously upon the enemy.

sĕrdadu, Port. a soldier.

sĕrdak, very fine dust—such as collects on undusted furniture.

sĕrdam, a native fife of bamboo.

sĕrdang, a tall fan-palm (*livistona cochinchinensis*).

sĕrdeh, sticking out (of the stomach or chest, when a man does not sit upright).

sĕrek, I. to be frightened off a risky business; to amend one's ways through a bad fright. II. (onom.) *sĕrok-sĕrek*, the cracking of the finger-joints.

serek, bluffing; threatening without intending to carry out one's threats.

sĕrĕmban, I. a game played by children. II. wearing the *sarong* high in front and low behind.

sĕrĕmpak, hastily and slovenly done (of work).

sĕrĕmpu, a rough keel shaped like a dug-out; *jalur s.*, a dug-out.

sĕrĕndah, I. a kind of banana. II. a kind of padi.

sĕrendeng, heeling over to one side; aslant.

sĕrĕngam, over abundance; excess; *bĕrsĕrĕngam*, in objectionable excess.

sĕrĕnjang, perfectly perpendicular (of a flagstaff, tree, etc.)

sĕrĕsah, rubbish, offal.

seret, dragging along; trailing along; *mĕnyeret*, to trail after one; to drag something over the ground behind one.

sĕrgah, *mĕnyĕrgah*, to startle anyone with a sudden sound or movement.

sĕrgam, standing out; in bold relief; conspicuous.

sĕrgap, *mĕnyĕrgap*, to surprise with a sudden onslaught.

sĕrgut, roughly finished; coarsely done (of bad work).

sĕri, I. Skr. charm, beauty, glory; the best of anything; the embryo; *s. nĕgĕri*, the pride of the city; *s. balai*, the heart of the audience hall; *s. muka*, the light of the countenance; *s. kaya*, the custard apple; *bĕrsĕri*, to brighten up (of the countenance). II. drawn (of a game).

sĕriap, a large bird (unidentified) frequenting mud banks.

sĕriat, an instrument with long trailers [the trailers are drawn through the water frightening shrimps and prawns, which are thereby induced to leap out of the water and fall into a boat].

sĕriawan, a sort of sprue.

sĕriding, side, border, edge, fringe.

sĕrigala, a jackal; *anjing s.*, a name sometimes given to the wild dog (*cyon rutilans*).

sĕrikat, Ar. the joint earnings of husband and wife.

sĕrikaya, see *sĕri*.

sĕrindai, an evil spirit.

sĕrindit, the love-bird (*loriculus galgulus*).

sĕring, I. stiff (of cloth or paper). II. the feeling of "goose-flesh"; *s. sĕram*, id. III. (onom.) the humming of a humble-bee. IV. Jav. *sĕring kali*, occasionally.

sĕringai, *mĕnyĕringai*, to grin (of apes).

sĕriwa, part of the title of a *bĕndahara*—i.e. *bĕndahara sĕriwa raja*.

sĕrja, a cloth-fabric; serge?

sĕrkah, torn apart, split.

sĕrkai, rinsing or wringing out; squeezing out.

sĕrkap, a coop-shaped fish-trap thrust down over a fish.

sĕrkup, enclosing under a dome or cup-shaped surface; catching with a *sĕrkap*.

sĕrlah, glowing white.

sĕrling, a pitfall.

sĕrmangin, a musical instrument.

sĕrobeh, dishevelled (of the hair).

sĕroda, a belt of thorns (also known as *sĕrangkak*) which is placed round a tree to stop thieves climbing it.

sĕrodi, filing down precious stones.

sĕroh, shrunken; reduced (of inflammation).

sĕroja, Skr. the lotus (*nĕlumbium speciosum*).

sĕrok, a measure of capacity, = about 10 *gantang*.

serok, a name given to a small variety of the fish-trap (better-known as *kelong*).

sĕrokan, a water-course; a stream.

sĕrombong, a funnel, a hollow cylinder; *pahat s.*, a chisel.

serong, askew, at an angle.

sĕronggong, cross beams used in mining.

sĕronok, (Kedah) pleasant, agreeable; = *sĕdap*.

sĕrpai, chipping, clipping, lopping off.

sĕrpeh, chipping; a chip.

sĕrta, Skr. with, together with; accompanying; while; and; *rajin sĕrta usaha*, diligent and industrious; *sĕrta-mĕrta*, at that very moment; immediately; on the spot; *bĕsĕrta*, along with, together with; *mĕnyĕrtai*, to co-operate with; to assist.

sĕrtup, closing; shutting up.

sĕru, I. Skr. all; *s. sakalian*, id.; *s. sĕmĕsta sakalian*, id.; also *sarwa*. II. exclaiming, calling out, shouting; *bĕrsĕru*, to call out loudly; *mĕnyĕru*, id.

sĕruit, a fishspear with a single barb.

sĕrul, inadhesive (of the grains of boiled rice).

sĕrunai, a name given to a number of musical instruments (especially to a wooden whistle with a slide for varying the pitch); *buaya s.*, a name given to the gavial.

sĕrunding, a Javanese preparation of ground coconut.

sĕruntun, *akar sĕruntun*, a medicinal shrub (*lepidagathis longifolia*).

sĕrut, (onom.) a dull scraping sound.

sĕsah, beating with a long flexible cane or rod.

sĕsak, close pressure, packing tightly; *pĕnoh s.*, full to crowding.

sĕsal, regret, sorrow, repentance; *sĕsalkan*, to regret (anything); *mĕnyĕsal*, to feel regret.

sĕsap, lapping up water (of animals drinking); *sĕsapan burong*, a pool frequented by birds in dry weather.

sĕsar, pushing or shoving aside; *yang hidup sĕsarkan mati*, the living displace the dead.

sĕsat, straying from the right path; losing one's way; going astray; *s. jalan*, to lose one's way; *s. barat*, confused; *di-pĕrsĕsat*, led astray.

sĕsawi, = *sawi-sawi*.

sĕsĕgan, = (*burong*) *sĕgan*.

sĕsĕma, = *sĕma-sĕma*.

sĕsorok, = *sorok-sorok*.

sĕsumpit, = *sumpit-sumpit*.

sĕta, Skr. a cubit; also *hasta*.

sĕtakona, = *astakona*.

sĕtambun, a small tree (*baccaurea parvifolia*).

Setan, Ar. a devil, an evil spirit, Satan; also *Shaitan*.

sĕtanggar, = *istinggar*.

sĕtanggi, Skr. incense; also *istanggi*.

sĕtawar, a name given to some medicinal herbs (*costus speciosus* and *forrestia* spp.)

sĕtĕrawan, = *sastĕrawan*.

Sĕtĕria, Skr. a Kshatriya; a member of the warrior-caste.

sĕtĕriman, a petty officer on a ship.

sĕtĕru, a personal (not national) enemy; *bĕrsĕtĕru* to be at enmity with; *pĕrsĕtĕruan*, a feud.

sĕtĕrup, (Dutch) syrup.

sĕtia, Skr. loyalty, fidelity, faith, constancy; *s. tĕgoh*, firm loyalty.

sĕtiawan, Skr. loyal, faithful, constant—cf. *sĕtia*.

sĕtinggi, a reef in a sail.

sĕtinja, = *istinja*.

sĕtoka, a fish (unidentified).

sĕtolop, (Dutch) a wall-lamp.

sĕtru, = *sĕtĕru*.

sĕtu, Jav. blessing (of a Hindu divinity or ascetic blessing a devotee); laying a transformation on a person; *sĕtui*, to bless; to lay a spell on.

sĕtua, Skr. an animal; *marga-s.*, animals generally; *s. angkara*, a fabulous wild beast.

sĕtul, a marine plant (*enhalus acoroides*).

sewa, hire, hiring, engaging, leasing; *sewaan*, obtaining on lease, leasing, engaging; *rumah sewaan*, a house held on leasehold tenure or intended for leasehold tenure; *mĕnyewa*, to hire.

sewah, I. a short curved dagger. II. a generic name given to a number of birds of pray; *s. bĕlalang* (*accipiter virgatus*); *lang s.*, the large kite (*pernis tweeddalii*); *s. tĕkukur*, the Indian koel (*eudynamis honorata*).

sewal, misfortune.

Shaaban, Ar. the name of a Muhammadan month.

shaer, Ar. poem.

shafaat, Ar. intercession.

Shafeï, Ar. Shafiite; appertaining to the Shafiite school of doctrine.

shah, Pers. king, sovereign; a royal title; *s. johan*, ruler of the world; *s. mardan*, king of men; *s. bandar*, master attendant, harbour master.

shahadan, Ar. this is to testify—a common exordium to a sentence.

shahadat, Ar. attestation; the confession of faith.

shahbandar, see *shah*.

shahid, Ar. *mati shahid*, to die a martyr for the faith; to be killed in a holy war.

shahuat, Ar. voluptuous sensation.

shaikh, Ar. a title given to Arabs who are not descendants of the Prophet.

Shaitan, Ar. an evil spirit; a devil; Satan; also *Setan*.

shajrat, Ar. a tree.

shak, Ar. doubt, suspicion.

shakar, Pers. sugar.

shal, Pers. a shawl.

shamsu, Ar. the sun.

shara' Ar. *hukum shara'*, Muhammadan law.

sharat, Ar. article or clause in a contract.

sharbat, Ar. wine, cooling drink; also *sĕrbat*.

shareat, Ar. ritual.

sharif, Ar. noble.

sharifah, Ar. noble; a title given to women who are descended from the Prophet; also *saripah*.

sharikat, Ar. the joint earnings of husband and wife; also *sĕrikat*.

Shawal, Ar. the name of a Muhammadan month.

shufaat, = *shafaat*.

shukur, Ar. thanks; *bĕribu shukur*, thousands of thanks.

shurga, Skr. heaven; also *sorga*.

si, a prefix (usually half contemptuous) to the names of persons and personified animals or things; *si-anu*, so-and-so; *si-apa*, who, what person; *si-ĕngkau si-aku*, a person with whom you can take liberties (using familiar words like *aku* and *ĕngkau*).

sia, *sia-sia*, idle, useless, futile, without result; *dĕngan sia-sia*, uselessly.

siah, bustling; *s. layah*, swaying about.

siak, I. the caretaker of a mosque. II. *akar siak*, a slender climber with white flowers (*physostelma wallichii*).

siakap, a fish (*lates nobilis*).

sial, bringing ill-luck; ill-omened; ill-starred.

sialang, *pokok sialang*, any large tree on which bees build a nest; *bĕrsialang*, to swarm (of bees).

siamang, the well-known long-armed ape (*hylobates syndactylus*).

siang, daylight; *s. hari*, during the daytime; *bulan kĕsiangan*, the moon in daylight—a symbol of pallor.

siap, bringing to readiness; preparation; *sudah s.*, it is ready; *siapkan*, to get ready; *bĕrsiap*, in readiness.

siapa, who; see *si*.

siar, I. Port. *bĕrsiar*, to stroll about. II. welding together; hammering pieces of metal into one.

siasat, Ar. chastisement, punishment, control.

siat, tearing into strips; *siatkan*, to tear to pieces.

siau, cooled down to a bearable temperature (of water, hot metal, etc.)

sibang, *sibang-sibok*, snatching at a thing as one passes by.

sibar, a border sewn on to a piece of embroidery.

sibok, I. a whirl, a rush (of amusements or work). II. *sibang-sibok*, snatching at a thing as one passes by.

sibur, a shallow ladle of coconut shell.

sida, castration; a eunuch; *sida-sida*, eunuchs.

sidaguri, = *sĕlĕguri*.

sidai, hanging out clothes to dry; *pĕnyidai kain*, a clothes-cord or rail; *tĕrsidai*, hung out to dry.

sidang, I. a gathering, a council; *s. mĕshuarat*, members of council; *s.*

Jumaat, the Friday meeting for congregational service. II. the sharpened edge of a knife (showing the scraping of the grindstone).

sidek, investigation; thinking out—cf. *sĕlidek*.

siding, a sharply defined edge; a low dyke or fence; a long low fence used in catching dwarf-deer.

sifat, = *sipat*.

sigai, *tangga sigai*, a sort of ladder made by lashing short pieces of wood to a tree-trunk.

sigap, I. bearing, pose; = *sikap*. II. Jav. to have one's weapons ready for use.

sigar, *kain sigar*, a head-dress worn by a bridegroom.

sigĕra, = *sĕgĕra*.

sigi, I. pointing the finger at any person or thing. II. a band of thin metal round the sheath of a *kĕris*. III. a torch of resinous wood.

sigong, *mĕnyigong*, to give a dig with the elbow.

sihat, = *sehat*.

sihir, = *seher*.

sikap, I. manner, bearing, pose; also *sigap*. II. *lang sikap*, a name sometimes given to small hawks. III. *baju sikap*, a jacket with tight sleeves.

sikat, combing, a comb; a harrow; *bĕrsikat*, combed.

sikin, Ar. a knife.

sikkah, = *sekah*.

siksa, = *seksa*.

siku, the elbow; a sharp angle; *s. jalan*, a sharp turn in the road.

sila, I. Skr. "welcome"; "please" (in "please sit down," etc.); a polite invitation; *s. dudok*, pray be seated; *bĕnang s.*, a thick white thread; *silakan*, be pleased to; kindly agree to; *bĕrsila*, to sit down politely and ceremoniously; *mĕmpĕrsilakan*, to invite. II. *batu mĕdang sila*, a kind of gypsum used medicinally.

silah, Ar. *silah-silah*, a genealogical tree; a table showing descent.

silam, gloom, darkness, nightfall; *tĕrsilam*, benighted.

silang, cross-wise; position at right angles; *bĕrsilang*, marked with cross-cuts or scars; *silang-mĕnyilang*, lying across each other.

silap, I. Ar. an error, a mistake. II. conjuring, sleight of hand, puzzling the eye; *tukang s. mata*, a conjuror.

silasilah, see *silah*.

silat, fencing (especially the mimicry of fencing in a Malay sword-dance); *main s.*, a sword-dance; *bĕrsilat*, to fence.

silau, the shimmer of light on water—cf. *kilau*.

sileh, making good; replacing; repairing a loss; *s. mata*, making good to the eyes—i.e. publicly paying over a large sum only to have it quietly returned later.

silir, *silir-sĕmilir*, waving (as the loose end of a garment).

silu, shyness, retiring modesty.

simbah, besprinkling from above; watering.

simbai, looking smart; an effective appearance.

simbang, I. a sea-bird (*procellaria* sp.); *simbangan*, id. II. unreliable; *musim s.*, the uncertain weather at the change of monsoon.

simbok, a small basin or finger-bowl.

simpai, I. fastening in a band; a rattan fastening on the handle of a chisel or any similar object; *rotan s.*, a piece of very flexible rattan used for this purpose. II. a monkey (*semnopithecus melalophos*).

simpan, retaining in one's possession; holding; keeping; preserving; *s. di-hati*, remembering; *mĕnyimpan*, to keep; to preserve.

simpang, = *sempang*.

simpir, letting the wings droop (of a peacock).

simpul, knotting, tying, fastening; *s. mati*, a fast knot; *s. puleh*, a slip-knot; *sĕnyum s.*, a smile accompanied by a blush; *simpulan*, a fastening; *mĕnyimpul*, to fasten.

simpur, a generic name for a number of trees (especially *dillenia indica*).

sinar, ray of light; radiance; *kĕna sinar matahari*, to be struck by the sun's rays.

sindat, a flat armlet worn by women.

sinding, = *sendeng*.

sindir, teasing, chaff; *s. nyanyi*, teasing in song; *mĕnyindir*, to chaff.

sindura, Hind. minium, red-lead.

singa, Skr. a lion; an ancient title.

singga, = *sa-hingga*.

singgah, touching at; stopping at on the way; breaking a journey; *s.-mĕnyinggah*, to keep stopping at places—e.g. as a pedlar trying to sell his wares.

singgang, fish cooked in salt.

singgasana, Skr. a throne or royal dais; *s. kĕrajaan*, id.

singgat, = *sa-hingga*.

singgul, a blow or knock with the side of the head.

singit, = *senget*.

singkap, drawing apart curtains or mosquito-nets; drawing aside a hanging cloth so as to make one's way past it; *mĕnyingkap*, to open or draw aside a curtain.

singkat, = *sengkat*.

singkek, Ch. a "new-comer;" a contract-coolie fresh from China.

singkil, I. *singkil gigi*, teeth "on edge." II. *tali singkil*, a cord holding up curtains.

singkir, to tread a hen (of a cock); to push slightly aside.

singkur, kicking aside; pushing aside; knocking out of the way.

singsing, rolling up the sleeves; *fajar mĕnyingsing*, the day is breaking.

sini, here; this way; this direction; *di-sini*, here; in this place; *ka-sini*, hither; *dari-sini*, hence; *di-sĕbĕrang sini*, on the nearer bank.

sinjoh, elbowing a man out of the way.

sintar, the blue-breasted banded rail (*hypotænidia striata*).

sinting, I. *sĕluar sinting*, short trousers. II. a thin shell (*placuna sella*).

sintok, a tree (*cinnamomum sentu*?) out of the fibre of which a kind of soap is made; *mĕnyintok*, to use this fibrous stuff in the bath.

sinyur, = *senyur*.

sioman, = *siuman*.

siong, tusks, large canine teeth; *gigi s.*, the canines; *bĕrsiong*, tusked.

sipahi, Hind. a sepoy; a soldier.

sipat, Ar. a ruled or marked line; attributes; qualities, charms; *tali s.*, a line drawn by a carpenter to guide him in his work.

sipi, position off the centre; wide of the mark.

sipir, (Dutch) a cypher.

sipu, shamefacedness; *kĕsipu-sipuan*, id.; *tĕrsipu-sipu*, put to the blush.

sipua, Ch. an abacus.

siput, a generic name for many shells; the whorls, loops, lines and markings on the hand; *s. bawang* (*bulla ampulla*); *s. bĕlang chĕchak* (*terebra mascaria*); *s. bulan* (*helix ovum*); *s. bulan puteh* (*natica mamilla*); *s. panjang* (*terebra maculata*); *s. subang* (*solarium trochleare*); *s. tudong* (*trochus pyramis*); other shells have generic names of their own—e.g. *rangkek*, *chongkak*, etc.

sir, I. Ar. secret. II. lust; the promptings of lust; *s. bĕrahi*, id.

sira, Jav. a title of inferior distinction; *Sira Panji*, the *nom de guerre* of the famous Javanese hero *Radin Inu Kĕrtapati*, Prince of Kuripan.

sirai, dressed (of the hair).

siram, besprinkling; pouring water over; the bathing of princes; *bĕrsiram*, to bathe (of a prince or princess); *sirankan*, to pour (a liquid over anything).

sirat, I. netting together; *mata s.*, a mesh; *siratan gigi*, the mesh-like appearance of regular teeth; *pĕnyirat kuku*, the thin line of skin covering the edge of the finger-nail. II. Ar. *sirat-ul-mustakim*, the razor-edged bridge over which the true believer passes into heaven.

sireh, the betel-vine (*piper betle*); *s. charang*, soft new shoots on the vine; *s. kadok* (*piper longum*); *s. kĕrakap*, coarse leaves from the vine; *junjong s.*, the pole or support of the *sireh* vine; *makan s.*, to chew betel; *santap s.*, id. (of princes chewing betel); *tĕmpat s.* or *bĕkas s.*, a betel-box; *pĕsirehan*, id. [The use of *sireh* in the betrothal formalities has given rise to the following expressions: *s. bĕrchakap*, the *sireh* sent to typify the formal proposal of marriage; *s. mĕminang*, the *sireh* typifying the formal acceptance.]

siring, an instrument something like a large tennis racquet. [It is used for catching shrimps—it is drawn through the water and the shrimps coming in contact with it leap out of the water and fall into a boat.]

sirip, the fin of a fish.

sisa, Skr. what is left over; surplus; residue; remains (especially the remains of a meal); *s. nabi*, a flat-fish; the sole.

siseh, quarrelling, dispute—cf. *sĕliseh*; *mĕnyiseh*, to quarrel.

sisek, I. the scale of a fish, or armadillo, or dragon; the scraping off of the scales of a fish; *bĕrsisek-sisek*, scale-like; *s. tĕnggiling*, the scales of the armadillo—a description of a shingle roof; *batok s.*, whooping-cough. II. a name for some turtles —e.g. *s. lilin* (*chelone imbricata*); *s. tĕmpurong* (*thalassochelys caretta*).

sisi, side, brink, edge; *di-sisi putĕri*, by the side of the princess.

sisil, turning up the ends of the sleeves or trousers—cf. *singsing*.

sisip, insertion between two flat surfaces (as one inserts a paper-knife between the leaves of a book); *sisipkan* or *mĕnyisipkan*, to so insert or slip in.

sisir, a comb, a harrow, a toothed instrument of any sort; *mĕnyisir*, to harrow; to comb; to rake up.

sitak, a bag, a valise.

sitar, Hind. an Indian three-stringed guitar.

siti, Ar. lady; *S. Hawa*, Our Lady Eve; *S. Mariam*, the Virgin Mary; *s. guru*, a lady teacher.

sitin, Eng. satin.

siting, = *sinting*.

sitti, = *siti*.

situ, that place, there; *di-situ*, in that place; at that place; *dari-s.*, thence; *ka-s.*, thither.

situn, a pot of black glazed earthenware.

siul, whistling; *bĕrsiul*, to whistle; *burong s.*, the crested wood-quail (*rollulus roulroul*); *punai s.*, the small green pigeon (*osmotreron olax*).

siuman, the recovery of a consciousness after a fainting-fit or drunken debauch.

siur, I. *sĕmpang siur*, zigzagging. II. *ta'-siur*, not to care about.

siut, I. singeing, burning up a small object. II. whistling; = *siul*.

soah, Ch. over, done with, finished.

soal, Ar. question; *bĕrsoal*, to enquire; *bĕrsoal jawab*, to question and get replies; to discuss.

sobat, Ar. friendship, friend.

sobek, a nip or pinch of anything; to nip off a piece.

sobok, *pĕnyobok*, a night-prowler; a sneak-thief who steals under cover of the darkness.

sodok, shovelling up; ladling up; a shovel—cf. *sudu*.

sofi, = *sufi*.

soga, a tree (*ormosia venosa*).

sogang, palisades, fencing.

sogeh, attempting work of which one lacks experience; the bungling of a beginner.

sogok, menyogok, to give a significant nod or wink; to direct by a sign.

soh, an exclamation to make buffaloes turn.

soja, kowtowing; tĕrsoja-soja, repeatedly kowtowing.

sokma, Skr. the soul (in contradistinction to the body); raga dan s., body and soul [the word is used of the soul in the Hindu sense].

sokom, smearing with paint or colouring; clouded-white (as a colour of a dog); sokomkan, to besmear.

sokong, propping up, buttressing, sustaining, supporting.

solak, inclined to, liking.

soldadu, Port. a soldier.

solek, foppish; pĕsolek, a dandy.

solok, pĕsolok, a gift to be returned in kind—e.g. a contribution to a feast to which one is to be invited.

som, I. a ship of an obsolete type. II. akar som, a Chinese strengthening medicine. III. tulang som, a pubic-bone.

sombong, arrogance; self-assertion; overbearing manner.

sompek, jagged at the edge (through injury).

sompoh, carrying on the neck and shoulders.

sonak, the "thorns" on a "thornback" fish; the barb-like sting of a ray.

sondeh, a tree (payena leerii); gĕtah s., gutta obtained from this tree.

sondol, lowering the head (as a threatening bull); mĕnyondol, to lower the head for a charge.

sondong, a kind of shrimp-net used in Singapore.

songar, Jav. affectation in dress or manner.

songel, sticking out (as the cheek, when a quid of betel is in the mouth).

songgeng, = sungging.

songket, = sungkit.

songkok, a small white cap worn by devout Malays.

songkom, mĕnyongkom, to bury the face in a mother's lap (as a weeping child); to cuddle up against.

songkong, = sokong.

songsang, = sungsang.

songsong, making way against; s. harus, a name given to a shell (murex ternispina); mĕnyongsong, to make head against (used of an eagle flying against the wind).

sontok, = suntok.

sopak, a skin disease, a form of psoriasis.

sopan, dignified modesty; a self-contained but respectful demeanour.

sopi, ayer sopi, liqueur.

sopoh, mĕnyopoh, to carry pick-a-back.

sorak, cheering; cries of elation; bĕrsorak, to cheer.

sorang, = sa-orang.

sore, Jav. evening.

sorga, Skr. heaven; also shurga.

sorok, I. concealment by withdrawal; harimau mĕnyorokkan kuku, a tiger hiding its claws. II. sorok-sorok, an insect very destructive to padi.

sorong, pushing forward under; shoving forward under; a surreptitious offer of a bribe; a bribe; s. dayong, backing water; sorongkan, to push anything forward under cover.

sotoh, Ar. the flat roof of a house.

sotong, a cuttle-fish.

soyak, rending in twain; tearing from top to bottom.

soyat, = soyak.

su, younger; = bongsu [in certain expressions, pak su, mak su, etc.]

sua, pushing an object towards another—e.g. holding a fighting-cock and pushing him towards his rival; bulu s., the feathers on the neck of a fighting-cock; pagar s., the paling

separating two buffaloes which are being matched against one another.
suah, searching by artificial light.
suai, I. fitting, matching. II. Eng. *tali suai*, sway-ropes.
suaji, the breech of a flag.
suak, an indentation; a slight hollow; the parting of the hair.
suaka, Skr. a place of refuge, a lodging; *orang bĕrsuaka*, poor people; people compelled to lodge with others; dependents.
sual, = *soal*.
suam, lukewarm.
suami, Skr. husband (more respectful than *laki*); lord (in the sense of husband); *bĕrsuami*, to be married (of a woman); *bĕrsuamikan*, to be married to.
suang, ease, facility; lightly done; *sa-suang-suang*, with the greatest possible ease.
suap, a mouthful; putting in the mouth; feeding a child; (by metaphor) bribing; *sa-suap dua*, a mouthful or two; *makan s.*, to take bribes.
suar, a fire-signal; a torch or lantern used to convey a message.
suara, Skr. voice; vocal sound; *dĕngan s. yang lĕmah-lĕmbut*, in a gentle tone of voice.
suarga, = *shurga*.
suari, *bantal suari*, an ornamental pillow used in marriage ceremonies.
suasa, gold much alloyed with copper.
suat, whimsical, capricious.
suatu, one; = *sa-watu* [*watu* being the Javanese form of *batu*]; *sa-suatu*, each every.
subal, discreditable.
subam, dull (of metallic lustre).
suban, a splinter.
subang, a large ear-stud. [In some places this stud is worn by maidens only and is discarded on marriage.]
subhana, Ar. praised be.
suboh, Ar. dawn; *sĕmbah-yang s.*, early morning service.

subur, rapid and healthy growth (of plants).
suchi, Skr. cleanliness, purity; pure, clean; *s. hati*, a heart free from malice or deceit; *Maha-suchi*, the All-pure; God.
suda, sharp-pointed bamboo splinters (used as caltrops).
sudah, Pers. completion, accomplishment; done, finished; *sa-tĕlah s.*, when it was finished; *sudahkan*, to complete, to finish off; *kĕsudahan*, the end of; *pĕnyudah*, the fulfilment of; the crowning of hope or desire; realisation, culmination.
sudang, = *sĕlodang*.
sudara, = *saudara*.
sudi, satisfied, contented, pleased, ready; approval; *jikalau s.*, if you like; *sudikan*, to like; to care for; to approve of.
sudip, a large rice-ladle.
sudu, a ladle; a coconut-shell spoon; the bill of a duck; *s. itek*, a duck's bill; *siput s.*, a shell (*haliotis* spp.); *tulang s. hati*, the xiphoid process.
sudut, a corner; an out-of-the-way nook.
suf, Ar. a cloth-fabric, camelot.
sufi, Ar. *ilmu sufi*, sufiism, mysticism.
suga, = *soga*.
sugar, I. *mĕnyugar*, to pass the fingers through the hair. II. Eng. sugar.
sugi, rubbing the point of a stick against anything; putting out a torch by rubbing off the burning portions; cleaning the teeth in the Malay way.
sugun, forcing down with violence; seizing the hair or throat and so forcing down an adversary.
suhun, *suhunan*, a Javanese royal title; also *susuhunan* and *susunan*.
suir, *lang suir*, a vampire.
suja, = *soja*.
sujana, = *saujana*.
suji, embroidery; fancy needlework.
sujud, Ar. bowing in prayer.

suka, Skr. liking, pleasure, enjoyment; *s. hati*, id.; *s. chita*, joy, delight; *s. raya*, uproarious delight; *s. hati tuan*, as you please; *sukaï*, to take pleasure in; to like; *sukakan*, id.; *kĕsukaan*, pleasure, enjoyment.

sukachita, see *suka*.

sukar, difficult, arduous; *s. di-chari*, hard to find; *s. bĕroleh dia*, id.

sukat, I. the measurement of area or capacity; mensuration. II. provided that, supposing that, if, when; *sukat ayer mĕnjadi batu*, if (or when) water turns into stone—i.e. never.

suku, a leg or limb; a quarter; a section; a tribe or division of the people; *s. jam*, a quarter of an hour; *rial dan s.*, dollars and quarter-dollars.

sukun, the bread fruit (*artocarpus incisa*).

sukur, = *shukur*.

sula, Skr. a pointed stick; an impaling-post; spitting, impaling; *sulakan*, to impale; to roast on a spit; *tĕrsula*, impaled; *tĕri-sula*, a trident.

sulah, bald, bare-headed; *lada s.*, white pepper.

sulalat, Ar. extraction, descent, origin; *s. us-salatin*, the ancestry of our kings—a Malay traditional history.

sulam, embroidery; *bĕrsulam*, embroidered.

sulang, I. joining in a drink; inviting another person to drink with you; *minum bĕrsulang-sulangan*, exchanging drinks time after time. II. sooty deposit.

sulbi, Ar. *tulang sulbi*, the coccyx.

suldi, Ar. Adam's-apple (in the throat).

suleh, a plant (*tittius*).

suli, a grandson or great-grandson; a descendant.

suling, a generic name for native flageolets.

sulit, obscure, out of the way, little known, secluded.

suliwatang, a Bugis title.

suloh, a torch; a spy; a scout.

sulong, senior, eldest, first in age; *anak s.*, eldest son; *gigi s.*, the four front teeth.

sultan, Ar. sultan; *s. al-muazam*, the august sultan—i.e. the Sultan of Turkey.

sulur, sticking up conspicuously; *s. tiang*, topmast.

suma, *daun suma*, a medicinal plant (unidentified).

sumbang, improper, revolting, incestuous; *s. di-mata*, an eye-sore; *anak s.*, a child of incest.

sumbar, challenging, reproaching, reviling.

sumbat, corking up; stopping an orifice; *sumbatkan*, to plug; to put a stopper into anything; to put cotton-wool into the ears.

sumbi, replacing an injured part; putting new planks into a boat; patching.

sumbing, notched, dented, jagged; *gĕlak s.*, a sickly laugh.

sumbu, I. a wick; a fuse; a slow match; *s. pĕlita*, the wick of a lamp. II. the horn of a rhinoceros.

sumbul, = *chĕmbul*.

sumpah, swearing, reviling, cursing; the taking of an oath; *bĕrsumpah*, to take an oath; *mĕmbĕri sumpah*, to administer the oath; *sumpah-sumpah*, a name given to the Malay "chameleons" (*calotes versicolor* and *calotes cristatellus*).

sumpil, stopping up; corking up; = *sumbat*.

sumpit, the use of a blowpipe; shooting with a blowpipe; *sumpitan*, a blowpipe; *sumpitkan*, to kill (anything) with the blowpipe; *mĕnyumpit*, to use the blowpipe; *sumpit-sumpit*, (1) the well-known shooting fish (*toxotes jaculator*), (2) a small *mĕngkuang* bag.

sumsum, Jav. marrow, pith.

sumur, Jav. a well.

sunan, = *suhunan*.

sunat, Ar. tradition, practice; the traditional law of the Prophet; circumcision; *tukang s.*, a circumciser; *sunatkan*, to circumcise.

sundal, a harlot; a common prostitute.

sundang, a broad short sword with a full-sized handle.

sundus, Pers. brocade.

sungai, a river; a flowing stream of some size; *anak s.*, a rivulet; *pĕrgi ka-s.*, a polite way of describing obedience to a call of nature.

sungga, Jav. a spur; a goad.

sungging, picturing flowers or ornamental patterns in paint (such as gold paint), etc.

sunggit, Jav. an attendant on a princess.

sunggoh, reality; genuine, true, real; *s. hati*, heartiness, strenuousness; *sunggoh-pun*, although; *sunggoh-sunggoh*, really, genuinely; *sa-sunggoh-nya*, in all truth; in all reality; *sunggoh-sunggohi*, to strive vigorously or strenuously.

sungkal, to turn up (as a ploughshare turns up the earth); *s. bajak*, a ploughshare.

sungkap, torn apart; pulled loose; *kuku tĕrsungkap*, a finger-nail or toe-nail torn from the quick.

sungkit, *kain sungkit*, silk cloth shot with gold.

sungkup, covering under a hollow bowl or vessel.

sungkur, rooting up; ladling up; scooping up; shovelling up; a net of triangular shape pushed through mud and water so as to catch shrimps; *s. sangkar*, sprawling.

sungsang, reversal; turning upside down.

sungu, Jav. horn.

sungut, I. murmuring, grumbling; *bĕrsungut*, to murmur. II. the antennæ.

sunjam, head downwards; *tĕrsunjam*, hung up by the heels.

sunteh, chipping off.

sunti, I. a sort of pickle made of the *bĕlimbing*. II. *anak dara sunti*, a very young maiden.

sunting, to wear stuck behind the ear (as flowers are occasionally worn); *suntingkan*, to wear in the hair; to "crop the flower in season."

suntok, insufficiency of time; failure through insufficiency; *waktu s.*, time is up; *orang tua s.*, an old man who still apes young ways.

sunyi, lonely, solitary, desolately quiet, deserted; *sunyi-lah labohan Mĕlaka*, the Malacca roadstead was deserted.

sup, (Dutch) soup, broth.

supai, = *sipahi*.

sura, I. Skr. hero; man of men. II. Ar. *bulan Sura*, a name given to the month *Muharram*.

surah, Ar. a subdivision or chapter of the *Kuran*.

surai, the combing or dressing of the hair; the hair itself (when speaking of a prince or princess).

suralaya, Skr. the abode of the gods; the Hindu Olympus.

suram, darkness, gloom, cloudiness; the obscuring of the brightness of the sun or of the beauty of the countenance.

surat, a writing of any sort; a letter; *isi s.*, the contents of a letter or document; *muka s.*, the written page; *s. kiriman*, a letter; an epistle; *s. mĕnĕgah*, a patent; *s. pĕlĕkat*, a poster; *s. tanda tangan*, a signed acknowledgment; (usually) an I.O.U.; *s. wakil*, a power of attorney; *s. wasiat*, a will; *suratkan*, to cause to be written; *tĕrsurat*, written.

surau, a private mosque in contradistinction to a mosque of general assembly.

suraya, Skr. the sun.

surdi, = *sĕrodi*.

sureh, *s.-s.*, (Perak) descent, lineage.

surga, = *shurga*.

suri, Skr. a queen; royal; = *pĕrmaisuri*; *rama aji ibu suri*, royal father and queenly mother; the parents of a prince.

surmah, Pers. a collyrium made of antimony.

suroh, ordering; giving instructions; *surohan*, an order, a command; an orderly; *suroh-surohan*, messengers; *surohkan*, to order; to instruct.

surut, the ebbing of the tide; *ayer s.*, the ebb-tide.

susah, trouble; difficulty; uneasiness; disquiet; *s. hati*, mental trouble; *susahkan*, to vex, to annoy; *kĕsusahan*, trouble; affliction.

susoh, the (natural) spur of a fighting-cock.

susok, I. to found (a city); *mĕnyusok*, id. II. manner, bearing, mean; *s. jijak*, id. III. a loop; a button-hole. IV. = *chuchok*.

susu, the breast; milk; *ayer s.*, milk; *susui*, to suckle; *mĕnyusu*, to be suckled; *s. bundar*, firm hemispherical breasts; *s. kopek* or *s. lanjut*, pendulous breasts; *s. rimau*, the sclerotium or resting-place of a fungus; *dapur s.*, the outer portion of the breast; *hujong s.*, the nipple generally; the extremity; *puting s.*, the nipple proper; *tampok s.*, the nipple and the dark circle round it.

susuhunan, = *suhunan*.

susul, pursuing; following up.

susun, laying in rows one above the other; *bĕrsusun-susun*, in layers.

susunan, = *suhunan*.

susup, position under; resting or passing or pushing under; *susupkan* or *mĕnyusupkan*, to place under; to insert under.

susur, skirting; edging past; the shirts, fringe or edge of anything; *mĕnyusur*, to skirt; to hug (the shore); to edge past.

susut, shrinking; diminution in size; attenuation; thinning down.

sutĕra, Skr. silk; *kain sutĕra*, a silk *sarong*; *payong sutĕra*, a silk umbrella.

T

taajub, Ar. to wonder.

taala, Ar. most high; *Allah t.*, God Most High.

taalek, I. to feed or fatten animals. II. Ar. to be enamoured of; to be taken with.

taalok, Ar. subdued; *mĕnaalokkan*, to bring into subjection.

taat, Ar. obedience, submission (to God's will).

tabah, a hand's-breadth.

tabak, Ar. a box, a casket; a present of food taken away by a departing guest.

tabal, Ar. a kettledrum used at the installation of a ruler; to instal; *bĕrtabal*, to ascend the throne; to be crowned (of a ruler).

taban, *gĕtah taban*, gutta percha; *pokok t.*, the gutta percha tree (*dichopsis gutta*).

tabaraka, Ar. may (he) be blessed.

tabek, greeting, salutation; *mĕmbĕri t.*, to greet; to courteously salute or recognise; *minta t.*, to respectfully excuse oneself; to apologise in advance for any unintentional breach of etiquette.

tabiat, Ar. character, nature.

tabib, Ar. a physician.

tabir, I. Ar. the interpretation or elucidation (of dreams). II. curtains against a wall; hangings; drapery.

taboh, I. a long cylindrical drum; *tabohkan*, to beat this drum. II. *tabohan*, = *tĕbuan*.

tabong, a cylindrical vessel of bamboo; a quiver; *t. bunga*, a shrub (*ixora pendula*).

tabur, I. the scattering of seed or flowers; sowing; dispersing; *taburkan* or *mĕnaburkan*, to sow; *bĕrtaburan*, scattered over. II. a square-sail.

tabut, Ar. the ark of the covenant; (Penang) a Hindu processional emblem.

tada, = *tiada*.

tadah, intercepting or catching a falling object; *tadahkan tangan*, to stretch out the arms with the palms of the hands turned upwards.

tadbir, Ar. government.

tadi, lately; just a moment ago; immediately past; *baharu t.*, a moment ago; *sa-malam t.*, this last night; *tĕrsĕbut di-atas t.*, aforesaid; also *tahadi*.

tadong, knocking the foot against anything; stumbling up against.

tafsir, Ar. commentary (on the Kuran).

tagak, putting off, procrastination.

tagan, the stakes in a sweep; the "pool."

tagar, a peal of thunder.

tageh, dunning, pressing, importuning; worrying; *kĕtageh*, the craving caused by constant indulgence in tobacco, opium or alcohol.

tah, a suffix expressing interrogation or doubt; = *ĕntah*; *ini-tah gambaran-nya*, is this his portrait?

tahadi, recently; just before this; see *tadi*.

tahan, I. holding out against, resisting, sustaining; *tahani* or *mĕnahani*, to restrain or resist; to bear up against; to stand (anything). II. setting (traps); *t. lukah*, to set a fish-trap.

tahana, greatness, majesty; *bĕrtahana*, to sit in majesty; to be present (of a prince).

tahar, to keep on a course in spite of unfavourable winds.

tahi, filth, mucus, dirt, ordure, feculence, lees, grounds; *t. angin*, light fleecy clouds; words of little account; windy talk; *t. ayer*, scum on water; *t. bĕsi*, rust; *t. chandu*, opium dross; *t. gĕrgaji*, sawdust; *t. harus*, driftwood; *t. kĕtam*, shavings; *t. lalat*, a freckle, a mole; *t. mata*, mucus from the eye; *t. minyak*, refuse in making oil; *t. panas*, prickly heat; *t. tĕlinga*, wax in the ear; *ular t. kĕrbau*, a snake (*coluber radiatus*).

tahil, a tael; 1⅓ oz.

tahu, knowing, knowledge; *bĕri t.*, to inform; *dĕngan sa-tahu-ku*, with my knowledge; *kĕtahuan*, knowledge, sense, capacity for understanding; *kĕtahuï*, or *mĕngĕtahuï*, to know.

tahun, year; *t. baharu*, the new year; *bĕrtahun-tahun*, for years, chronic.

taj, Ar. crown, diadem.

tajak, a sort of scythe—used for cutting down long grass, weeds, etc., in the rice-fields.

tajam, sharpness; sharp; *akal-nya t.*, he was sharp mentally; *tajamkan*, to sharpen.

tajang, I. stamping; thrusting down the heel. II. *kĕris tajang*, a straight-bladed Patani *kĕris*.

tajau, a large earthenware jar.

taji, the artificial spur of a fighting-cock; *mĕmbulang t.*, to fasten the spurs on.

tajok, an aigrette; a tuft; a sheath (with flowers in it) worn in the hair; *t. makota*, the aigrette or apex of a crown.

tajur, running out into the sea; *pĕnajur*, a row of fishing-stakes to drive fish into a trap.

tajwid, Ar. grammatical accuracy; writing (Arabic) correctly.

takak, *takok-takak*, notched—v. *takok*. II. *kain bĕrtakak*, a sarong made up of two pieces.

takal, Eng. a pulley; a block.

takan, = *ta'-akan*.

takar, an earthenware vessel with a narrow neck.

takat, as far as; up to; *t. pinggang*, up to the waist; *t. lutut*, up to the knee.

takbir, Ar. to bury.

takdir, Ar. will, decree; the decree of providence.

takek, a cleft; a slight cut—such as that made in a tree-trunk by a single blow with a chopper.

takhta, Pers. a throne.

takok, a notch; a sort of step created by cutting out a piece from the outer portion of a tree-trunk; *t. takak*, notched, jagged; *kĕpala pĕnakok*, the cleft at the top of a screw.

takong, keeping anything for fermentation; *minyak t.*, crude oil.

taksir, I. Ar. negligence, carelessness. II. (Dutch) estimate, valuation, assessment.

takut, fear; *takuti*, to fear; *takutkan*, to frighten; *kĕtakutan*, panic, fright; *pĕnakut*, a coward; timorous.

takwim, Ar. calendar; almanac.

tala, I. harmonious response; *bĕrtala-tala*, taking up a strain in turn. II. a padlock.

talai, negligence; = *lalai*.

talak, divorce; *tiga t.*, the full divorce; the triple divorce.

talam, a tray or platter.

talan, a shrub (*saraca* sp.)

talang, I. a fish (*chorenemus* sp.) II. *bujang talang*, a bachelor or childless widower; a man "without encumbrances."

talar, permitting, letting, allowing; = *biar*.

tali, I. cord, rope; anything of a cord-like appearance; *t. ayer*, a runnel; *t. harus*, the thin line of drift-wood marking the flow of a current; *t. kulit*, a strap; *t. pinggang*, a girdle; a waistband; *t. pusat*, the umbilical cord; *t. tĕmali*, cordage. II. a money value—about 7½ cents.

talkin, Ar. a prayer or formula recited at a burial.

talu, *bĕrtalu-talu*, continuous, uninterrupted, in unbroken succession.

talun, echoing back.

tama', Ar. covetousness; greed.

tamah, affability.

taman, a garden; a pleasure-ground.

tamar, Ar. *tamar hindi*, tamarind.

tamasha, = *tĕrmasa*.

tamat, Ar. end; termination; "finis."

tambah, increase by repetition or by continuation; *nasi t.*, a second helping of rice; *tambahan pula*, again; furthermore; *tambahkan* or *mĕnambahkan*, to increase; *pĕnambahan*, an addition, an appendix.

tambak, banking; filling; levelling up; *jalan t.*, a causeway; a road raised above the level of the surrounding fields.

tamban, a generic name given to a number of sardine-like fish.

tambang, I. ferrying for money; a ferry-boat; *tambangan*, a regular trip. II. keeping medicine overnight so as (according to Malay belief) to improve its efficacy.

tambat, fastening up; tying up; tethering; *tambati*, *tambatkan*, or *mĕnambatkan*, to tie up; *tĕrtambat*, tethered up (of an animal).

tambi, Tam. a messenger; a peon; an orderly.

tambul, I. refreshments (especially drinks). II. *bĕrtambul*, to act; *pĕnambul*, an actor; a juggler.

tambun, plump, sleek.

tambur, Eur. a drum.

taming, Jav. a small buckler used by heroes of romance.

tampak, visibility; being visible; *tampak-nya sa-rupa mas*, it looks like gold.

tampal, plastering, pasting, posting up; *tampalkan*, to stick on; to paste on.

tampan, I. handsome, looking well, suitable, befitting; *tiada sa-tampan*, it does not seem right or look well; *tampan-tampan* or *tětampan*, a sort of shoulder-cloth worn by Malays on ceremonial occasions. II. stopping the progress of a moving body (as a boy stops a football with the side of his foot).

tampang, I. flat; *pěnampang*, the flat side of anything. II. a tin token or medium of exchange. III. cutting and tying up (as the umbilical cord is severed). IV. a tree (*artocarpus gomeziana*); *t. burong*, id. (*ficus vasculosa*).

tampar, slapping; a slap; *tampari*, to slap; *tamparan*, the giving of a slap.

tampas, I. lopping off (small prominences). II. blowing in (of wind entering a house).

tampek, fault-finding; censure.

tampi, winnowing by tossing up and down on a winnowing sieve; *měnampi*, to winnow; *měnampi dada*, the heaving of the breasts; *to' kětampi*, an owl (*ketupa javanensis*).

tampil, to come forward; to come out in front.

tampin, a receptacle for sago; *sagu t.*, pearl sago.

tampok, the point of junction of stalk and fruit; the little bit of stalk usually left on plucked fruit; the central point of converging lines; *t. susu*, the teat and the dark circle round it; *ikan tampok-tampok*, a fish (*gerres oblongus*).

tampong, I. patching; piebald; *badak t.*, a tapir. II. to catch a falling object (as a cricket-ball is caught); *tahan t.*, id.

tamsil, Ar. likeness, example, metaphor.

tamu, to entertain a guest—cf. *jamu*.

tan, Hind. *tan kuda*, a stable.

tanah, earth, ground, land; a country; *t. ayer*, territories; *t. liat*, clay;
t. těnggala, arable land; *tupai t.*, a small animal (*tamias lysteri*); *urat t.*, certain snakes (*typhlops* spp.)

tanak, the boiling of rice; *běrtanak*, to cook (rice); *sa-pětanak nasi*, the time it takes for rice to boil—a primitive measure of time.

tanam, burying in the ground; planting; *t. tanaman*, things planted; agricultural growths; *tanamkan*, to plant.

tanda, I. sign, token, mark, emblem; *t. bachaan*, the vowel points; *t. tangan*, a signature; *ikan tanda-tanda*, a fish (*lutianus sillaoo*). II. *pěrtanda*, an executioner.

tandak, dancing; *běrtandak*, to dance.

tandan, a cluster, a bunch; the main stalk of a cluster or bunch of fruit.

tandang, I. wandering in search; travelling; *orang t. desa*, a vagrant. II. *běrtandang*, to visit.

tandas, a privy.

tandil, Tam. the head of a gang of coolies; a petty officer—subordinate to the serang on a ship.

tanding, a subdivision; a lot; *sa-t.*, equality in size.

tandok, horn (of two-horned animals); goring, butting; *t.-t.*, a creeper (*strophanthus dichotomus*); *běrtandok*, horned; *měnandok*, to butt.

tandu, a hammock-litter.

tandun, *zaman tandun*, the immemorial past.

tandur, I. Jav. to plant. II. holding up by means of a string; *tali t.*, a string for pulling up chicks.

tang, an abbreviation for *těntang*.

tangan, hand; forearm and hand; handle; sleeve; possession; *t. baju*, sleeve; *t. kěmudi*, the handle of a rudder; *ibu t.*, thumb; *sapu t.*, handkerchief; *tanda t.*, signature; *tapak t.*, palm.

tangas, fumigation; steaming; heating.

tangga, ladder, staircase; *anak t.*, a step; a rung of a ladder; *rumah t.*, a homestead; *bĕrtangga-tangga*, at fifth or sixth-hand.

tanggah, *pĕnanggah* or *pĕnanggahan*, a kitchen in a royal palace.

tanggal, loosening; spontaneous severance or fall; *tanggalkan*, to remove; to take off; *mĕnanggalkan*, id.; *pĕnanggalan*, an evil spirit; a flying head and viscera.

tanggam, a groove at the end of a beam; *tĕrtanggam*, bound together.

tanggang, propping up, buttressing; = *sagang*.

tanggar, undertaking a duty successfully; "putting through" work; managing to get things done.

tanggi, = *tangki*.

tanggoh, putting off, postponing; *bĕrtanggoh*, to postpone.

tanggok, a landing-basket used by fishermen.

tanggong, supporting; bearing up under; standing security for; *tanggongkan*, to support a burden; *tĕrtanggong*, to be borne; supportable; sustained.

tanggul, the bobbing of a boat's bows—cf. *anggul*.

tangis, weeping; *tangisi*, to weep; to shed tears; *mĕnangis*, id.; *tangiskan*, to mourn for anyone; *pĕmĕnangis*; a mourner; *tulang rimau mĕnangis*, the manubrium.

tangkai, stalk, haulm, stem; *t. hati*, a term of endearment.

tangkal, protective (of a spell or charm); *azimat tangkal sawan kanak-kanak*, a talisman against convulsions.

tangkap, seizure, capture, arrest, gripping, clasping; *tangkapan*, toils, captivity, arrest; *mĕnangkap*, to seize, to grip, to capture; *tĕrtangkap*, captured.

tangkas, agility, nimbleness.

tangki, Eur. the water-tanks on a ship.

tangkil, superposition; sticking one tenuous object (e.g. paper) on another.

tangkis, parrying, warding off, guarding; *mĕnangkis*, to guard, to parry; *tangkiskan*, to intercept (a blow); to ward off.

tangkul, a name given to ground-nets, or nets and screens which catch fish by being pulled up with a winch; *pukat t.*, a wide ground-net [the sides of which are raised up when fish are over the net, thus preventing their escape].

tangkup, capture by dropping a concave object over anything.

tanglong, Ch. a Chinese lantern.

tangsi, I. Ch. a strong gut used in fishing-lines. II. barracks; the canteen.

tanjak, projecting up; sticking up; *bĕrtanjak kaki*, standing on tiptoe.

tanjong, a cape, a promontory, a headland.

tanju, a bracket-lamp.

tanjul, a sort of fishing-rod with a noose instead of a hook at the end.

tanti, wait a moment—cf. *nanti*.

tanya, enquiry, questioning; *bĕrtanya*, to ask a question; *bĕrtanyakan*, to enquire about.

tapa, asceticism; austerities undergone by hermits; *bĕrbuat t.*, to practise these austerities; *bĕrtapa*, id.; *pĕrtapa*, austere, ascetic; *ikan tapa*, a large fish (unidentified).

tapai, a preparation of steamed *pulut* rice fermented with native yeast; *arak t.*, a native spirit made from this preparation.

tapak, the palm (of the hand); the sole (of the foot); *sa-tapak*, a step; *bĕkas t. gajah*, an elephant's footprints; *t. itek*, a herb (*floscopa scandens*); *t. kaki*, the sole of the foot; *t. Sulaiman*, the seal of Solomon; the pentacle; the five-pointed star-fish.

tapeh, tying up the *sarong* in the way Malay women fasten it up; *sĕluar t.*, drawers worn by Javanese.

tapi, = *tĕtapi*.

tapis, I. filtration; passing a liquid through cloth; *sa-tapis*, a generation; *tapiskan*, to filter (water). II. the Ceylon iron-wood (*messua ferrea*).

tapok, a scab, a scar, a pock-mark, the remains of the pistil in a fruit—cf. *tampok*.

tara, equality of altitude; evenness; parity; *sa-tara*, on a level with; *tiada tara-nya*, peerless; *pĕnara bukit*, the ridge of a range of hills.

tarah, rough-hewing; *mĕnarah*, to rough-hew.

taram, gloomy, overcast (of the sky).

tarang, *pĕtarangan*, a hen's nesting-place.

tarbil, a pellet-bow.

tarek, drawing to or after oneself; pulling; *mĕnarek* or *mĕnarekkan*, to draw; to pull; to drag; to draw in (a long breath) or prolong (a note in singing).

tari, dancing (by swaying the arms and body); *mĕnari*, to dance.

tarikh, Ar. date; era; period of time; *pada t. itu*, at that time; *bĕrtarikh*, dated.

taring, the projecting and visible tusk of a wild-boar; *misai bĕrtaring*, a turned-up moustache.

taris, fastening, tying up, = *ikat*.

taroh, depositing; receiving or placing in a safe place; staking; *bĕrtaroh*, to stake; *mĕnaroh*, to retain or preserve; to keep; to harbour; *pĕtarohkan*, to entrust or confide.

tarok, a shoot; a young sprout.

tarong, (onom.) a deep booming sound.

taru, *bĕrtaru*, to sound (of the *nafiri*).

tarum, the indigo plant (*indigofera tinctoria*).

tas, a tree (*kurrimia panniculata*) the wood of which is believed to frighten away tigers.

tasak, the stopping of bleeding; *mĕnasak*, to stop bleeding.

tasbeh, Ar. a rosary; *buah t.*, prayer-beads.

tasek, a lake, a mere; (rarely) the sea; *t. pauh janggi*, the great ocean; *tasek-tasek*, a plant (*adenosma capitatum*).

tashdid, Ar. the diacritical mark signifying that the letter over which it is placed is doubled.

tashrih, Ar. *ilmu tashrih*, the science of anatomy.

tatah, inlaying, embedding, sticking into; *bĕrtatahkan ratna mutu manikam*, studded with gems.

tatal, a shaving.

tatang, carrying on the upturned palm of the hand, or any similar flat or slightly concave surface; carrying with extreme care; cherishing.

tatap, close visual examination (such as a watchmaker gives to the works of a watch); *mĕnatap*, to examine; to watch; to keep a look-out.

tateh, the stumbling walk of a very young child; *bĕrtateh*, to toddle along.

tatkala, Skr. the time when; at the time when; *pada t. itu*, at that time; *t. ia lagi muda*, while he was still a child.

taubat, Ar. repentance; giving up (an evil practice); also *tobat*.

tauchang, Ch. a Chinese queue; a pig-tail.

tauge, Ch. bean sprouts.

tauhid, Ar. the doctrine of the unity of God.

tauke, Ch. a "towkay," an employer of labour.

taul, securing an oar by attaching it with cord to the gunwale.

taulan, Tam. friend, comrade.

taun, Ar. a murrain, an epidemic.

Taurit, Ar. the Pentateuch; the books of Moses.

taut, a night-line with a rod.

tawa, *tĕrtawa*, laughing, laughter.

tawak, *tawak-tawak*, a small unmelodious gong or sounding-board used to summon people to a meeting.

tawakkul, Ar. surrender to God's will; trust in God.

tawan, capture; enslavement; subduing; *tawanan*, a captive; *mĕnawan* or *mĕnawankan*, to subdue, to take captive; *tĕrtawan*, taken prisoner; led captive.

tawar, I. tastelessness; absence of flavour or distinctive characteristic; *ayer t.*, fresh water (as distinct from salt); *t. hati*, nausea; *lauk yang t.*, insipid or tasteless food; *tĕpong t.*, rice-flour and water used as a cooling or healing paste for the skin; *tawari* or *mĕnawari*, to meet a spell with a countercharm; to futilise; *pĕnawar*, an antidote; a protective talisman. II. bargaining; *t. mĕnawar*, haggling over a price.

tawas, alum.

tĕbah, beating a flat surface—e.g. beating the breasts or beating a carpet.

tĕbak, a heavy cutting or chopping blow; *sa-t.*, a piece (of wood) lopped off from a log.

tĕbal, thick (of cloth, paper, planking, etc.); *muka t.*, brazen-faced; *t. hati*, hard-hearted.

teban, stakes in gambling; money deposited.

tĕbang, felling heavy timber; *mĕnĕbang*, to fell.

tebar, scattering, sowing, or spreading by a sweeping round-arm motion; *t. jala*, to throw a casting-net; *mĕnebar*, to scatter.

tĕbas, felling small scrub, clearing undergrowth—cf. *tĕbang*.

tĕbat, damming; barring; barricading; closing to traffic.

tebeng, spread out; expanded (as a *sarong* or piece of embroidery is spread out to show the pattern).

tĕbĕrau, a name given to several large grasses (especially *sacharum arundinaceum*, *sacharum ridleyi* and *thysanoloena acarifera*).

tĕbing, a bank by a cutting; the bank of a river or canal.

tĕbok, boring; making a cylindrical hole in anything; sinking a shaft or well.

tebok, a heavy thrust.

tĕbu, sugar-cane; *ular katang t.*, the banded karait (*bungarus fasciatus*).

tĕbuan, a hornet.

tĕbus, redemption; release from mortgage or pawn; the purchase of a slave from someone else; *mĕnĕbus*, to redeem.

techi, = *tezi*.

tĕdas, a raised ring round a pillar.

tĕdoh, the stilling of storm and rain; *bĕrtĕdoh*, to take shelter.

tĕdong, *ular tĕdong*, a generic name given to hooded snakes and to some snakes resembling them; *ular t. sĕndok*, the cobra (*naia tripudians*); *ular t. sĕlar* or *ular t. abu*, the hamadryad (*naia bungarus*); *ular t. matahari*, a small brilliantly coloured snake (*doliophis bivirgatus*); *ular t. liar*, the snake *zamenis korros*.

tĕfĕkur, absent-minded; plunged in meditation.

tĕgah, hindrance, prohibition; *tĕgahkan* or *mĕnĕgahkan*, to prohibit.

tĕgak, stiffly erect; bolt upright; also *chĕgak*.

tĕgal, *tĕgal apa*, why; = *karna apa*.

tĕgang, taut; fully outstretched; at its full span.

tĕgap, = *tĕgak*.

tĕgar, stiff, unyielding, obstinate, inflexible; *t. hati*, stiff-necked.

tĕgarun, a silk *kain lĕpas*.

tĕgoh, firm; fast; tight (of a knot); rigidly adhered to (of a promise); *di-ikat-nya tĕgoh-tĕgoh*, he tied it very tightly.

tĕgok, gulping; a mouthful; *sa-tĕgok*, a mouthful; as much as one can gulp down.

tĕgun, an expectant attitude.

tĕgur, address, greeting, salutation; *t. sapa*, courtesy; *tĕguri*, to address.

teh, I. Ch. tea; *daun t.*, tea (in leaf form); *ayer t.*, tea (prepared for

drinking). II. an abbreviation for *puteh* as a proper name.
teja, Skr. glowing rain-clouds.
teji, Pers. *kuda teji*, a Pegasus; a winged steed; also *tezi*.
tĕka, Skr. *tĕka-tĕki*, riddles; conundrums; *tĕkaan*, guess-work.
tĕkak, I. *anak tĕkak*, the uvula. II. obstinacy. III. = *tĕka*.
tĕkan, pressure with the flat of the hand or leg; pressure to test strength or to obtain a squeeze or impression of an old inscription or mould—cf. *tĕkap*.
tĕkang, a thwart; a cross-beam to resist pressure at its extremities and not to support a weight resting on it.
tĕkap, resting the flat of the hand on anything—e.g. closing a child's mouth in jest to prevent him speaking—cf. *tĕkan*.
tĕkat, embroidery; *bĕrtĕkat mas*, embroidered in gold.
tĕkĕbur, Ar. pride; arrogance; haughtiness.
tĕkek, I. a drug used in dyeing. II. = *to'kek*.
tĕki, *tĕka-tĕki* or *kĕtĕki*, riddle, conundrum.
tĕkoh, (Kedah) period; = *masa*; *t. mana*, when?
tĕkua, *baju tĕkua*, a long sleeveless jacket worn by women.
tĕkukur, the little Malay grounddove (*geopelia striata*); *padang t.*, a plain abandoned to doves, a desolate place; *burong sewah tĕkukur*, the Indian koel (*eudynamis honorata*); *ular sawa tĕkukur*, a name given to a snake (*coluber melanurus*).
tĕkun, assiduous attention; *bĕrtĕkun mĕngaji*, to study attentively or assiduously.
tĕkup, covering with the hand; catching by covering with the hand.
tĕla, a passage in a Malay house connecting the kitchen with the main building.
tela, the pan of a firearm.

tĕladan, model; example; a copy to follow.
tĕlaga, Skr. a well, tank, or basin of water; a small mere.
tĕlah, did, was—a word giving a preterite meaning to the passage in which it occurs; *maka tĕlah di-lihat itu*, when that was seen; when he saw that; *sa-tĕlah*, being past or over; after.
tĕlampong, drift-wood; a float.
tĕlan, swallowing; *mĕnĕlan*, to swallow; *pĕrtĕlan*, a draught.
tĕlang, long patches (as a pattern); *buloh t.*, a bamboo (*gigantochloa* spp.)
tĕlangkai, a marriage-broker.
tĕlanjang, naked, stripped; *t. bulat*, stark-naked; *t. bugil*, id.; *bĕrtĕlanjang*, in a state of nudity; bare.
tĕlanjur, projecting; stretching out.
tĕlantar, stretched; prone; lying at full length.
tĕlap, penetration, incision, wounding.
tĕlapakan, *duli tĕlapakan*, a royal title; = *duli*, *kaus*, etc.
tĕlatah, manners, behaviour, ways.
tĕlau, patchy (of colouring or of light).
tĕledur, idler, sluggard—a term of reproach.
tĕlĕkan, *bĕrtĕlĕkan*, to rest one's head on one's arms.
tĕlĕkong, a praying-veil—used by Muhammadan women.
tĕlĕku, *bĕrtĕlĕku*, to lean on one's elbows.
tĕlĕmpap, *sa-tĕlĕmpap*, a hand'sbreadth.
tĕlĕnan, a cleaning-frame—used by a native copper-smith.
teleng, cocked on one's side (of the head).
tĕlĕpa, = *chĕlĕpa*.
tĕlĕpok, printing on cloth; geometric pattern generally; marquetry.
tĕlerang, *mas tĕlerang*, reef-gold; quartz outcrop.

tĕlinga, the ear; the handle of a vessel; *t. bĕdil*, the pan of a gun; *t. kĕra*, a plant (*henslowia lobbiana*); *anak t.*, the tympanum; *chuping t.*, the lobe of the ear; *daun t.*, the outer frame of the ear; *lobang t.*, the orifice of the ear; *ikan korek t. buaya*, a fish (*gastrotoceus biaculeatus*).

tĕlingkah, ways, behaviour, conduct —cf. *tingkah*.

tĕlipok, the lotus.

tĕlok, I. a bay, a bight, a curve, a bend; *t. rantau*, bends and reaches (in a river); territories generally. II. = *tĕlut*.

tĕlukup, = *tĕlangkup*—v. *langkup*.

tĕlunjok, the index-finger.

tĕlur, egg; fish-roe; *t. asin*, preserved eggs; *t. buaya*, a crocodile's egg; *t. tĕrubok*, a sambal made of the roe of the *tĕrubok* fish (*clupea kanagurta*).

telur, lisping; inability to articulate certain letters properly.

tĕlut, I. *bĕrtĕlut*, to kneel. II. = *lut*.

tĕmabur, besprinkled, scattered, dispersed; *bintang t.*, a constellation —cf. *tabur*.

tĕmali, *tali tĕmali*, cordage.

tĕman, attending on, waiting on, accompanying a companion of higher rank; *tĕmani*, to attend on.

tĕmandang, garb; get-up; general appearance.

tĕmaram, *tĕrang tĕmaram*, dusk, gloom, doubtful light.

tĕmarang, = *tĕmaram*.

tĕmbadau, a name given in Borneo to the small wild ox (*bos sondaicus*, and also in some dialects to *bos mindorensis*).

tĕmbaga, Skr. copper, bronze, brass; *t. kuning*, polished brass; *t. merah*, dull bronze; *t. puteh*, nickel; *t. suasa*, an alloy of gold and copper.

tembak, shooting, firing shots; *mĕnembak*, to fire shots.

tĕmbakau, Eur. tobacco; *t. jawa*, locally grown tobacco; *t. bĕlati*, tobacco imported from Europe.

tĕmbakul, a fresh-water fish (unidentified). [It has a very large head.]

tĕmban, puffy (of the cheeks).

tĕmbang, songs sung by dancing-girls.

tĕmbatu, the fruit of the *nipah* palm.

tembek, close (of a shot); nearly hitting; just missing; just avoiding.

tĕmbekar, = *tĕmbikar*.

tembel, a stye in the eye.

tĕmbĕlang, rottenness (in eggs).

tĕmbĕliong, = *puting bĕliong*.

tĕmbelok, an edible marine worm which eats into wood exposed to the action of salt water.

tĕmberang, the stays of a mast.

tĕmbĕreh, a fish (unidentified).

tĕmberek, = *tĕmbikar*.

tĕmbereng, a bit; a section; a curved or sharp edge; *t. tajam*, a sector.

tĕmbĕsu, a tree (*fagræa fragrans*).

tĕmbi, an outward elbow-thrust.

tĕmbikai, a water-melon (*citrullus edulis*).

tĕmbikar, sherds; broken pottery; the pieces of broken earthenware used by children in playing games—such as *tuju lobang*.

tĕmbilok, = *tĕmbelok*.

tĕmbiring, = *tĕmbereng*.

tĕmbok, perforated, rent, torn; rotten or hollow (of the teeth); eaten through.

tembok, I. a wall; *kaki t.*, the foundations of a wall. II. *mĕnembok*, to cool a liquid by stirring it or by pouring it from one vessel to another.

tĕmbolok, the crop of a bird.

tĕmbokor, = *bokor*.

tĕmbong, a long cudgel or quarter-staff.

tĕmbosa, folding up; *kueh lipat t.*, a sort of pie or patty.

tĕmbuku, a knob; a hard projection —cf. *buku*.

těmbun, = *tambun.*
těmbuni, the caul; *t. kěchil,* the placenta.
těmbus, broken through; perforated; holed.
těmbusu, = *těmběsu.*
těměnggong, a Malay dignitary of high rank.
těměnong, a fish (unidentified).
těmiang, a liana (*lettsomia peguensis*).
těmilang, a plant (*aglaia odoratissima*).
těmin, an iron joint or ferrule connecting the spear-head with its shaft; a ferrule at the base of a *kěris*-sheath.
těmoleh, a fish (unidentified).
těmpa, hammering, beating; working metal with the hammer—cf. *těmpawan.*
těmpah, engagement in advance; retaining services; *pěněmpah bidan,* the fee paid in advance to a midwife.
těmpala, the hop or spring of a fighting chevrotin.
tempang, chronic lameness; limping; halt.
těmpap, bringing down the flat of the hand forcibly on any surface.
těmpat, place, locality; *t. dawat,* an inkstand; *t. měngaji,* a school; *t. sireh,* a *sireh*-box.
těmpaus, *ikan těmpaus,* a whale; also *paus.*
těmpawan, hammered, beaten, wrought (of metals); *mas t.,* hammered gold—the pale yellow colour of which is a simile for a much admired tint of the complexion.
těmpayak, the larvæ or grubs of wasps, bees, etc.
těmpayan, a large earthenware jar used for storing water.
těmpek, cheering; cries of joy or of self-encouragement; the war-cries of an advancing army.
tempel, close approach, nearing; *jangan běrtempel děngan dia,* do not go close to him.

těmpělak, twitting a person with a blunder or mistake; teasing a man who has made a fool of himself.
těmpeleng, a box on the ears.
těmpěras, scattered about by leakage; spilt all about a place.
těmperas, a biting insect (unidentified).
těmpěrau, surly answering; an angry tone.
těmpiar, *běrtěmpiar* or *běrtěmpiaran,* fleeing in all directions; scattering.
těmpias, beating in (of rain).
těmpinah, the water balsam (*hydrocera triflora*).
těmpinis, a well-known hard-wood tree (*sloetia sideroxylon*).
těmpit, = *těmpek.*
tempo, Port. time (especially in the sense of further time for payment; extension of time).
těmpoh, a violent onslaught; charging; *měněmpoh,* to assault, to storm.
těmponek, the monkey-jack (*artocarpus rigida*).
tempong, I. throwing at a mark. II. pushing off at right angles; pushing off a boat from a bank.
těmporok, = *porok.*
těmporong, = *těmpurong.*
těmpoyak, a preserve made of salted durian.
těmpua, *burong těmpua,* the weaverbird; *ikan t.,* a fish (*barbus apogon*).
těmpui, a tree yielding a good fruit (*baccaurea malayana*).
těmpuling, a barbed fish-spear.
těmpunai, = *těmponek.*
těmpuras, = *těmpěras.*
těmpurong, a piece of coconut-shell; a bit of a skull; the body of a mandoline-like musical instrument; *t. lutut,* the knee-pan; *sisek t.,* the logger-head turtle (*thalassochelys caretta*).
těmu, I. meeting; coming together at the same spot; *běrtěmu,* to meet; *pěrtěmuan,* meeting; the act or place of meeting. II. a generic name

given to a number of wild gingers (*scitamineæ*); *t. kunchi*, a small cultivated ginger (*koempferia pandulata*); *t. kunyit*, turmeric (*curcuma longa*); *t. lawak*, a white turmeric, the zedoary (*curcuma zedoaria*).

těmuchut, = *chěmuchup*.

těmukus, = *kěmungkus*.

těmukut, = *lěmukut*.

těmurun, *turun těmurun*, descent, pedigree, lineage.

těmut, the throbbing of the fontanel.

těnang, calm, smooth, still (of the surface of the water).

těnar, an uproar; a row; a family row—such that neighbours can hear; "washing dirty linen in public."

tenda, Port. an awning.

těndang, kicking out; *běrtumbok běrtěndang*, with cuffs and kicks.

těndas, decapitation; cutting off a man's head.

teng, Ch. a Chinese lantern.

těngadah, looking upwards; to look up.

těngah, midst, middle; the half, the centre; in the middle of (in point of time); whilst; *t. hari*, midday; *t. naik*, half-grown; *t. měngajar*, while he was teaching; *sa-těngah*, a half; a fair quantity of; some.

těngar, a tree of the mangrove type —the bark of which is used for tanning (*ceriops candolleana*).

těngek, rancid (of oil).

těnggala, Skr. a plough; *tanah t.*, arable land; *padi t.*, seed-padi; *měněnggala*, to plough.

těnggalong, a civet-cat (*riverra tangalunga*); *pagar t.*, a name given to the railing round the stern-gallery of a native trading-ship.

těnggan, rolls of fat on the limbs or body.

tenggang, share and share alike; equally divided.

těnggara, south-east; *timur měněnggara*, E.S.E.; *sělatan měněnggara*, S.S.E.

těnggat, limit, extreme point; *dari těnggat ini ka-těnggat itu*, from this extremity to that.

těnggek, tossing rice up and down when winnowing.

tenggek, I. squatting, perching; sitting like a bird or ape. II. wearing the head-dress at a rakish slant.

těnggělam, to sink; to be submerged; to disappear from the surface; *matahari t.*, sunset; *suratannya timbul těnggělam*, the written characters on it were partly visible, partly effaced; *těnggělamkan*, to submerge.

těnggělong, a (Kedah) variant of *pěnanggalan*—v. *tanggal*.

tengger, = *tenggek*.

těnggiling, a sort of ant-eater or armadillo (*manis javanica*); *atap batu sisek t.*, tiled roofing.

těnggiri, a generic name for a number of fish which make excellent eating (*cybium* spp.)

těnggulong, a millipede which rolls itself up into a ball when touched; also *sěnygulong*.

těngkalak, a long narrow fish-trap with inturning spikes at the broader end, or else (*t. onak*) made of sticks with inturning thorns.

těngkalok, unripe but edible (of fruit).

těngkalong, = *těnggalong*.

těngkang, the space between the eyes.

těngkar, altercation, quarrelling; *běrtěngkar*, to quarrel, to have a squabble with; *těngkari*, to stir up a quarrel; *pěrtěngkaran*, an altercation.

těngkawang, a (Borneo) tree (*diplocnemia sebifera*); see *kawang*.

těngkelang, = *kelang*.

těngkerong, a fish (*sebastes stolizkæ*) —also known as *kerong-kerong*.

tengkes, unequal in size to its fellows; insufficiently developed.

těngking, snarling; an angry tone; *měněngking*, to speak angrily.

tengkoh, Ch. opium-dross prepared for re-smoking.
těngkolok, a head-wrapper; a kerchief starched and used as a headdress.
těngkorak, a skull; the cranium; *ringgit t.*, the 2½ guilder piece.
těngku, a royal title of the highest rank; a prince of the first grade.
těngkuyong, I. a shell (*cypræa* sp.) II. sago-bark.
tenglong, = *tanglong*.
těngoh, (onom.) *měněngoh*, to low (of oxen).
tengok, seeing, looking at, peering at; (in bazaar Malay) to see, = *lihat*.
těngsi, Ch. a soup-spoon.
těnok, a tapir (*tapirus malayanus*); also *badak těnok*—cf. also *badak tampong*.
těnong, abstraction absent-mindedness; *pětěnong*, a (Singapore) fortune-teller.
tenong, a flat-topped circular box of Javanese make.
těntang, opposite, facing; *běrtěntangan*, vis-à-vis; *měněntang*, to face (as a man faces an opponent).
tentang, a window (the hinges of which are at the top and not at the side).
těntawan, *akar těntawan*, a water-producing vine (*conocephalus suaveolens*).
těntu, certainty; definitiveness (as opposed to vagueness); indubitable, positive; *khabar yang t.*, reliable news.
těntuban, = *tuban-tuban*.
těnturun, a (Riau) equivalent for *běnturong*.
těnul, a tree (*myristica laurina*).
těnun, weaving; the art or process of weaving; *těnunan*, method or style of weaving; *salah těnunan*, a fault in the fabric; *běrtěnun*, to weave.
těpak, (onom.) a slight slap, pat or blow with the flat of the hand.

tepak, a rectangular (Palembang-made) box containing *sireh*-chewing requisities.
těpam, laying the palm of the hand on anything or passing the palm of the hand over anything (as a man in the dark trying to make out the character of some object).
těpas, I. brimful; full up. II. *ěmpat těpas dunia*, the four quarters of the earth; = *ěmpat pěnjuru alam*.
těpat, exactly; full; *barat t.*, due west; *matahari t.*, exactly noon; *pěnoh t.*, just exactly full; *běrtěpat*, to carry out in its exactness—e.g. *běrtěpat janji*, to carry out one's promise to the letter.
těpayan, = *těmpayan*.
tepeh, an edible salt-water shell-fish (unidentified).
teper, = *cheper*.
těpi, edge, border, margin, brink; *měněpi*, to step to the edge; to edge off; to step aside.
těpis, pushing aside; knocking aside; warding off; *těpiskan*, to strike or push anything aside; *těpis měněpis*, to fence.
těpok, a heavy blow with the flat of the hand; clapping, slapping, patting; *měněpok*, to slap; *měněpok dada*, to beat the breast; *t. lalat*, the flap which Malays use for catching grass-hoppers.
tepok, lameness due to a bad leg and not to amputation.
těpong, flour; meal; powdery substance; a generic name for a large number of cakes; *t. běras*, rice flour; *t. gandum*, wheaten flour; *t. tawar*, a powder used for cooling the skin.
těpu, full to the brim; full (of the sails).
těra, the royal seal, stamp or impression; *bělum běrtěra*, it is still unsealed; it lacks the official confirmation; *mětěraï*, to seal; to stamp an official mark on documents or on coins in the mint.

tĕrada, a (Batavia) equivalent of *tiada*.

tĕrajang, trampling under foot; stamping down the foot on anything; *tĕndang t.*, kicking and stamping (of an angry horse).

tĕraju, Pers. scales; a balance; the loose string joining the extremities of a kite.

tĕrak, I. a fowl's laying-place. II. tin refuse after smelting. III. *pĕnoh tĕrak*, absolutely full; chockful; *elok t.*, perfectly beautiful.

tĕral, insistence; verbal pressure or importunity.

tĕraling, I. a bird (unidentified). II. a wood used in house-building (*tarrietia simplicifolia*).

tĕran, straining (in easing oneself); the impulse in labour.

tĕranas, good anchorage; firm sea-bottom.

tĕrang, clear, bright, obvious, evident; *t. hati*, clear-sightedness; *t. bĕndĕrang*, shining brightness; *t. chuacha*, clear daylight; *di-tĕngah-tĕngah t.*, quite openly; in broad daylight; *kĕtĕrangan*, elucidation, clearing up, explanation.

tĕrap, I. a hollow moulding running along a *kĕris*; *kĕris tĕtĕrapan*, a *kĕris* with this hollow running along the blade. II. a tree (*artocarpus kunstleri*) the bark of which is used by Sakais as cloth; *kulit t.*, the bark so used.

terap, = *tiarap*.

tĕrapang, a metal covering for the *kĕris*-sheath.

tĕras, hard wood in a tree; the harder portions of a good timber-tree; *bĕrtĕras*, having a solid core.

tĕrasi, a preparation of fish and prawns (better known as *bĕlachan*).

tĕrasul, Ar. letter-writing; *ilmu t.*, a knowledge of epistolary forms; *kitab t.*, a treatise on letter-writing.

tĕrat, a boundary.

tĕratai, the lotus (*nelumbium speciosum*).

tĕratak, a lean-to; a humble hut; a depreciatory way of describing one's own dwelling.

tĕratu, Port. torture; *tĕmpat t.*, a torture-chamber.

tĕrau, spinning; *mĕnĕrau*, to spin thread.

tĕrbang, flying; to fly; *bĕlum t. lalat*, before the flies are astir—i.e. the very early morning; *t. arwah* or *t. sĕmangat*, "the flight of the spirit of life"; loss of consciousness; sudden stupor; *bĕtĕrbangan*, flying about.

tĕrbis, slipping down at the side (as earth after a landslip).

tĕrbit, issuing out of; exit from; *matahari t.*, the rising sun; *t. rimba*, issuing from the forest; *yang tĕrbit dari pada hati yang jĕrnch*, proceeding from a pure heart.

tĕrbul, a fresh-water fish (unidentified).

tĕrbus, Ar. tarboosh; a fez.

tĕrbut, a heavy wooden bolt used in ship-building.

tĕrek, I. extreme, excessive; *panas t.*, extreme heat. II. *burong tĕrek chanai*, a bird, the Indian oriole (*oriolus indicus*).

tĕrĕnang, a sort of decanter made of earthenware.

tĕrendak, a conical sun-hat worn by Chinese as well as Malays; *t. China*, the Chinese pattern of sun-hat (which is not a perfect cone but slopes inwards); *siput t.*, a shell (*phorus solaris*).

tĕrĕntang, a large forest-tree (*campnosperma auriculata*).

tĕri, Skr. three, triple (in certain expressions only—e.g. *tĕri-buana*, the three worlds; *tĕri-sula*, a trident).

tĕriak, a cry; a shout; *bĕrtĕriak*, to cry out.

tĕriba, *akar tĕriba*, a medicinal plant (*rhinacanthus communis*).

tĕrigu, Port. flour.

tĕrima, reception, acceptance; receipt into one's possession; *t. kaseh*, the acknowledgment of the receipt of kindness; thank you; thanks; *mĕnĕrima*, to receive, to obtain.

tĕripang, a sea-worm—much prized by Chinese as a delicacy (*holothuria edulis*); *ikan t.*, a fish (*saurus indicus*).

tĕrisula, Skr. a trident; see *tĕri* and *sula*.

tĕritek, dripping; dropping continually in small drops—cf. *titek*.

tĕritip, a small sea-slug (which eats into piles and ships' bottoms).

tĕrjal, the flapping of a kite.

tĕrjĕmah, Ar. translation; interpretation; *mĕntĕrjĕmahkan*, to translate.

tĕrjun, rapid descent; leaping or jumping down; *ayer t.*, a waterfall; *t. dari atas kuda*, to leap off a horse; *tĕrjunkan*, to let drop.

tĕrka, Skr. guess-work; *mĕnĕrka*, to guess—cf. *tĕka*.

tĕrkam, leaping or springing forward; *sĕpĕrti singa hĕndak mĕnĕrkam*, like a lion about to spring.

tĕrkap, catching under a concave surface.

tĕrkul, *sĕnapang tĕrkul*, a rifled gun.

tĕrkup, (onom.) the dull clash of flat non-metallic substances; the butting of rams.

tĕrmasa, Pers. a show; a spectacular festival; the sights of a place.

tĕrnah, unprecedented, unusual, extraordinary; *si-tĕrnah*, a dressed-up idiot—a term of abuse.

tĕrnak, *orang tĕrnak*, aborigines.

tĕrok, severe (of illness or of a beating).

tĕrompah, = *tĕrompak*.

tĕrompak, wooden clogs.

tĕrompet, Eng. trumpet; *siput t.*, a shell (*triton variegatus*).

tĕrona, = *tĕruna*.

tĕrong, a vegetable; the brinjal or solanum; *t. asam* or *t. pĕrat* (*solanum aculeatissimum*); *t. mĕranti*, (*solanum nigrum*); *t. pipit* (*solanum torvum* and *solanum verbascifolium*); *t. tikus* (*solanum sarmentosum*).

tĕrongko, Port. a prison; a lock-up; a cell.

tĕropong, a tube; a tubular or telescopic instrument; a telescope; *t. api*, a bellows; *t. tuma*, a microscope.

tĕrpa, a hasty forward movement; an impulsive spring forward; *mĕnĕrpa*, to dart forward.

tĕrpal, Eng. a tarpaulin; a driving-apron.

tĕrtawa, to laugh; see also *tawa*.

tĕrtib, Ar. order, rank, fitting precedence; *t. sĕmbahyang*, the order of prayer, ritual. [The word *tĕrtib* is also used in the sense of "becoming modesty,"—i.e. of people who know their proper place and do not presume or push themselves forward.]

tĕrubin, a fish-trap with a falling door; also *tubin*.

tĕrubok, a fish (*clupea kanagurta*); *tĕlur t.*, the roe of this fish used as a sort of caviare.

tĕrubong, a granary; a padi-barn.

tĕrubul, a tree (*ixora grandifolia*).

tĕrum, a word of command given to elephants to make them sit down.

tĕrumba, a pedigree; a genealogical tree.

tĕrumbu, a reef or rock visible at low tide but covered at high water.

tĕruna, Skr. an unmarried youth; *muda t.*, a stripling; *ayam t.*, a cockerel.

tĕruntum, a sea-shore shrub (*ægiceras majus*).

tĕrup, I. main *tĕrup*, a game played with European cards. II. *kuda tĕrup*, a troop-horse.

tĕrus, right through; in a direct line through or across; *baju itu-pun t.*, the coat was pierced right through; *tĕrusan*, a canal or cutting joining two reaches of a river.

těrusi, Tam. vitriol, sulphuric acid.
tesi, Ch. a tea-spoon.
tětak, hewing, hacking, slashing; *tětakkan*, to strike (anything) with a cutting weapon; *měnětakkan*, id.; *měnětak*, to give a cutting blow.
tětal, close (of the pattern of a cloth); without wide interstices; *kueh t.*, a cake made of *pulut* rice with coconut-milk, sugar and egg.
tětampan, a sort of napkin or kerchief of silk cloth worn ceremonially on the shoulder by certain court officials.
tětap, I. permanency; fixity (of tenure or residence); definitely decided; *sa-tělah t. bichara itu*, when that matter was settled; *měnětapkan*, to give security or permanency to anything; *pěrtětap*, confident, assured. II. blotting up; sucking up moisture; *kain t. tuboh*, a towel.
tětapi, Skr. but; however; still; nevertheless.
tětas, broken or forced open by internal forces (as an egg is hatched); *měnětas*, to be hatched (of eggs).
tete, watching his chance (of a wrestler or fighting-cock).
tětěgok, a small owl—perhaps a dialectic name for the *punggok* (*glaucidium brodii*).
tetek, the breast of a suckling woman; *měmběri t.*, to suckle.
tetel, inferior meat (sinews, soft cartilage, etc.), consumed by the poor.
tětibau, (onom.) a bird (unidentified) —so called from its note, which is sometimes represented as *ta'-tidur*.
tětirok, see *tirok*.
tětkala, = *tatkala*.
tewas, failure; being worsted; *t. pěrang-nya*, the battle was going against him.
tezi, Pers. *kuda tezi*, a Pegasus, a winged horse; also *teji*.
thabit, Ar. truth revealed; also *sabit*.
thalatha, = *sělasa*.
thalju, Ar. snow.

tiada, is not; not to be; *tiada-lah ia di-sini*, he is not here.
tian, Jav. the lower abdomen in a pregnant woman.
tiang, a pillar; a post; a mast; a vertical support; *t. agong*, the mainmast; *t. běndera*, a flagstaff; *t. sěri*, the central pillar in a Malay house.
tiap, *tiap-tiap*, every; *pada tiap-tiap hari*, every day; *tiap-tiap měreka-itu*, everyone of them.
tiarap, lying on one's face (of a man); lying bottom upwards (of a boat); face downwards; *tiarapkan*, to turn (anything) face downwards; *měniarap*, to assume such a position.
tiba, I. sudden arrival or occurrence; an unexpected development; "putting in" at a port (of a ship); "landing" (of a blow); *tiba-tiba*, suddenly, unexpectedly. II. *pětiban sampir*, a gift, a present—in Javanese tales only.
tibar, = *tebar*.
tidak, no, not; *tidakkan*, to deny the existence of; *kětidakan*, non-existence.
tidur, sleep; *t. lělap*, deep sleep; *těmpat t.*, a bed; *tiduran* or *kětiduran*, sleep; being asleep; *tidurkan*, to put to sleep.
tiga, three; *běrtiga*, in a party of three; *kětiga*, all three; *yang kětiga*, third.
tijak, = *pijak*.
tika, a reel of thread.
tikal, a Siamese "tical."
tikam, stabbing; spearing; striking with a pointed weapon; piercing with thorns; *mati kěna t.*, death from a stab or from a spear-thrust; *tikamkan*, to drive (a pointed weapon) into anything.
tikar, a mat; *běntangkan t.*, to spread a mat; *běrtikarkan*, to use (anything) as a mat;. to sleep on.
tikas, the line of sea-weed and driftwood on a beach, showing the extreme point reached by the tide.

tikus, a generic name for rats and mice; *t. ambang bulan*, Raffles' gymnura; *t. Bĕlanda*, the (imported) guinea-pig; *t. buloh*, a name for the bamboo-rat (*rhizomys sumatrensis*), better *dĕkan*; *t. mondok*, = *t. ambang bulan*; *t. rumah*, the common house-mouse (*mus musculus*); *t. tanah*, the field-mouse (*mus decumanus*); *t. turi*, the musk-shrew (*crocidura murina* and *crocidura cærulea*); *angin t.*, uncertain winds; *gigi t.*, small regular teeth; *lobang t.*, the cavity in which the body is laid in a Malay grave.

tilam, a sleeping-mattress; *tilaman*, id.

tilan, a fish (*mastacembelus armatus*); *t. pasir* (*trypauchena vagina*); *t. rumput* (*pinclepterus cinerascens*).

tilek, looking long and fixedly at anything; carefully examining; *tĕmpat t.*, a cynosure of all eyes; *tukang t.*, a man gifted with second-sight; a fortune-teller.

tilu, an insect (unidentified).

tim, Ch. stewing; *pĕtiman*, a stew-pan.

timah, tin; lead; zinc; *t. puteh*, tinned iron; *t. hitam*, lead; *t. sari*, zinc; *bijeh t.*, alluvial tin; *ikan timah-timah*, a fish (*lutianus lineolatus?*); *pokok timah-timah*, a small tree (*ilex cymosa*).

timang, balancing; tossing up and down (as an adult playing with a very young child); *timang-timangan*, a pet name or nursery name.

timba, a small bucket; a dipper; *t. ruang*, the bucket for baling out water from a boat; *mĕnimba*, to bale.

timbal, equilibrium, balancing; *bĕr-timbalan*, in equipoise; matching.

timbang, weighing; estimating the weight of anything; considering the pros and cons of a question; *batu timbangan*, measure of weight; *tim-bangkan*, to weigh; *pĕnimbang*, the weigher.

timbau, adding a piece so as to lengthen anything.

timbok, a downward blow with the flat of the fist.

timbul, appearing on the surface; floating; emerging from below; *t. tĕnggĕlam*, appearing and disappearing—of the letters of a half-erased inscription; *bulan t.*, the new moon; *gambar t.*, a statue; *timbulkan*, to bring out in evidence; *mĕnimbulkan*, id.; *pĕnimbul*, that which causes a thing to come to the surface—used especially of a charm of invulnerability (*kĕbal pĕnimbul* or *pĕnimbul raksa*) [based on the belief that quicksilver absorbed into the system will rush to any spot struck by a weapon and so prevent the weapon penetrating beneath the skin].

timbun, heaped up; a heap; heaping or piling up; *timbuni*, *timbunkan*, or *mĕnimbunkan*, to heap up anything; *bĕrtimbun-timbun*, in heaps; piled one on top of the other.

timbus, filling up or blocking an orifice or cavity; *timbusi*, to fill up (a grave).

timpa, falling down on; striking in its fall; *di-timpa batu*, struck down by falling stones; *t. rasa*, to bear the brunt of anything; *t. pĕrasan*, id.; *di-timpa daulat*, struck down by the power of dead kings; *mĕnimpa*, to strike in one's fall; to fall upon.

timpang, = *tempang*.

timpas, low-water; *t. pĕrbani*, very low tide.

timpoh, sitting on the ground with the legs turned to the right and bent back towards the body, while the left arm rests on the ground; sitting as Malay women often sit.

timpus, disproportionate narrowness; lacking in beam (of a boat).

timu, by right (*de jure*); *timu-timu*, id.

timun, a gourd; a pumpkin; *t. China*, the cucumber; *t. dendang*, a passion-flower (*passiflora fœtida*); *t. hutan*, the grenadilla; also *mĕn-timun*.

timur, east; *t. laut*, N.E.; *t. padang*, S.E.; *t. měněnggara*, E.S.E.

tinas, = *tindas*.

tindan, lying loosely one on the other (of a pile of books or similar objects); *sa-tindan*, a disorderly heap.

tindas, the cracking of a flea on the thumb-nail.

tindeh, lying one over the other; superimposed; *yang rěbah di-tindeh*, what is fallen is pressed under (still further); the unfortunate are exposed to oppression; *běrtindeh*, one lying over the other (as bodies on a battle-field).

tindek, pricking through a thin surface.

tinggal, remaining over or behind; abandoned; abiding in a place; *rumah t.*, an abandoned house; *t. nadi*, with life alone left one; ruined completely; *tinggali*, to leave behind; to abandon; *tinggalkan* or *měninggalkan*, id.; *kětinggalan*, abandonment; severance; *pěninggalan*, absence; *sapěninggalan*, in the absence of (so-and-so); *těrtinggal*, left behind; abandoned.

tinggi, height; loftiness; *t. hati*, pride.

tinggil, *pěninggil*, a gallery.

tinggong, squatting; sitting on one's heels; squatting like a toad, or as a dog sitting on its hind legs only; *běrtinggong*, to squat.

tingkah, ways, behaviour, manners; *t. laku*, id.

tingkal, Skr. solder.

tingkap, a long low native window.

tingkat, a deck, a flooring—taken as a measure of height or size; *kapal tiga t.*, a three-decker; *běrtingkat-tingkat*, in storeys; in stages.

tingkil, a bunch; a cluster (of fruit).

tingkis, sad, sorrowful.

tingting, to hop.

tinjau, stretching out the neck; *měninjau*, to look out; *pěninjau*, a scout.

tinju, boxing; *běrtinju*, to box.

tinta, Port. ink.

tinting, winnowing with a swaying motion.

tiong, the mynah (*gracula intermedia* and *gracula javanensis*); *t. batu* or *t. bělachan*, the Eastern broad-billed roller (*eurystomus orientalis*).

tipis, thin, delicate; = *nipis*.

tipu, deception, fraud; *bohong dan t.*, lies and misrepresentations; *měnipu*, to deceive; *pěnipu*, deceptive.

tir, I. Eur. tar. II. the rook or castle in chess.

tirai, Tam. a curtain; *t. kělambu*, mosquito-curtains.

tiram, an oyster.

tiri, "step"—in expressions like step-child (*anak t.*), step-father (*bapa t.*) and step-mother (*ma' t.*)

tiris, oozing through; dripping from.

tirok, a long unbarbed fish-spear; *burong t.*, the snipe (*gallinago stenura* and *g. coelestis*); *burong tětirok*, id.; *měnirok*, to spear fish—cf. *tirus*.

tiru, the imitation of a model or copy; copying; *tiruan*, a model for imitation.

tirus, thin and tapering to a point *padi měnirus*, the ear of rice in its earliest stages—cf. *tirok*.

titah, the utterance of a prince; *t. sultan*, the sultan says; *běrtitah*, to speak (of a prince speaking).

titar, = *titir*.

titek, I. a drop; a liquid particle; *sa-titek ěmbun*, a drop of dew; *měnitek*, to let fall in drops. II. a heavy racking blow in administering torture.

titi, motion over a narrow plank, branch, or bridge; a crossing-plank; a bridge; *měniti*, to pass over a narrow footway; *titian*, a narrow footway; a narrow bridge.

titir, a swift rapping movement; the beating of certain drums with the knuckles.

titis, slow dropping; the dropping of sticky liquids—cf. *titek*.

tiup, blowing; the action of a current of air upon anything; *buntal di-t.*, a blown-out *buntal* fish; *bĕrtiup*, to blow (of the breeze).

to', a contraction for *dato'*, q.v.

toakang, Ch. puffed up with self-conceit.

toalang, the swarming of bees; *bĕrtoalang*, to swarm (of bees); *pokok t.*, a tree where bees have made a nest.

tobak, square-cut; trimmed square (of the nails).

tobat, Ar. repentance; giving up (an evil practice); also *taubat*.

todak, a fish (*belone strongylura* and *hemiramphus* spp.)

togel, = *dogel*.

togok, limbless; with stumps for limbs; *bĕlayar t.*, to sail with only a storm-sail set; *si-togok*, the long-nosed clown in a wayang.

tohok, a sort of harpoon with a rope attached to it; *tĕnggiri t.*, a fish (unidentified).

tohor, shallow; *kapur t.*, whitewash.

tojang, a temporary prop or support; *pĕnojang kaki*, a foot-rest.

tokak, I. an ulcer on the shin. II. biting (in fighting and not for eating). III. hairy patches on the head.

to'kek, (onom.) the gecko.

toko, Ch. a large warehouse or store; a big godown.

tokoh, character, quality, type—of goods; *sa-tokoh ini*, up to this sample.

tokok, a small increase; throwing something in over and above.

tokong, I. a treeless rock; a barren island. II. Ch. a Chinese temple. III. shaving the head of a woman.

tolak, repelling or pushing back; keeping off; rejecting; shedding; *t. bara*, ballast; *t. bala*, a propitiatory offering against misfortune; *tolakkan*, to push away; *mĕnolakkan*, id.

toleh, a side-look; *mĕnoleh ka-bĕlakang*, to look back; *pĕrtolehan hari*, the turning point in the sun's course (when he seems to descend precipitately).

tolo, I. impulsiveness. II. *anyam sa-tolo*, a quadruple plait.

tolok, I. matching; a peer or equal; *tiada tĕrtolok*, matchless. II. (Dutch) an interpreter.

tolong, aid, assistance; (in the Straits) favour, mercy, help; *tolongan*, assistance; *mĕnolong*, to lend a helping hand; *tolongkan*, to assist (a person or animal); *mĕnolongkan*, id.

tom, (Dutch) the bridle; *tali t.*, the reins.

toman, a fish (*ophicephalus striatus*).

tombak, a spear; a pike; a halberd; *t. bĕndĕrang*, spears with horse-hair attached to them (as emblems of rank); *t. kĕrajaan*, state-spears of any sort; *t. rambu*, a spear with a fringe or tassel under the spear-point; *t. sayang*, a gaff for close-hauling a sail.

tombol, the knob on a door; *ikan t. mas*, a fish (*thynnus thunnina*).

tombong, I. the seed-bud in a coco-nut-shell. II. arrogance; = *sombong*.

tomong, a short squat gun; a sort of native howitzer.

tompok, *sa-tompok*, a small heap.

tondong, banishment; hounding a man out of a place.

tong, (Dutch) a tun; a wooden tub; a barrel.

tonggak, I. a snag. II. aerial roots —such as those of the banyan.

tonggek, hanging head downwards —cf. *tunggit*.

tonggeng, lifting the posterior (as in leap-frog).

tongget, = *tunggit*.

tonggok, heap; *sa-tonggok*, a heap; a pile; = *sa-tompok*.

tonggong, heaping up—cf. *tonggok*.

Tongkah, I. a town in Junk Ceylon; *rĕlau t.*, a common type of smelting-furnace. II. *papan tongkah*, a plank used to make one's way over mud-flats. III. to lengthen a garment by sewing on a piece at the top.

tongkang, a barge; a lighter; a very large open boat.

tongkat, a vertical prop; a crutch; a stick; propping up from below; *t. kětiak*, a crutch; *měnongkat*, to sustain, to prop up.

tongkeng, I. the rump; *tulang t.*, the coccyx. II. *bunga tongkeng*, the Tonkin creeper (*pergularia minor*).

tongkol, a knob; a roundish lump or clod; *mas t.*, nugget gold.

tongkong, = *tongkol*.

tongong, slowness of wit.

tongtong, a clapper; a sounding-board.

tonjol, a big bump or protuberance on the forehead.

tonyoh, rubbing one substance on another; rubbing dirt roughly on a boy's face, etc.

top, a vessel with very bluff bows; *layar t.*, a lug-sail with a long yard.

topang, the forked supports of a *kajang* in a native boat; a forked stick of any sort; *layar t.*, a foresail.

topekong, Ch. a Chinese joss.

topeng, masked Javanese dancers.

topes, a precipitously sloping bank.

topi, Hind. a sun-hat; a hat generally.

topong, a small bag for holding *bělachan*.

torak, I. *anak torak*, the spool (in weaving); *batang t.*, the spool rod. II. *ubi torak*, a kind of potato.

torang, the knot at the corner of a mesh.

torek, a running at the ears.

totok, I. full-blooded (*pur sang*). II. a fish (unidentified).

toya, physical weakness.

toyah, a long pole used as a thrusting-pole in fighting.

toyoh, = *tonyoh*.

tu, = *itu*.

tua, old, matured; age, seniority; depth (of colouring); *orang t.*, an old man; the head of a family; a village elder; *kětua*, a village head-man; *pa' t.*, an uncle older than one's father; *merah t.*, deep red; dark red.

tuah, luck; prosperity that can only be ascribed to chance and not to labour or foresight.

tuai, a peculiar cutter used for reaping padi (a few stalks only being cut at a time).

tuak, fermented spirit made from palm-juice.

tuala, Port. a serviette; a napkin; a towel; *t. mandi*, a bath-towel.

tualang, see *toalang*.

tuam, the application of a hot dry poultice to a diseased part.

tuan, master, lord, lady; a term applied to Europeans (men only), to Malays (men and women) of some position who have not higher titles, to a *haji* of either sex, to all descendants of the Prophet, and by a lover to his mistress or vice versa; *běr-tuankan*, to take service under; to acknowledge (someone) as a master; *tuan-ku*, a title used in addressing a reigning prince; *yang-dipěrtuan*, the supreme lord; the sovereign; *yam-tuan*, id.

tuang, I. pouring out; emptying out a liquid; *měnuangkan*, to pour out. II. *tuang-tuang*, a bamboo blown into noisily by way of signal.

tuap, a splint of rattans.

tuar, a riverine fish-trap made of thorns which turn their points towards the interior.

tuas, I. leverage; the application of leverage in torture. II. a name given in Penang to a form of fishing in which branches of foliage are anchored so as to attract fish by the food and shelter they provide [the fishing is done by hook and line—cf. *unjam*].

tuat, I. a mark indicating a good fishing ground. II. *kětuat*, a **wart**.

tuba, a plant (*derris elliptica*) with a root the sap of which has stupefying properties and is used in fishing; *mĕnuba*, to fish in this way.

tuban, *tuban-tuban*, the discharge preceding delivery; the *liquor amnii*.

tubi, devotion to anything; giving oneself up heart and soul to anything.

tubin, a fish-trap with a falling door; also *tĕrubin*.

tubir, a very steep river-bank or shore.

tuboh, the body in the anatomical sense; the bodily frame; the seat of physical sensation; *panas rasa tuboh-ku*, I feel cold; *bĕkas t.*, a garment that has actually been worn; *sa-tuboh*, carnal intercourse.

tubok, a wooden lance for spearing *tĕripang*.

tuding, aslant; at an angle; a "pulling" stroke in contradistinction to a straight drive.

tudoh, accusation (especially slanderous accusation); bringing charges against a person; *mĕnudoh*, to accuse.

tudong, a veil; a hollow cover; covering up; *t. saji*, a large dish-cover; *siput t.*, a shell (*trochus pyramis*); *tudongan*, a veil; *tudongi* or *tudongkan*, to enshroud.

tugal, a pointed stick used for making holes in the ground in which padi-seed is dropped.

tugar, = *tugal*.

tugas, steady and strong (of a breeze).

Tuhan, God.

tuhfat, Ar. *tuhfat ul-ajnas*, "a gift of miscellanies"—a term used in polite letter-writing to describe the letter and the gifts which theoretically accompany it.

tui, a tree (*ixonanthes icosandra*).

tuil, a lever for tilting up a heavy mass.

tujoh, seven.

tuju, pointing at; aiming at; making for; *sa-t.*, in harmony; *tujui*, to aim at; to make for; *mĕnuju*, to point towards; to injure by turning evil spirits upon.

tukal, I. a measure for thread; a parcel of skeins. II. a dent or mark left on the skin, the skin not being broken.

tukang, a craftsman; a skilled workman; *t. bĕsi*, a blacksmith; *t. chap*, a printer; *t. chukur*, a barber; *t. kasut*, a shoe-maker; *t. kayu*, a carpenter; *t. mas*, a goldsmith; *t. tilek*, a fortune-teller.

tukar, change by substituting one thing for another; *tukarkan*, to exchange.

tukas, *mĕnukas*, to accuse of immorality.

tukil, a bamboo vessel for carrying liquid.

tukul, a small hammer.

tukun, a sunken rock—cf. *tokong*.

tul, Eur. a thole-pin.

tuladan, = *tĕladan*.

tulah, Ar. a calamity consequent on sacrilege or extreme presumption; *t. papa*, the curse of poverty generally.

tulang, a bone; *t. bĕlakang*, the dorsal vertebræ; *t. bĕlikat*, the shoulder-blade; *t. dayong*, id.; *t. chaping*, the xiphoid process; *t. kĕring*, the tibia; *t. rusok*, the ribs; *t. sĕlangka*, the collar-bone; *t. sulbi* or *t. tongkeng*, the coccyx.

tulat, the third day after this; the day after the day after to-morrow.

tuli, I. deafness, deaf; *mĕnulikan*, to deafen; *tuli-tuli*, a sort of *kĕris*-band of bead-work or fancy-work.

tulis, writing, painting, figuring; *juru t.*, a scribe, a clerk; *tulisan*, handwriting; *mĕnulis*, to write (intransitive).

tulong, = *tolong*.

tulus, sincerity; earnestness.

tuma, a small insect; a sort of louse.

tuman, = *toman*.

tumang, a wooden tent-peg; a tethering peg; an arrangement of three sticks for cooking.

tumbang, falling heavily; toppling down (of a large tree).

tumbas, to the bitter end; to the last drop—a strong expression of completion.

tumboh, sprouting up; springing up (of any growth); *tumboh-tumbohan*, plants generally; *kĕtumbohan*, an eruptive disease; small-pox; *bĕr-tumboh*, to sprout (of plants).

tumbok, a heavy pounding blow; *t. lada*, a small knife.

tumis, cooking in oil and seasoning.

tumit, heel (of the foot); *t. tiang*, the truck of a mast.

tumpah, spilling; shedding; *t. ruah*, poured out; *tumpahkan*, to pour out; to empty out.

tumpang, lodging; temporary residence; *mĕnumpang*, to lodge; to take shelter with; to take up one's abode with.

tumpas, utterly; head over heels (of a bad fall).

tumpat, stopped up; filled up (of a hollow); *mĕnumpat*, to stop up an orifice.

tumpu, having a footing on; resting on; *mĕlompat bĕrsatumpu*, to jump from a standing position; *bĕrtumpu*, to have a footing somewhere; to have a place to "take off" from.

tumpul, bluntness, blunt.

tumpur, loss by leakage; frittering away.

tumu, a sea-shore tree (*didymocarpus crinitus*).

tumus, falling on the face; sprawling.

tun, an old Malay title.

tuna, Skr. a wound; = *luka*.

tunai, ready (of money); cash down; *wang t.*, ready money; *tunaikan* or *mĕnunaikan*, to realise (one's hopes).

tunak, definite attachment; fixity of tenure.

tunam, the match applied to a cannon.

tunang, troth; betrothal; *pĕluru t.*, a bullet pledged (by sorcery) to take effect; *bĕrtunang*, to be engaged to be married.

tunas, a young shoot sprouting from a branch.

tunda, towing; *sampan t.*, a dinghy; *panching t.*, a tow-line.

tundok, stooping, bowing, lowering the head; *t. mĕnyĕmbah*, to bow in salutation; *t. tĕngadah*, to look down and then up (as a man trying to compose a letter); *mĕnundokkan kĕpala*, to bow the head; *ilmu pĕnundok*, a magic art for procuring the submission of a person.

tundun, the pudendum muliebre.

tungau, a small insect-parasite infesting fowls.

tunggal, unity; sole; the one; *anak t.*, an only child; *babi t.*, a solitary boar; *Sany-yang t.*, the one God.

tunggang, I. astride; riding; *mĕnunggang kuda*, to ride. II. upside down; *t. langgang*, head over heels; *t. balek*, id.; *t. tunggit*, bowing very deep; bobbing up and down.

tungging, = *tonggeng*.

tunggit, *tunggang-tunggit*, bowing very low; bobbing up and down.

tunggu, watching over; keeping an eye on; *tungguï*, to watch over; *bĕrtunggu*, to be on the watch; *pĕnunggu*, a watchman; *pĕnunggu pintu*, a porter.

tunggul, I. the stump of a tree; *tunggul-tunggul* or *tĕtunggul*, the upstanding stump of a rainbow (believed to be portentous). II. a flag-staff; a standard. III. *pĕnunggul*, a hostage, a propitiatory offering made by the vanquished to the victor. IV. *pĕnunggul*, a heavy lump of wood to which an animal is tethered to prevent him running away.

tungkap, tongue-tied; dumb-foundered; silent through nervousness; opening the mouth and saying nothing.

tungku, an arrangement of stones constituting a primitive stove; *batu t.*, the stones so used.

tungkus, deeply imbedded in anything.
tuni, = *tuna*.
tunjal, a thrust downwards to give impetus to an upward motion.
tunjang, that portion of the root which goes vertically downwards.
tunjok, showing; indicating; *tunjokkan* or *mĕnunjokkan*, to point out; to show; to display—cf. *tĕlunjok*.
tunjong, the water-lily.
tuntong, a turtle (*callagur picta*).
tuntun, I. leading, conducting, guiding—by means of some connecting link as a man leading a horse with a rope. II. *mĕnuntun*, to flock in crowds (to any performance).
tuntut, following after; following up; intently seeking; *t. ilmu*, the pursuit of knowledge.
tunu, burning up; consuming by fire.
tupai, I. a generic name for squirrels; *t. biji nangka*, the tupaia (*tupaia ferruginea*); *t. galang pĕrahu*, Raffles' squirrel (*sciurus rafflesi*); *t. jinjang*, = *t. nandong*; *t. kampong* (*sciurus notatus*); *t. nandong* (*sciurus bicolor*); *t. tanah* (*tamias lysteri*). II. a cooking-place on a native ship.
tupang, = *topang*.
turap, covering, plastering, lining.

turas, filtration; straining through cloth.
turi, Skr. *tikus turi*, a name given to the musk-shrews, = *tikus kĕsturi*.
turis, scratching (a line or mark).
Turki, Turkish.
turun, descent; coming down; *turunan* or *kĕturunan*, descent, origin; *t. tĕmurun*, genealogy; line of descent; *turunkan* or *mĕnurunkan*, to lower.
turus, erect; the uprights of a fish-trap; *t. nĕgĕri*, a pillar of the state.
turut, following in succession after; following advice or instruction; *turutan*, an example; *turutkan* or *mĕnurutkan*, to take anything as an example to follow.
tutoh, *mĕnutoh*, to lop off the branches from the trunk, after or before felling a tree.
tutok, I. breaking or crushing rattans into a sort of fibrous pulp. II. a tree (*hibiscus macrophyllus*).
tutul, Jav. spotted; *machan t.*, the leopard; = *harimau bintang*.
tutup, closing up; covering; shutting; a lid or cover; *sa-tahun t.*, a full year; *t. bumi*, a weed (*clephantopus scaber*); *tutupkan*, to close, to shut up; *mĕnutupkan*, id.
tutur, utterance; *bĕrtutur*, to utter, to speak.

U

uak, *mĕnguak*, to low; to bellow.
uap, vapour, steam; also *wap*.
uar, *uar-uar*, public proclamation; publishing widely; " proclaiming from the house-tops."
uba, a sago-vat.
ubah, change, alteration; *ubahkan*, to alter (a thing); *bĕrubah*, to be altered.
uban, greyness of the hair; *bĕruban*, to be or become grey or grizzled; to age; *chiak uban* or *pipit uban*, the white-headed munia (*amadina maja*).

ubang, to cut a curved groove in a log so as to fit it to another.
ubar, *bĕrubar*, to become loose; to open out; *bĕrubar hati*, to speak from the heart.
ubat, a drug, a medicine, a chemical, a magic simple, a philtre; *u. chaching*, a remedy for intestinal worms; *u. bĕdil*, gunpowder; *u. guna*, a philtre; *tukang u.*, a druggist; *ubati*, to apply medicine to; to treat; *mĕngubati*, id.; *pĕngubat*, a remedy.

ubi, a generic name for yams and tuberous roots; *u. Běnggala*, the common potato (*solanum tuberosum*); *u. karu*, tapioca (*manihot utilissima*); *u. nasi*, the common yam (*dioscorea alata*); *u. pasir* (*dioscorea pentaphylla*).

ubin, *batu ubin*, a floor-tile; (also) hard granitic stone for road-metal.

ubong, = *hubong*.

ubun, *ubun-ubun*, the fontanel.

ubur, *ubur-ubur*, a large jelly-fish; *payong ubur-ubur*, a fringed umbrella.

uchap, *menguchap*, to utter; *menguchap shukur*, to give thanks; *menguchap tasbeh*, to tell one's beads.

uda, = *muda*.

udam, dulled; faded (of colouring); dimmed (of brilliancy).

udang, a generic name for prawns, shrimps and lobsters; *u. galah*, the lobster; *u. geragau*, a very small shrimp; *u. lobok*, the prawn; *u. sungai*, the fresh-water prawn; *raja u.*, a name given to kingfishers in the south and to large sandpipers in the north of the Peninsula.

udap, *udap-udapan*, ingredients of all sorts that go to make up a salad.

udara, Skr. the atmosphere; the heavens.

udoh, = *odoh*.

udut, *mengudut*, to smoke tobacco or chandu.

uet, = *wet*.

ufti, Skr. tribute; also *upěti*.

ugahari, Skr. fairness; evenness; equality; parity.

ugama, Skr. creed, religion; also *igama* and *agama*.

ugut, menacing, frightening.

ujan, = *hujan*.

ujar, utterance, speech, saying; *ujarnya*, he (or they) said.

uji, testing; applying a touchstone to anything; *batu u.*, a touchstone.

ujong, = *hujong*.

ujud, Ar. personality; individuality; self; the body; *u. anggota*, the body and limbs.

ukas, a generic name for shells of the genus *malleus*.

ukir, engraving; incised patterns; *ukiran*, id.

ukup, perfuming (cloth, etc.), with incense; *pěngukup* or *pěrukupan*, the framework over which the cloth is laid and under which the incense is burnt.

ukur, linear measurement; *mengukur*, to measure.

ulam, = *hulam*.

ulama, Ar. learned men generally; one learned in the Scriptures.

ulang, repetition of action; *ulangkan*, to repeat; *běrulang*, repeatedly; *ulang-aling*, backwards and forwards.

ulap, *ulap-ulap*, broth made of coconut-milk and *kěladi* (*colocasia antiquorum*).

ular, a generic name for snakes—e.g. *ular sawa*, a python; *ular tědong sěndok*, a cobra; *u. danu*, (Kedah) a rainbow; *u. naga*, a dragon; *u.-ular*, a pennon, a streamer.

ulas, a covering; a wrapper; *ulasan*, id.

ulat, a generic name for a number of worms; a maggot; *u. bulu*, a hairy caterpillar; *u. sutěra*, the silk-worm.

uleh, = *oleh*.

uli, kneading, squeezing down, pressing or ramming down.

ulit, lulling, crooning, or singing to sleep; *ulitkan*, to sing (a person) to sleep; *mengulitkan*, id.; *mengulit*, to croon; to sing a lullaby; *pěngulit*, a lullaby.

ulu, = *hulu*.

ulun, I. servant; your servant; I; II. a name given to some Celebes shells (*conus miles* and *conus lithoglyphus*).

uman, *uman-uman*, long-winded; a bore; *menguman*, to drag on a story monotonously.

umang, *umang-umang*, a hermit-crab.

umat, Ar. people; mankind.
umbai, dangling; hanging down loosely.
umban, *umban tali*, a sling.
umbang, colossal; *naga u.*, a great sea-dragon.
umbas, = *humbas*.
umbi, the roots of a tree; *akar u.*, id.; "to the very roots."
umbut, I. the soft heart of the upper portion of a palm; the palm-cabbage. II. *ikan umbut-umbut*, a fish (unidentified).
umpama, Skr. likeness; example; instance; similar case; *sa-u.*, for instance; *umpamaan*, a proverb; *umpamakan*, to liken to; to compare.
umpan, bait; food to attract fish or animals; *u. těkak*, an appetiser.
umpat, abuse; evil-speaking; cursing; *umpati*, to revile; *měngumpat*, to be abusive.
umpil, *měngumpil*, to lever up.
umum, Ar. obscure, involved, complicated, difficult.
umur, Ar. life; *sa-umur-ku*, as long as I live.
unai, soft, moist and odorous—as perfumed oil.
unam, an edible shell-fish (*murex* sp.)
unchang, I. *unchang-unchit*, by driblets, by fits and starts. II. a travelling-bag for money; a small wallet of plaited-work.
unchat, lifting and lowering; moving a thing up and down.
unchit, *unchang-unchit*, by driblets; by fits and starts; *bayar u.*, payment in instalments.
unchui, Ch. a pipe.
undak, *měngundak*, not to make headway (of a ship); *laut pěngundak*, a choppy sea against which it is difficult to make headway.
undan, I. *burong undan*, a large bird (*pelecanus philippensis*). II. *běrundan*, to be protracted; to drag on.
undang, *undang-undang*, laws, statutes, ordinances, codified enactments.

undi, lot; die to determine chances; *buang u.*, to cast lots; *buah u.*, die, dice.
undil, a money-box.
undok, I. *undok-undok*, the sea-horse (*hippocampus* sp.) II. *undok-andal*, in swift succession.
undur, giving way, retreat, loss of ground; *měngundur*, to give way.
ungak, *ungak-angek*, bobbing up and down.
ungap, gasping for breath (as a dying fish).
ungar, an edible salt-water fish (*lutianus argentimaculatus*).
unggal, = *tunggal*.
unggang, = *ungkang*.
unggas, a bird; *u. dewata*, the bird of paradise.
unggat, stiffly erect.
unggis, *měnggunggis*, to gnaw, to nibble.
unggit, = *ungkit*.
unggun, banking a fire.
ungka, a gibbon (*hylobates lar* or *hylobates agilis*).
ungkang, *ungkang ungkit*, see-saw motion; *kursi ungkang ungkit*, a rocking-chair.
ungkap, gaping; exposing a large orifice; *těrungkap*, id.
ungkil, levering up—cf. *umpil*.
ungkit, bringing up again; raking up old stories; *ungkang ungkit*, see-saw motion.
ungku, = *ěngku*.
ungkur, *běrungkur-ungkuran*, retreating in different directions; dispersing.
ungu, purple; deep reddish brown; rich dark colouring.
ungum, mumbling to oneself.
unjam, I. thrusting anything vigorously into the ground. II. (Pahang) an arrangement of branches and leaves anchored with stones on a fishing-ground to afford shelter to fish; *buang u.*, to place this arrangement in position—cf. *tuas*.
unjap, a (Kedah) variant of *injap*.

unjok, giving out (anything); putting (a thing) forward; *unjokkan* or *měn-unjokkan*, to hold out, to thrust out.

unjong, I. *měngunjong*—v. *kunjong*. II. *pěrunjong*—v. *runjong*.

unjun, lifting and lowering a bait in order to draw the attention of fish to it.

unjur, stretching out; projection; *unjurkan*, to thrust (anything) forward—cf. *unjok*.

untai, hanging down loosely, dangling.

untak, *untak-anti*, convulsive movement; also *ěntak-anti*.

untal, I. *untal-antil*, swaying loosely. II. *sa-untal*, an armful.

untang, pendulous, swaying; *untang-anting*, id.

until, *sa-until*, a small ball or pill; a small quantity.

unting, a small skein or bunch; a unit of measurement for thread.

untok, share, allotted portion.

untong, profit, gain, advantage; fortune; natural destiny; *měndapat u.*, to derive profit.

untut, elephantiasis.

unus, = *hunus*.

upah, payment for service rendered; fee, wage, bribe; *upahkan*, to engage a person's services; *měngupahkan*, id.

upak, I. *měngupak*, to stir up a smouldering heap of ashes. II. *upak-apek*, inconsequent (of talk); mischievous or inconsistent talk.

upam, burnishing, polishing, giving lustre to stones and metals.

upama, = *umpama*.

upas, Jav. poison generally; the poison of the upas tree (*antiaris toxicaria*) in particular.

upat, = *umpat*.

upaya, Skr. means, resources; *tiada u.* or *tiada daya u.*, destitute of all means; helpless; moneyless.

upeh, the tough flower-sheaths of certain palms. [These sheaths are used for making small buckets or dippers.]

upěti, Skr. tribute; also *ufti*.

ura, *běrura-ura*, to talk over anything; to discuss the *pros* and *cons*.

urai, loose, dishevelled, inadhesive; *mas u.*, gold dust; *uraikan*, to undo, to unloose, to explain; *měnguraikan*, id.; *měngurai*, to open out, to become loose, to unfold; *těrurai*, undone, dishevelled (of hair).

urap, *urapan*, cosmetics; ointment for application to the skin; *běrurap-urapan*, to be adorning oneself with these cosmetics.

urat, I. nerve, sinew, fibre, vein, muscle; *u. bělikat*, the dorsal muscles; *u. tanah*, a snake (*typhlops* spp.); *salah u.*, a strained sinew. II. Ar. *gila u.*, lasciviousness.

urdi, = *ordi*.

uri, the afterbirth; *urian*, a brazier's mould, after use.

urna, = *warna*.

urong, crowding; *batu mas u.*, iron pyrites; *di-urong sěmut*, covered with ants.

urup, *kědai urup-urup*, a money-changer's shop; *měngurup*, to change money.

urus, rubbing, scrubbing—more refined in use than the word *gosok*.

urut, massage, rubbing with the hands, shampooing; *janggut di-u.*, a forked beard.

usah, *ta'-usah*, needless; it is unnecessary; never mind; don't; *usahkan*, so far from; = *jangankan*.

usaha, Skr. diligence, industry; *běr-usaha*, industrious; *měngusahakan diri*, to exert oneself.

usang, shrivelled up internally (of grains of padi, etc.); *rumah u.*, an abandoned house (of which the outer shell only remains).

usap, plating, coating.

usat, *ikan usat*, a fish (unidentified); *ular tědong u.*, a snake (*simotes octolineatus*).

usek, teasing, chaffing, worrying with impertinent questions.

usia, Skr. length of life, duration of life; *sa-panjang usia*, all one's life.
usir, pursuit, following up, pressing after; *měngusir*, to pursue, to harrass.
usong, carrying in a litter or slung from a pole; *usongan*, a litter.
usul, I. Ar. beginnings, origins—the plural of *asal*; *asal u.*, the antecedents or early history of anything. II. manner; *u. jijak*, bearing; *u. sipat*, ways; *u. měnunjokkan asal*, manners display descent.
utama, I. Skr. excellence, eminence; *yang těrutama*, the most eminent. II. Skr. the breath (of life); *u. jiwa*, id. (a term of endearment); *ayer u. jiwa*, the water of life.
utan, = *hutan*.
utang, = *hutang*.
utara, Skr. the north; *u. těpat*, due north; *u. barat laut*, N.N.W.; *u. timur laut*, N.N.E.; *angin u.*, a northerly wind; *musim u.*, the N.E. monsoon.
Utarek, Ar. the planet Mercury.
utas, I. a coil, a skein, a string; *sa-utas manek-manek*, a string of beads or corals. II. skilled labour, craftsmanship; a craftsman.
utus, sending on an embassy; *utusan*, an envoy, a mission.
uyong, shaking, swaying.

W

wa, Ar. and.
waad, Ar. bond, contract; = *janji*.
waba, Ar. plague, pestilence.
wadun, Jav. a woman.
wafat, Ar. to die.
wah, an exclamation of surprise.
wahai, an exclamation of appellation; hey there!
waham, Ar. surmise, conjecture.
wahid, Ar. sole, single.
waja, = *baja*.
wajah, Ar. countenance, visage.
wajek, a kind of sweetmeat.
wajib, Ar. pledged to, bound to.
wakaf, Ar. devoted to religious purposes; *tanah wakaf*, mosque land.
wakap, I. the name of a bird (unidentified). II. = *wakaf*.
wakil, Ar. agent, attorney, representative.
waktu, Ar. time, occasion, opportunity.
walakin, Ar. and yet; but; still.
walang, Jav. sad, sorrowful, melancholy.
walau, Ar. although.
wali, I. Ar. a vicegerent; a guardian of an unmarried woman; a deputy; *w. allah*, a saint. II. *pisau wali*, a small lancet-like knife. III. a shoulder-cloth.
walimana, Skr. a harpy.
Wallah, Ar. God!—an exclamation of astonishment.
wa'llahu, Ar. *wa'llahu aalam*, God is all-knowing; God knoweth best.
wan, a title of high rank given to the descendants of great chiefs not of royal rank.
wang, money, cash; *w. tunai*, ready money.
wangi, fragrant, odorous, perfumed.
wangkang, a Chinese junk.
wanta, Skr. nature; = *anta*.
wap, vapour, steam; also *uap*.
war, = *uar*.
warangan, white arsenic.
waras, Jav. cure, convalescence, good health.
warga, Skr. family, people.
warip, Jav. alive; *w. waras*, alive and well.
waris, Ar. heir; inheritor; officers

in Menangkabau entrusted with the administration of hereditary custom.
warkat, Ar. a writing; a letter.
warna, Skr. colour; shade of colour.
warong, Jav. a booth or stall.
warta, Skr. news, tidings; *warta-nya*, the report was.
Waruna, Skr. the god of the ocean, Varuna.
wasangka, = *sangka*.
wasi, Ar. an executor of a will.
wasiat, Ar. a will.
wasir, = *bawasir*.
waswas, Ar. care, worry, anxiety.
wat, (Siamese) a watt; a Buddhist temple.
watas, = *batas*.
wati, Skr. the firmament; the universe.
watu, = *batu*.
wau, a kite flown by boys.
wayang, Jav. a theatrical performance whether by living actors (*w. wong*) or by puppets (*w. kulit*).
wazir, Ar. a vizier, a minister.

weh, an interjection of address or appeal.
wěrna, = *warna*.
wet, turning (a boat) with a stroke of the paddle.
wetan, Jav. the east.
wijaya, Skr. and Jav. victorious; *bunga wijaya mala*, a legendary flower which brought all it touched to life.
wijil, Jav. a gallery in an audience-hall.
wijong, Jav. the large squirrel (*sciurus bicolor*), = *tupai nandong*.
wilada, *mandi wilada*, a ceremonial washing of the abdomen in pregnancy.
wilahar, a pool, a mere; also *lahar*.
wilis, Jav. green; dark green.
wira, Skr. a man, a hero; *pěrwira*, heroic.
wong, (Sundanese) a man; = *orang*; *wayang wong*, a play with living actors (in Java).
wujud, = *ujud*.

Y

ya, yes; that is so; = *ia*.
yaani, Ar. that is to say; i.e.
yad, Ar. hand.
yahudi, = *jaudi*.
yaï, Jav. younger brother or sister; = *adinda*.
Yajuj, Ar. the giant Gog.
yakin, Ar. certain, positive, definite.
yakut, Ar. a jacinth.
yamtuan, sovereign; = *yang-di-pěrtuan*.
yang, I. divinity god-head; *sěmbah-yang*, worship; *kěyangan*, the abode of the old divinities; paradise; fairy-land; *sang-yang*, holy god—a title given to the major divinities only; *yang-yang*, god of gods; a similar title. II. an expression having the force of a relative bringing the word or clause following it into relation with that which precedes —e.g. *masa yang baik*, a fortunate time, a lucky moment. III. a title of little distinction; an abbreviation of *dayang*.
yangyang, see *yang*.
yani, = *yaani*.
yarkan, Ar. jaundice.
yatim, Ar. orphaned, desolate, fatherless; *anak y.*, a fatherless child.
yaum, Ar. day; *yaumu'l-kiamat*, the day of judgment.
yogia, *sa-yogia-nya*, as is fitting; properly; appropriately; next.
yojana, *sa-yojana* = *saujana*, q.v.
yong, driving domestic animals or poultry into a pen, house, or confined area of any sort.

yu, a generic name for sharks, dog-fishes and rays resembling sharks; *y. bengkong*, the hammer-headed shark; *y. gila* (*chyloscillium indicum*); *y. laras* (*mustelus manazo*); *y. rimau* (*galeocerdo rayneri*); *y. sambaran*, the ground shark.
Yunan, Ionia, Greece.
yup, a designation, = *kulup*.
yuta, = *juta*.

Z

zabad, Ar. civet.
zabib, Ar. raisins, dried fruit.
zabur, Ar. the psalms of David.
zadah, Pers. sprung from, son of; *haram z.*, ill-begotten, illegitimate; *halal-z.*, legitimate.
zahid, Ar. a hermit, an ascetic.
zaitun, = *zetun*.
zakar, Ar. the male organ of generation; also *dzakar*.
zakat, Ar. alms; *měmběri z.* and *běrzakat*, to distribute charity.
zaman, Ar. long period of time, age; also *zěman*.
zamrud, Ar. emerald.
Zamzam, Ar. the Zemzem well at Mecca.
Zanggi, I. Pers. Zanzibari; African; *pauh z.*, the tree believed to grow at the "heart of the seas"; *buah pauh z.*, the double coconut. II. Pers. warlike.
zěman, Ar. age, long period of time; also *zaman*.
zetun, Ar. *buah zetun*, the olive.
ziarat, Ar. a pilgrimage to a tomb or shrine.
zina, Ar. illicit intercourse.
zirafah, Pers. a fabulous monster.
zirah, Pers. *baju zirah*, a coat of mail.
zu, Ar. possessed of; endowed with; *zu'l-karnain*, the possessor of two horns; also *dzu*.
Zuhal, Ar. the planet Saturn.
Zuhrah, the planet Venus.
Zulikha, Ar. the traditional name of Potiphar's wife.

PRINTED AT THE
F.M.S. GOVERNMENT PRESS,
KUALA LUMPUR.

ADDENDA.

A

ablok, piebald, = *hablok*.
akhwan, Ar. brothers; also *ikhwan*.
antah-antah, a descendant in the fifth generation.
ap, a Chinese purse; also *hap*.
apa, II. *buloh a.*, a dwarf-bamboo growing on river-banks.

arghawani, Pers. red.
arkus, a guinea-pig.
asar, help, assistance.
asli, Ar. original, primal.

B

bangbun, (Perak) the Malayan mongoose, = *bambun*.
bebek, the pursing of a child's lips.
bĕlĕkok, *burong b.*, a bird (*porphyrio poliocephalus ?*)
bĕmbĕreng, *ikan b.*, a fish (*platax vespertilio*).

bĕriang, the large monitor-lizard (*varanus salvator*).
bĕruyang, = *bĕriang*.
bibi, the queen (in cards).
bodong, I. a lean-to. II. a squall.
bos, the noise made by a crocodile.

C

chaku, *pisau ch.*, a pocket-knife.
chambai, a coarse leaf used as inferior *sireh*.
chatok, III. a measure of capacity, = ¼ *leng*.
chĕlut, *pĕnchĕlut*, a thief.

chĕmpiang, a raid, a gang-robbery.
chĕnaku, (Patani) a were-tiger.
chĕnayang, (Kedah) the medium or interpreter at a *bĕrhantu* seance.
chiku, a well-known fruit.

D

dari-dari, (Kedah) a small hill-tortoise.
dĕlan, a snag.

didal, Port. a thimble.
doyak, (Riau) a large cuttle-fish.

G

gabus, II. *g. kaki*, a Malay door-mat.
gatek, (Patani) I, me.
gĕmonglai, = *kĕmalai*.
gĕndali, a Palembang type of shoe.
gĕnjala, lamp-black.
gĕntang-gĕntit, wavy and tapering to a point (like a wavy *kĕris*).
gĕntit, see *gĕntang*.
gĕrambi, a curved dagger.
godek, *tĕrgodek-godek*, wagging like a dog's tail.
guli, *main g.*, to play marbles.
gundi, *kĕmbal g.*, (Perak) ornamental boxes used at weddings.

H

hap, a Chinese purse; also *ap*.
holi, (Hind.) nautch-dancers.

I

ikhwan, Ar. brothers.
ilachi, (Tam. ?) the cardamom.

J

jabing, *tĕlinga j.*, very prominent ears—cf. *jĕbang*.
jais, *kalis j.*, very irreceptive or inattentive.
jĕbang, *tĕlinga j.*, rather prominent ears—cf. *jabing*.
jĕlu, *j. masak pisang*, a name for the weasel (*putorius nudipes*).
jĕman, = *zaman*.
jĕrunyas, rough-surfaced.
jilak, lockers in a ship.
jipan, a tapir; also *kipan*.
jose, Ch. silk crêpe.
jut, a trace (harness).

K

kadsi, = *kadi* or *kali* II.
kanjipĕrak, (Tam. ?) a singlet.
karok, a torch of dry leaves.
kayau, III. a snag.
kechek, a game played with coins.
kĕpiran, scored-off, "done in the eye."
kĕsuir, hairy in the nostrils.
kĕtis, the immediate stalk of a fruit that grows in clusters.
kĕtong, *sĕmut k.*, a large black ant.
kĕtun, *ringgit k.*, the "pillar" dollar.
kilah, (Perak) *bĕrkilah*, to picnic.
kimbah, cleaning with sand and water.
kuar, II. *siput k.*, a large land snail.
kunyah, II. Ar. the naming of a father after his son.

L

lading, II. *ikan lading-lading,* a fish (*pellona* sp.)
landar, a slightly-sloping beach.
langsir, a hanging door-curtain.
latok, II. *mĕlatok,* to quiver; to chatter (of teeth)—cf. *gĕlatok.*
legeh, (Pahang) a dividing line, a watershed.

lokchuan, Ch. smooth shining silk.
lop, (Perak) a titular prefix to the names of men of good family.
luak, III. (Negri Sembilan) a territorial subdivision.
lumi, *ikan lumi-lumi,* a fish (*echineis neucrates*).

M

mek, (North Malaya) a titular prefix to the names of girls of good parentage; = (South Malaya) *yang.*
mĕrangas, spoilt by air-bubbles (in smelting).

mĕrual, a long oblong flag or pennon with two metal balls at the further end.
muntil, full-bodied, fat.

N

nilong, a slow loris.

nusus, Ar. recalcitrant (of a woman refusing to live with her husband).

P

pĕpatur, the extreme outer plank on which a roof rests.
pĕrĕgar, (Patani) the serow.
piang, II. a preparation of *pulut* rice.
pias, *ikan p.,* a fish (*chatoessus* sp.)
pistaka, II. *balai p.,* (Perak) a throne-room or hall-of-audience.

piutang, a debt; see *hutang.*
pong, *buloh p.,* a toy (the paper membrane of which is broken by air-pressure and goes off with a bang).
pos, *buah p.,* (Riau) the testes.
puloh, a group of ten; *sa-puloh,* ten; *dua-puloh,* twenty.

R

riau, *mĕriau mas,* to wash for gold.

rugas, *ayam mĕrugas,* a fowl that is about to lay.

S

saki, Pers. a cup-bearer.
sapar, (Perak) a lean-to.
sĕlĕmbada, *sĕmut s.*, a large ant (sp. unidentified).
sĕlodok, *mĕnyĕlodok*, to worm one's way through jungle.
sĕmbap, to swell (with dropsy).
sĕmpudal, filth.
sĕngkau, *s. pĕrahu*, the Malay weasel (*putorius nudipes*).

sengsut, (Malacca) a fabled man-eating ape that walks with its head between its legs.
serak, II. *tumboh s.*, young sprouts in water.
siak, *bakul s.*, a tiffin-basket.
solok, II. the outer portions of a stretch of rice-field.
sureh-sureh, (Perak) descent, lineage.

T

ta, (ta^n) the report of a gun.
takah, a Kedah name for the slow loris.
takup, a small tuberous jungle-plant.
tambak, II. *ikan t.* or *bawal t.*, the fish *stromateus niger*.

tĕbis, *sa-t.*, a particle.
tĕmbĕlah, a quiver for darts.
tĕsak, the bull's-eye in a target.
tumbong, the hairless patches on the hindquarters of certain monkeys.

U

ukek, a game played with coins.

W

wayang, *ikan w.*, a fish (*zanclus cornutus*).

www.ingramcontent.com/pod-product-compliance
Lightning Source LLC
Chambersburg PA
CBHW060117170426
43198CB00010B/929